WITHDRAWN

Augustin Cardinal Bea: Spiritual Profile

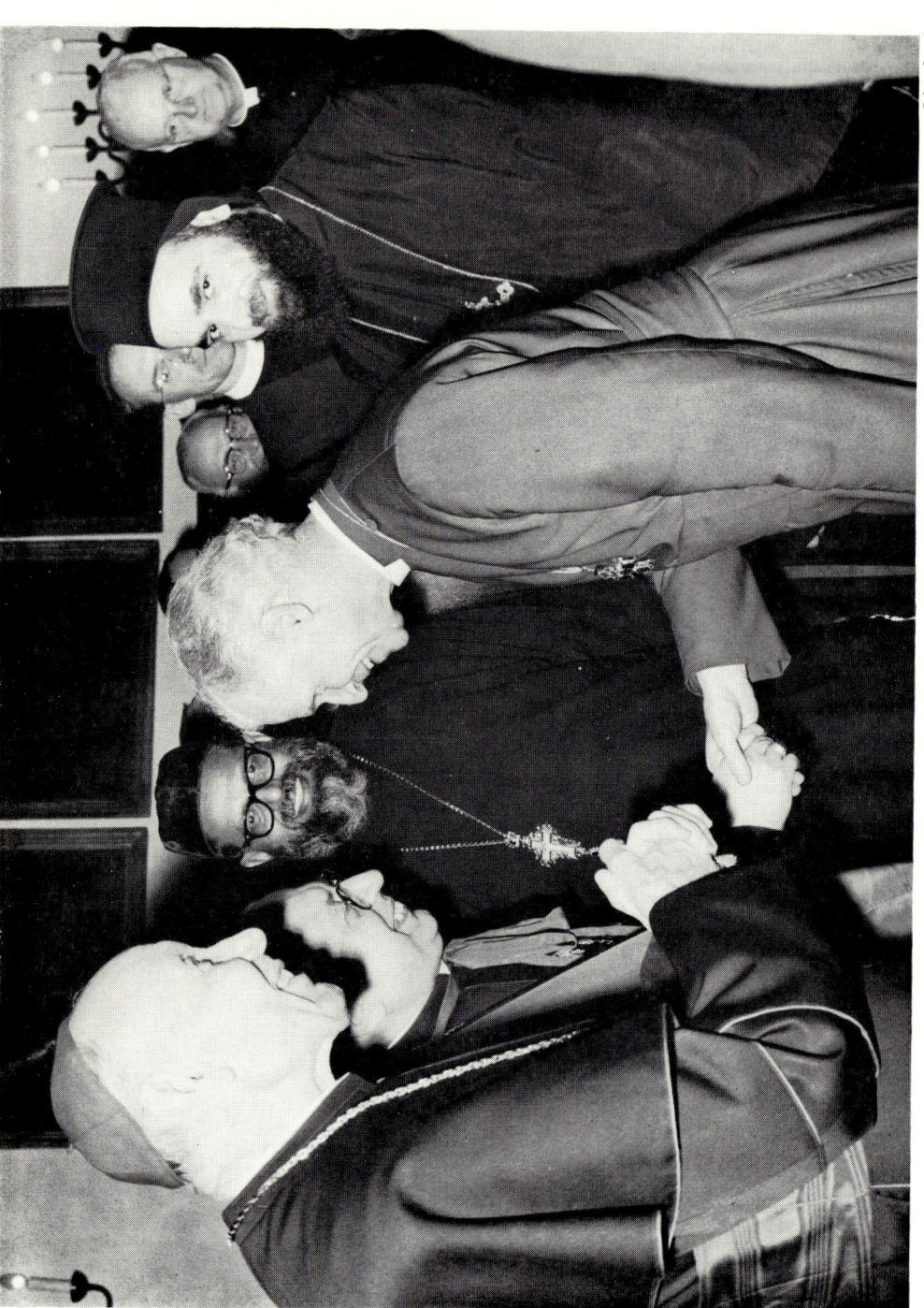

Cardinal Bea with a group of non-Catholic observers at the Vatican Council. In the foreground is Rt Rev John Moorman, Anglican bishop of Ripon, England.

AUGUSTIN CARDINAL BEA: SPIRITUAL PROFILE

Notes from the Cardinal's diary
With a commentary

EDITED BY STJEPAN SCHMIDT SJ
Translated by E. M. Stewart

 GEOFFREY CHAPMAN
LONDON DUBLIN MELBOURNE 1971

Geoffrey Chapman Ltd
18 High Street, Wimbledon, London SW 19

Geoffrey Chapman (Ireland) Ltd
5–7 Main Street, Blackrock, County Dublin

© 1970 Geoffrey Chapman Ltd

English edition, first published 1971
ISBN 0 225 48863 9

Quotations from the *Exercises of St Ignatius* are from the version translated by Thomas Corbishley, SJ, and published by Burns & Oates, London. Used by permission.

This book is set in 10 on 12 pt Baskerville
Made and printed in Great Britain by Butler and Tanner Ltd, Frome and London

Contents

Editor's Note	vii
Preface by Cardinal Willebrands	viii
Chapter 1 A happy discovery	1
Chapter 2 The meaning of a busy life	12

PART ONE NOTES FROM THE ANNUAL RETREATS 1959–1968

Chapter 3 Three months before he became a cardinal 1959	21
Chapter 4 A cardinal in retreat 1960	45
Chapter 5 The number of responsibilities is constantly increasing 1961	67
Chapter 6 In sight of the Council 1962	87
Chapter 7 The first session of the Council—the death of Pope John 1963	106
Chapter 8 The first year of the new pontificate 1964	123
Chapter 9 'Let us run with perseverance the race that is set before us' 1965	142
Chapter 10 'Now the time for a hidden life has come for me' 1966	156
Chapter 11 'Accept everything with tranquillity and energy' 1967	174
Chapter 12 'A life of quiet humble faith' 1968	187

PART TWO A SPIRITUAL PROFILE OF CARDINAL BEA

Introduction	202
Chapter 13 God has been 'extraordinarily generous to me'	203
Chapter 14 'I must be a praying cardinal'	218
Chapter 15 'My life and work must be centred on Jesus'	221
Chapter 16 'The Church must be the norm'	228
Chapter 17 'The family of God'	234
Chapter 18 'Servants of Christ and stewards of the mysteries of God'	239
Chapter 19 Servants of Christ in the holy Eucharist	249
Chapter 20 Creation, 'the world', the cross	254
Chapter 21 Eyes fixed firmly on the goal and on the cross	266

Chapter 22 'Watch and pray, that you enter not into temptation' 274
Chapter 23 'The first and most perfect of Christ's assistants' 278
Chapter 24 The Holy Spirit: 'my life, my light, my strength' 286
Chapter 25 'My death will not be lonely' 291

Epilogue 296

Editor's Note

In the text of the retreat notes in Part One, the numbered paragraphs refer to the day of the retreat and the number of the meditation, e.g. I/1 means: first day, first meditation. These numbers, together with the year, are also used in cross-references, e.g. 1959/I/1.

The footnotes are the work of the editor. Occasional additions made in the text of the retreat notes are signified by square brackets. The author's text is clearly presented in the first part of the book. Quotations from the notes in the second part are made without these signs, for the sake of simplicity.

Preface

by Jan Cardinal Willebrands

When I first got to know Cardinal Bea, in 1957, he was rector of the Pontifical Biblical Institute and a consultant to the Congregation of the Holy Office. After the death of Fr Grendel SVD, he also made himself responsible in the 'Consulta' (the consultative body) for all questions appertaining to the relations between Catholics and evangelical Christians, particularly in Germany. His interest in ecumenical matters prompted me to pay him a visit, which was subsequently to be repeated about once a year, until the foundation of the Unity Secretariat by Pope John brought us permanently together in the service of Christian unity.

Fr Bea SJ was undoubtedly the man who made the deepest impression on me during my many visits to Rome, the one to whom I most readily returned. The reason for this lay not in his vast store of information on the ecumenical movement—information which at that time was mainly confined to German problems—nor in the depth of his theological knowledge, however much his familiarity with holy scripture prepared him for an understanding of the separated Christians, but rather in his spiritual approach to the mystery of the unity of the Church and the disunity of Christians.

A few years before the Second Vatican Council issued its Decree on Ecumenism, Bea was already fully alive to the spiritual nature of the ecumenical movement. 'There can be no ecumenism worthy of the name without a change of heart. For it is from newness of attitudes, from self-denial and unstinted love, that yearnings for unity take their rise and grow towards maturity. We should therefore pray to the divine Spirit for the grace to be genuinely self-denying, humble, gentle in the service of others and to have an attitude of brotherly generosity towards them' (*Decree on Ecumenism*, 7). 'This change of heart and holiness of life, along with public and private prayer for the unity of Christians, should be regarded as the soul of the whole ecumenical movement' (id, 8).

He made his annual retreats not merely because they are customary with Jesuits, but because they answered his need for reflection for and with God. The quality that struck me most in Bea was the sincerity of his personality and way of life. The source of it is found in his spiritual notes. 'Towards my fellow-men: kindness, gentleness, understanding, not in any artificial way for the sake of diplomacy, but the result of a genuine supernatural love of neighbour' (1959/V/2); 'not as a matter of tactics but because of an interior spirit and a sense of apostolate' (1959/V/3; 'not lust for power, no earthly interest, no mere busyness, no matter of routine, but the genuine spirit of Christ' (1960/VI/3).

His spirituality goes further, and sees that not even the modern human sciences but only God offers an adequate foundation here: 'It is not only a question of psychology, however: behind it all there are two powers: God and Satan' (1961/V/3). He saw the social task of the Church, and particularly of her priests, in the same perspective. The Lord gives the multitude 'first of all, the bread of doctrine . . . but also wants to provide bread for the body. Not, it is true, personally, but through his apostles: "*You* give them something to eat!" . . . the social concern of the Church. This too flows from our Lord's heart. But he works through us, his priests and faithful. Everything must remain on the level of the supernatural; even the social welfare work of the Church should help souls' (1966/VI/2).

Bea always sought a secluded life: 'a retired life in my room' (1959/IV/1). This involved an absence of every ambition to be 'the sort of cardinal who looks for popularity and publicity' (1960/V/2), and a desire in his relations with others to 'show myself a colleague, not stressing the prince of the Church' (1962/IV/3). It also meant a life of concentration, of study—in so far as there was any time left for it—and of prayer: 'The *strength* to do all this is given me by the "Word of God". Above all, I must aim at an interior life, based on the "Word of God"' (1960/V/2).

From this introspection he drew real strength. Despite his advancing years, he set out to give lectures and pay visits in the service of the Gospel. This he preached unabridged: 'putting forward the doctrine of the Church, without any falsification and without any abridgement, but also in such a way that it may be "tasty", that it may appeal and take hold of mind and heart. I am preaching the "good news", not a code of law!' (1964/IV/4). He was conscious of his responsibility and authority as a cardinal. He regarded this status as a task and a service, as an obligation to greater loyalty. He never sought a personal victory, but a victory for the cause which he served, the cause of God and the Church. In this service he could be very strong, to the surprise of his friends and of those who did not share his thinking. 'There are also times when I have to say a clear and decisive no (or yes), whoever the person concerned may be. The deciding factor is the will of God: about my Father's business' (1961/IV/3). He never allowed himself to be tempted into personal criticism. 'An apostle who criticizes, and criticizes the Master himself to some extent, is a public scandal. When I criticize, even if it is justified and well meant, I always give scandal' (1964/VI/2).

The cardinal followed the post-conciliar developments with confidence, and invariably inspired fresh hope. He had no wish to be over-optimistic, but always based his realism on providence, on his prayers and on the enormous effort made by the pope, and especially by the entire Church. He also recognized certain tendencies which did not rest on the theological and pastoral basis of the Council. 'Force is no use against this, the only answer is to work earnestly, unassumingly, not giving oneself airs and asserting oneself, but straightforwardly, simply content with everything, doing the work where it is accepted and leaving it where it is rejected, as Paul did with the Jews' (1961/V/4). In his latter years he was particularly aware that the faith had suffered, either from glowing half-truths (1967/II/3) or from a rationalistic secularism, that recognizes no 'mystery'. 'My task is to oppose this spirit of the times, and see that justice is done to the faith' (1968/IV/1).

On reading these spiritual notes, one may wonder at the great significance which Cardinal Bea attached to his annual spiritual exercises, always in strict accordance with the basic plan laid down by St Ignatius. But anyone who has known his love of men, his love of God, and his unwavering devotion to his given task, will recognize here the Cardinal Bea who stimulated and inspired him, and, more than that, he will find here the sources of this life: God's Word, the faith, and an immense love. While opposing certain contemporary tendencies with his evident awareness of sin, and the predominance which he gives to prayer, he lives intensely in the present, listening to what younger generations have to say, and above all listening for the message that God's Spirit holds for the present age.

One may perhaps be surprised that the questions which fill his other books—ecumenical theology and ecumenical activities—receive such scant mention here. But the spirit of his books, his thinking and his labours does find expression in these notes. Bea alone with God (the most authentic picture of him), Bea in his struggle with God, like Jacob with the angel, and in his love of God, like John and Paul. This constant inward renewal in a leader of the ecumenical movement is the greatest ecumenical gift his life had to give.

He went, as he had hoped he would, in full harness. His parting words to me were: 'I am ever grateful.' These words were a reflection on his whole life. In deep faith, I can express them to God for everything he gave us in Cardinal Bea.

CHAPTER 1

A happy discovery

Much has been written about Cardinal Bea, especially after he became President of the newly created Secretariat for the Promotion of Christian Unity in June 1960. From that time until his death his activities were more in the public eye than those of almost any other cardinal. In 1960, he had just entered his eightieth year; in spite of his age, he travelled extensively inside Europe, went once to Constantinople and four times to the USA. He gave many interviews to press, radio and television: twenty-five, for example, in the first nine months of 1962 alone. At the Council he presented four official reports in the name of the Secretariat for the Promotion of Christian Unity and spoke nineteen times in his own right as a Council father. Besides all this, he was almost incredibly active as a writer: from 1960 to his death his publications exceed 260 in number, and of these eight were books translated on average into four or five different languages. Surely enough is already known about this man, and there is nothing particularly new to be discovered about him.

Certainly, the editor of this book was the last person to expect that anything was left to be discovered. For nearly a quarter of a century I had the privilege of close friendship with Father, later Cardinal, Bea. For nine years, as the cardinal's secretary, I lived in the same house. I assumed that I knew him very well and in every way. So, on going through his papers not long after his death in my capacity as executor, I was surprised to come across various exercise books containing his spiritual notes mainly from his annual eight-day retreats! I had had conversations with the cardinal on every possible subject and we had talked a great deal about the theoretical and practical questions of the spiritual life—and never a word, not even a hint, that these notes existed! He was always very reticent on the subject of his own spiritual life, and his relationship with God and Christ, but I really never imagined that reticence would go so far!

The greatest surprise was to come with the first reading of the notes. Cardinal Bea always gave the impression of being a man of God, and this had drawn frequent comment, especially since his death. But it remained an impression, unsupported by specific instances, precisely because the cardinal was so reticent, almost shy, in these matters. And now these notes reveal a richness and depth of the spiritual life which could scarcely have been imagined of one who was such a man of action. He never tires of reminding himself before God that amongst all the other claims on his time the cultivation of a deep spiritual life is the decisive thing, not only for his own salvation but also for the fruitfulness of his apostolic work. The more intimately he is united to Christ, as an instrument, to be used, the more effectively the apostle works. Hence the tireless, even relentless, energy and persistence in his efforts to make his prayer in its various forms really living and personal. Hence too the constant cultivation of the love of God and Christ. Again and again he insists that Christ must be the centre of his spiritual life. Love for Christ, however, also means a constant effort to become like him in all things and especially in true love of neighbour, in humility and in a cheerful readiness to bear his cross.

These few disjointed references to the rich content of these spiritual notes will give the reader at least some slight idea of my happy surprise, indeed astonishment, when I first read the late cardinal's notes. And the more closely I studied them, the more my joy increased. The obvious conclusion was to think of publishing them, in order to share this growing joy with the many others who knew the cardinal in one way or another, and to increase their understanding of the spirit and personality of this unique man, and the principles by which he was guided. The impression made by these notes should be all the deeper since the author wrote them before God and for the benefit of his own soul alone. With this publication I hope to continue to be of service to the cardinal, as I was in his lifetime, and to give him the opportunity of carrying on his apostolic work even after death, in order to convey to more people the spirit which inspired his world-wide activities in the Church of the Council.

It was decided to limit this publication to notes from the years when their author was cardinal; this period forms a natural unity in his life, and is the part of it most familiar and of greatest interest to the general public. The notes from this period are in themselves sufficient to make a book. And there is another reason too: people probably take it for granted that a member of a religious order should lead a deep and serious spiritual life. But the average reader may not so readily expect one of the highest dignitaries of the Church to do so, especially when his life was outwardly one of such extraordinary dynamic activity as Cardinal Bea's.[1]

Most of the notes published here are from the author's annual retreats, while the rest are from his 'monthly recollections'. In the Society of Jesus, of which Cardinal Bea was a member, it is customary to devote eight days every year in silence and seclusion to mental prayer, following the

---

[1] The retreat of August 1959 is included in this book, although Bea did not become a cardinal until December 1959. This retreat is included because it was made only three months before he became cardinal; and it is quite certain that he lived on the strength drawn from it in the first year after his elevation.

well-known method of the Spiritual Exercises of the founder, St Ignatius of Loyola. It is not required that anything should be put down in writing on these occasions, though in fact this is very often done, depending to a large extent on the character of the retreatant. But Bea was generally in the habit of putting things into writing in other matters, and he did the same in his retreats.

In addition to the notes from the retreats there are short notes from the 'monthly recollections', usually a brief phrase to jog the memory. These monthly recollections are customary in the Society of Jesus (and in many other orders); they help a person to make a brief review of the state of his spiritual life and to make resolutions for the future on those points that are important for him in his particular situation. To the very end, the cardinal kept faithfully to this custom of his Society. In his retreat notes he speaks repeatedly of this practice and resolves to observe it regularly ('on the first Sunday of the month' cf 1962/II/2). So for example in 1967 after he has meditated on the 'disorders' in his life, he writes: 'So I must always keep a check on myself, daily through a carefully made examination of conscience, weekly through confession and monthly through the recollection. Only by using these means shall I be able to keep myself free from faults' (1967/II/3; cf also 1959/II/2). The proof that he kept this resolution can be seen in the brief jottings from the monthly recollections that follow each set of retreat notes. These occur practically every month; the last is dated 29 September, six weeks before his death. In his recollections it was his custom to go through one or other of the meditations of the previous annual retreat, and with his characteristic precision to note at the end of that meditation the date on which he had again reflected on this theme.

It should already be clear that the jottings from the monthly recollections do not as a rule add any new ideas to the retreat notes. Their significance is, firstly, as concrete proof of the uninterrupted efforts of the author to keep the resolutions of the previous retreat alive in his mind and to shape his spiritual life accordingly. They also indicate which points gave him more trouble, or which were of more concern to him due to particular circumstances or for some other reason: in other words, they reveal the general direction in which his spiritual life was moving or, rather, was being moved by the Spirit of God.

This is not a strictly scientific and critical publication. It is designed for a wide circle of readers. In practice, this means that the text of the notes has been published complete and in chronological order, without omission or abbreviation, but leaving out technicalities (e.g. Greek or Latin phrases) that are of no importance for the text and might make the going heavy for the general reader. The critical apparatus has been restricted to essentials.

The transcription of the retreat notes (written in ordinary school exercise books) presented no problem. The author's writing is precise and clear, so that there were virtually no difficulties in reading the text. In a very few cases a word, for example a pronoun or a verb at the end of the sentence, is missing. In such cases the missing words have simply been supplied. In cases of doubt, there is a footnote.

The transcription of the notes from the monthly recollection was rather different. These notes are contained in a small, handmade (octavo) booklet with an old envelope as a cover. The booklet bears the title 'Recoll. Mensilis' ('Monthly Recollection'). Various passages were written in shorthand. Since I was not familiar with the old Gabelsberger shorthand used by the author, two experts were called in to decipher these passages: A. Grauer (Doctor of Law and Political Sciences, Stuttgart) and Mrs E. Spath (Villach, Austria). They read and deciphered the shorthand independently, and the texts they arrived at were almost completely in agreement with one another. In most cases of doubt, it was possible to get at the meaning by comparison with the retreat notes, to which the monthly recollections refer. In the few remaining cases of doubt a question mark in the text tells the reader of some uncertainty in the reading.

The frequent use of Latin expressions or passages from scripture, the Spiritual Exercises, the Constitutions of the Society of Jesus or the *Imitation of Christ* raised a problem: in most cases these are passages familiar to the author, and the use of the Latin does not have any special significance for the meaning. To avoid making the reading unnecessarily burdensome these quotations are translated in the English text. In the few cases where the use of the Latin is of particular importance, it is given in a footnote. The same applies with the much less frequent Greek phrases, which usually come from the New Testament.

The cardinal had a habit of underlining passages, usually to impress a point on his mind or maybe to direct attention quickly to the important points on re-reading the notes. The underlining is seldom an essential part of the text, and has been ignored, unless necessary for the understanding of the text itself.

It was not my intention to write a thorough-going commentary on the notes; for one thing, I did not feel that this was necessary. I simply wanted to offer the help needed to read the notes, as it were, in the spirit of the author himself. To this end it seemed necessary or at least useful to add a few biographical details, some information about the Spiritual Exercises of St Ignatius, which the author normally followed, and to explain or give references to the biblical passages or ideas quoted or used in some way by the author.

The biographical framework

Chapter 2 gives a short biography of the cardinal, in which the main emphasis is on events which are important for the understanding of the notes. Each year's notes are preceded by a short review of the main events of the period since the last retreat—giving them more or less as the cardinal himself would have looked back over them during the retreat.²

The framework of the Spiritual Exercises
Cardinal Bea followed the Exercises of St Ignatius in his retreats not because there is no other method, but because he was a member of the Society of Jesus which was founded by Ignatius, and the Exercises are the basic source of the Society's spirituality. His notes always refer to at least the key meditations of the Exercises. Where there is a direct reference, this is given in the text, in brackets.³ Characteristic ideas from the Exercises are explained in the footnotes, as are details from the Constitutions of the Society of Jesus.

In order to give the reader a general grasp of the content and structure of the Exercises, their main outline is described here, and certain passages from the most important meditations, particularly helpful for understanding the cardinal's retreat notes, are given in full.

1) The retreat notes usually begin with the meditation on God as the goal of men, on the salvation of a man's soul and the use of created things in the service of these two goals. We find these themes of the Exercises briefly and neatly summarized in the 'fundamental principle'.

> Man has been created to praise, reverence and serve our Lord God, thereby saving his soul. Everything else on earth has been created for man's sake, to help him to achieve the purpose for which he has been created. So it follows that man has to use them as far as they help and abstain from them where they hinder his purpose. Therefore we need to train ourselves to be impartial in our attitude towards all created reality, provided we are at liberty to do so, that is to say it is not forbidden. So that, as far as we are concerned, we do not set our hearts on good health as against bad health, prosperity as against poverty, a good reputation as against a bad one, a long life as against a short one, and so on. The one thing we desire, the one thing we choose is what is more likely to achieve the purpose of our creating (23).

The words 'we need to train ourselves to be impartial in our attitude towards all created reality, provided we are at liberty to do so, that is to say it is not forbidden' need some special explanation. This is the Ignatian 'indifference', unfortunately so often misunderstood because it is interpreted as some kind of cold, stoic detachment from things. To grasp the real Ignatian meaning of this attitude it is enough to read Bea's profound theological and psychological explanation of it: ' "We

---

² The notes for each year form a single chapter which, in order to give each year some sort of shape and to make it easier for the reader to find his way, has been given a descriptive title.

³ For passages quoted from the Exercises in the course of the notes, references are given only if they are *not* from the meditation noted at the beginning of each entry.

need to train ourselves to be impartial": this means I must have a great aim in life and let nothing, except the clearly recognized will of God, turn me from it. I have this great goal: to serve God and only him, always, everywhere and in everything. And what I have to do now is to protect this ideal from every hindrance, which can come from me or my environment or from outside. I must be "indifferent" to all this, that is without any inclination or preference' (1964/1/3). Then even more profoundly: 'Indifference does not stop me advancing in wisdom and prudence. On the contrary it excludes whatever is merely emotion or a matter of feeling and in its place it puts considerations of faith and reason, which I can follow, unhampered by personal considerations. It gives me, then, true freedom of spirit, independence of every influence that is not willed by God, and therefore energy and strength. The energy with which the saints pursued their goal would not have been possible without this interior freedom, that is without indifference. But indifference itself presupposes a great love of God, by which all self-love is, so to speak, burned up and supplanted' (1959/I/4).

2) The 'fundamental principle' is followed by the meditations on sin; firstly one on the 'threefold sin', that is the sins of the angels, of our first parents and of mankind in general; then one on the sins of the retreatant himself; and finally the meditation on the doctrine of hell. These meditations, which could be called the classical meditations of the Exercises, are frequently followed by others on death, judgment etc. Although these are not mentioned in the Spanish manuscript of the Exercises, they are in the much-used first Latin translation, which was also used by Ignatius, and there they are put at the end of the meditation on hell.

3) From this point in the Exercises onwards the meditations—with only one or two exceptions—all revolve round Christ, his incarnation, his life, sufferings, glorious resurrection and ascension, and of course his teaching. The famous meditation on Christ the King and his kingdom forms the prelude to these meditations on Christ. This reaches its climax in the invitation which Ignatius only puts before those retreatants who 'wish to be outstanding in the service of Christ':

> Those who are anxious to show greater enthusiasm still and distinguish themselves in unstinted service of their eternal King and Lord of the universe will not be content to offer themselves without reservation for the enterprise. Going against their natural weakness and their love of the world and of the flesh, they will make their dedication of themselves still more valuable and worthwhile, in these terms: 'Eternal Lord of the universe, in the presence of your own infinite goodness, of your glorious mother and all the saints of heaven's courts, by your grace and help, I make this my offering: I intend and desire, and it is my deliberate resolve, granted it be for the more perfect service and greater praise of your Majesty, to imitate you in

putting up with all injustice, all abuse, all poverty in reality no less than in spirit, should your most sacred Majesty be willing to choose and admit me to this stage of life' (97 f.).[4]

4) This idea of imitating Christ in poverty and humiliation is so dear to Ignatius, that he comes back to it in different forms on two further occasions. Firstly in the 'meditation on the two standards', where the retreatant is invited to compare the tactics of Lucifer on the one hand and of Christ on the other. Lucifer urges his helpers to

> have their traps and fetters in position, tempting men first with eagerness for money (his usual procedure) as the easiest means to acquiring some worthwhile position in the world, and eventually to overweening pride. Notice the three steps, money, position, pride; from these three steps he leads men on to all other vices (142).

Christ's approach is the direct opposite. He encourages his servants and friends that they should

> aim to help everybody, leading them first to perfect poverty in the spirit, and even to poverty in reality, if this be his divine Majesty's pleasure, and he should, of his graciousness, so choose them; then to

---

[4] Ignatius intended that the retreatant's offer 'to imitate you in putting up with all injustice, all abuse, all poverty in reality no less than in spirit' should form a clear contrast with 'natural weakness and their love of the world and of the flesh'. Ignatius' exact meaning in these last words is clear: they are *not* to be understood in the modern sense, but refer to everything loved and sought after by the lower nature ('flesh') and the 'world'. And by this, as Ignatius frequently tells us, he means riches and honours. Instead, the retreatant is offered the choice of putting up with injustice and shame, and material as well as spiritual poverty. The best and simplest explanation of Ignatius' thought is to be found in the following passage from the General Examination, proposed by the Founder for the consideration of candidates wishing to enter the Society:

> All who are being examined (to see if they are suitable for the Society) must diligently observe, esteeming it of great importance and of the highest moment in the sight of our Creator and Lord, how much it helps and contributes to progress in spiritual life, to abhor wholly and not in part what the world loves and embraces, and to accept and desire with their whole strength whatsoever Christ our Lord loved and embraced. For as worldly men, who follow the things of the world, love and with great diligence seek honours, reputation and the credit of a great name upon earth, as the world teaches them, so those who are advancing in spirit and seriously follow Christ our Lord, love and earnestly desire things which are altogether the contrary; that is, to be clothed with the same garment and with the livery of their Lord for his love and reverence; insomuch that if it could be without offence of the divine majesty and without sin on the part of their neighbour, they would wish to suffer reproaches, slanders and injuries, and to be treated and accounted as fools (without at the same time giving any occasion for it), because they desire to imitate and resemble in some sort their Creator and Lord Jesus Christ, and to be clothed with his garments and livery; since he clothed himself with the same for our greater spiritual good, and gave us an example, that in all things, as far as by the assistance of God's grace we can, we may seek to imitate and follow him, seeing he is the true way that leads men to life.

This text is so important to the Society that the whole passage has been adopted as the famous rule 11 in the 'Summarium', the short summary of the Constitutions of the Society.

want to be laughed at and looked down upon. From these two comes humility. Notice the three steps: poverty, as against money: being laughed at and looked down on as against being looked up to by men of the world: humility, as against pride. From these three steps men can be led on to all the virtues (146).

This special form of the imitation of Christ is offered as a subject for meditation and thoughtful prayer in a positive way in the so-called third way or degree of subjection. This degree is achieved

> supposing that I have attained to the first two ways, and granted an equal measure of praise and glory to God, I desire to be poor along with Christ in poverty, rather than to be rich, to be insulted along with Christ so grossly insulted, rather than to be thought well of. I would rather be thought a helpless fool for the sake of Christ who was so treated, rather than to be thought wise and clever in the world's eyes (167).

As usual at important points in the Exercises, Ignatius recommends here too that God's grace should be implored with the help of the three 'colloquies', that is with the mother of God, with Christ and with the heavenly Father: 'begging our Lord to will to choose him for this higher and more perfect subjection, if the service and praise of his divine Majesty be equal, if not greater' (168).

5) It only remains to mention the final meditation in the Exercises, on 'achieving love' of God, a meditation with which Cardinal Bea always without exception concludes his retreats. In this meditation Ignatius firstly makes the retreatant

> recall the good things I have had from creation, my redemption, personal gifts. I will rouse myself to reckon how much our Lord God has done for me, how much that is his own he has shared with me: I will further consider the divine plan whereby this same Lord wants to give me all that it is in his power to give (234).

The first meditation ends with the prayer known by its Latin opening words 'Sume et suscipe':

> Take, Lord, into your possession my complete freedom of action, my memory, my understanding and my entire will, all that I have, all that I own, it is your gift to me, I now return it to you. It is all yours, to be used simply as you wish. Give me your love and your grace; it is all I need (234).

After this Ignatius makes the retreatant

> see God living in his creatures: in matter, giving it existence, in plants, giving them life, in animals, giving them consciousness, in men, giving them intelligence. So he lives in me, giving me existence, life,

consciousness, intelligence. More, he makes me his temple, since I have been created wearing the image and likeness of God' (235).

Thirdly:

Think of God energizing, at though he were actively at work, in every created reality, in the sky, in matter, plants and fruits, herds and the like: it is he who creates them and keeps them in being, he who confers life or consciousness, and so on (236).

Fourthly:

Realize that all gifts and benefits come from above. My moderate ability comes from the supreme omnipotence on high, as do my sense of justice, kindliness, charity, mercy, and so on, like sunbeams from the sun or streams from their source (237).

Finally, a remark in passing to avoid a possible misunderstanding. To talk of following a method in the spiritual life, and especially the Ignatian method of the Exercises, can give rise to the fear that such methods, which are after all, basically human, might restrict the freedom of the soul and become a barrier between it and God or Christ. A first answer to this is to recall the fact mentioned above, that apart from the meditation on the 'fundamental principle' and on sin—which are in any case based on the teaching of Christ—all the other meditations in the Exercises have Christ, his life, sufferings, glory and teaching as their real object and therefore their centre. On closer observation it emerges, perhaps particularly today, how central the Ignatian method of meditating on Christ in poverty and the shame of the cross is to the Gospel. Cardinal Bea's retreat notes are clearly centred on God and Christ. In fact he refers more than once to Christ himself in the meditation of the 'fundamental principle' and sees man's vocation and his relation to creation essentially in Christ (cf 1960/I/1; 1963/I/2; 1968/I/2), although there is actually no mention of Christ in the corresponding text of the Exercises. Finally, it is significant to note that his meditations are thoroughly based on the written word of God, indeed they are woven out of God's word.

It might be thought that the notes, by following the Exercises, would become tedious or monotonous. Now it is in the nature of things that certain thoughts should be repeated, because the author had to struggle with the same or similar difficulties again and again, and to keep renewing his efforts in order gradually to achieve certain goals. It is also true that to some extent the same general meditations keep on occurring; but there are also changes, some small, some considerable. For example, the retreats sometimes start with the thought of creation, sometimes with the idea that man is from God and exists for God, and sometimes again even with the general thought of man's calling to holiness because of God's holiness (cf 1965/6/I/2; 1968/I/1–4).

Again, the general themes are expressed by means of different texts from scripture and so appear in a constantly new light. It is noticeable that the notes are thoroughly penetrated by pauline thought. It is the influence of the apostle of the Gentiles that gives these entries their world-embracing breadth and their obvious warmth, sometimes restrained, sometimes glowing. By these means the cardinal is able to meditate on even the most ordinary and one might almost say, trite themes of the Exercises and give them a very personal flavour. To take just one example: he regards the idea of death, so often used in the meditations of the Exercises as a means of exciting fear, in a pleasant light: death is a welcome friend, come to take him to Christ.

Moreover, the notes are assured of variety and interest from the 'application' in the sphere of the spiritual life. The author never remains lost in mere contemplation: he repeatedly directs his attention to himself and asks himself how the insights he has gained in the meditation can help him to love God more and serve him better in the Church and in his neighbour. In this way he sees new facets of even the most commonplace meditations and the notes gain actuality and awaken interest.[5]

Notes on the Biblical Content

We have remarked more than once that the retreat notes are to a great extent couched in the language of the Bible. The footnotes are largely concerned with elucidating this biblical frame of reference.[6]

Often, the quotations are literal; but also, very often, they are free renderings of a Bible passage, sometimes no more than the use of a typically biblical idea. It seemed important to draw attention to these points and to explain them, since this very biblical language is so characteristic of the author, and gives the notes added depth and attraction for the reader. His biblical language reveals the extent to which the cardinal lived on the written word of God; so much so that in the end (perhaps without being fully conscious of it) he expressed his thoughts naturally in the language of the Bible.

It scarcely needs to be said that this prominence of the biblical elements is of considerable ecumenical significance. Sacred scripture is, as Vatican II says, a precious instrument 'in the mighty hands of God for attaining that unity which the Saviour holds out to all men' (*Decree on Ecumenism*, 21). Here, more than anywhere, divided Christian brothers can find common ground. Perhaps to some extent this could also be said

---

[5] Frequently, between the entries for the third and fourth meditations of the day, we find notes on a 'consideratio status': this is mainly a practical examination of the state of the spiritual life.

[6] Passing mention must be made of two other small groups of quotations and references with which the notes deal. The first comes from the liturgy or other ecclesiastical texts, and to this belong also the occasional texts from Vatican II which underline the significant connection between the retreat notes and the thought of the Council. There are also a few texts from the Fathers of the Church; the precise references will not be given, to avoid making the notes too technical.

of these notes, in so far as they speak the language of the Bible to an extraordinary degree—perhaps particularly so because they speak the language of St Paul, so dear to the heart of so many non-Catholics, and are penetrated by the thought and spirit of the apostle to the Gentiles.[7] This biblical and pauline language will be a source of special joy to so many of our non-Catholic brethren who knew and loved the cardinal and who included his work in their prayers. It will make it easier for them to recognize him again in these notes and to meet and follow him.

In explaining the biblical passages or ideas in the notes, we will give the full text in footnotes where this seems necessary. Many references will already be familiar, and others will gradually become so as the reader progresses, and to these references only are given, within the text, in square brackets.[8]

On more than one occasion the spiritual relationship between Pope John and Cardinal Bea has been stressed, together with the fact that the cardinal—more than most—made the concerns of the Council, its aims and its spirit his own. This is why he understood so well and supported so firmly the plans the pope had for the Council. It may, then, be said with confidence that these notes show the spirit in which he co-operated so whole-heartedly in making the Council a success. In order to help the reader to gain a better understanding of this spirit, we shall try in the second part of this book to arrange the many points arising from the notes in some sort of order around certain themes, and where possible to set them in the context of the spiritual profile of the cardinal. May the notes in this way be a happy reminder to the many people who knew and loved their author, and at the same time may they provide a permanent guide in the faithful and persevering service of what was the great concern of both Pope John and Cardinal Bea: the Second Vatican Council and especially the unity of those baptized in Christ.

[7] This pauline influence may seem surprising in Bea, who was principally an Old Testament exegete. As a young Jesuit student his spiritual director was Fr Wilhelm Eberschweiler S.J., whose spirituality was thoroughly penetrated by pauline theology —which at that time was not at all usual (cf W. Sierp, *Pater Wilhelm Eberschweiler*). The frequent conversations I had with the cardinal in the last decade of his life made clear how great an impression this spiritual direction made on the young student, and that it probably contributed far more to his spiritual formation than his years in the noviciate and the influence of his novice master. Father Bea lectured on New Testament theology during his first years at the Pontifical Gregorian University in Rome, and extensive notes from these lectures still exist.

[8] Gospel references are normally to the Gospel on which the particular meditation is mainly based. Where there are references in the course of the meditation to an individual passage, the source will be given only if it is not from the passage quoted at the beginning.

CHAPTER 2

The meaning of a busy life

On 18 August 1968 Cardinal Bea celebrated the Golden Jubilee of his solemn vows. This celebration took place in Switzerland in the presence of a small group of people. At his request I made the speech, which could be described as a few thoughts on the life of the jubilarian. To begin with I related what the cardinal himself had told his young brethren in America about his own early years in the Society. I said: 'It is a well known fact that the authorities in the Society ask themselves at the beginning of a young student's studies what will later become of him and for what sort of work he is suited. When young Augustin Bea finished his noviciate in Holland and began the study of philosophy, he was told that one of his professors was preparing a work on the worship of God in the history of mankind and that he should study in the related faculty of ethnology in order to help with this work. So he began to study ethnology together with philosophy. Then, after the conclusion of his philosophical studies and a spell of teaching in a college, he was given new instructions. He was to study classical philology in Innsbruck, in order to become professor of Latin and Greek later on. What they had in mind was the Jesuit College in Feldkirch. After only six months of these studies the highest authority in the Society issued a regulation that studies of this sort should no longer be done before theological studies but afterwards. So the young student had to leave Innsbruck to study theology in Holland. It is evident that in the course of his theological training new qualities and talents became apparent, and so it was decided that he should lecture in theology or scripture and not in Latin and Greek. After the completion of his theological studies he was, therefore, sent to Berlin University to study ancient oriental history and languages. But events led to the interruption of these studies too after only six months, for World War I broke out, with all its difficulties. After the war young Father Bea was at last able to begin lecturing on sacred scripture, as far as the post-war situation allowed.' I went on to say: 'I believe I am right in saying that the events just described are symbolic for the jubilarian's later life and work, for this too is full of variety, movement and change.'[1]

When he was rector of the Pontifical Biblical Institute, the author,

---

[1] The text of this speech was circulated in manuscript form to a small circle.

meditating on the calling of the apostles in his annual retreat in 1944, wrote of his background: 'To dream of turning the carpenter's son from Riedböhringen into what he has become would have seemed madness.' He was born the only son of Karl and Maria (née Merk) on 28 May 1881 in the village of Riedböhringen in South Baden, at that time a village of about six hundred inhabitants. As we know, his father was a carpenter. He also had a small plot of land. The family was really very poor and he must have felt this poverty especially in his student years. In a speech made in his home village in 1966 at the opening of a school named after him, the cardinal spoke of the financial help his fellow-villagers had given him as a student: 'During my studies I received a great deal of help, financial help, from my fellow-villagers, from the families known to me. When I took leave of my relations and acquaintances after the holidays, they always opened their purses and I could almost always return to school with the next nine months taken care of.'[2] He also helped himself by giving lessons. Amongst the papers he left were also found documents relating to certain financial grants that he received from various charitable institutions: from the 'Fürstliche Fürstenbergische Kammer' (1899) and from the 'Grossherzoglicher Oberschulrat' of Karlsruhe, from the Joachim Letz Foundation in Constance (1898). When he entered the theological college in Freiburg (1900), he was given a certificate of poverty.

He attended the local primary school and learnt a little Latin from the parish priest; then he was accepted in 1893 by the Catholic college, the 'Lendersche Heimschule', in Sassbach/Baden, where he stayed until 1897. As time passed he seems to have become dissatisfied with various things in this school and so in 1897 he transferred to the *Gymnasium* in Constance. He lodged in the 'Konradihaus', but as this hostel was to be rebuilt he had to leave here too after a year, and spent his last school years (1898–1900) in the classical *Gymnasium* at Ratstatt, where he matriculated.

Very early on he felt a desire to be a priest and gradually this became a firm resolve. This had really been his motive in pursuing his studies. In the last years before matriculation he began to think of entering a religious order, and finally this crystalized into a desire to enter the Society of Jesus. This choice did not please his father, partly because since Bismark's time the Society of Jesus had been banned in Germany, and to enter it would mean leaving the country. His father suggested that he should first try his vocation at the seminary in Freiburg-im-Breisgau and begin to study theology at the Catholic Theological Faculty at Freiburg University. But as Augustin remained firm in his decision, his parents finally let their only child go.

So, on 8 April 1902, he entered the Jesuit noviciate in Blyenbeek in Holland. After two years' noviciate he took the vows and began the

[2] This address was not written down, and exists only in the transcript of a tape recording.

usual Jesuit training: three years of philosophy in the Society's house of studies in Valkenburg (Holland) (1904–7), a few years' teaching practice as a teacher of Latin and Greek, etc., in a college for boys in Sittart in Holland (1907–10); and during this time there was also the six months of Latin and Greek studies at Innsbruck University, which has already been mentioned. Afterwards came the theological studies, also at the house of studies in Valkenburg (1910–12); and because of his studies in the theological faculty in Freiburg before his entry into the Society, his theology course was shortened by two years. He was ordained priest on 25 August 1912. It was during this period that his superiors changed their dispositions so often, as I mentioned at the beginning of this chapter, and so the young student had one assignment after another in quick succession, with the result that no sooner had he settled down and done some work than they changed their minds again.

For three years during World War I he was superior in Aachen (1914–17), and after that was at last able to begin his lectures on Old Testament exegesis in the house of studies at Valkenburg. At the same time he was prefect of studies for all the students. After four years he had to give up this work too, for his superiors in Rome made him provincial of the newly founded Jesuit province of Upper Germany (1921–24). It is not difficult to imagine what the direction of a newly created province meant in terms of exhausting work, the travelling it involved and the difficult decisions it demanded. After only three years came yet another job: the direction of the international house of studies in Rome for Jesuits specializing in philosophical and theological studies, who would later teach these subjects in the houses of studies in the various provinces of the Society all over the world. At the same time he was made professor of New Testament theology at the Pontifical Gregorian University (1924–28), and was also lecturing on inspiration and the introduction to the Old Testament at the Pontifical Biblical Institute. In 1928 he was relieved of responsibility for the house of studies, so that he could take over lectures on Old Testament exegesis as well at the Pontifical Biblical Institute. At this time (1929) he was sent by the General as 'Visitor' (inspector) to the Japanese province of the Society in the Far East, which took up six months of his time. Because of conditions at the time he travelled via Russia, Siberia and Korea, returning by ship via Indonesia, India and the Mediterranean.

On 2 July 1930 he was appointed rector of the Pontifical Biblical Institute, an office of great importance that required every ounce of his strength; he was there for nineteen years, until 1949. Being rector meant that he had to organize all the academic work of the Institute and also take care of the religious community who worked there. Anyone with experience of running a religious community will know how many individual tasks this involves. And the conduct of an academic institute is considerably more complicated and was not made any easier by the fact that this institute was situated in Rome, at the very heart of the Catholic Church. So it was inevitable that the rector of the Institute should become more and more involved in the work of the central government of the Church. Even before he became rector he was consultor to a papal commission for the reform of higher ecclesiastical studies. The result of this commission is contained in the famous papal bull *Deus scientiarum Dominus*. In 1931 he was also made a consultor to the Pontifical Biblical Commission. Apart from his activity as a professor, which he continued without any curtailment, he was for more than twenty years chief editor of the Institute's periodical *Biblica*. Under his direction a new faculty was added to the Institute, for the study of the ancient East, its languages, history, culture etc. The Institute also conducted excavations at Teleilat Ghallul in the Jordan valley, which brought to light an entire culture of the period 3500–3200 B.C., which was hitherto unknown and was therefore simply called the Ghallul culture, after the name of the site.[3]

Apart from all this Fr Bea still found time for his own academic work and published books on the problems of biblical inspiration and the Pentateuch, and also many articles and smaller contributions. Yet it is also true that anyone who knew Fr Bea well over a period of years was aware that many of his personal academic interests had to be set aside, many plans had to be given up and many manuscripts had to remain in the drawer.

During this period of his rectorship two events in which Fr Bea had a decisive role to play stand out especially. First, in 1943 there appeared the papal encyclical *Divino afflante Spiritu* dealing with the latest biblical studies, a document that has rightly been called the Magna Carta of modern Catholic scripture studies. The part played by Bea in this document—although only later, if ever, will documentary evidence of this appear—was even at the time an open secret, so much so that the word went round among the students at the Biblical Institute that a great deal of what had appeared in Fr Bea's book on the inspiration of scripture, especially on the literary genres in the Bible, without quotation marks, would from then on have to be printed with quotation marks, so clear and extensive was the agreement between the papal encyclical and what he had been teaching for years.

The second event was the publication of a new Latin translation of the psalms from the Hebrew originals (March 1945), called the 'Pian Psalter' after Pius XII. On the instructions of Pius XII, it had been prepared by the professors of the Pontifical Biblical Institute under the direction of their rector in three years of quiet and difficult work.

About the time of the publication of this new translation of the psalms, Fr Bea had to take on a new duty. When his confessor, Fr A. Merk S.J., became seriously ill, Pius XII took Fr Bea as his confessor;

---

[3] Cf Stefano Schmidt, 'Cinquant'anni del Pontificio Istituto Biblico' in *La Civiltà Cattolica* 1960, I, 615–23, which gives further bibliographical details.

he held this post for more than thirteen years until the death of the pope in 1958. True, the new post did not mean any great increase in work in the usual sense of the word, but it was a very unusual responsibility. Four years later Fr Bea was also made an adviser to the Holy Office. Meetings took place every week and lasted three hours or more. Once Fr Bea told me privately that for months the preparation for these sessions took up half of his time. I give just two examples, which are common knowledge now, to show how serious and responsible this work was. It is well known that the preparation for the dogmatic definition of the bodily Assumption of Mary into heaven was the responsibility of the Holy Office. The commission of twelve, amongst whom was Fr Bea (even before he became a regular adviser to the Holy Office), worked about ten years on the task which had been entrusted to it. The Holy Office also studied and discussed for months the possibility of an ecumenical Council, and later its preparation. Fr Bea had been proposed as the secretary of one of the four preparatory commissions.[4] Since he was still carrying on his work as professor, it became quite impossible for him to continue as rector of the Institute. So he was relieved of this duty at his own urgent request. There now followed a long period of quiet, even hidden, work: apart from his teaching there was the very important and increasing participation in the central government of the Church. In 1950, in the midst of the liturgical reform that was then beginning, he also became a consultor of the Congregation of Rites. In spite of all this he still found time for personal academic work. The biography that was composed in 1959, at the end of this period of his life and on the occasion of his elevation to the cardinalate, lists altogether one hundred articles and smaller contributions apart from the full studies on inspiration and the Pentateuch mentioned above.

Looking back on all the fruitful and varied activity of this man we have to marvel that he did all this in a state of health that could really be described as weak. It had been so since his childhood: at the age of eleven he had tuberculosis in both lungs, and the village doctor gave him only three months to live. As a young philosophy student he had to spend some months in a sanatorium for a lung complaint. In 1913, when he was about to begin his studies at the newly founded Pontifical Biblical Institute in Rome, the doctor X-rayed him and told him that he would not be able to stand the climate in Rome. During his years as professor at Valkenburg (1917–21) he had a heart attack and had to convalesce for some months. In 1956 too, during his annual retreat, he suffered a severe cardiac infraction from which he really never fully recovered: and as a result he had a permanent blockage in his left leg.

On the occasion of the jubilee mentioned at the beginning I spoke with the cardinal about many aspects of his busy life, and he told me that it

[4] Cf G. Caprile, 'Pio XII e un nuovo progretto di Concilio Ecumenico' in *La Civiltà Cattolica* 1966, III, 214.

was only when he became president of the Secretariat for Promoting Christian Unity that he fully understood the real meaning of all the changes, of the repeated orders that he received to leave one job and start a new one. This task demanded so much intellectual flexibility, so much pliability and constant changes of approach, that he would scarcely have been able to manage it without the long remote preparation that his previous busy life had been. But at the point in his life that we have reached, things looked quite different. At this time Fr Bea was in his seventy-eighth year and two weeks before the death of Pius XII he fell seriously ill himself, so that he was unable to assist his dying penitent. Even after he had recovered, he remained decidedly weak. So it was quite understandable that people should wonder whether this man had not come to the end of his great apostolic activity or even the end of his life on earth.[5]

[5] For further biographical details cf E. P. Jung-Inglessis, Augustin Bea, *Kardinal der Einheit*, Reclinghausen 1962, 152: B. I. Leeming S.J., *Augustine Card. Bea*, Notre Dame, USA, 1964, 48; L. A. Dorn, 'Augustin Kardinal Bea' in *Porträts Katholischer Bischöfe Deutschlands*, Osnabrück 1963, 39–46.

PART ONE
Notes from the Annual Retreats
1959–1968

CHAPTER 3

Three months before he became a cardinal

1959

In 1959 Fr Bea made his annual retreat about two months before 16 November, the day on which he heard that the pope intended to make him a cardinal. His notes show that he had not the slightest idea of what the future held for him. His attitude and frame of mind is clear from the details of his life and work following the death of Pius XII.

In the autumn of 1958 Fr Bea was living about twenty-two miles from Rome in the German College's 'Villa San Pastore' (near Gallicano), and he made his annual retreat there. He had visited Pius XII beforehand, to ask 'leave' to make the forthcoming retreat and also to ask his special blessing. He had no idea this was the last time that he would see the pope. Toward the end of his retreat Bea became seriously ill—the eventual diagnosis was intestinal poisoning—and had to be brought back to Rome in haste. At the end of the retreat notes for 28 September 1958 he wrote: 'The last meditation is missing on account of illness.' About a week later Pius XII succumbed to the disease that was to bring about his death. It was very distressing for his confessor that he was unfit to be with the pope during these final hours. Yet he maintained that death would be a blessing to him. When I said to him—in a burst of rather youthful enthusiasm—that we could still ask God to work a miracle for the pope, he answered significantly: 'I know the burden the poor man has to carry and I would not ask him to carry it any longer.'

Bea grew slowly better, and on the afternoon of 28 October he got up for the first time to receive the televized blessing of the newly elected pope, John XXIII. But in the next few months the results of his illness were still noticeable, and the death of Pius XII—especially as it had happened so relatively suddenly and under such painful circumstances —was deeply felt by his confessor. He did resume his usual lectures on inspiration and the two courses on the method of studying scripture and teaching it in the seminaries. He also took part regularly in the weekly session of the Holy Office, but was still quite weak. Before the summer holidays he told me: 'You know that I have travelled a lot during my life, but now I really dread each new journey.' So he tried to convalesce at the Biblical Institute itself and made his 1959 retreat there.

His condition and frame of mind can be seen in the retreat notes themselves, although his expression is restrained. Constantly we meet references to his 'weakened powers' or the 'frailty of old age': 'So I must bear physical discomfort, whatever its origin, not only with patience but in union with the physical sufferings of our Lord, and so for his intention too and following his example (3rd way of subjection). The transfiguration, of the body too, will only come when I rise from the dead' (VI/2). 'I must pursue this goal (the faithful fulfilment of God's will) even with weakened powers, and my great model in this is Pius XII' (1/4). His examination of conscience showed: '. . . there is a lack of energy and determination. I shall need these all the more as the weakness of old age becomes more of a hindrance and makes it more difficult to be faithful in doing what is right. So I must make a great effort to summon up and preserve this energy and must not hold back or look for excuses' (II/1).

At the same time we meet thoughts of death: 'The seventy-nine years that he has given me tell me that he will soon be calling me to eternity. So no hesitation in carrying out the programme, always keeping in sight the greater thing that he wants to give me, namely himself' (I/3).

But it can be seen that this was not a sign of mere resignation. One might almost say that the feeling of weakness even aroused new energy and so became a starting point for renewed faithfulness. This is why he drew up a clear and definite programme, corresponding to his circumstances and conditions as he was able to see them at that time. 'Our Lord lived and worked quietly in Nazareth . . . this is the model for the years God may still grant me. I live (he later added as a precaution: "as far as I can") a retired life in my room; I only appear in public when I have to, and I do not talk about myself. My life is devoted to work for the Church, in whatever way I am needed. . . .' (IV/1). But he added at once: 'So I must make constant efforts to advance in wisdom and grace. Wisdom: human and worldly wisdom—I must not fall behind in my knowledge and in my subject, but must try at least to keep up with developments, and for apostolic reasons: I must not endanger the standing of authority by knowing too little' (id.). Twice he comes back to this idea of progress and explains it: in the meditation on those words of our Lord 'you are the salt of the earth' (Mt 5:13), he writes: '. . . I must try to give men a taste for Christ's teaching and so always show the attractive and inspiring side of Christian truth and of Scripture: but at the same time preserve them from corruption: teach and champion sound doctrine but also see the difficulties and in disputed questions find a sensible middle way' (V/3). And even more clearly: 'Study and academic work: neither progressive nor reactionary but serving the truth, weighing everything up carefully and prudently: straightforward in everything, even in my position of authority: pray for the right insight: great reverence for Scripture. In my teaching I must take up a position with regard to all new questions, and not so much from the historical point of view. Truth without exaggeration and without concealment! Truth is love for the Church and for my neighbour. Modest: "semper paratus doceri"—"always ready to be taught"' (V/consid. of state).

In conclusion: it was his wish: 'May it (death) come to me in the midst of my work' (II/4). But the summary of his programme was this: 'The years that I have left I must and I will spend energetically and with my eyes fixed on the goal, in apostolic work, apostolic prayer, apostolic example and apostolic suffering' (IV/4).

RETREAT 1959

Rome, 31 August–7 September

I/1 *God created me* [Exercises 23] God's real motive for creating me was not any desire to receive glory from me—his glory is not increased by anything I can do—it was his love. Everything that is good wants to communicate itself and allow others to share in its goodness.[1] If that is the case with us men, how much more must it be so with God, who is infinite goodness. This self-communication cannot simply be a perfect natural knowledge of God, for this will never be more than a weak analogical representation; it must be a share in the divine nature, and that means a supernatural raising to a quasi-divine level. This is the 'share in the divine life',[2] which means too a share in the divine happiness. This is why the angels and our first parents were created in a state of grace, and why the redemption restored this divinely willed state of grace to mankind. Everything, therefore, depends on this divine will to love, through which I too was created. But the way to fulfil this divine will to love is through praise, reverence and service, that means through the loyal and, if possible, perfect fulfilment of God's will, in a way it is already an 'identification' with him here on earth. And at the same time this is the response to his love: the most perfect compliance with his will to love and the desire that this will should be fulfilled in the most perfect possible way. O God I love thee.[3]

I/2 *Thereby saving his soul* [Exercises 23] The share in God's happiness depends on the measure of grace that God in his divine providence gives. In this matter no one can argue[4] with him and we shall never

---

[1] This phrase is often used in scholastic philosophy.

[2] Cf 2 Pet 1:4: God has 'called us to his own glory and excellence, by which he has granted to us his precious and very great promises, that through these you may escape from the corruption that is in the world because of passion, and become partakers of the divine nature'.

[3] The Latin, 'O Deus, ego amo te!', is the beginning of a famous hymn attributed to St Francis Xavier.

[4] Cf St Paul: 'But who are you, a man, to answer back to God? Will what is moulded say to its moulder, "Why have you made me thus?"' (Rom 9:20.)

comprehend his mysterious decisions.⁵ The question for me is this: what has God decided for me? I can tell this by looking at the graces and the help that he has given me and continues to give me, which are incomparably greater than those he has given to so many others. This obliges me to use all these graces and all this help with the greatest care, even where that calls for self-control and sacrifice. My 'praise' must be in proportion to the great knowledge that I have of God: others know much less about him and yet are more faithful in prayer, in meditation. . . .

My 'reverence' in worship, in the liturgy, especially in the celebration of Mass, must be more fervent, corresponding to my knowledge of the greatness, nobility and holiness of God. My 'service' must not simply be a matter of avoiding sin, of doing what is essential; it must be the most perfect possible fulfilment of the vows and rules, all the duties of my position, all the daily work and tasks: by choosing what is more likely to achieve the purpose of my creation! How others do this is no concern of mine: I do not know how much grace they have—but I do know how much grace I have and I must make the most of it.

I/3 *Everything else on earth has been created for my sake* [Exercises 23]
But I must weigh all these things up according to supernatural principles, not according to nature.⁶ Everything must help me to achieve my goal, but it must be the goal that I have recognized as *mine*: the most faithful fulfilment possible of God's will. Any dependence on creatures, any lack of self-control in my way of life and my relations with others, any love of ease or of self: anything of this sort holds me back in my pursuit of my goal, as my own experience and observation of others show.

I must pursue this goal even with weakened powers and my great

---

⁵ There is an echo of St Paul here too: 'O the depth of the riches and wisdom and knowledge of God! How unsearchable are his judgments and how inscrutable his ways! For who has known the mind of the Lord, or who has been his counsellor?' (Rom 11:33 f.)

⁶ It is essential to understand the ascetic concept of 'nature' used here by the author. The best explanation is to be found in the following passage from the *Imitation of Christ* by Thomas à Kempis in the chapter 'On the corruption of nature and the power of God's grace'. In this chapter the author says, speaking to God: 'Yes, I need your grace, and a lot of it at that, if I am to overcome nature, always bent on evil from youth upwards (Gen 8:21). It was through Adam, the first man, that it fell and was spoiled by sin; and the penalty for that blemish upon humanity has come down upon all men. That very nature which, as made by you, was good and upright, now stands for something vicious, for the weakness of a nature given over to corruption; that is because its instincts, left to themselves, drag the man in whom it is found towards evil and base desires. What little strength has remained is like a little spark hidden among ashes. This is natural reason itself, which, though shut off by intense darkness, can still tell good from evil, still separate truth from falsehood. Yet it is powerless to carry out all it approves of, and now no longer possesses the full light of truth nor the wholesome affections it once had' (III, 55, 2).

In other words this concept of 'nature' as used in ascetics corresponds fairly precisely to the Pauline idea of the 'flesh'. It comes from that painful experience of man's moral and religious consciousness expressed by Paul in the famous chapter 7 of Romans.

model in this is Pius XII.⁷ Not for one moment unfaithful to the programme. As a check I have my examination of conscience: how have I made this? How will I keep it till the next time? My model is our Lord. I am a child of God and so I must be like him, the first-born Son of God.⁸ It is something more that God wants to give you and that is himself, he who made these creatures (St Augustine). Nor must I forget that God is going to give me this *soon*. The seventy-nine years that he has given me tell me that he will soon be calling me to eternity. So no hesitation in carrying out the programme, always keeping in sight the greater thing that he wants to give me, namely himself.   4.X.1959

Consideration of state. The most important thing for me is to aim at perfection with all my strength. And the best way to do this is by love— to imitate the love of God who gave his Son for us,⁹ the love of our Lord who gave himself up for me.¹⁰ I must, therefore, refuse God nothing: whatever God wants, however he wants it and as long as he wants. He has been so generous with me: I must not bargain with him. 'You must give me all for all, keep no aspect of yourself as your private concern' (*Imitation* III:27). Increase your love in me!

I/4 *Indifference* [Exercises 23] This is not just for beginners; the more I want to advance in the spiritual life and the more I want to work for the Church and for souls, the more I need it, to become free from myself, free from the hindrance of any regard for myself, when carrying out what I recognize clearly as God's will. In this respect the great saints are my model: St Paul in his apostolate, St Ignatius in his foundation.¹¹ And I can recognize the will of God clearly through the commands of my superiors, through the circumstances and conditions in which I have been placed, and through clear interior promptings.

Indifference does not stop me advancing in wisdom and prudence. On the contrary it excludes whatever is merely emotion or a matter of feeling and in its place it puts considerations of faith and reason, which I can follow unhampered by personal considerations. It gives me, then, true freedom of spirit, independence of every influence that is not willed by God, and therefore energy and strength. The energy with which the saints pursued their goal would not have been possible without this interior freedom, that is without indifference. But indifference itself presupposes a great love of God, by which all self-love is, so to speak,

---

⁷ Bea was confessor to Pius XII from 1945–58.
⁸ Cf Rom 8:29: 'For those whom he foreknew he also predestined to be conformed to the image of his Son, in order that he might be the first-born among many brethren.'
⁹ Cf Rom 8:31 f: 'If God is for us, who is against us? He who did not spare his own Son but gave him up for us all, will he not also give us all things with him?'
¹⁰ Cf Gal 2:20: 'I have been crucified with Christ; it is no longer I who live, but Christ who lives in me; and the life I now live in the flesh I live by faith in the Son of God, who loved me and gave himself for me.'
¹¹ Ignatius of Loyola (1491–1556), founder of the Society of Jesus.

burned up and supplanted. This love does not need to be a matter of feeling: it must be in the will, which wants to give itself up wholly to God. O God, I love thee!

II/1 *My own sins* [Exercises 55–61] I can only commend my past confidently to God's mercy. He knows how things stand, and I have been through this often enough in my general confessions. Have mercy on me, O Lord, in thy great mercy [cf Ps 50:1]. As for the present, my main fault is that I have not made full use of so many graces or that I have not won more grace by greater attention to my spiritual exercises. Nor have I always given the good example that a person of my age and position should give. On both these scores there is a lack of energy and determination. I shall need these all the more, as the weakness of old age becomes more of a hindrance and makes it more difficult to be faithful in doing what is right. So I must make a great effort to summon up and preserve this energy and must not hold back or look for excuses. This too I owe God for the many graces he has shown me in the seventy-eight years of my life and which he continues to show me. The more faithfully I use these graces, the more fresh graces the Lord will give me, and he will give me also those which I need most in particular circumstances.

II/2 *Venial Sin* Even when it is not a matter of completely deliberate sin, it is still always a serious matter. For example, I lose many graces through distraction in prayer: I give less than good example on many occasions through lack of punctuality and humility: I dissipate my energy and weaken my will through indulgence. The line between the two sorts of venial sin is not so easy to draw and so the question of their consequences is not so clear and simple. If I am serious about making constant progress in the spiritual life, I must fight the sins of thoughtlessness constantly and perseveringly. To help me in this I have once again the examination of conscience and the monthly renewal, when I must come back to this point again and again. In my case there is a special reason for good example, my age, my position, my authority demand that I should in all things be exemplary and faithful. This is also an apostolate, especially as I can scarcely exercise any other apart from that of academic work. But the last and highest motive here too is the love of God: for him and his honour and in gratitude to him I must aim at the highest, and should not ask: what can I do without actually sinning, but: how can I advance even more in love and virtue? Then the Lord will be generous toward me and shower his graces upon me.[12]

---

[12] St Ignatius has this to say on the meaning of generosity towards God in one of the introductory notes to the Exercises: 'The retreatant will greatly benefit if he starts with a large-hearted generosity towards his Creator and Lord, surrendering to him his freedom of will, so that his Divine Majesty may make that use of his person and possessions which is in accordance with his most holy will' (5). In the Constitutions of the Society of Jesus, he is even more specific: 'In general the more closely anyone binds himself to God and the more generous he shows

II/3 *Penance and trust* I must not forget the past: whatever it may have been, it cannot have been pleasing to God, and like the apostle I have to say: 'I am the least of all.'[13] That I have become what I am today is not through any merit of mine but through God's grace. By the grace of God I am what I am. But this consideration must not depress me or paralyse my efforts, any more than it paralysed St Paul, who, far from being faint-hearted, derived the greatest driving force from it to work tirelessly for God. 'I have laboured more.' So too my conclusion from the past must be to work for our Lord to the last breath! What work I have to do for him is not for me to decide: it is God's will, which reveals itself in the orders and commissions of superiors, in the circumstances of life and in my own heart, when I meditate on supernatural things. I am, therefore, exactly where I ought to be. I can say with St Augustine: give me the strength to do what you ask and ask what you will. Peter, Paul, Augustine all did great things in spite of their earlier sins. He who has loved much . . .[14] But this also shows me how humble I must be: 'Not I but the grace of God which is in me' (1 Cor 15:10). And this grace is not deserved.

Consideration of state: examination of conscience. Make the effort to serve God better and to love God more, above all in the faithful performance of my duties. Prévoir, pourvoir, revoir. *Prévoir:* the duties and obstacles that lie ahead—I must have a plan; *pourvoir:* I must choose the means [in the presence of God]. I must ask advice[15] and not try to do everything on my own; *revoir:* what were the mistakes of the past, the reason for past success?

II/4 *Death and judgment* It is clear that my death is not far off, even though I cannot in any way determine when and how it will come. May it come to me in the midst of my work. I must not be 'unprepared' even if it comes 'unexpectedly'. Every single day that the Lord gives me should be a preparation for death: an ever-growing detachment from the 'world', that means from everything the world could give me—honour, recognition, position, and at the same time it means a love of God that is always growing and nourished by an ever-increasing faith-

---

himself towards God's majesty, the more he will experience God's great kindness towards himself and day by day will himself become more capable of receiving still greater spiritual gifts and graces' (III, 1, 22).

[13] Cf St Paul writing of those to whom Christ appeared after his resurrection: 'Last of all, as to one untimely born, he appeared also to me. For I am the least of the apostles, unfit to be called an apostle, because I persecuted the Church of God. But by the grace of God I am what I am, and his grace towards me was not in vain. On the contrary, I worked harder than any of them, though it was not I, but the grace of God which is with me' (1 Cor 15:8-10).

[14] Compare our Lord's words about the repentant sinner in the house of Simon the Pharisee: 'Therefore I tell you, her sins, which are many, are forgiven, for she loved much; but he who is forgiven little, loves little' (Lk 7:47).

[15] In the Ms two words are in shorthand here. Probably we should read (ask) 'others for' (advice).

fulness in carrying out God's will. Even in my last years this will not be possible without a struggle and self-denial. Nor must I forget my sins: examination of conscience, monthly recollection, confession and, as a penance, great patience in the face of the difficulties and obstacles that old age brings with it. I can draw strength from the Church, whose child I am, and from the sacraments, especially the Eucharist, and I can draw light from the Church's teaching. Then let death come. I am not afraid of it; in fact I welcome it because it will take me to the Lord, to whom the Church prays: 'May Christ Jesus smile upon you and welcome your coming: may he appoint a place for you amongst those who stand near him',[16] and at this moment Mary will 'turn her eyes of mercy towards me'.[17] In this way I shall be able to face death and also my judge with confidence: 'as already judged and not waiting to be judged I wish to appear before thee, Lord' (St Bernard).

III/1 *The kingdom of Christ* [Exercises 91-98] Here it is not God calling (that was in the first week) but our Lord, who is God but has become in all things like us men, except for sin,[18] and who has taken upon himself the infinitely burdensome work of redemption for our sake. He can point, then, to his own example: 'to anyone, then, who chooses to join me, I offer nothing but a share in my hardships; but if he follows me in suffering he will assuredly follow me in glory.' And he is calling us to share what he did for us: to make us subject to God! To enable me to do it he became man, he suffered and was hungry and thirsty. So now it is more than reasonable that I too should share in the work that he did for me and which could not have any concrete success without my cooperation (free will!). But for me this is not just reasonable. He has done far more than is necessary for me and to me; his graces and his help have really been showered on me. So it is only fitting that I should do more than is absolutely necessary; that I should be outstanding in sharing his work for me; that I should be firm in overcoming all obstacles within me—take positive steps[19]—and that I should make faithful use of all available help against them, especially his example, so that I may achieve the purpose for which he came into the world, in the most perfect possible way. Once again then, I must strive after perfection in all things, just as I resolved in the first week. In thy company, Lord!

[16] Cf Ordo commendationis animae in the *Roman Ritual*, Tit. VI ch. vii.
[17] Cf the prayer, 'Hail, holy Queen.'
[18] Cf Heb 4:15: 'For we have not a high priest who is unable to sympathize with our weaknesses, but one who in every respect has been tempted as we are, yet without sinning.'
[19] An idea which is very significant for the spirituality of the Exercises and for Ignatius in general. At the very beginning, in one of the twenty 'preliminary remarks' the retreatant is warned of the difficulties that he will meet in prayer: '. . . whilst it is easy and pleasant to complete the full hour of contemplation in time of comfort, in time of distress it is very hard to finish it. So, in order to counter the distress and overcome the temptation, the retreatant must always go on a little longer than the full hour. In this way he will get used not only to resisting the enemy but to routing him completely' (13).

III/2 *The incarnation—the annunciation* [cf Lk 1:26–38] The incarnation in its concrete form is nothing but the realization of the programme that the meditation on the kingdom of Christ puts before me. The redemption is not brought about by a simple act of God's will but also by a work that repairs the damage done by the Fall. And so the Second Person [of the Trinity] became man, but a man who took to himself and upon himself all the wretchedness caused by sin [cf Heb 4:15]. The opposite of what the 'world' seeks: instead of ambition, the Servant of the Lord;[20] instead of riches, poverty-stricken Nazareth; instead of self-satisfaction and pleasure, work and self-denial. And since man cannot be saved without cooperation on his part, Christ calls him to share his work. The first and also the most perfect of his assistants is his mother, Mary. She is the ideal for collaboration with the divine King; the handmaid of the Lord at the side of the Servant of the Lord, the poor woman of Nazareth at the side of the one who had nowhere to lay his head;[21] the purest, the holiest, the immaculate at the side of the one who was the pure God-Man. This is her real greatness and at the same time the key to the mystery of Nazareth. The others who cooperate with him, the apostles and the priests, are copying her and only in this way are they real apostles. 'Prelates' with worldly jurisdiction, popes as temporal sovereigns, abbots as estate-owners may have been a consequence of the conditions of their time: but they were not the ideal: the Society [of Jesus] with its concept of poverty, purity and obedience may perhaps come as close as possible to this ideal, and *I* must make an effort to bring this about in my own case as perfectly as possible. Fiat, fiat!

III/3 *The nativity* [cf Lk 2:1–7] The meaning of Bethlehem is expressed in the angels' song, glory to God and peace to men [cf Lk 2:13 f]; it is the programme the heavenly King has drawn up for himself. But the path towards this goal is quite different from the way in which we men, and also those directly concerned at the time, had imagined it. Mary has made all sorts of plans about bringing up and caring for her child, but God confounds them all. Fiat! Her job is only to cooperate. The decision is made in Rome;[22] it is the result of completely worldly interests; for hundreds of thousands it is a heavy burden, but for our Lord it is the way to the fulfilment of what has been prophesied about him. To criticize would be to misunderstand divine providence. On the journey they feel all the effects of poverty—'in utter destitution' [Exercises 116], but they go in the spirit of faith, remembering the great events of sacred

---

[20] The famous songs in Isaiah about the Messiah as the 'Servant of the Lord' are frequently applied in the New Testament to Christ. Cf, e.g., Mt 12:17 f: 'This was to fulfil what was spoken of by the prophet Isaiah: "Behold my servant whom I have chosen, my beloved with whom my soul is well pleased. I will put my spirit upon him, and he shall proclaim justice to the Gentiles. . . ."' (cf Is 42:1).

[21] See what Christ said in Lk 9:58: 'Foxes have holes, and birds of the air have nests; but the Son of man has nowhere to lay his head.'

[22] Cf Lk 2:1–4: 'In those days a decree went out from Caesar Augustus that all the world should be enrolled.'

history. In Bethlehem Mary suffers because her child is not an ordinary child of man; this consideration leads her to take shelter in a stable. And there at last the greatest event of world history takes place, and not a soul pays any attention. These are the ways of God, which bypass our ways and show us that we are *only* collaborators in God's work, but *real* collaborators.

General confession (Fr Vacci) 2.IX.1959

Consideration of state; mental prayer Preparation: what grace? What are the main thoughts to be? Application to the needs of the moment.

The meditation itself: 'friendly conversation with God' (St Teresa). Affections: ejaculatory prayers. Drawing inspiration from the liturgy! 'All the saints became saints by the practice of mental prayer' (St Alphonsus).

III/4 *The presentation in the temple—Simeon* [cf Lk 2:22–32] For Mary this day is the beginning of her share in her Son's sufferings, her 'compassion'. Joyfully she goes up to the Temple, not because she has to, but because her heart leads her there. But she cannot yet read the heart of her child, who today once again and now in concrete circumstances utters the words: 'Lo, I come to do your will ... your law is in my heart'.[23] He offers himself on the altar without any reservations: Behold I come. Old Simeon's words reveal to the mother the thoughts of her Son. Simeon knows that he is the salvation, the light and the glory but he knows too that this means struggles, suffering and death. This is what Simeon now tells the mother: 'set for the fall and rising of many in Israel, and for a sign that is spoken against', and his mother is to have her share in this: 'and a sword will pierce through your soul also'. So begins the mother's way of the cross at the side of her suffering Son, and it will end on Calvary: 'By the cross stood his mother Mary.' She is the first and noblest of those who join in the Lord's work; and so she must make the same sacrifices as he does. To share our Lord's work means to share his sufferings and his cross: 'to anyone, then, who chooses to join me, I offer nothing but a share in my hardships; but if he follows me in suffering he will assuredly follow me in glory' (Exercises 95). But that means imitating our Lord in 'putting up with all injustice, all abuse, all

---

[23] A reference to Hebrews, where the words of the psalmist are put into the mouth of Christ: 'Consequently, when Christ came into the world, he said, "Sacrifices and offerings thou hast not desired, but a body hast thou prepared for me; in burnt offerings and sin offerings thou hast taken no pleasure. Then I said, 'Lo, I have come to do thy will, O God, as it is written of me in the roll of the book' (Ps 40:7 f) ... and by that will we have been sanctified through the offering of the body of Jesus Christ once for all" ' (Heb 10:5–7, 10). We come across this text repeatedly in the cardinal's meditations. The Latin phrase he uses, 'lex tua in medio cordis mei', does not occur in this form in Hebrews, but in Ps 40:8 (legem tuam in medio cordis mei); it is used as the offertory verse in the votive Mass to the Sacred Heart at Eastertide, with reference to the heart of Christ.

poverty . . .' (Exercises 98). This is my lot too. 'Holy mother, pierce me through, in my heart each wound renew of my Saviour crucified.'[24]

IV/1 *Life at Nazareth* Our Lord lived and worked quietly in Nazareth. No one who was not aware of his secret could even guess who he was. And he was only known at all within his own narrow circle of acquaintance. This is the model for the years God may still grant me. As far as I can I live a retired life in my room; I only appear in public when I have to and I do not talk about myself. My life is devoted to work for the Church, in whatever way I am needed—just as our Lord did the things that were required of him. So I must make constant efforts to advance in wisdom and grace [cf Lk 2:52]. Wisdom: human and worldly wisdom—I must not fall behind in my knowledge and in my subject, but must try at least to keep up with developments, and for apostolic reasons: I must not endanger the standing of authority by knowing too little. But also supernatural wisdom: everything must help me on my way to the final goal by the most suitable means. And favour with God and man: nor must I discount people's opinions, for in my work they are of importance. But the most important thing is to increase in grace and holiness.   25.VII.1960

IV/2 *In the temple* [cf Lk 2:41–52] Our Lord goes to Jerusalem. In his omniscience he sees how often he will go there in the years to come and how worried he will be about Jerusalem ('how often would I have . . .'),[25] and all this concerns him deeply. How well I can imitate our Lord in *my* ways: not thinking vain thoughts but thinking of God's ways and of my supernatural tasks. The Lord gives everyone his share: in work and in prayer. At this point he interrupts his work because of a call to something higher. He must go to his Father and give an example of leaving all things, that he may be about his Father's business. And it is wonderful to see how many imitators his example has found. Hundreds of thousands of young people have left home to consecrate themselves to God's service and to echo those words: 'Do you not know that I must be in my Father's house?' By God's grace I too once said that, and now every day I must make a serious effort to keep my heart free from any dependence on natural things and devote myself totally to the service of God—in whatever concrete form the opportunity may present itself. But at the same time like our Lord I must be modest and humble: 'hearing and asking them questions', not 'teaching', although he knew infinitely more than all the teachers facing him. I must show understanding,[26] towards everything that I hear from others; I must not

---

[24] From the hymn 'Stabat Mater', used in the liturgy on the feast of the Seven Sorrows of our Lady.

[25] Cf Jesus' words to the city of Jerusalem: 'How often would I have gathered your children together as a hen gathers her brood under her wings, and you would not!' (Mt 23:37).

[26] Bea used the Greek word, *synesis*, as used by the Evangelist: 'and all who heard

be stubborn and exclusive, unless that should be necessary for higher reasons.

IV/3 *The baptism* [Mt 3:13-17 and parallels] When I meditate on this mystery I must thank the Lord from the bottom of my heart for the example he has given me: 1) *Freedom* from all earthly attachments, even from his holy mother whom he loved so much: and all this in order to be able to carry out his task without any hindrance. 2) *Humility:* although he is the purest and the holiest he stands in the midst of sinners and waits his turn. In this way it really does come about that he bore our sins: 'the Lamb of God who takes away the sins of the world'.[27] He bore them: but he takes them away from us. 3) *The gift of baptism:* he has himself baptized so that we should be baptized and by baptism become, like him, beloved sons of God [cf Eph 5:1], in whom God is well pleased. But by no means all men receive this grace: out of 2,600 millions only 878 millions, that is one third, and of these again half are separated from the true Church! And so only one sixth are Catholic—would that they all were! Thus the baptism of our Lord awakens the desire to spread the faith, a task to which our Society, together with many others, devotes itself. In my position I can only help by my apostolic prayer and I must practise this more and more.

IV/C *Consideration of state* I. *Union with God:* 'I have seen God in a man' (Ars). 1) Faithfulness in my daily spiritual exercises. 2) Prayer before every important action. 'In thy company, Lord: through thee: for thee!' 3) Visits to the Blessed Sacrament, even if they are short. 4) Self-denial: prayer and self-denial are the main ways of achieving this end and have a mutual influence on one another.   5.I.1960

II. *Affective prayer:* the will must control the mind: 'more attention must be paid to the affections (of the will) and to interior appreciation.[28] Very active prayer, precisely through the affections.

[the child Jesus] were amazed at his understanding (*synesis*) and his answers' (Lk 2:47).

[27] Cf Is 53:7, 12. The elements of Isaiah's prophecy are linked together in the words used by John the Baptist to introduce Christ: 'Behold the Lamb of God, who takes away the sin of the world' (Jn 1:29; cf also 1:36).

[28] Directory 14, 3. This is the practical introduction for the retreat-giver. The idea of 'interior appreciation' is set out in the suggestion for the retreat-givers in Exercises 2: 'The person who gives another the method and outline for meditation or contemplation must faithfully recount the historical subject of such a contemplation or meditation, just running over the headings in a brief and summary explanation.' This is in order that 'when the person making the contemplation is given the basic facts of the story and then goes over it and thinks about it for himself, any discovery he makes which sheds light on the story, or brings it home to him more, will give him greater delight and more benefit of soul. Such discoveries may be due to his own reflection or to the divine action, but they are better than if the giver of the exercises had gone into great detail and expounded at length the significance of the story. Nor does the soul's full satisfaction come from wide knowledge so much as from the personal appreciation of and feeling for things.'

IV/4 *The call of the apostles* [cf Mk 3:13–19 and parallels] In the vocation of the apostles I see my own vocation. You have not chosen me, I have chosen you,[29] not because of natural qualities—he could find these in a thousand others; not for my merits—I have none; but because 'he desired'.[30] The conditions in which I lived when he called me were ordinary, so that I might appreciate better the gratuity of my vocation. Now, as I near the end of my life, I must be especially grateful for this vocation and have only one thing to regret, that I have not cooperated with this vocation as much as he might have expected. He called me that I might be with him[31] and in fact there cannot have been one month even in my fifty-seven years in the Society that I have not lived under the same roof as our Lord. But being with him also means that I had his example always in front of me (meditation, reading) and heard his teaching—to a degree which few enjoy. And finally the words 'go and bear fruit' [Jn 15:16] apply to me too. I had to leave my parents, my home, my country in his apostolic service in order to 'bear fruit'. Only he knows how much fruit I have borne. I hope there was some at least. And now I can only pray: 'that my fruit may remain', the fruit deep inside me, but also whatever apostolic fruit my efforts may have produced. And if I had to bear crosses and face difficulties—and really there has not been much of that, almost too little—then here too the words of scripture apply: the disciple is not above his master [cf Mt 10:24 f; Jn 15:20]. The years that I have left I must and I will spend energetically with my eyes fixed on the goal, in apostolic work, apostolic prayer, apostolic example and apostolic suffering. Give me your love and your grace! [Exercises 234.]

V/1 *The training of the apostles* All my activity must come from within, from a religious supernatural foundation. Otherwise it is activism, pretence, without any real foundation and hence without lasting success, 'a noisy gong or a clanging cymbal'.[32] And the final and deepest foundation must be love: a love of God striving to give him the greatest possible honour and glory, and a love of service towards my fellow-men, for I wish to be of service to them in their apostolic work and for the good of their souls. Precisely in this respect there is still much that I can do by advice, help and encouragement, and in this way I am also working apostolically, at least indirectly. But all this will only have any real effect if it comes from an interior life and a serious striving after perfection, and in this way seeks not self but God. This was the first thing the

---

[29] From our Lord's farewell address after the Last Supper: 'You did not choose me, but I chose you' (Jn 15:16).

[30] The freedom of choice exercised by Christ is expressly stated by Mark: 'And he went up into the hills, and called to him those whom he desired' (3:13).

[31] Cf Mk 3:14: 'And he appointed twelve, to be with him, and to be sent out to preach.'

[32] Cf Paul's hymn of love: 'If I speak in the tongues of men and of angels, but have not love, I am a noisy gong or a clanging cymbal' (1 Cor 13:1).

apostles had to learn, to overcome their ambition, their eagerness to have the first place, their impatience, in order to become genuine stewards of God's mysteries [cf 1 Cor 4:1]. The example of our Lord (meditation!) and his warnings trained them, but it was the Holy Spirit coming on them at Pentecost who completed the work. Come, Holy Ghost.

V/2 *The Sermon on the Mount (I)* [cf Mt 5:3–12] The most important thing for me is to hunger and thirst, that is to have a great desire for 'justice', for the perfection demanded by my vocation and position. Everything else follows from that. For me the question is not knowing what I have to do, but carrying out what I have long known to be my task with determination, resolution and perseverance. Above all, then, pay attention to the will, and do not forget that perseverance is a grace, so I must pray for it. In detail: *those who mourn*—a life that is mortified, overcoming self, one that does not attract attention, spent quietly without any special comforts in my room and without anything special in the way of food and drink: *pure in heart*—very conscientious, not because of scruples but because of love, in all things (careful custody of the eyes).

Towards my fellow-men: kindness, gentleness, understanding [cf Lk 6:27–38], not in any artificial way for the sake of diplomacy, but the result of a genuine supernatural love of neighbour. In particular, must always do my best to encourage peace and cooperation. *Persecutions* [cf Mt 5:11 f]: I shall scarcely be called upon to face these, but I must bear opposition and disagreements in a spirit of love and patience. The great example in all this is our Lord, so I must learn to know and love him more and more in meditation and spiritual reading etc.: make my heart like thine!

V/3 *The Sermon on the Mount (II)* [cf Mt 5:13–16] *Salt of the earth:* I must try to give men a taste for Christ's teaching and so always show the attractive and inspiring side of Christian truth and of scripture. But at the same time preserve them from corruption: teach and champion sound doctrine,[33] but also see the difficulties and in disputed questions find a sensible middle way.

---

[33] This is a biblical (or more precisely pauline) idea. Just as there can be bodily ill-health, which can basically be a contradiction to life, and can damage it, even endanger it, so also in the sphere of faith. There exists 'sound doctrine', a 'healthy word, be urgent in season and out of season, convince, rebuke, and exhort, be unfailing doctrine. Thus Paul gives Timothy the famous warning: 'I charge you in the presence of God and of Jesus Christ who is to judge the living and the dead . . . preach the word, be urgent in season and out of season, convince, rebuke, and exhort, be unfailing in patience and teaching.' Why? 'For the time is coming when people will not endure sound teaching, but having itching ears they will accumulate for themselves teachers to suit their own likings, and will turn away from listening to the truth and wander into myths' (2 Tim 4:1–4).

The idea of sound doctrine is emphasized in Tit 1:9: among a bishop's other qualities: 'he must hold firm to the sure word as taught, so that he may be able to give instruction in sound doctrine and also to confute those who contradict it.' Titus is urged: 'therefore rebuke them [the faithful] sharply, that they may be sound in the faith' (Tit 1:13). And again: 'But as for you, teach what befits sound doctrine. Bid the older men be temperate . . . sound in faith' (Tit 2:1 f).

Light: I must be aware that my words have a certain authority and so a certain responsibility. So must pray for light for myself. Come, Holy Ghost! *A city:* I am now in a position where people look up to me, in small things and in great; in my own community and elsewhere. Therefore I can never 'let myself go' in any way; I must always 'observe restraint', not as a matter of tactics but because of an interior spirit and a sense of apostolate. For me there can be no 'unimportant details', about which I do not need to bother: everything, words, bearing, my room, my relations with others must be considered under the heading of 'good example'. And all this demands decisiveness—'if thy hand scandalize thee' [cf Mt 5:30]—and therefore sacrifice. These are the little daily sacrifices that I offer in union with the sacrifices of our Lord.

V/C *Consideration of state   Study and academic work*   Neither progressive nor reactionary but serving the truth, weighing everything up carefully and prudently: straightforward in everything, even in a position of authority: and praying for the right insight: great reverence for scripture. In my teaching must take up a position with regard to all new questions, and not so much from the historical point of view. Truth without exaggeration and without concealment! Truth is love for the Church and for my neighbour. Modest: always ready to be taught.[34] From my contact with others must, wherever possible, increase my knowledge.

V/4 *The multiplication of the loaves* [Mk 6:31-44]   The goodness of our Lord is boundless: towards the disciples and towards the people. At all times I must be gentle and thoughtful. I must learn from this episode. I must not become a hermit making myself unapproachable; on the contrary, I must show myself always ready to help everyone, my own brethren, people from outside, the students. From the people I can learn how to be eager to hear our Lord and be with him: in meditations, visits and spiritual reading. For me too he is the Good Shepherd [cf Jn 10:11], particularly where I cannot see my path clearly. Jesu shepherd, bread indeed, take thou pity on our need![35] The disciples are obviously afraid that they might lose their night's rest after losing their rest that day. Our Lord does not allow *this* particular fear to be realized but he does not spare them the burden of the night. In his great goodness he knows how to protect them and preserve them from dangers.

---

[34] This was the motto of a famous Roman cardinal, Michael Mercati, a prefect of the Vatican library. The author was fond of quoting this motto, and in these notes it occurs more than once. In an autobiographical essay on his own road to Ecumenism, he wrote on this point: (it is necessary to have) 'a sincere and firm will always to understand, according to the motto of that well-known orientalist, Cardinal G. Mercati (1866-1957), Prefect of the Vatican Library: "paratus semper doceri", always ready to be taught. The desire for a continual intellectual renewal is needed' (cf *Saturday Review*, New York, 8 July 1967, p. 9).

[35] From the liturgical hymn to the Blessed Sacrament, in the Roman Missal for the feast of Corpus Christi.

Our Lord is not just kind-hearted, he is also powerful and wise. The most comforting thing, however, is that he makes them 'stewards of the mysteries of God' [cf 1 Cor 4:1], for it is in their hands that the bread is multiplied: whether one or thousands eat. . . .[36] It is the same today in the Mass, where he teaches the faithful through the mouth of his priests and then lets them work the great miracle of the consecration and distribute the bread of life. We are no longer 'like sheep that have no shepherd' [cf Mk 6:34]. He is the good shepherd and we priests share his pastoral office. 6.III.1960

VI/1 *The calming of the storm* [cf Lk 8:22–25 and parallels] In all storms in the Church, in the Society and in my own heart two things must help us: our own work and fervent prayer. That my work may be successful, God's help is needed. This is more powerful than any human effort, but as a rule God does not help unless I make a serious effort myself. Much that is harmful could have been avoided in the Church if people who were responsible and held positions of authority had intervened actively, energetically and promptly. So whenever I have to deal with difficulties, whether they are my own or the Church's or whether it is in some matter confided to my care, I must act with all my strength, but in all this I must not forget prayer. 'And there came a great calm' [cf Mk 4:30]. The Lord can come to my aid in a moment. The miraculous draught of fish [cf Lk 5:1–11] shows us St Peter's pre-eminence. Although there are other apostles there with their boats, it is Peter's boat that our Lord chooses to step into: it is to him that he gives the command to launch out into the deep; it is to him (and only him) that he says: 'From now on you will catch men.' I must consider it an honour and a joy to work for the successor of St Peter.

VI/2 *The transfiguration* [cf Mt 17:1–9] 'The gates of hell shall not prevail':[37] the Church remains and will endure, but the cross awaits its servants: let a man take up his cross [cf Mt 16:24 f]! This is for them the condition of following Jesus, and the more closely we follow him, the more we must bear his cross which is our cross. The transfiguration affects the body as well, so the cross must also have its physical side; this, too, because the kingdom of God will not be spread without hard physical effort. Another reason is that our Lord himself suffered so much physically, to give us an example, but also to give us strength. So I must bear physical discomfort, whatever its origin, not only with patience but in union with the physical sufferings of our Lord, and hence for his

---

[36] Idem.

[37] 'And I tell you, you are Peter, and on this rock I will build my church, and the powers of death shall not prevail against it' (Mt 16:18). It is to be noted that the author in this meditation (as so often) sees the main object of the meditation in a wide context. In Matthew for instance this promise and the assurance of Christ are followed by the anouncement of his suffering and death; there follows the warning on the necessity for self-denial, and only after that the account of the transfiguration of Christ.

intentions too and following his example (3rd way of subjection [Exercises 167]). The transfiguration, of the body too, will only come when I rise from the dead. But prayer must be added to the cross: 'while he was praying on the mountain' [Lk 9:28 f], and that means prayer in solitude, apart from the world. If I do not share our Lord's prayer I shall not share his transfiguration. Here too it is a case of 'let him follow me'! These, then, are the three words that must shape my life: prayer, work, cross, and all three must be joined together in my daily life, including the cross. And if it does not come from without, then I must take it upon myself: 'let him take up his cross',[38] that means take up and carry.

VI/3 *The Blessed Sacrament* [Mt 26:26–29 and parallels] That the Eucharist is the greatest thing that we have here on earth, I know well enough theoretically. But in practice my daily Mass and reception of communion becomes a habit, something almost mechanical. Therefore I must make a new resolution to be practical above all and show how much I value the Blessed Sacrament by a good and fervent preparation, great recollection and care in the Mass itself, a good and lively thanksgiving and finally great devotion and care in my daily visits to the Blessed Sacrament. Only in this way can I share in the great fruits of the holy sacrifice and holy communion, so that the Eucharist may really nourish and strengthen my spiritual life. I shall need this strength especially now after this retreat, so that I can carry out and persevere in carrying out the programme and practical resolutions that this retreat has produced. I must make an effort, then, to grasp more and more clearly the great importance of the Eucharist for my spiritual life and to receive a full share of all the grace that our Lord has attached to it.

VI/4 *Thoughts from the farewell discourse* 'He remains in me and I in him' [cf Jn 15:5]: this is a constant and profound union with our Lord, not merely a moral union but an ontic one, as the branch is united to the vine. From this union I receive strength, power and joy. It makes it possible for me to bear fruit, and indeed, as our Lord says, much fruit. But all this does not depend on our Lord alone, he says: remain in my love [cf Jn 15:9 f]; so I can destroy this union, I can also make it grow less. There are degrees of this remaining in Christ, just as there are degrees of love in a friendship or in marriage. The norm is: keep my commandments; the more faithfully, perfectly and energetically I keep our Lord's commandments, the more this union with him will be deep, firm and fruitful. Can I, then, keep on coming to every confession with the same sins and failings, when I could overcome them if I made a greater effort? I must also give proof of this union with Christ by suffering. He himself is the suffering Saviour and says here too: if I your Lord and master ... (cf Jn 13:14). Suffering may come from without: but

---

[38] To underline his meaning the author uses the Greek word *airo*.

in any case infirmities, hardships, ill-health are also forms of suffering that I must bear in union with the sufferings of our Lord. Must bear and can bear, for it is only a drop in the full and overflowing cup of *his* suffering. Even if it is difficult: have faith—I have overcome (the world) [cf Jn 16:33].

Finally he gives me the Holy Spirit, who dwells in my soul as in a temple[39] and gives the strength and grace that our Lord allots me. The Spirit of fortitude but also the Spirit of truth [cf Jn 16:13]: may I keep the faith always before my eyes and so live from faith. You in me and I in you! Come, Holy Ghost.   3.IV.1960

VII/1 *The high-priestly prayer* [Jn 17:1–5] 'The hour has come': it is the hour of his suffering, when he must drink the cup his Father offers him. This suffering, borne with devotion and endurance, is a glorification of the Father: in fact it is *the* glorification: the great sacrifice of praise, thanksgiving, supplication and expiation, by which mankind is reconciled to him once again. In every Mass he offers this glorification to the Father again and in this I am his instrument. This is yet another reason for celebrating the Mass with the greatest possible devotion. The hour of suffering is, however, also the hour of our Lord's own glory, in the heroic example he gives in the first place, but also through the merits which he wins through his human nature: for which cause God has exalted him and given him a name. 'The work thou gavest me to do': to preach his name 'the one true God and him whom thou hast sent' . . . this is the message our Lord announces to mankind. Sacrifice and love is the glory that I too must offer the Father. May the Lord grant that I too at the end of my life, in my 'hour', the hour of death, may be able to say: I have finished the work thou gavest me to do!

VII/2 *In the garden of olives* Even if all do, I shall not . . .[40] How shamefully this promise was broken! So often I have promised our Lord loyalty—in every retreat!—and then? May he give me grace this time to keep faithfully the promises I have made him. But it also depends on my cooperation. The point of devotion to the Sacred Heart is to 'comfort' our Lord, not only for the past but also for all the injuries done to him today, and perhaps today more intentionally than in the past when sins were so often matters of weakness not hatred of God. Our Lord in the Garden of Olives foresaw all this and suffered for it, but he also saw the comfort offered him by people piously honouring his Sacred Heart. So the devotion to the Sacred Heart must be an object of particular importance for me. I must not look for comfort among men but with God in prayer, and in prayer as such, even when the Lord hears me in

---

[39] Cf 1 Cor 3:16: 'Do you not know that you are God's temple and that God's spirit dwells in you?' (Cf also 2 Cor 6:16; Rom 8:9.)

[40] Cf Mt 26:31, 33: 'Then Jesus said to them, "You will all fall away because of me this night . . ." Peter declared to him, "Though they all fall away because of you, I will never fall away".'

a way different from what I have asked. Not my will but thine be done [cf Lk 22:41-44]. The main thing is that his angel strengthens me, so that I can bear all that he sends me and in whatever form he sends it to me. Passion of Christ strengthen me.[41] In our Lord's case the strength brought by the angel produced the sweat of blood through the intensity with which he spoke those words: thy will be done.

VII/3 *The fruits of the passion* 'He suffered for your redemption, enlightenment, justification and glorification. So always think of this great favour too, as if he suffered it for you alone' (St Bonaventure). The sufferings of the Lord teach me to have a horror of sin and of my sins, for he has given me such preferential treatment. Should I commit the same sins again and again? The sufferings of our Lord also teach me how good and wise God is: he did not simply want to redeem us, but also to give us a model and a source of strength. Passion of Christ, strengthen me. And in fact the martyrs—that unique phenomenon in the religious life—derived strength from the sufferings of our Lord and his example, so that they too could bear extreme pain. What Christ demands of us is not that we should aim at any stoic ideal, but something that he himself practised in his life and for which he also gives his disciples strength. I can also learn zeal for souls: if he suffered so much for souls, should I not also work for them, pray and suffer for them?[42] But all this must not be just insights and understanding, not just a matter of feeling and emotion. 'It is effective love that our Lord demands' (St Francis of Sales): faithfulness in my resolutions, then, and faithful imitation in suffering and endurance. Passion of Christ, strengthen me!

VII/4 *Suffering and love on the cross* This meditation is inexhaustible. I must meditate on it deeply in the week after Passion Sunday and in Holy Week. Our Lord's pain is expiation for all the lust of the world, his poverty and nakedness the expiation for all the selfishness, his shame (quite literally) the expiation for all ambition. But this expiation also bore great fruit in the form of the countless people who have followed him in every century, in poverty, humility and obedience. Through the shame and pain of the cross he really did reform the world, and the cross will now give me once again strength and perseverance in following him. His words are so many proofs of his love, an inexhaustible love, and also of his suffering and of his power. In particular his words to his mother [Jn 19:26 f]. It is difficult even to imagine all that entered into and weighed on his mother's heart at that hour. Only she and our Lord

---

[41] From the famous prayer 'Anima Christi, sanctifica me'. This prayer was particularly familiar to St Ignatius and it is regularly recommended to the retreatant in the 'triple colloquy', at the end of the colloquy with Christ (cf Exercises 63).

[42] Cf St Paul: 'For the love of Christ controls us, because we are convinced that one has died for all; therefore all have died. And he died for all, that those who live might live no longer for themselves, but for him who for their sake died and was raised' (2 Cor 5:14 f).

know that. But our Lord does not say anything about it: he lets her bear this pain in silence. He gives her only one sign of his love; he takes care of the mother he is now leaving behind and gives her his favourite disciple as a son. This is a scene of such godly dimensions that it is difficult to think of it in human terms. Our Lord concludes his life with these words of power: 'Father, into thy hands I commend my spirit' [Lk 23:46]. He gives up his life; he does not die of his wounds nor of a broken heart: I lay down my life . . . and I have the power to lay it down . . . (Jn 10:17, 18). He gives his life for me: I must sacrifice my life and give it up for him. This is the meaning of my 'decision'.

VIII/1 *The heart of Jesus is pierced* [cf Jn 19:33–37] The evangelist shows that this event is not just a chance happening or the natural sequence of events, but that God willed that it should happen in this way. He willed it in order to give us in the pierced[43] Heart of our Lord and the blood and water that flow out an image of that inexhaustible love of our Lord, in which he gives up everything for us. Thus devotion to the Sacred Heart is above all devotion to the love of Jesus, this generous, kind, forgiving love. They looked upon him whom they had pierced: we have pierced the Heart of our Lord ourselves, but we can look to him with confidence and hope. He is all things to all men: rest for the good—the contemplative souls—a refuge for sinners, but for us all through the Church and the sacraments, a torrent of mercy (baptism, confession) and of grace (Eucharist etc.).[44] This is why this devotion is of such great importance to the Society of Jesus as well, for it is precisely *its* task to convert sinners and channel the treasures of grace into all hearts. If our Lord has entrusted this devotion to us in particular, that means that he wants to bless in a special way the apostolic work we have undertaken as our vocation. But we must also 'draw our inspiration from this source that can never be exhausted', as St Margaret Mary says. Meditation on and imitation of the Heart of Jesus is therefore my special duty and task. 1.V.1960

VIII/2 *The meaning of the resurrection* In the first place it had a meaning for our Lord himself (christological meaning): his victory over his enemies, his exaltation (he exalted him), the reward for his sufferings and death (he gave him a name . . .).[45] So he became a model for us all;

[43] Here the author stresses the meaning by using the original Greek word *enyxen*, pierced.
[44] These are thoughts from the preface of the Mass of the Sacred Heart: 'In your divine plan your only Son was pierced by a soldier's lance as he hung on the cross; from his wounded heart flow out living waters of compassion and love. That heart has never ceased to beat with love for us, bringing peace to those who love him and salvation to those who turn in sorrow from their sins' (translation: International Committee on English in the Liturgy). This prayer, in which the Church speaks, is based on theological insights going back to the early Fathers of the Church, Augustine, Cyril of Alexandria and, later, St Bonaventure. Cf S. Tromp, 'De nativitate Ecclesiae e Corde Jesu in Cruce', in *Gregorianum*, XIII, 1932, 489–527.
[45] A reference to the famous hymn in the Epistle to the Philippians: [Christ]

and we will follow him along this way too if we have followed the way of the cross with him.⁴⁶ But more important is the soteriological meaning: he rose for our justification [cf Rom 4:25]. He did indeed earn us forgiveness of our sins and win grace for us, but all this has to be applied to us and for this an instrument was needed, the Church founded on the apostles and especially on Peter. The apostles, then, were the first who had to be convinced of his resurrection, first Peter (he appeared to Peter) [cf Lk 24:34], then all the others, so that no one, not even Thomas [cf Jn 20:24-29], was in doubt any longer. Then they had to be equipped with all the gifts and powers: the sacraments and the Holy Spirit. All this depends on our Lord showing himself to them with absolute certainty, and thus the feast of Pentecost is nothing but the completion of his life on earth and the beginning of his mystical life in the Church. The fact that I am called to work for this Church is a great grace, especially since I have the privilege of working directly for the Vicar of Christ. This calls for joyful and ungrudging cooperation in the work of the Church.

VIII/3 *The last instructions* Our Lord concludes his earthly work with the apostles with the promise 'I am with you', with the command to await the power of the Holy Spirit coming upon them, and with his blessing.⁴⁷ Thus I too can conclude my retreat in happy confidence: our Lord will be with me, the Holy Spirit will give me light and strength and the blessing of our Lord will follow me through the year. My job is the same as the one he gave the apostles: to work for his Church through teaching and through the sacraments. The fact that I am myself a member of this Church is the great grace of my life, and the fact that I have the privilege of working for this Church—and in fact only for it —is the special calling that he has given me. So like the apostles I can conclude the retreat 'with great joy', in the expectation that the Holy Spirit will give me light and strength, that he will be the 'power from on high' making it possible for me to be a true and faithful apostle of the Lord: 'you will be witnesses to me': and that I can always and everywhere bear a genuine and fitting witness to our Lord.

VIII/4 *On achieving love* [Exercises 230-237] God has given me and continues to give me so very much for my body and soul, and the response to this is relatively easy and clear: to dispose of all these according to your will [cf Exercises 234]. For my part I have decided once again

---

humbled himself and became obedient unto death, even death on a cross. Therefore God has highly exalted him and bestowed on him the name which is above every name, that at the name of Jesus every knee should bow, in heaven and on the earth and under the earth, and every tongue confess that Jesus Christ is Lord, to the glory of God the Father' (Phil 2:8-11).

⁴⁶ Cf Rom 8:17: 'and if children, then heirs, heirs of God and fellow heirs with Christ, provided we suffer with him in order that we may also be glorified with him.'

⁴⁷ In this sentence, elements are linked from several accounts of the Lord's farewell to the apostles: cf Mt 28:18 ff; Acts 1:4 f, 8; and Luke 24:50, 52.

in the 'decision' the ways and means by which I am going to use these gifts of God better and better, and thus advance to greater perfection. Under this 'decision' I can only write: 'Give me your love and your grace: it is all I need' [id]. But beyond that there is something more—'to seek God in all things',[48] and the result—'to find God in all'. The second and third points of the meditation tell me this. If God is present in all things, in every flower and work of art and in every great spiritual achievement, then I must find him there and see him there too. In this way everything that is great on earth loses its value and is nothing but a sign to me, a reflection, an image of the infinitely greater beauty, wisdom and power of God. Then nothing in the world can really impress me, for God is great, infinitely greater. Not even great deeds and achievements, for they only happen because God has produced the effect and because his activity is of an infinitely higher and greater order. This is the spirit of faith that enables one to see all things in a supernatural light. And through this I must eventually be led to the final thing: to the love of God for the sake of his own infinite greatness. I do not need to 'despise' the world, for it is a ladder than leads to God, and whatever greatness I see in the world, I see something still greater in God. May I arrive at this profound and exalted understanding of all things and thus at the perfect love of God! 27.VII.1960
Rome, 7 September 1959

FROM THE MONTHLY RECOLLECTIONS

4.X.1959
1. The little sins of transgression too. Examination of conscience: 'restraint', orderliness, cleanliness, punctuality, politeness. Criticism—avoid it even when it is justified. Prayer—meditation (affective!).

I/1 Created out of love: self-communication: sharing the divine nature, imitation in my life at this moment too (act from love!).

I/2 Greater graces—greater achievements!—greater sanctity. Corresponding to the great knowledge and love!—for the purpose for which I was created [Exercises 23].

---

[48] These words are taken from part III of the Constitutions of the Society of Jesus, where the founder describes the 'right intention' with which members of the Society must let themselves be guided in all things. The text is as follows: 'All should endeavour to have a right intention, concerning not only their state of life in general, but also in all its details. In these they should always sincerely aim at serving and pleasing the goodness of God for its own sake and in return for the love and the extraordinary favours it has so liberally bestowed on us, rather than for fear of punishment or hope of reward (though they should benefit by these considerations too). They should seek God in all things, and strip themselves as far as is possible of the love of all created things, in order to give their hearts entirely to the Creator of them by loving him in all his works and all his works in him; for this is his most holy and divine will' (III, 1, 26). The sense of this passage of the notes obviously derives from this text.

Most faithful possible fulfilment of God's will—not unfaithful to the programme for a moment!—'it is something greater that he wants to give you, namely himself, the one who created these things' (St Augustine, cf I/3).

1.XI.1959

Spiritual exercises—precise, punctual, recollected, especially the examination of conscience. Custody of the eyes—unobtrusive but consistent work, no waste of time on unimportant things. Good example in all things—'of help and service' to all.

I/ Refuse God nothing: whatever, however and as long as he wants.

I/4 Detached from myself, 'I shall not seek the things that are my own' (cf 1 Cor 13:5), independent of every influence that is not willed by God.

II/2 Distraction, unpunctuality, vanity; in all things exemplary and faithful—how can I advance in love and virtue?

II/3 'I have laboured more'—not I but the grace of God that is in me.

II/4 Every day a greater and deeper love of God, patience in ill-health.

25.XII.1959

Aim at perfection in the faithful performance of God's will in all things. Unobtrusive, calm work without making any fuss—apostolic example in accordance with my position. 'Restraint' in all things; help and service, apostolic prayer.

III/1 God has showered me with graces, and has given me an influential, important task, so I must be outstanding in all things. Must aim then at the greatest possible perfection.

III/2 A servant of the Lord, work and self-denial, like 'the handmaid of the Lord', not a 'prelate' in the worldly sense. Altogether a man of God!

III/3 I must not seek to be anything but one who cooperates with God, a steward of the mysteries of God. The ways[49] of God which often bypass our ways.

6.III.1960

IV/ Consideration. Regular visits in the morning to the Kerenda; in the afternoon: after the breviary (3.50).

IV/4 Because he desired—gratuity of vocation.

V/1 Love as the last foundation; based on an interior life.

V/2 Kindness, love, understanding from a supernatural love of neighbour.

V/3 Pray for light—not let myself go: restraint.

3.IV.1960

Faithful carrying out of God's will each day. Prayer: careful arrange-

---

[49] The word 'ways' was missing but without it the sentence hardly makes sense: it is taken from the end of the relevant meditation, where it says: 'These are God's ways that bypass ours.'

ment, recollected, preparation for meditation. Visits to the Blessed Sacrament. Small sacrifices in community life, patience, love (not criticism), not sarcastic. Quiet peaceful work. Apostolic example in all things. Help and service to all.

VI/1 Prayer and work—apply myself to it with all my strength.

VI/2 His cross = my cross! Prayer—work—cross.

1.V.1960

As faithful as possible in doing God's will in all situations. Love for God. Not allowing any obstacles in my spiritual life (punctual, perfect, recollected): good example in all things. Encourage love and harmony everywhere. Apostolic prayer. Patience and love.

VII/1 Sacrifice and teaching: to accomplish the work! Doing it as perfectly as possible.

VII/2 Every day with energy; thy will be done.

VII/3 'Amour effectif'.

VII/4 Perseverance.

27.VI.1960

VIII/2 Called to work for the Church (and to pray!).

VIII/3 Work for his Church—witness for our Lord.

25.VII.1960

Faithfulness in the life of prayer—examination of conscience (5 points!) and meditation. Apostolic example everywhere. Prudence in speaking, kindness, and patience towards all. Humility and restraint in my dealings with others.

III/1 To work with me: to follow me—showered with graces and help—outstanding.

III/2 Contrast to world. To achieve the ideal of the Society as well as possible. 'In all poverty'—even as cardinal!

IV/1 Work just as I am asked! Growth in grace and sanctity.

CHAPTER 4

A cardinal in retreat

1960

On Monday 16 November 1959, just as Fr Bea was setting out for the usual session at the Holy Office, a member of the Secretariat of State of His Holiness handed him what is known as a 'Lettera autografa', telling him of the pope's intention to make him a cardinal on the following 14 December. This news was followed by days of strenuous preparation for the creation of the new cardinal. I played a part in all this and found it a very exhausting experience, while the cardinal—in spite of the weariness from which he had suffered since his illness—took it all and the difficult transformation that it meant for a member of a religious order surprisingly easily.

In his new position he had responsibilities in the Congregation of Rites (where beatifications and canonizations form the major part of the work), the Congregation for Seminaries and Church Universities and the Pontifical Biblical Commission. The first half of 1960 passed quite uneventfully. As early as March 1960 it had been decided in principle to create the Secretariat for the Promotion of Christian Unity, but it was not until the end of May that the cardinal learned in confidence that he was to be its president. On 5 June, Pentecost Sunday, the formation of the preparatory commissions for the Council and also of the Secretariat was announced. In the afternoon of that day the cardinal flew for the first time to New York, where he was to receive an honorary doctorate of law at Fordham University, which is run by the Society of Jesus. It was there on 6 June that he heard of the public announcement of his nomination as the President of the Secretariat. The following day he held a sort of press conference to talk about the work and prospects of the new Secretariat.

In July he met the famous French Jew, Professor Jules Isaac, who had already asked Pope John XXIII if the Council could do something to counter anti-semitism and to further Jewish-Christian understanding. Pope John listened to him sympathetically, and suggested he should discuss his problem with Cardinal Bea. From this modest beginning matters developed until, at an audience with Pope John on 18 September 1960, Cardinal Bea received an official commission to prepare a draft document on the Church and the Jews for the Council to discuss.

On 28 June, Monsignor Jan Willebrands was named secretary of the Secretariat for the Promotion of Christian Unity. The first half of July was occupied in preparing the lists of members and advisers for the Secretariat to be submitted to the pope. At the end of July and beginning of August the cardinal took part in the International Eucharistic Congress in Munich and there too he gave an interview on the possibilities and prospects of bringing about Christian Unity. After a visit to his native diocese, Freiburg-im-Breisgau, and to his village, he returned at the end of August to the noviciate of his own province in Neuhausen an den Fildern (Stuttgart) to make his annual retreat. This retreat must be seen in the context of his new position, but also in the light of the great prospects for the future: the preparation for the Council in general and the special task entrusted to the cardinal in the Secretariat for Unity in particular.

RETREAT 1960

Neuhausen, 24–31 August

I/1 *My task* If it is my duty to promote God's glory at all times, then I must do so more than ever in my present position, in which I have been placed for God's interests and nothing else. So I must belong to him. 'To him', that means to the Church, through which and in which all honour is given to God, 'through Jesus Christ our Lord'. The Church offers to God the glory and honour that I pay him: it is the Mystical Body of Christ, and therefore in a certain way of God himself. So all my works, sufferings and prayers go up to God through the Church. I can never really pray 'privately', for it is always the living member of Christ's Body who is praying and therefore Christ himself. This gives my prayer a unique dedication and dignity, but it is also a warning to me that I must always pray reverently and not superficially and thoughtlessly. Totally for him: not thinking of my own reputation or convenience. I exist only for him and for his interests, and the consequences of this for me, whether recognition and praise or blame and scorn, are of no account. For God and God alone!

I/2 *The fundamental principle: in Christ* I must not meditate on the 'fundamental principle' as a purely logical consequence of 'being a creature': I am a creature 'in Christ', that is as part of him, one of his members, and so I share the task that God by his eternal decree gave to him, the 'Word made flesh'. All praise, reverence and service is an image of his ministry, a share in his ministry and in the work of his ministry. This gives all my actions, words and thoughts his dignity, but also his stamp, his form and his character: not simply human, but 'Christ-like', in so far as this is at all possible for a finite creature. My praise too goes through Christ to the Father, but must be like the praise of the Son of

God. My reverence must be the reverence of Christ for his Father, as he showed it in his life and Passion (Garden of Olives!). My ministry is like Christ's ministry: not just fulfilling God's will but fulfilling it with sacrifice and suffering, in fact self-sacrifice, just as our Lord offered himself for us (Lo, I come, 'a body hast thou prepared for me'[1]), and as the 'handmaid of the Lord' offered herself ('fiat') [cf Lk 1:38]. As a priest I also have the privilege of offering to the heavenly Father the sacrifice of all the others and even the sacrifice of our Lord himself. All this is what the phrase 'in Christ' means for my thoughts and actions.

Consideration of state 'Go through (Christ) the man and you will find God' (St Augustine, Sermo 141, N.4, PL 38, 77). 'You come to a man crucified: you should come already crucified or ready to be crucified' (St Peter Damien).

Walk in the presence of God, especially in these times of great responsibility.

I/3 *'Thereby saving his soul'* (Exercises 23) The salvation of my soul is not simply a matter of logic or reason. In the state of affairs that has existed since the first sin of our first parents it is no longer enough simply to observe the natural moral laws. The 'salvation of my soul' is part of the great will of God that all men should be saved. 'And by that will we have been sanctified through the offering of the Body of Jesus Christ' (Heb 10:10). Christ spoke his 'Lo, I come' to this 'will of God to save all men', received his body from the Virgin Mary, and lived and died for our 'salvation'. 'For us and our salvation.'[2] This is my task too, both for my own salvation and in my work for the salvation of others. For my own salvation. Because of sin this is and always remains, to my last breath, in danger. So I must go the way our Lord went before me: self-conquest, the cross, misfortune, with Christ and like Christ. There is no other way for me either. Body of Christ, save me![3] For the salvation of others. Treading the path Christ trod in order to save them: praying, working, suffering and sacrificing myself for them. I will most gladly spend myself and be spent for your souls.[4] This is the meaning of my priesthood and of my whole vocation to the apostolate. I must be prepared to let it cost me something, just as our Lord did. 2.X.60

I/4 *'Everything else on earth'* (Exercises 23) This meditation pro-

---

[1] Consequently, when Christ came into the world, he said, "sacrifices and offerings thou hast not desired, but a body hast thou prepared for me; in burnt offerings and sin offerings thou hast taken no pleasure." Then I said, "Lo, I have come to do thy will, O God" ' (cf Ps 40:7 f) (Heb 10:5 ff).

[2] From the Nicene-Constantinopolitan Creed, recited at Mass.

[3] From the prayer 'Soul of Christ, sanctify me', in the Exercises.

[4] These words are from St Paul, writing to his beloved Corinthians: 'Here for the third time I am ready to come to you. And I will not be a burden, for I seek not what is yours but you; for children ought not to lay up for their parents, but parents for their children. I will most gladly spend and be spent for your souls' (2 Cor 12:14–15).

vides me with an absolutely essential programme for my life: to see everything in a supernatural light, i.e. with the eyes of Christ: 'all things were created through him and for him'.[5] It is he who guides my life and shapes it; so I must not become attached to anything. If he disposes of it differently, through no fault on my part, then it is no matter whether I like it or not, whether it fits in with my plans or not. It is not I who am 'the measure of things', but Christ. For me the only thing that matters is that I should do my part faithfully and honourably, whatever position I am given, and leave the outcome and success to God. I should think things over, make plans and decisions, but must not become attached to my plans. In my spiritual life I must cultivate this interior supernatural frame of mind and not let myself become wrapped up in the externals of everyday life: above all I must take care not to let external things get in the way of my meditation, examination of conscience and breviary. Give to God what is God's . . .[6] and so in spite of all external work try to remain inwardly recollected and not lose myself in externals. Whatever is *more* likely to achieve the purpose:[7] as far as my own soul is concerned it is clear that this idea of 'more likely' means what our Lord himself chose: if a man wants to follow me, let him take up his cross and follow me [cf Mt 16:24]. In my concern for others and in my job: I must think things over before God and choose whatever circumstances demand, without any thought of reputation or convenience, and try to make the best choice. Everything else must be left to the Holy Spirit. Come, Holy Ghost. 7.V.61

II/1 *Sin* I must take this question of sin seriously. In the first place because sin still remains a possibility for me too. I must have no illusions on this score, on the other hand, however, there must be no over-vivid imagination. The concupiscence of the flesh and the pride of life[8] are still in me. And I have a free will that can refuse God's command. In every Mass I pray: take away from us our sins.[9] In order to avoid sin I must aim at perfection by every means at my disposal.

As a priest I am also obliged to fight sin. That is why I must detest it in myself and keep far from it. The good example that a priest gives inspires people and encourages them to imitate him: while the sin of a priest, even if it is only a venial sin, has a corrupting effect. The life of a

[5] The basic theme of the christological hymn in Colossians: 'He is the image of the invisible God, the first-born of all creation; for in him all things were created, in heaven and on earth, visible and invisible, whether thrones or dominions or principalities or authorities—all things were created through him and for him' (Col 1:15 f).

[6] Christ's words to the Pharisees: 'Render therefore to Caesar the things that are Caesar's, and to God the things that are God's' (Mt 22:21 and parallels).

[7] In the opening chapter of the Exercises, entitled 'Fundamental Principle', Ignatius sets out the principle: 'The one thing we desire, the one thing we choose is what is more likely to achieve the purpose of our creating' (23).

[8] Cf First Epistle of John: 'For all that is in the world, the lust of the flesh and the lust of the eyes and the pride of life, is not of the Father but is of the world' (2:16).

[9] Prayer following the prayers at the foot of the altar, in the Tridentine Mass.

priest by itself, if it is good, is an encouragement, but it is a temptation and a snare if it is corrupted by sin.—Finally as a priest I must above all never forget what the crucified Lord did to destroy sin [cf 1 Jn 3:8; Rom 8:3]. Follow me!

II/2 *The sin of the angels and of our first parents* Refusing 'to make the most of their free will' (Exercise 50): every sin is a denial of one's own freedom. God gave us our freedom to be used in his service and so really in our own best interests. Of course there is grace: but I must cooperate with grace for my salvation and by 'honouring and obeying (the) Creator' (id). And I really cannot complain of lack of grace; indeed God showers his graces on me; but for that reason my obligation to cooperate is all the greater, and also my responsibilty to avoid even the slightest sin and to aim at perfection.

The realization of the social effects of sin is an important point. Particularly in the case of people in high places this is never really a purely personal affair. The history of the Church shows how much damage the Church, individuals and whole peoples have suffered from the sins of prelates and professors. Probably there would have been no split in the Church but for these sins.[10] In my position all eyes are on me. I can do a great deal of good by my actions but also a great deal of harm. People notice even the smallest things. 'And they watched him'[11]—and above all in the case of people of a different faith!

Consideration of spiritual state Prayer and spiritual exercises. Recollection: at least briefly before praying: what? to whom? Even in the midst of work!—Preparation for meditation (something in writing)— 'Ask for what I need'.[12]

II/3 *The story of my sins* [cf Exercises 56] If I look back over my life, I can never thank God enough for his goodness in forgiving me my past sins, in preserving me from so many sins and in showering so many graces on me. I am really 'a sinner manqué' and I can repeat a thousand times with St Paul: 'by the grace of God (and only by the grace of God) I am what I am' [1 Cor 15:10].

But this obliges me, and now in a special way, to aim at perfection and holiness. In this meditation I have drawn up a programme, which I will complete and perfect in the course of the next few days.

I. *A man of prayer:* order in my spiritual exercises (breviary!): great devotion, care and reverence at Mass: visits in the morning and after-

---

[10] Written about two months after his appointment as President of the Secretariat for the Promotion of Christian Unity.

[11] As the Gospels tell us, the Pharisees frequently had Christ 'under observation': e.g. Mk 3:2; Lk 6:6; 14:1; 20:20.

[12] This phrase is used in the Exercises to denote the grace to be asked in every meditation, according to its object (Exercises 44, etc).

noon. Good preparation for meditation; examination of conscience at the appointed times. In short, good order in my spiritual life.

II. *Work:* tranquillity, method, care, no haste. At the same time preserving recollection.

Trusting cooperation with others, with consideration and patience.

III. *The cardinal's household:*[13] fatherliness, kindness, patience, spiritual care.

IV. *Relations with others*

1. With cardinals: respectful, ready to help, modest, understanding, but also open and straightforward in all things.

2. With subordinates: always friendly, patient, kind, but not familiar: firm and clear.

3. With strangers: friendly but discreet and serious: ready to help and kind, not familiar.

V. *For myself*

1. Food: as much as is necessary, nothing special, restrained (better too little!). Diet.

2. Sleep: 9.30–4.30: in the afternoon $\frac{3}{4}$ hour.

3. Dress and behaviour: always discreet and dignified.

II/4   *The triple colloquy*[14]   There was no sin in Mary's life, not even venial sin. That was her privilege. It must be my concern to reduce the number of venial sins all the time, especially deliberate venial sins. These sins offend our Lord, wound his Sacred Heart and his love. They are an abomination to the heavenly Father. The heavens are not pure enough for him. They are ingratitude in response to the love that was so great that he gave us his only-begotten Son.

There were no disorders in the life of Mary or of Jesus. As described by scripture everything in her life is ordered and well-weighed, down to the last detail. Nor should there be any slovenliness, shabbiness or any-

---

[13] The usual expression not for the relatives of the cardinal, but for those people normally in his personal service, e.g. his chaplain, private secretary etc.

[14] This is another characteristic example of the method of the Exercises. In cases where God is to be asked for a particularly important grace Ignatius suggests to the retreatant the use of the 'triple colloquy'. First he should ask our Lady to intercede with Jesus on his behalf: then he should ask Jesus to be his mediator with the Father: and finally he should ask the heavenly Father himself for the grace. The object of this colloquy obviously varies according to the object of the meditation and of the grace desired. As a brief example we quote the following text, where the triple colloquy is recommended and explained for the first time: this is to be found in the third 'exercise' of the first week, which consists in the repetition of the first two meditations on sin. After the material for the exercise has been given, it continues 'First Colloquy: With our Lady, that she may obtain from her Son the grace for three things: a) a deep-felt consciousness of my sins and a profound disgust with them; b) an appreciation of the irregularity of what I have done, so that, by hating that, I may lead a better and more regular life; c) a knowledge of the world such that I may come to hate it and so give up all wordliness and folly. Then a *Hail Mary*.
'Second Colloquy: With the Son, asking him to obtain the same graces from the Father, and ending with the *Anima Christi*.
'Third Colloquy: With the Father, that the same eternal Lord may grant my prayer. Then an *Our Father*' (63).

thing slipshod in my life. And not just for the sake of good example. The heavenly Father, who created everything and preserves it in order, is order itself. Every disorder must displease him.

World: Mary did not know this 'world': her joy and her happiness—*my soul has rejoiced in God my Saviour* [cf Lk 1:46 f]. And her divine Son never tires of warning against the world: the lust of flesh and of the eyes and the pride of life (cf 1 Jn 2:16). 'The world hates me.'[15]

So it is best to leave these three requests in the hands of Mary and Jesus, and they will take them to the Father.

III/1 *Hell* Near hell stands the cross. It is entirely thanks to the crucified Lord if I am preserved from eternal damnation.[16] But I must also cooperate faithfully with the grace that he has won for me. 'Faults and defects', that is venial sins and giving in to evil desires, lead to hell.[17] Therefore I must avoid these first signs. I think the most frightening thing about hell is not the pain of the senses but the pain of loss: to be separated for ever from God, who here on earth meant everything to me. After spending my whole life with him, what should I be without him for all eternity! But now I must be very earnest about 'being with him': no half-measures, half-heartedness, no slackness in his service, which is the service of the crucified Lord. I shall be able to talk of 'victory' when I am a 'victim',[18] just as he did not ascend to heaven until he had suffered on the cross and died.[19] If I want to belong to the glorious Messiah, I must first follow the 'Servant of the Lord'.[20]

III/2 *The kingdom of Christ* [Exercises 91–99] This meditation has an entirely new meaning for me now. The King and Lord of all things is now the only one who, through his Vicar, can give me orders. I am, then, his closest and most direct instrument and exist only to offer him the most immediate and direct service. This is the result of my position:

[15] In Jn 7:7 Jesus says to his family: 'The world cannot hate you, but it hates me because I testify of it that its works are evil' (cf also 15:18).

[16] Paul refers to himself with the same kind of humility: 'We were by nature children of wrath, like the rest of mankind' (Eph 2:3), 'we are waiting for his son from heaven . . . Jesus who delivers us from the wrath to come' (1 Thess 1.10).

[17] The reference seems to be to the following passage from the Exercises: 'Asking for what I want. Here it will be to obtain a deep-felt consciousness of the sufferings of those who are damned, so that, should my faults cause me to forget my love for the eternal Lord, at least the fear of these sufferings will help to keep me out of sin' (65). According to commentaries on the Exercises, Ignatius uses the Spanish word translated by 'faults' to refer to the deliberate venial sins that pave the way for serious sins.

[18] Cf St Paul, 1 Cor 15:54–57: 'When the perishable puts on the imperishable, and the mortal puts on immortality, then shall come to pass the saying that is written: "Death is swallowed up in victory." "O death, where is thy victory? O death, where is thy sting?" The sting of death is sin, and the power of sin is the law. But thanks be to God, who gives us the victory through our Lord Jesus Christ.'

[19] 'Was it not necessary that Christ should suffer these things and enter into his glory?' (Lk 24:26).

[20] Cf the passage where Matthew applies to Christ the words of the Suffering Servant songs of Isaiah (Mt 12:17 f; cf Is 42:1).

but it must be in my will: I desire to show greater enthusiasm and distinguish myself in the unstinted service of the eternal king. The special task he has entrusted to me is very great indeed. But I know that I am working 'with him' ('a share in my hardships'). So I must approach it with courage and be on the look-out for anything and everything that concerns it in any way; I must listen, encourage, help and spare no effort in this task. Not thinking of myself: no 'sensuality', but a reasonable and practical care for my health and strength, yet without indulgence or laziness:[21] no love of the flesh or of the world and above all no seeking for vain honour or recognition. And if honour and recognition come my way they are not to be directed to my own person but to the thing achieved. So, altogether unselfish and serving only the great cause. And so with our Lord putting up with any abuse, every cross and self-denial. Behold I am here: dispose of me! 6.XI.60

General confession (Fr Frank) 26.VIII.

III/3 *The incarnation* [cf Lk 1:26–38] Here we see God's 'tactics' revealed. Mankind has totally rejected God, but he does not condemn it and destroy it; he wants to save it. And for this purpose he decided to send his own Son: he is to become man, to teach men by his word and example, to suffer and die for them and then to set up an institution to make sure that the effects of his life and suffering reach men: the Church. And he has placed me in this institution, not in an unimportant position but in an important one, with a great job to do, as one of his primary assistants. I must cooperate in this work in the spirit of the first assistants, the angel (humility), Mary (absolute surrender: fiat), and our Lord himself: 'a body hast thou prepared for me . . . lo, I have come to do thy will O God'. Externals do not count: Bethlehem, not Jerusalem or Athens or Rome: a poor girl, wife of a manual labourer; a miserable little house in despised Nazareth. God does not work by external means, but with men ready to serve and surrender themselves. Lo, I come.
2.VI.61

III/4 *The nativity* [cf Lk 2:1–14] God the Father arranged everything in a wonderful way: even the power of Rome had to serve him without realizing it, so that our Lord might be born in utter destitution;[22] unknown, not famous; in a stable, with poor shepherds not kings and princes as his first worshippers. The darkness of the stable keeps safe

[21] The word 'sensuality' is used by the Exercises in a particular sense to mean the opposite of the right attitude with regard to the body in general, hence the author sees reasonable care for health, self-control and a certain hardness as the opposite of 'sensuality'.

[22] 'See and reflect on what they are doing. Here it is the journey they have to make, the hardships they have to put up with, before our Lord is born in utter destitution. After all his labours, after suffering from hunger and thirst, heat and cold, being treated with injustice and insulted, he is to die on the Cross—and all for me' (Exercises 116).

(and conceals) the one who was 'the true light that enlightens every man, coming into the world'.[23] Patiently Mary leaves everything to God, however difficult and incomprehensible she finds it all. It is her good fortune and joy to be allowed to serve the one she now carries in her chaste arms. She does not ask for more. And the angels—they bend the knee before the incarnate Son of God; because of him their lot was decided at the beginning of time: they know that he is giving glory to God the Father and bringing peace to men (gloria—pax). And our Lord: Lo, I come to do thy will. Nothing else matters. This is my motto too in my position: not honour or recognition or possessions, but to do the will of the Father in any situation in which he places me.

IV/1 *Presentation in the temple* [cf Lk 2:22–38] This is the day of sacrifice. When our Lord is taken to the temple he sees and he knows what will happen to him in this temple and in spirit he also sees Golgotha, which is only a few yards away, and hears the cry 'crucify him'. But here too he speaks his 'Lo, I come' and repeats the offering that he made on the day he became incarnate.

Mary, at his side, obviously does not see so clearly, but here too she offers her first-born absolutely and unconditionally. And old Simeon tells her explicitly that she is to join in her Son's sacrifice, and so closely that a sword will pierce her own soul [cf Lk 2:34 ff]. And she too, worthy of her Son, without hesitation pronounces her 'fiat'. I must share the sacrifice of the Son and his mother—through my self-sacrificing work for him and his Church, even if this entails effort, strain and all sorts of suffering for me. In his unsearchable wisdom God has destined me for this in a special way and I have expressed my readiness and I repeat it with all its consequences. Lo, I come—ecce, venio!

IV/2 *Nazareth* Here is a wonderful programme for my daily work. I must not go out of my way to appear much in public; I will be a quiet, working cardinal, as far as circumstances permit. Even if the work is monotonous, dull or tedious: this is God's will and that is enough. When I receive visitors, I must be friendly, kind, ready to help, but dignified, discreet and serious; and only pay visits if they have some apostolic purpose. Towards the people who work with me, kind, considerate, trusting and like a father. Not bothering about what people say: it is enough to do God's will and carry out the task given me to the best of my ability. I must forgo my private interests (academic work, study), in so far as my professional work demands. The main thing is that of my work and of my household it may be said: 'and the favour of God was upon him' [Lk 2:39 f].

Consideration of state: prayer and activity 'To contemplate and then hand on' (St Thomas). To see God in my neighbour; and draw strength

---

[23] Cf prologue to St John's Gospel.

from prayer [Constitutions, X, 2]. And let my work help me in my prayer!

IV/3 *In the temple at Jerusalem* [cf Lk 2: 41–52] This is the first real revelation of our Lord; but it occurs in the framework of everyday ordinary life. So it is important for me also to use everyday opportunities of doing good and carrying out my work: in audiences, meetings, correspondence and so on. No one should leave me without taking away with him something important for his soul, his spiritual life and his vocation. I must not forget those words of Pius XII: 'It is always the pope who speaks.' So I must not look for 'great opportunities'! Nor expect that I shall always have lasting success. They were amazed at our Lord but then they let him go. After the multiplication of the loaves they wanted to make him king and the next day many even of his disciples left him [cf Jn 6:14, 66]. Don't look for applause. Do my duty without curtailment! Our Lord does not let his great love for his parents keep him from doing his Father's will and doing it as *he* wants.[24] It is the 'Father' in whose name he is acting; and the 'Father' comes before everything, even the closest ties on earth. So no false considerations! The will of God without curtailment, without limitation.

4.XII.1960
9.VII.1961

IV/4 *Departure of Jesus from Nazareth* The public life of our Lord begins with a really great sacrifice: the separation from his holy mother and for good. Even at the foot of the cross he reaffirms this separation by giving her John as a son [cf Jn 19:26 f]. His mission requires him to devote himself totally to his task. Mine makes the same demands on me: I must never let myself be guided by mere feelings in anything; they must never prevent me from carrying out my duty to the full. Our Lord leaves the 'house of God' in Nazareth and joins the sinners by the Jordan, as if he was one of them. For he has 'come to call the sinners and save them', and he never refuses anyone coming to him openly and honestly (the Good Thief [cf Lk 23:43]). He even had a kind word for Judas: 'Friend'.[25] In my position I shall be in contact with all sorts of people, either personally or by letter. I must always receive them and treat them with love and kindness, seeing them as children of God and also as members of the Mystical Body and treating them as such.

Our Lord goes into the desert (cf Lk 4:1 f). He gives up what little comfort the house in Nazareth offered. His servant must not be demanding in his own household or wherever he happens to be a guest. I am not

---

[24] 'How is it that you sought me? Did you not know that I must be in my Father's house?' (Lk 2:49).

[25] Cf Mt 26:49 f: 'And he (Judas) came up to Jesus at once and said, "Hail, master!" And he kissed him. Jesus said to him, "Friend, why are you here?" '

a cardinal in order to lead a life of luxury. My model must be our Lord in his wonderful modesty and unpretentiousness.

V/1 *The baptism of Jesus* (Mt 3:13–17) Our Lord stands among the sinners, as if he was one of them, and if John had not had a special revelation he would have baptized him like any other.[26] In fact: he is the lamb of God who 'takes away' the sins of the world—takes away = takes them upon himself, bears them in order to wipe them out by his cruel death.[27] He allows me too a share in this expiation after taking on himself the more difficult part: the load of sin and the suffering. The sacrament of baptism is the fruit of this 'taking away'. And because he does this, his Father declares him his beloved Son, with whom he is well pleased, and the Holy Spirit comes down upon him and stays with him. This is the anointing of our Lord as Messiah. It is also the basis of my mission. I have a share in his power of expiation and so I must share too his humility, his suffering and his self-immolation. I am his 'servant' and nothing else.[28] All external glory is superficial and means nothing. The only important thing is that the Holy Spirit has come upon me too and that I too am a beloved son of the heavenly Father. Therein lies my true dignity and greatness.

V/2 *The temptations in the desert* [cf Lk 4:1–13 and parallels] It was the 'Spirit', the Holy Spirit, who led our Lord into the desert, in order that he might be tempted [cf Lk 4:1; Mt 4:1]. This temptation was to show that we are not safe against the attacks of the evil spirit even in the holiest places (if our Lord is not, should an ecclesiastical dignitary be!), and where the temptations lie. There are three temptations: to a comfortable life, to glory and honour, and to power. I must not be a 'prince of the Church', having a good time, leading a comfortable life and not exerting myself; on the contrary I must lead a simple, moderate and modest life, as far as this is consistent with my position. I must not be the sort of cardinal who looks for popularity and publicity, always wanting to be in the limelight and anxious to have people dance attendance. If my job makes it necessary for me to appear in public, then I must be modest, rather restrained and not make a fuss. Lastly, not power-loving. Worldly power is, thank God, out of the question in these days, but I must not be domineering, authoritarian, insisting on controlling everything, but must carry out the tasks of my position with love.—

---

[26] 'I saw the Spirit descend as a dove from heaven, and it remained on him. I myself did not know him; but he who sent me to baptize with water said to me, "He on whom you see the Spirit descend and remain, this is he who baptizes with the Holy Spirit!" ' (Jn 1:32 f).

[27] Cf Jn 1:29: 'The next day he saw Jesus coming towards him and said, "Behold, the Lamb of God, who takes away the sin of the world!" ' See above, p. 32, 1959/IV/3.

[28] Paul usually introduces himself in his epistles as 'Paul, a servant of Jesus Christ, called to be an apostle . . .' (Rom 1:1; cf Phil 1:1; Tit 1:1; Gal 1:10).

The strength to do all this is given me by the 'Word of God',[29] that is the supernatural way of looking at things. Above all I must aim at an interior life, based on the 'Word of God', and further a life of prayer. I shall always receive strength and grace from this source.

V/3 *The two standards* [Exercises 136–148] The resolutions I have made in the preceding meditations amount to a plan of action with three points. But it is not just a matter of psychology; behind everything there are the two great powers: God and Satan. The latter's interest lies in preventing me from carrying out this plan fully. So all the more watchfulness, perseverance and prayer. The basic driving force must be love for our Lord, who goes before me with his noble example.

V/4 *The choice and training of the apostles* [cf Mk 3:13–19 and parallels] Since I share the mission and needs of the apostles to a great extent, like them I must also be an 'example to the flock'.[30] 'The life of the leader should be as far above the life of the people, as that of a shepherd is above his flock' (St Gregory, *Cur. Past.* II/1). Being a model to the flock means above all: example (be imitators of me[31]), care (I spend myself . . .[32]), work (like a good soldier of Jesus Christ[33]), love (caritas Christi urget nos[34]). I must grow all the time in perfection in these four points, following above all the example of our Lord himself.— Then I must remember that I am an 'apostle', an 'envoy', so must do not my will, but say and do what he wants.[35]

VI/1 *The Sermon on the Mount* The eight beatitudes [cf Mt 5:1–12] are more or less the programme that I have once again learned to understand better during the last few days. If I carry this plan out, I shall really be 'blessed', unlike the world, where the ideal is to be rich enough to be able to lead a life of luxury, to indulge one's passions and have one's own way in all things. The apostles' programme is directly and

---

[29] In the course of the temptations Jesus repeatedly had recourse to the Word of God, until the tempter was moved to use the same weapon—and, of course, misused it.

[30] 'So I exhort the elders among you, as a fellow elder and a witness of the sufferings of Christ as well as a partaker in the glory that is to be revealed. Tend the flock of God that is in your charge, not by constraint but willingly, not for shameful gain but eagerly, not as domineering over those in your charge but being examples to the flock' (1 Pt 5:1–3).

[31] A thought often expressed by Paul: 'I urge you then, be imitators of me, as I am of Christ!' (1 Cor 4:16 and 11:1; Phil 3:17; 1 Thess 1:6).

[32] Cf 2 Cor 12:15: 'I will most gladly spend and be spent for your souls.' This is one of the author's favourite thoughts, which we meet again and again in his writings.

[33] Cf Paul's admonition to Timothy: 'Take your share of suffering, as a good soldier of Christ Jesus' (2 Tim 2:3).

[34] 'For the love of Christ controls us, because we are convinced that one has died for all' (2 Cor 5:14).

[35] As Jesus himself did: 'My teaching is not mine, but his who sent me . . . He who speaks on his own authority seeks his own glory; but he who seeks the glory of him who sent him is true, and in him there is no falsehood' (Jn 7:13–16).

diametrically opposed to this. And this programme is more binding on me, the higher my position. Now more than ever I am a city set on a hill and a light lit on a stand, and everyone has the right to expect me to be a light and salt for him [cf Mt 5:13–16]. So I must 'embody' this plan, so to speak, not just by conforming to these rules outwardly, but through a genuine interior spirit, out of which these externals can, so to speak, grow. My perfection must not be just a legal matter, it must flow from a deep interior spiritual poverty, humility and self-sacrifice. Finally it must be the expression of a great and deep love of God and neighbour.

VI/2 *The mission of the apostles* I look upon the task that I have been given as the real 'mission' our Lord has now given me, which I must fulfil with utter devotion. The idea of being 'without a shepherd' is only too true of the separated Christians.[36] So I too must have 'compassion on the crowd' [cf Mk 8:2]. In this thoroughly apostolic spirit I see my work: 'for souls'—to build up the body of Christ.[37] So I must do everything to make the quest for unity worth their while, and offer them every help to achieve this goal. But above all I must show my love; in my relations with people, in my conversation, correspondence and dealings with people. They should recognize that it is only the love of Christ that inspires me. And I will make every effort to instil this frame of mind into all the people who work with me. The work must be done with fervour (of spirit) and in the spirit of power: with supernatural strength.[38] Everyone must see: here is no lust for power, no earthly interest, no mere busyness, no matter of routine, but the genuine spirit of Christ.

If it is definitely entrusted to me, I shall treat the Jewish question in this spirit too.

When I have carried out these tasks I can sing my 'Nunc dimittis'. May

[36] 'When he saw the crowds, he had compassion for them, because they were harassed and helpless, like sheep without a shepherd' (Mt 9:36; cf Mk 6:34). In applying this to non-Catholics there is no attempt to sit in judgment on any persons or Churches, but simply a statement of the absence of that full unity that Christ willed for his Church. Basically the same thought is set out in Vatican II's Decree on Ecumenism: '. . . our separated brethren, whether considered as individuals or as Communities and Churches, are not blessed with that unity which Jesus Christ wished to bestow on all those whom he has regenerated and vivified into one body and newness of life—that unity which the holy scriptures and the revered tradition of the Church proclaim. For it is through Christ's Catholic Church alone, which is the all-embracing means of salvation, that the fulness of the means of salvation can be obtained. It was to the apostolic college alone, of which Peter is the head, that we believe our Lord entrusted all the blessings of the New Covenant, in order to establish on earth the one Body of Christ into which all those should be fully incorporated who already belong in any way to God's People' (3).
[37] Cf St Paul: 'And [Christ's] gifts were that some should be apostles, some prophets . . . for the equipment of the saints, for the work of the ministry, for building up the body of Christ' (Eph 4:11 f).
[38] 'For our Gospel came to you not only in word, but also in power and in the Holy Spirit and with full conviction. You know what kind of men we proved to be among you for your sake' (1 Thess 1:5); cf also 1 Cor 4:20: 'For the kingdom of God does not consist in talk but in power.'

he uphold my strength, health, energy, so that I may carry them out fully.

VI/3 *Three ways of subjection* [Exercises 164-168] My asceticism must have nothing extravagant or vague about it, which in practice will be nothing but emptiness. My present position imposes certain conditions on my life and for me these are the will of God and the glory of God, and I must not neglect them. My age and my state of health have also got a part to play in this. So this shows me at once what the condition for the greater or at least equal glory of God is, both in the second as well as in the third way of subjection. It is the same with respect and honour. But it is important that I should not take all this in a comfortable bourgeois sense, as a cover for natural laziness etc., but accept it as God's will, and at the same time cultivate love of the cross and of the crucified Lord as a permanent and basic attitude.[39] As far as depends on me, would I not prefer things to be more difficult, more like our Lord on the cross? There will always be opportunities of this sort, when I can put this love into practice, either by my own choice or through circumstances: environment, fitting in with difficult characters, ill-health, contradictions, misinterpretations and misunderstandings and so on. I must take all this upon me in the spirit of the third way for love of the crucified Lord and like him. This would be a genuine and practical way of practising the third way of subjection.

VI/4 *The last supper* [cf Mt 26:26-29] The holy Eucharist should always be the centre and focal point of my interior life and of my apostolic work. Now I celebrate Mass with greater external ceremony; so I must now also say it with greater interior reverence and devotion. For me this is the epitome of our divine Lord's whole life of love; everything that he did on earth for the poor, the sick, the blind, the lame, for children and for sinners, he continues here tirelessly and he does it through my hands. This is the sacrament of humble love and service, as he showed before he instituted the Blessed Sacrament by washing their feet [cf Jn 13:1-11]. Mass is the hour when I can lay all my own intentions, problems and needs on the altar, but also all the intentions and

---

[39] To understand this one must keep in mind what the Exercises have to say on the second and third ways of subjection: 'The second way of subjection . . . means that I so submit myself that I neither seek nor desire to be rich rather than poor, I do not try to be well thought of rather than disregarded . . .'; 'The third way of subjection . . . I desire to be poor along with Christ in poverty rather than rich, to be insulted along with Christ so grossly insulted, rather than to be well thought of . . .' (166 f). So now, when the author reviews his life in the light of this, he states: 'My present position imposes certain conditions on my life and for me these are the will of God and the glory of God, and I must not neglect them.' This shows at once where the greater glory of God lies. Thus the author concludes that he cannot *choose* poverty or scorn in such cases; but at the same time he insists that he must accept the conditions imposed on him by his position in the right spirit and so at the same time foster love of the cross and love for the crucified Lord.

problems of the Church and of each one of the faithful. Every day it is for me, for the Church, for the world the great hour of grace, and I must make fresh use of it every day. How many of the separated brethren envy us this grace! Every day, then, I must renew my strength in the devout, recollected and reverent celebration of Mass. This is the great hour of each day for me and for the life of the world. The moment of the consecration is the greatest in all my day's work.

VII/1 *Jesus in the Garden of Olives* Hours like those our Lord experienced in the Garden of Olives can always come upon me, either through interior dryness, lack of consolation and so on, or from without through failure, misunderstandings, misinterpretations, opposition, attacks and so on. In itself this has no direct bearing on the state of my soul: our Lord was and remained the beloved Son of the heavenly Father even in these difficult hours when his soul was sorrowful unto death. And it was precisely here that he turned to the Father with special fervour: 'Father . . .'[40] For me too there is no other consolation in such cases except confident prayer. Men cannot be relied upon in these situations: and they slept; although he had told them that his soul was sorrowful unto death, they were tired and wanted their sleep. But the Father is watching over him and at the most difficult moment sends an angel to comfort him. And the Lord of Angels gratefully accepts the consolation of the angel sent by the Father [cf Lk 22:43] and braces himself to meet the enemy. In thee, Lord, I shall put my trust and I shall never be confounded.[41]

VII/2 *The capture and trial before Caiaphas* Here I can see the all-out attack that was made on our Lord. He stands alone: the masses, who were once so enthusiastic, are silent; after an untimely effort to defend him the apostles have abandoned him, Judas betrays him, and his judges are his mortal enemies, who have already determined on his death.[42] This is the picture, not so much of the individual soul, but of the persecuted Church as it appears in every century, with a different emphasis at different times. I should have to doubt the Church if it did not suffer this fate even today. In fact it suffers it today more than ever. While its reputation has grown in one part of the world and it is recognized in its greatness, attacks on it from the other side are all the more fierce and ruthless. It has to be that way. But I must not forget what our Lord said [to the High Priest]: 'You have said so. But I tell you, hereafter you will see the Son of Man seated at the right hand of Power and

---

[40] In his prayer in the Garden of Olives Jesus said: 'Abba, Father, all things are possible to thee; remove this cup from me; yet not what I will, but what thou wilt' (Mk 14:36).

[41] The last verse of the 'Te Deum'.

[42] Two days before the Pasch 'the chief priests and the elders of the people gathered in the palace of the high priest, who was called Caiphas, and took counsel together in order to arrest Jesus by stealth and kill him' (Mt 26:3 f).

coming on the clouds of heaven' (Mt 26:64), which means that in the end victory will be his.

VII/3 *Before Pilate and Herod*   Our Lord went through all that his Church had to suffer later and still suffers today. And worse than anything there is the implacable hatred with which the Jews pursue their aim and which is satisfied with no half-measures.[43] It is the 'écrasez l'infâme' of the later persecutors of the Church: Pilate's half-measures and Herod's mockery do not satisfy them: take him, take him and crucify him is their cry. And yet all this happens in order that God's plans may be realized. They want to see him on the cross and they get their way; but 'when I have been raised up from the earth I shall draw all things with me' [cf Jn 12:32]. What would the world be today without that image of our Lord on the cross! The accusation of the Jews only helped to set Christ's kingdom in its true perspective: 'my kingdom is not of this world', but he is a king. You say it: I am a king [cf Jn 18:36 f]. And the picture of heavenly tranquillity that our Lord presents in every situation has become a source of strength and an example for the countless people who have followed the king of martyrs to death.[44] So this hatred has turned into the cause of countless numbers following our Lord in love and offering him their lives in work and, if it must be so, in death.

VII/4 *The way of the cross and Calvary*   While on the one hand hatred imagines it is celebrating its triumph, it is really love, a love that knows no limits, that is triumphantly celebrating in our Lord the fulfilment of those words of St Paul: 'he loved me and gave himself up for me',[45] he gave himself up to the most painful and shameful death. He could go no further in generosity. There is nothing left for me to do but to copy this generosity and generously to accept and bear the crosses that life brings me: to grow in faithful love for the crucified Christ and the cross, even if for love of our crucified Lord I must reach out for the cross (third way), as I have resolved, 'granted an equal measure of praise and glory to God' [Exercises 167].

[43] It should be said here, once and for all, that when the author here and in other places speaks of Jesus' persecutors as the 'Jews', this has nothing to do with anti-semitism: it simply reflects the historically conditioned and usual usage of the Gospels, especially John. On this habit of St John, Bea wrote in his study *The Church and the Jewish People* (Chapman, London 1966):

'For John the term "Jews" denotes *not* just the Jewish people but the *leaders* who opposed Jesus (cf Jn 2:18, 20; 3:25; 5:10, 16, 18; 7:13; 8:22; 9:22; 10:24; 11:8; etc). It must not be forgotten that St John wrote at the close of the first century and therefore after a whole series of very painful experiences on the part of the early Christian communities. This special usage of St John's must naturally be kept in mind lest we misinterpret what he says and conclude that he is referring to the whole Jewish people as such' (p. 79, note)'

[44] Jesus made no further answer to all the accusations, or to any of Pilate's questions, 'so that Pilate wondered' (Mk 15:15).

[45] This is Paul's creed: '. . . the life I now live in the flesh I live by faith in the Son of God, who loved me and gave himself for me' (Gal 2:20).

At the foot of the cross Mary became my mother [cf. Jn 19:26 f]: I must belong to her as her crucified Son does. The devotion to the mother of sorrows is familiar to me from my childhood: I must remain faithful to it now in the last years of my life as well, until I can say with our Lord: 'It is finished' [Jn 19:30] and can join him in saying with some truth: I have accomplished the work which thou gavest me to do, and then, too, pray confidently: 'now, Father, glorify thou me in thy own presence' [Jn 17:4 f]. 5.III.61

VIII/1 *After Jesus' death* His triumph begins at once: the earthquake, the opening of tombs, the tearing of the curtain and the Roman centurion: 'indeed this is the Son of God' [cf Mt 27:51–54]; the fear of the Jews that he might rise from the dead [cf Mt 27:62–66] and so on. The opening of Jesus' side is already one of the fruits of the Redemption: the opening of the way to the treasury of love,[46] to the living waters of compassion and love, to the place of peace for the good and salvation for the repentant. Since that moment how many graces have flowed into the world out of our Lord's heart, beginning with the Church, which was born out of his side as his pure bride.[47] The moment he bows his head in death, his glorious life begins. I belong to a kind, powerful and gracious Master indeed! And from that moment his holy mother at the foot of the cross, the 'pietà', became the mother of mercy, our life, our sweetness and our hope.[48] I will take this devotion to the Sacred Heart and to Mary his mother with me from this retreat as two sources of strength and grace.

VIII/2 *Our Lord as comforter* In the first place he comforts the apostles. He had prophesied quite clearly that he would rise again on the third day [cf e.g., Mt 16:21; 20:19], but they had not grasped the idea and were still confused by what had happened. 'We had hoped.'[49] Now he must make them understand. By his presence—his wounds—his behaviour. Only gradually do they grasp it, and not fully until after the Pentecost event. Often enough it is the same with me. I am so wrapped

[46] Cf Preface of the Sacred Heart (see above, p. 40, note 44).

[47] An insight familiar to the great Fathers of the Church: Augustine, Cyril of Alexandria, and later St Bonaventure. Cf S. Tromp, art. cit., p. 40, note 44 above. The idea is also expressed by Vatican II in the Constitution on the Church, para. 3: 'The Church or, in other words, the kingdom of Christ now present in mystery, grows visibly in the world through the power of God. This inauguration and this growth are both symbolized by the blood and water which flowed from the open side of the crucified Jesus (cf Jn 19:34), and are foretold in the Lord's words concerning his death on the cross: "And I, if I be lifted up from the earth, will draw all men to myself" (Jn 12:32, Greek text).' And, even more explicitly, in the Council's Constitution on the Liturgy: 'For it was from the side of Christ as he slept the sleep of death upon the cross that there came forth the wondrous sacrament which is the whole Church' (5). The Council confirms this idea with a text of St Augustine ('Enarr. in Ps 138' 2, Corp. Christ. XL).

[48] From the prayer 'Hail, holy Queen'.

[49] The two disciples on the way to Emmaus said: 'But we had hoped that he was the one to redeem Israel' (Lk 24:21).

up in material things and difficulties—but I must not be so superficial! I am now at the end of my life. So I look forward with confidence to this end and to what comes after. As long as I can work, I shall do so with all my strength, and suffer and endure too. But then I hope to hear the words 'enter into the joy of your master'.

Comfort too for Mary. It is true that she does not need it in the ordinary sense of the word; she has suffered with him, but also hoped and realized that he would rise again. And now he is with her and shows her, his mother, what is to happen in the future: she who suffered with him is now to be the mother of the Church as well. The Lord's brethren are her children too and she will accept them as she accepted our Lord. So I must put my work under her special patronage. All the baptized are her children, whether they are aware of it or not.[50] Under your patronage!

VIII/3 *The appearances* They reveal the tender love and thoughtfulness of our Lord for all those who are unhappy and weak (Emmaus, Peter, Thomas). But above all care for his Church. This is based on the handing over of 'all power in heaven and on earth' [Mt 28:18]. This is, so to speak, the foundation of the building: unshakable and invincible. The historical basis is the truth of his Resurrection (Emmaus, Thomas). The link that holds everything together is Peter, the Shepherd, and his successor, the pope, whose exercise of authority does not come from any lust for power or ambition but from a love that must be greater than the love of all the others.[51] The closer I am to St Peter's successor, the more the question: 'Do you love me? Do you love me more than these?' applies to me too, and in all humility I must be able to reply: 'Lord, you know everything; you know that I love you.' Then our Lord gives the Church the precious gift of baptism, its consecration to the Blessed Trinity,[52]

---

[50] An old tradition of the Church, based on Jn 19:26 f: 'Woman, behold your Son . . . Son, behold your mother.' Cf also Vatican II, Constitution of the Church, para. 56: 'By thus consenting to the divine utterance Mary, a daughter of Adam, became the mother of Jesus. Embracing God's saving will with a full heart and impeded by no sin, she devoted herself totally as a handmaid of the Lord to the person and work of her Son. In subordination to him and along with him, by the grace of almighty God she served the mystery of redemption. Rightly therefore the holy Fathers see her as used by God not merely in a passive way, but as cooperating in the work of human salvation through free faith and obedience. For, as St Irenaeus says; she, "being obedient, became the cause of salvation for herself and for the whole human race". Hence in their preaching not a few of the early Fathers gladly assert with him: "The knot of Eve's disobedience was untied by Mary's obedience. What the virgin Eve bound through her unbelief, Mary loosened by her faith." Comparing Mary with Eve, they call her "the mother of the living", and still more often they say: "death through Eve, life through Mary".'

[51] See Christ's threefold question to Peter after the resurrection: 'Do you love me?' and Peter's replies (Jn 21:15–17).

[52] Cf Jesus' commission of the apostles on his appearance in Galilee: 'Go therefore and make disciples of all nations, baptizing them in the Name of the Father and of the Son and of the Holy Spirit, teaching them to observe all things that I have commanded you' (Mt 28:19 f). 'Baptizing them in the Name . . .' implies consecrating to the Blessed Trinity.

and the sacrament of peace, the sacrament of penance.⁵³ And finally the guarantee for the whole future: 'Lo, I am with you always, even to the close of the age' [Mt 28:20]. This divine guarantee also accompanies me as I go from this retreat back to the service of the Church and of the Mystical Body of our Lord.

VIII/4 *Love* In the course of my eighty years God has given me and continues to give me every day a stream of favours, graces and help, more than is given to the average person. My life is a chain of guidance and providence, which I can only contemplate with astonishment. If anyone ever had reason to say with St Ignatius: 'All that I have, all that I own: it is your gift to me, I now return it to you. It is all yours, to be used simply as you wish,'⁵⁴ then I am that person. This is the meaning of my 'decision': I belong only to God and the Church. The things I have decided on in this retreat are not just 'resolutions': they form a programme of restitution, to which I am bound. All the more since our Lord worked and suffered so much in his life to win these graces for me. I too, then, must work and suffer for him, again so to speak by way of restitution! But the most important thing is that I should now seek him and see him in everything: the raising of the mind to God (cf Augustine, Bernard, Francis of Assisi, Bonaventure, Ignatius, Francis Xavier, Bellarmine, Canisius); that I should love him in everything and everyone, and love everything and everyone in him and only in him.⁵⁵ This will be the truly fervent interior life that I have resolved on in my 'decision' and it must, so to speak, penetrate everything. I must pray for this and make it grow deeper and more perfect in my spiritual exercises (meditation, Mass). Fiat, fiat!

17.IV.61

31 August 1960

FROM THE MONTHLY RECOLLECTIONS

2.X.1960
Devotion, sacrifice, self-conquest. In public: dignified, composed, reserved, not domineering—kind, fatherly—good example, genuine fervour, faithfulness in spiritual exercises, recollection (short visits).

I/1 For no other purpose than God's honour; all my work, life and prayer through the Church to God! The dignity and consecration of prayer comes: through Christ. I exist only for God.

⁵³ ' "Peace be with you. As the Father has sent me, even so I send you." And when he had said this, he breathed on them, and said to them, "Receive the Holy Spirit. If you forgive the sins of any, they are forgiven; if you retain the sins of any, they are retained" ' (Jn 20:21 ff).
⁵⁴ From the prayer concluding the meditation on the favours received from God (Exercises 234).
⁵⁵ Cf above, pp. 41–2.

I/2 Share in Christ's mission: Christlike behaviour in the Lord! In praise, reverence and service in Christ!

I/3 Christ's way is the way of salvation!—for others; I must let it cost me something.

6.XI.1960

Not authoritarian; courteous and considerate towards those who work with me, fatherly, trusting: work quietly without haste and irritability. Spiritual exercises faithfully and punctually: recollection all day long.

I/4 God guides and shapes my life, not I; no waste of time on the externals of everyday life.

II/2 Social effect of sin—never a purely personal matter!

II/3 Order and arrangement in the spiritual life.

II/4 Not slovenly and nothing slipshod—example!!

III/1 First a victim, then victory.

III/2 To work with me: recognition and honour not to be directed towards myself personally.

4.XII.1960

Not authoritarian, domineering, courteous, considerate, kind: good example for all: reserved in speech: work without haste and irritability, meditation (preparation) and visits: not taken up with external matters.

III/3 Work for the Church: humility and devotion, not so dependent on external means.

III/4 Let God guide me: Lo I come to do thy will (not mine!) in every situation.

IV/1 Mary offers her Son absolutely and unconditionally: an unconditional yes to everything! Share in the sacrifice of the Son and of the Mother.

IV/4 No looking for approval!! No false consideration!

6.I.1961

Considerate and kind; give everyone something good; work quietly, without irritability and haste: the greatest faithfulness in spiritual exercises. Prepare meditation (16.00!) daily offering: three ways of subjection.

IV/4 Must not allow myself to be influenced by feelings: unpretentious in all things!

V/1 All external glory is merely superficial.

V/2 Not a 'prince of the Church' but 'a servant of the servants of God'! Must not seek the limelight! In the strength of God's 'Word'.

12.II.1961

Courteous, considerate, kind especially to those about me; good example in everything. Restraint—indifferent to people's opinions.

Dealings with God: familiarity with God in prayer and deed (examination of conscience).

VI/1 Heavier responsibility because of higher position. A city set on a hill. But coming from an interior spirit.

VI/2 'I have compassion on the crowd'[56] with a view to the building up of Christ's Body—I am spurred on by the love of Christ—for souls.

VI/3 No natural love of ease, etc, but for the greater glory of God. Contradictions, misrepresentation—in the spirit of Christ: third way!!

IV/4 Mass with greater reverence and more fervour.

5.III.1961

Courteous, considerate and kind—particularly towards those who work with me. Always give good example. Cautious and restrained in speech, particularly when it is a question of authority.

Work without haste or irritability. Spiritual exercises without haste, restlessness or negligence.

VII/1 Misunderstandings, misrepresentations, etc! Consolation in the supernatural—Prayer—in thee, O Lord, I have put my trust . . .

VII/2 Our Lord left alone!—in his Church—in me! I am he!!

VII/3 The hate directed against our Lord had the opposite effect!

VII/4 Bear crosses and reach out for the cross—Mary Mother of the crucified Son!!

7.IV.1961

A man of genuine interior life: hence . . . spiritual exercises. In public, composed, dignified, reserved, because all eyes are on me. Patience when working with others. Union with God in the Holy Ghost during the day. Prayer, recollected, simple, practical.

VIII/3 The Church has power in heaven and on earth—historical basis of our belief. Resurrection. Institution: Peter and the Apostles. Gifts: sacraments—I am with you. . . .

7.V.1961

1) In public, dignified, composed, reserved especially in speech, but kind and friendly to all.
2) Towards the people who work with me fatherly, kind and trusting.
3) Interior life: recollected, careful, ordered prayer.

I/1 For God and only for him.

I/2 Share in Christ's mission—like Christ.

I/4 No waste of time on externals! Must not get wrapped up in them.

2.VI.1961

Courteous, considerate and kind to all. Good example in all things. Work calmly, carefully and methodically. Meditation and examination of conscience, visits to Blessed Sacrament.

---

[56] i.e. of the separated brethren. See above, p. 57, especially note 36.

II/1 Avoid sin: it has a corrupting effect on others.

II/2 In my case there is no lack of grace—oceans of grace! In my position all eyes are on me: people notice the smallest things.

III/1 Must be serious about life with Christ—victory—victim.

III/2 'Show greater enthusiasm and distinguish myself . . .' (Exercises 97).

9.VII.1961

Must never seek my own ends in anything. In public gracious, composed, reserved (in speech!). Good example and spiritual encouragement for all: faithful to spiritual exercises.

III/4 That I may do the Father's will.

IV/1 Unconditional sacrifice! A sword will pierce. Fiat! Must not be worried about what people say!

IV/1 Make good use of daily opportunities: 'it is always the cardinal who speaks';[57] no looking for approval! God's will without curtailment or restriction.

---

[57] An allusion to something Pius XII once said to the author, to explain why he prepared his speeches so carefully: 'è sempre il Papa che parla' (cf IV/3). The pope was very conscious of his position and responsibility. And the cardinal applies the words to himself, to express the great opportunities that his position in the Church offers him.

CHAPTER 5

The number of responsibilities is constantly increasing

1961

From this time onwards there began a period of the most intensive work for the cardinal: activity, travel, lectures and meetings—not to mention the reception of all sorts of important people—all these increased at such a rate that one wondered whether a man in his eightieth year could stand the strain. After his annual retreat, at the end of August, he did not take any holiday. And on 6 September 1960 he was already in Rome, only to start again on his travels on 20 September, when he addressed some words of welcome to the International Catholic Conference for Ecumenical Questions, which was meeting at Gazzada near Milan. This conference had been founded in 1951 by the then Monsignor Jan Willebrands, Professor of Theology in Roermond; the Secretariat for Unity had chosen quite a number of its members and advisers from it. Being in Milan also gave the cardinal the opportunity of meeting for the first time the General Secretary of the World Council of Churches, Dr Willem Visser't Hooft, on 'neutral' ground, far from curious eyes. One of the most important subjects of the conversation was religious freedom.[1]

On 9 November in Ferrara (it is significant that this was the town where the Unity Council of Ferrara–Florence took place, 1436–9!) he gave his first public lecture on the problem of ecumenism, addressed especially to university circles. 13 and 14 November (in the morning) saw the ceremonial inauguration of the work of the preparatory commission and on 14–15 November the Secretariat for Unity held its first plenary session. The main purpose was to enable them to get some idea of the themes and tasks that faced the Secretariat and to divide the work among the members of the commission, so that they could discuss in small groups of three to four men and prepare rough drafts.

Soon after this came the first of a series of exciting ecumenical events that took place during these years: on 2 December, the Anglican Archbishop of Canterbury, Dr Geoffrey Fisher, paid the 'courtesy visit' to

---

[1] Cf the introduction by J. Willebrands to Augustin Kardinal Bea, W. Visser't Hooft, *Der Friede zwischen Christen*, Freiburg i. Br., 1966, p. 14 f.

Pope John XXIII that had been announced at the beginning of November. The Secretariat made the preparations for this very unusual visit, and Cardinal Bea followed it up with an extensive commentary in the *Civiltà Cattolica* (10 December 1960).

From the time of the world octave of prayer in 1961 onwards the number of interviews and in particular of public lectures given by the President of the Secretariat began to increase. On 21 January in the great hall of the Dominican University in Rome, the Angelicum, he gave one of a series of talks arranged by the 'Studium Christi' on the theme: 'The Catholic and the ecumenical problem'. In this address he dealt for the first time with the burning question of the relationship of non-Catholics to the Church, still a delicate question in those days. A week later, on 29 January, in Genoa, he spoke about the attitude of Reformed Churches to the Council, which was in many cases very positive, and also of the contribution that the Council could make towards unity.

In the meantime the work of the small advisory groups had progressed so far that the Secretariat was able to hold another plenary session during the first half of February (6–9). During the whole of this session the participants lived together in the Pauline retreat house 'Casa Gesù Divin Maestro' in Aricia near Rome, a procedure which was copied by other commissions on some later occasions. The fact that they lived together not only saved time but was a great help in creating a family spirit and encouraging mutual understanding in the difficult questions that were debated at the meetings. The members repeatedly expressed their surprise at the lively and attentive way in which the eighty year old President chaired the meetings, which lasted from six to seven hours every day.

In March there followed an ecumenical lecture tour with lectures in Milan (8 March), Lugano (9 March), Turin (11 March), Chievi (12 March). Everywhere, but especially in Turin, the lectures were followed with the closest interest.

Alongside these duties directly connected with ecumenism, there were others no less important and tiring. Apart from plenary sessions of the Secretariat for Unity (16–21 April) there were the lectures he gave as part of the nineteen hundredth anniversary celebrations of the arrival of St Paul in Rome. On 9 April in Naples he gave a lecture as part of a 'Christological course' on the theme: 'The History of the Church in the World after Paul'. At the beginning of June he was in Reggio Calabria for the nineteen hundredth anniversary celebrations of St Paul's arrival in that town. In the same month, after a journey to Sardinia, he took part in a week long meeting of the Central Preparatory Commission for the Council (12–19 June). At the end, on 19 June, he addressed the Missionary Union of Clergy on the theme: 'The Priest according to the mind of St Paul: the servant of Christ.' From 20 July–10 August he allowed himself a few weeks' holiday outside Rome. And after that he flew to Germany where the first thing he did was to make his annual retreat.

RETREAT 1961

Neuhausen, 16–23 August

I/1 *Created* [Exercises 23] This one word tells me everything: from me comes nothing and from God comes all that I am and all that I have. My physical abilities: their nature, quality and endurance, are from him; my intellectual powers are from him, and my supernatural life is altogether his gift. And then there is the special guidance and direction I have received throughout my life. Neither I nor anyone else could foresee how my life would turn out in fact—neither in the world, nor even in the Society. God took me into his hands and led me the way he wanted. My formation and the way I have been used are his work; what I did was only cooperation and I needed his grace and help for that. What shall I offer in return? [Ps 115:12.] Clearly I must use all that he has given me according to his will, for him, in his interests and for his Church. And this with special zeal because he has given me special gifts. So never under any circumstances must I seek my own ends, neither my own honour nor my own convenience or comfort. I exist only for him to the last moment of my life and wherever he wants to have me. This is my duty but also my privilege and salvation for now and all eternity.

I/2 *By doing these things he will save his soul* [Exercises 23] *These things:* I do not have to do anything except what God asks of me every day, whether pleasant or unpleasant, easy or difficult, and whatever he sends me. Here too I have no need to make a choice: complete devotion to God's will!

Doing: No dawdling, hesitating or wasting time, just doing my job with all my energy. I must do all my work thoroughly and perform my spiritual duties fully; and accept everything that comes my way in everyday life, whatever its source.

He will save: not from earthly discomfort, unpleasantness or distress, etc: for these are parts of God's will for me—but 'save', that means make my soul safe, and happy! Everything that I have to do and to suffer for this is only a 'slight momentary affliction'.[2] And after that I shall be freed from all this and enjoy God and everything in God: to a degree that is impossible on earth, and securely, for no one will be able to take it away from me again. But I must not rely on the last moment, instead I must be ready every moment, and I shall be if I carry out God's will every moment totally and cheerfully.

---

[2] Paul, who had so much to suffer in his apostolic activity, describes it all as a 'slight momentary affliction' compared with the future glory and says: 'This slight momentary affliction is preparing for us an eternal weight of glory beyond all comparison, because we look not to the things that are seen but to the things that are unseen; for the things that are seen are transient, but the things that are unseen are eternal' (2 Cor 4:17 f).

Consideration of spiritual state   Must not seek my own ends or any creature (sympathies or antipathies). Supernatural outlook: all things must lead to God! Gratitude for all that the Lord has given me. 'Stop being a lover of yourself, and become instead a zealous doer of my will' (*Imitation* III/11).

I/3   *Creatures* [Exercises 23]   The world I love is not bad in itself: it is made by God and should lead me to God. It only becomes bad when it is untrue to this purpose for which it was created or is used by men or the devil for a bad purpose (irrational nature) or when I myself use it against its purpose. In the long run it depends on me, on my free will and self-discipline, whether it is good or bad for me. I can make use of everything that comes my way, every day, from morning to evening, of the pleasant things and of the unpleasant things; but I must be in control, exercise a certain sovereignty over things, and not live through it all without a thought. So there must be *reflection* on what I meet every day or what I can see is likely to happen (examination of conscience). In this way I can derive great benefits from the use of things but also from renunciation (sacrifice). But above all I must see the 'signs of God' in all things: in their beauty, order and activity, and so be raised up to God by them: 'the mind's journey to God' (St Boniface), St Bernard, St Robert Bellarmine,[3] St Ignatius ('what harm can the world do me, when I am looking at heaven?') and so many other saints. This is the real 'sense of the supernatural'. 'They should seek God in all things . . . give their hearts entirely to the Creator, by loving him in all his creatures and all his creatures in him'.[4] 'And so by this mutual consideration they would grow in devotion . . . and give praise to God.'[5] Fiat, Fiat!

I/4   *Indifference*   Impatience, sensitivity, desire to make a name for oneself, lack of recollection in prayer and in my spiritual exercises, lack of order in my work and so on: all this proves that I am not free deep down in my heart, as I should be. And behind these failings lie inclinations against which I do not struggle enough. And so even now in my old age I must pay attention to these tendencies and fight them systematically. My examination of conscience must be a real self-examination and at the same time a constant effort to overcome these tendencies. Basically it is the search for the 'four things that bring great peace' (*Imitation* III/23):

1) to do the will of others rather than your own;
2) choose to have less rather than more;

---

[3] St Robert Bellarmine's work, 'De ascensione mentis ad Deum per scalas rerum creaturarum', Biblioteca ascetica edita a Francisco Brehm, Bonn 1925, was found among the cardinal's papers.

[4] From the Constitutions of the Society of Jesus (part III, chap. 1, nr. 26). Already quoted in chap. 3, note 48.

[5] The general principle of seeking God in everything is applied in the Constitutions of the Society of Jesus to the relationship between the members (part III, chap. 1, nr. 4).

3) always make for the lowest place and take rank below others;
4) let your constant prayer and desire be that the will of God may be perfectly accomplished in you.

This is true even in my present position, sometimes perhaps more in my frame of mind than in external actions. It tells me that I must fight every urge to do my own will, every inclination to look for approval and recognition, every irregular desire to have and possess something, at its very beginning, at its root, so that I can face all these things with inward freedom. 'They do not take long to say (those few words), but they are full of meaning and rich in results' *(Imitation* III/23). 'Give me, Lord, a greater store of your grace, to enable me to keep your word' [id].

8.X.61

II/1 *The religious state and the fundamental principle* The main thing to notice here is how intensively the presence of God is realized in the religious life. The whole day is sanctified by the various 'exercises of piety' and in particular by the constant recollection and union with God resulting from them. On both scores I must renew my resolutions firmly: in the first place to perform my spiritual exercises fully, faithfully and in a spirit of recollection; they are the most important part of my day, even in my position. Next I must make great efforts to cultivate the spirit of recollection and union with God all day long, much more than I have done.—And I must be grateful to the Lord for making my life a continuous service. All my daily work is after all nothing but 'the work of God':[6] its whole purpose is to give glory to God, whether in the service of the Church or work for souls, whatever it may be. I do not have to go and look for opportunities: they are there from early morning to late at night. My task is simply to perform this service faithfully, conscientiously and with the right intentions: then I too can say after all this: 'I have accomplished the work which thou gavest me to do' (John 17:4).

II/2 *Conversion* [Mk 1:15; Lk 7:36–50] 'The kingdom of God is at hand; repent, and believe the Gospel.'[7] These words are addressed to me too and in a very special way. When one is in one's eighty-first year the 'kingdom of God' really is near, and so the heart must be completely turned to God, in faith and in love. The 'story of the sins' (Exercises 56) of my past life must not be a source of worry any more: 'your sins are forgiven you' (cf Lk 7:48); our Lord has said that to me too and I must believe his divine word. And now I must give him everything in love, as the sinful woman did, and the degree of loving devotion determines

[6] An expression used in many religious orders to describe the divine office in choir, the praise of God in the strict sense.
[7] In this meditation the author connects the basic theme of Christ's preaching (Mk 1:15) to his meeting with the sinful woman in the house of the Pharisee (Lk 7:36–50).

the degree of forgiveness: 'her sins, which are many, are forgiven, for she loved much' (Lk 7:47). Her love was generous: she made a sacrifice of everything that she had found her pleasure in before, and without a word she put her trust in our Lord's love. The prodigal son, the repentant Peter, the good thief on the cross, all did the same—the main thing is to begin and to carry on a life of trusting, believing, devoted love. 'Late have I loved thee', but I have loved and I do love thee!

Consideration of spiritual state A life of piety. 'Have the highest regard for the spiritual life.' 'Find devotion according to the degree of grace given.'[8] Divine office: attentively, devoutly and at the right time.[9]

II/3 *Venial sin* Of all the reasons that are usually put forward two are of special importance for me: in the first place the many graces that our Lord has showered on me and which have imposed on me a special debt of gratitude—and I show this gratitude best when I do not neglect any of these daily graces, but make full use of them all with the greatest care: meditation, Mass, spiritual reading, and my religious exercises in general. Hence unpunctuality, distractions, superficiality and negligence are particularly serious in my case.

The second point is: my position. Not only as a priest and a Jesuit, but above all as a cardinal I am a lamp set on a lampstand: hasty words, criticisms of high dignitaries, fits of impatience, irritability, taking offence, carelessness in my attitude, thoughtless speech and so on: all this is of much more importance in my case than with anybody else and destroys a great deal of the success of my work. If Trent says of clergy in general: 'Let them avoid venial sins, which in them could be serious', that is particularly true of someone in my position.

And lastly lack of care in avoiding these venial sins extinguishes the fire of love in me, prevents me from giving myself totally to God and his service, and makes me less pleasing to God. So in the coming year I must pay special attention to these points.

II/4 *Death* In my eighty-first year death must not be a stranger to me, but rather a welcome guest whom I expect every day. When it will come I cannot tell and I do not need to know. The main thing is that I must be prepared: prepared by my life and my work for God, and be able to say with our Lord: I have finished the work thou gavest me to do (Jn 17:4).

---

[8] The first quotation comes from a decree of a 'General Congregation of the Society of Jesus' (the highest law-making body in the Society): 'Let all have the highest regard for the spiritual life, *and indeed for all our concerns*; let them put this before all else and be convinced that the good estate of the Society rests on this regard' (cf Epitome Instituti Societatis Jesu, nr. 181, 1).

The second is from the Rules themselves: 'All (members) should spend the due amount of time on their spiritual exercises and try to find devotion in them according to the degree of divine grace given to them' (part III, chap. 1, nr. 20).

[9] The Society requires from its members who are priests: 'Priests should recite the divine office carefully, attentively, devoutly and at the correct time' (Epitome, nr. 188).

I have nothing to leave behind: I know that all fame etc is vain, and I have long since left flesh and blood, money and property. In my will I shall soon dispose of what I have as cardinal. As for what I take with me: their deeds follow them [cf Rev 14:13]. I shall place them confidently in our Lord's hands, for whom I have done them. I appeal to God's mercy for my sins and failings. So I hope to be ready every day to be called: and preferably in the midst of my work. Death holds no fears for me; it is death that frees me from the worries and labours of this life: 'eternal rest give unto me, O Lord';[10] it is death that leads me to our Lord, to the Blessed Trinity. I wait for it, not in idleness but working all the time until the Lord calls me. And then I hope the prayer may be answered: 'May Christ Jesus smile upon you and welcome your coming; and may he appoint a place for you among those who stand ever near him.'[11] Come, Lord Jesus [Apoc 22:20].

III/1 *The particular judgment* When the Lord calls me I shall stand before his judgment seat as I am at that moment. His mercy has accompanied me until death and even in death. But now I am not standing in front of the merciful Saviour but in front of the stern judge who sees right through me and judges me according to what I am at that moment. So everything depends on my ability to pass the test at that moment. The sins that have already been forgiven in confession do not count any more, nor do the venial sins of which I have earnestly repented. On the other hand there are the merits that I have gained in my life: 'for their deeds follow them'. They will determine the degree of blessedness that will be my lot. So it is fortunate that I have been able to serve our Lord for so many years! These, then, are the conclusions I can draw from this: 1) do my best to avoid all venial sins, even the slightest; 2) always do God's will faithfully, in whatever form it comes to me; 3) always make my examination of conscience and confession well; 4) cultivate the love of our Lord in myself more and more. Enter not into judgment with thy servant Lord! [Ps 142:2.] 3.XII.61

III/2 *The kingdom of Christ* (Exercises 91–98) Our Lord is the 'eternal Lord of all things' (Exercises 98); he must rule:[12] over me and over everyone else. But the world is against him, for it has turned away from his will and his rule.[13] He wants to win it back,[14] every single soul,

---

[10] From the liturgy: the introit for Masses for the Dead.
[11] From the liturgy: Ordo commendationis animae in the Roman Ritual.
[12] Cf St Paul, 1 Cor 15:24 f: 'Then comes the end, when he (Christ) delivers the kingdom to God the Father after destroying every rule and every authority and power. For he must reign until he has put all his enemies under his feet (Ps 110:1).'
[13] Cf the messianic Ps 2: 'Why do the nations conspire, and the peoples plot in vain? The kings of the earth set themselves, and the rulers take counsel together, against the Lord and his anointed, saying, "Let us burst their bonds asunder, and cast their cords from us" ' (Ps 2:1–3).
[14] Cf the mandate our Lord gave the apostles on the occasion of his appearance in Galilee: 'Go therefore and make disciples of all nations . . .' (Mt 28:18 ff).

including me. So his struggle is a struggle for souls, for my soul too, which he wants to free and save from the influence of the world. But he cannot do it without me. I must take up the struggle, but not by myself, for he fights with me—by his help (grace) and by his example. I do not have to do anything that he himself does not do. So I must and I can keep my soul pure and holy. But I must not just avoid doing evil; I must make his control over me as perfect and as full as possible— must 'distinguish' myself in his service [Exercises 97], because he did and still does 'distinguish' himself in serving me: vocation, special graces, special mercies. He did not confine himself to essentials; he could have redeemed the world with one divine–human act of the will; but he became a man like us, led a life of poverty and need, worked hard, suffered in body and soul.[15] In this way he became a model for me: to imitate you in putting up with all injustice, all abuse, all poverty in reality no less than in spirit [Exercises 98]. To follow him is, even now in my present position, my duty and my task, which I must not forget or neglect for one day even in the midst of all exterior pomp and ceremony: 'I will follow you wherever you go' [cf Mt 8:19].

General confession 18.VIII (Fr Schmitt)

III/3 *Incarnation and annunciation* [cf Lk 1:26–38] The boundless love of God and the greatness and humility of Mary. How far beyond all reckoning thy loving kindness! To ransom thy slave, thou gavest up thy Son![16] The actual moment is known only to God, but he has arranged everything with a view to this moment: the Roman empire and the central position of Palestine. Not Rome, Athens, Alexandria but Nazareth. The wisdom of God. Mary: she is not aware of the dignity and greatness that is already hers (Immaculate Conception); she is pious, humble and pure. She speaks little and thinks all the more. On hearing the angel's message, she has no answer but this: 'the handmaid of the Lord' (Lk 1:38) and the 'fiat', which is so rich in consequences, but at the moment she does not think of all the difficulties that it involves. It is the will of God and this is why she agrees, not because of the dignity and greatness that are connected with it and on the other hand in spite of the worries and sufferings that this fiat involves. It is enough for her that God wills it this way. If her son is to be the 'Servant of the Lord' then she will be the handmaid (of the servant) of the Lord.

III/4 *The Nativity* [cf Lk 2:1–7] 'Glory to God and peace among men' (cf Lk 2:14) is the song at the birth of the Saviour. But all this will be achieved by means of unspeakable disappointment, opposition, discomfort, inconvenience, which Joseph and Mary and the Child himself

---

[15] Cf Heb 4:15: 'For we have not a high priest who is unable to sympathize with our weaknesses, but one who in every respect has been tempted as we are, yet without sinning.'

[16] From the liturgical hymn 'Exultet' sung on the Easter Vigil.

will have to bear. Humanly speaking everything should have been quite different. But our Lord wanted it this way and chose to do it this way, and all this to give all of us, who are in the service of God's honour and want to bring peace to me, a model, a motto as it were. For me too! My present life is really too comfortable and easy. So I must make an effort to accept the unpleasantnesses and opposition that my work and my job bring me in the spirit of faithful imitation of our Lord, as Mary and Joseph accepted them. With what love and happiness and care did Mary take the child in her arms! In the Mass I hold the same Saviour in my hands—with faith, as Mary bore him in faith, but also with love, as she loved him with a mother's love. 17.I.62

IV/1 *Presentation in the temple* [cf Lk 2:22–35] The *Saviour* could not be redeemed by a vicarious sacrifice: thou hast given me a body; lo, I come to do thy will. And this will of the Father was the cross. 'Lo, I come.' I too say this over and over again. I want to carry the cross, in whatever form it comes, until 'it is finished' [Jn 19:30]; then I too shall rise again with my crucified Master. Mary was also shown her way of the cross on this day; a sword shall pierce thy soul (cf Lk 2:35). Up to this moment no doubt she had a general idea of what was involved: now she knew it through the words of a man speaking to her as a prophet. And soon she was to experience it: the flight into Egypt, Jesus lost in the Temple, the separation. . . . Sorrowful Mother, pray for me. Simeon was a saint of the Old Testament: just, pious, waiting for the Messiah, full of the Holy Spirit [cf Lk 2:25]. And for that reason he was allowed to take the Saviour into his arms. Day after day I take him into my hands too: my eyes see thy salvation [cf Lk 2:30]. I know the Saviour and his work of salvation better than Simeon. And so I must take him into my hands and bear him in my heart (Mass) with greater reverence and love. Only then shall I be fully justified in singing the 'nunc dimittis' [Lk 2:29].

IV/2 *The hidden life* A real programme for me.

1) No looking for publicity, but a quiet, industrious, retiring life, as far as that fits in with my position. You must set out to be unknown![17]

2) *Life in the house:* a) work systematically, calmly, constantly, with a definite programme for the day. b) *'the cardinal's household'*: like a father, patient, considerate, obliging, forbearing; not impatient, ready to take offence or irritable. c) *visitors:* always kind and friendly but without being weak. d) *Secretariat:* twice 10.15–12.15 (Wednesday and Saturday).[18]

[17] This is the advice given in the *Imitation of Christ* in the chapter 'on taking a low view of oneself': 'If you want to learn an art worth knowing you must set out to be unknown, and to count for nothing' (I/2).
[18] These were the definite times when the cardinal was present in the office of the Unity Secretariat—apart of course from the day-long plenary sessions and his other duties in the Roman Congregations and elsewhere.

3) *In public:*
a) *Ceremonies:* always recollected, dignified, precise, apostolic.
b) *Celebrations:* punctual, attentive, dignified.
c) *Receptions:* sedate, friendly to all.
d) *Invitations:* reserved, moderate, modest, friendly.

4) *Care for the interior life* can and must always be my aim: my daily solicitude must be to advance in God's favour. So I must pray a great deal; and preserve recollection and an interior life even when I appear outside in public.

Consideration of spiritual state Conversation with strangers: there should be an atmosphere of piety and edification.[19]

IV/3 *The twelve year old Jesus* [in the temple: Lk 2:41–50] Here two worlds meet in our Lord: on the one hand his kind, considerate, loving attitude to all—on the other the almost cold, almost harsh 'I must', that knows no bonds, not even the tender bonds of love for parents. This is a lesson for me. As a rule I must be kind, obliging and considerate to all: but there are also times when I have to say a clear decisive no (or yes), whoever the person concerned may be. The deciding factor is the will of God: about my Father's business! And in my case too people will not always understand: 'they did not understand the saying when he spoke to them'. But that is not the point. The important thing is always that I should be quite clear in my mind that this is God's will. I have at my disposal ways of finding this out, consultation or careful consideration. I must never act out of caprice.

IV/4 *The baptism* [Mt 3:13–17 and parallels] Our Lord prepares for his public life by cutting himself off completely from all that had gone before (his mother, his home, his occupation), by an infinite act of humility ('and they were baptized ... confessing their sins' [Mt 3:6]), and by prayer ('and when Jesus also had been baptized and was praying' [Lk 3:21]). Through his baptism he receives his mission: he is revealed as 'my Son', so he is full of divine power; the Spirit of God comes down on him and he becomes 'full of the Holy Spirit' (Lk. 4:1), as Isaiah had prophesied.[20] In this way he became the model and the source of my mission too: by God's authority and in the fullness of the Holy Spirit.[21]

Heaven, which was till then shut because of the sin of our first parents, is opened to us by baptism: we are made adopted sons of God (and that

---

[19] Cf St Paul to the Romans: 'Let us then pursue what makes for peace and for mutual upbuilding' (Rom 14:19); or to the Thessalonians: 'Therefore encourage one another and build one another up, just as you are doing' (1 Thess 5:11).

[20] 'There shall come forth a shoot from the stump of Jesse, and a branch shall grow out of his roots. And the Spirit of the Lord shall rest upon him, the spirit of wisdom and understanding, the spirit of counsel and might, the spirit of knowledge and the fear of the Lord. And his delight shall be in the fear of the Lord' (Is 11:1 ff).

[21] Cf 1 Thess 1:5; 2:13.

is our great dignity), sharers in the divine nature [cf 2 Pet 1:4]; by baptism we are filled with the Holy Spirit and so equipped for our new supernatural life. All this our Lord earned for us by his baptism, and I am to pass it on to others.

V/1 *The calling of the apostles* [Jn 1:35–51] There were certainly many others among John the Baptist's followers. Our Lord chooses only five. Why? 'The men whom thou gavest me' [cf Jn 17:6]. The vocation to be an apostle and to do apostolic work is an unmerited grace, the result of God's eternal decree.[22] But I may be sure that if he gives me this grace he will also give me all the help I need to live up to this grace and cooperate with it. This is a great consolation and at the same time a powerful encouragement. 'I am praying for them . . . for those whom thou hast given me, for they are thine . . . keep them in thy name, which thou hast given me' (Jn 17:9, 11). Our Lord's prayer is for me too.—Our Lord knows so well how to adapt himself to the character of each of them: Philip he orders: 'follow me' [Jn 1:43]. To John and Andrew he says: 'come and see' [cf Jn 1:39]; to Peter 'you shall be called Cephas' [v. 42]. To Nathanael: 'an Israelite indeed' [v. 47]. In the same way I must adapt myself with love and prudence to each of the people who work with me.—'I chose you that you should bear fruit' [cf. Jn 15:16]. They all bore rich fruit, each in accordance with the talents the Lord had given him. 'Because thou hast been faithful over a few things . . . enter into the joy of thy Lord' (cf Mt 25:21).

V/2 *The Sermon on the Mount* [Mt 5:1–16] A great programme for my work. My position: as the salt of the earth I must preserve from false doctrine, false interpretations, and try to ensure that everyone is pleasing to God: that is a very spiritual task. And in doing it I am in the public eye: a city set on a hill, more than ever. So I must give no cause for criticism, for objections, whether in something I do or the way I do it, on the other hand I must not be afraid of criticism. *The light of the world*: I must enlighten by solid, well-founded and clear teaching, expressed clearly, understandably and impressively. *A lamp set on the lampstand*: good example for those around me and all who come into contact with me.

My own *preparation and training*: free from any attachment to money or possessions and earnestly striving after justice [cf Mt 5:6] (sanctity and perfection in accordance with my position), clean of heart (free from serious and venial sin); kind, sympathetic and merciful, peaceable and peace-making towards my neighbour. And in all this: ready for hatred, scorn, calumny and detraction 'for my sake'. And not just 'ready'

---

[22] St Paul speaks in this sense of his own calling with reference to the calling of the prophet Jeremiah (Jer 1:5) and that of the Suffering Servant (cf Is 49:1): 'But he who had set me apart before I was born, and had called me through his grace, was pleased to reveal his Son to me, in order that I might preach him among the Gentiles . . .' (Gal 1:15 f).

but 'rejoice and be glad'. Our Lord points to the fate of the prophets: in front of my eyes I have the fate of the apostles and of all apostolic workers. Blessed are you!

V/3 *Calming the storm* [Mk 4:35-41 and parallels] Today all over the world there is a storm, a violent storm against God and the Church. This must not mislead me. The thing is to fight the storm and fight it with courage and confidence. Our Lord does not sleep but he wants us to work and fight for him. He could still all storms with one word, one sign, of his power: Peace! be still! and there was a great calm [v. 39]. But he does not do so, or rather he does it through the work of his apostles by strengthening their arms. And so we can and must pray to him, not like sinking men in a shipwreck but like good oarsmen. The history of the Church teaches me that he has overcome a thousand storms through his disciples, and often he has intervened suddenly himself: and there came a great calm. So faith, courage and confidence.

Our Lord's example shows me how I too should take care of my strength: 'he was in the stern, asleep on the cushion'. I owe the Church a reasonable concern for my strength and capacity for work. Certainly no one is indispensable, but it is often difficult enough for the authorities to find a replacement and so perhaps create a vacancy somewhere else. So I must rest in order to be able to work, but after my rest I must work all the harder. And in my work do what I have to do, leaving all the rest to the others.

V/4 *The mission of the apostles* [Mt 10:5-16 and parallels] What our Lord says to the apostles is just as essential today, however much times have changed. We must preach the 'kingdom of God', that is the Gospel with all that it contains, not philosophy or social science, etc. We must 'cast out devils'—but the devil dresses differently today:[23] in scientific clothes, in the guise of false humanism, in all sorts of philosophical systems. We must unmask him. The diseases of our time are greed, desire for material prosperity, the lust of the senses in all its forms, among the youth and in married life, to the ruin of the family and of human society. Force is no use against this, the only answer is to work earnestly, unassumingly, not giving oneself airs and asserting oneself, but straightforwardly, simply content with everything, doing the work where it is accepted and leaving it where it is rejected, as Paul did with the Jews.[24] Today too we often find ourselves in opposition to material

---

[23] The idea of the devil disguising himself comes from St Paul, who speaks of his opponents in this way: 'For such men are false apostles, deceitful workmen, disguising themselves as apostles of Christ. And no wonder, for even Satan disguises himself as an angel of light. So it is not strange if his servants also disguise themselves as servants of righteousness' (2 Cor 11:13 ff).

[24] Cf Acts 13:45 ff: 'But when the Jews saw the multitudes [who wanted to hear Paul preaching], they were filled with jealousy, and contradicted what was spoken by Paul, and reviled him. And Paul and Barnabas spoke out boldly, saying, "It was necessary that the word of God should be spoken first to you. Since you thrust it from

power, against which we cannot defend ourselves with material means but by being as cunning as serpents, trying to save what is essential, and, like the simple doves, coming back again and again. All this is true also of my great work for Christian Unity. 4.III.62

VI/1 *Multiplication of loaves* [Mt 14:13–21] Here more than anywhere I can see all the consideration and kindness of our Lord: towards his weary apostles, but also towards the people, whom he does not want to send away and whom he teaches till late in the evening. Then his friendliness towards the disciples: he talks to them as if he was one of them. Then his concern for the material well-being of his audience. Here we have the principle of subsidiarity: where the usual methods are not enough, he steps in with his help, just as the Church ought to do and does.[25] His love of order: 'make them sit down in companies, about fifty each',[26] and the gathering up of the remnants. Finally the dignity with which he does everything. It is as if he was pronouncing the words of consecration at Mass and performing a liturgical ceremony. And lastly: his humility: when the crowd gets enthusiastic about him he withdraws: 'he went into the hills by himself to pray' [v. 23]. He also protects his disciples from doing anything silly: 'he made the disciples get into the boat' [v. 22]. The whole scene is so indescribably grand and yet so simple and friendly. It is a fine model for me and my appearances in public.

VI/2 *The Transfiguration* [Mt 17:1–10 and parallels] Hours like those on Mount Tabor are not lasting here on earth, particularly not in my position. As soon as the retreat is over, humdrum everyday life will begin again, as with our Lord and the three apostles when they had come down from the mountain. The main thing is the testimony of the Father, which still echoed in Peter's ears, even when he was an old man: 'This is my beloved Son . . . listen to him'.[27] In this retreat I have listened

---

you, and judge yourselves unworthy of eternal life, behold, we turn to the Gentiles" ' (see also 18:6 and 28:8). The apostles were following our Lord's own instructions; for when he sent them out he said: 'And if anyone will not receive you or listen to your words, shake off the dust from your feet as you leave that house or town. . . . When they persecute you in one town, flee to the next . . .' (Mt 10:14, 23).

[25] The principle of subsidiarity means that society or its larger groupings should not replace the individuals or smaller groupings but assist them. Consequently society (or the larger social groupings) should leave to the individuals (or smaller social bodies) everything that they can do by themselves, and only intervene when they can no longer manage on their own.

[26] These words are from Lk 9:14. The author is using Matthew's account at the beginning of the meditation, but has the parallel passages in mind also, as a good exegete should.

[27] In 2 Pet 1:16 ff, Peter calls the transfiguration to mind and explains it more fully: 'For we did not follow cleverly devised myths when we made known to you the power and coming of our Lord Jesus Christ, but we were eye-witnesses of his majesty. For when he received honour and glory from God the Father and the voice was borne to him by the Majestic Glory, "This is my beloved Son, with whom I am well pleased," we heard this voice borne from heaven, for we were with him on the holy mountain.'

to him once again and should follow his word and put his inspirations into practice. And when it is difficult and I feel like saying with Peter: 'God forbid—this shall never happen to me' [Mt 16:22], then I must think of the transfiguration that is awaiting me too but only when I am with our Lord like Peter, John and James. John did not forget it either: 'we have beheld his glory . . . full of grace and truth' [Jn 1:14]. The picture of the transfigured Lord must go with me too into everyday life, 'if he follows him in suffering he will assuredly follow him in glory' [cf Exercises 95].

VI/3 *Last supper* The institution of the Eucharist takes place in an atmosphere of sorrow and yet also of love: sorrow, which fills our Lord's soul because of the sufferings he is going to face, because of Judas's treachery, the imperfection of his disciples and finally because he can foresee the abuse and dishonour to which he will be exposed in the Blessed Sacrament. But none of this stops his love from leaving us this great gift as a parting gift, as a source of grace, as a constant renewal of his death on the cross and as the application of the fruits of that death. 'Having loved his own . . . he loved them to the end' [cf Jn 13:1]. I must always keep this in my mind so that I do not approach the altar as a matter of course, cold and indifferent, but conscious every morning that as our Lord's instrument I am renewing his sacrifice of praise, thanksgiving, supplication and expiation and am really and truly receiving him into my heart in holy communion. My whole attitude, composed, earnest and reverent, should bear witness to this fact. The Mass is the greatest thing that I do and can do every day. So I must celebrate it with the greatest devotion and care.

VI/4 *The high-priestly prayer* [Jn 17] This is the night prayer of our Lord's life on earth and the morning prayer of the Mystical Christ, the Church. He has carried out his earthly mission: to give God glory by preaching the truth and by dying on the cross, which gives God the greatest glory. 'I have finished the work' [v. 4].

And now '*the men whom thou gavest me*': for the apostles firstly he asks unity [vv. 6–19]. The enemy of unity is the world: through its spirit and through its hate. Just as in the college of apostles there is a Judas who gives in to the world, so it can be in later times too. But our Lord prayed for the unity of the college, for the unity of the apostles around Peter; he, or the Father, preserves them in the truth and in unity, and Christ himself sacrifices himself.[28] This is the guarantee of the unity of the Church.

Then finally: 'for those who believe through their word': *the faithful* [vv. 20–26]: they too should be one and in particular so that they may bear witness through their unity, 'that the world may believe that

---

[28] As a confirmation of this interpretation of his the author quotes the Greek original '*hagiazo emauton*' (Jn 17:19).

thou hast sent me', 'that the world may know that thou hast sent me'. This unity should give them the truth ('that they may behold my glory') and above all love ('that the love with which thou hast loved me may be in them and I in them').

It is my great vocation to work for this unity.

VII/1 *In the Garden of Olives* Our Lord's soul, left to itself, is overcome by pain and fear. Its only consolation is still prayer, but he prayed 'saying the same words' [Mt 26:44]; his soul is full of fear and not capable of doing more. Nor does he find any comfort in his disciples: 'he found them sleeping'. They had all assured him: 'we are ready to go with you to prison and death' [Lk 22:33], and now they cannot even stay awake one hour with him. So much for human promises and resolutions. Mine too?—The only help our Lord receives is from the Father. He sends an angel to strengthen him [Lk 22:43], not to tell him that the Father is going to relieve him of the suffering but only that it is his will. And he repeats: 'not what I will, but what thou wilt' (Mk 14:36). Still the agony in his soul is so great that it forces the blood out of his veins [Lk 22:44]. But now he is ready: 'Rise, let us be going; see, my betrayer is at hand' [Mt 26:46]. Prayer is my strength too, whatever I have to bear. 'Watch and pray' [Mt 26:41].

VII/2 *Arrest and Jewish trial* What happens to our Lord happens again and again to his Church. Renegades, men of violence, diplomats, ambitious men and so on often rise up against it, even using physical force. But what happens to it is only as much as the Father wills, and he has more than 'twelve legions' at his disposal [cf Mt 26:53]. The main thing is that the Church, like our Lord himself on that occasion, is only persecuted because it preaches the kingdom of God, so that it can never be accused of secret intrigues ('secretly')[29] or revolutionary plans ('I will destroy this temple'), and it suffers all this for witnessing Christ: 'out of hate for the faith'.[30] Then let men judge it: it will always rise again. And the same goes for each of its servants and apostles —Peter has not yet understood this 'interior aspect'. He is caught up in the inward struggle between love for the Master and fear. But his love is imprudent: first he tries force and then boldness[31] but it is futile. He still has to learn and he learns by his fall: 'he went out and wept bitterly' [Lk 22:62]. From now on his self-confidence is broken: 'Lord, you know everything: you know that I love you' [Jn 21:16]. One glance from the Master was enough [cf Lk 22:61 f].

[29] A reference to Christ's answer to the High Priest: 'I have spoken openly to the world; I have always taught in synagogues and in the temple, where all Jews come together; I have said nothing secretly' (Jn 18:20).

[30] A technical expression used particularly about a martyr's death to indicate that the person in question was really martyred and suffered death on account of the faith.

[31] Mk 14:54: 'And Peter followed Jesus at a distance, right into the courtyard of the high priest; and he was sitting with the guards, and warming himself at the fire.'

VII/3 *Jesus before Pilate and Herod*   Here too our Lord shows the Church how to behave. Accusations of political activity: revolt, inciting rebellion, attempted coups d'état and so on, where the opposite can easily be proved. Stirring up the masses, the 'mind of the nation', after the people have so often cheered him, been taught and fed by him and on Palm Sunday have organized a triumphant procession for him. An object of politics and concessions: they became friends—they had been enemies before;[32] a plaything in the hands of an earthly ruler: Herod, the worldling, the unscrupulous murderer and so on. Time and again all this has happened in the history of the Church and of the leaders of the Church. Our Lord is silent, and so the Church too must be silent, however much it may be in the right. He only speaks when he is questioned about his religious position. 'King of the Jews' but a kingdom that is not of this world, a kingdom of truth, which the world will never understand anyway.[33] But in the end it was he who was victorious.

VII/4 *Way of the cross and crucifixion*   There will have been many who felt and thought like the holy women, and the sympathetic words of our Lord are addressed to them all: 'Weep for yourselves and for your children' [Lk 23:28]. But for many those tears will not have been shed in vain. Amongst the many people who became followers of the crucified Lord after the resurrection, many must have been members of this 'crowd'. The cross is the most visible and most striking symbol of Christ's religion. It spreads its arms over the whole world and calls all to itself, as it were. It is particularly noticeable how in the midst of all the pain and agony of the cross our Lord thinks of others and takes care of them, first of all, his enemies and crucifiers: 'Father, forgive them'; then the repentant sinners: the good thief; and finally his blessed Mother, who has followed him to the foot of the cross: 'Behold your son'. In her he gives his beloved disciple and us all a mother, his mother, who has now become our mother too—only then does he think of himself, and then only to fulfil what has been prophesied of him.[34] Then he can utter his 'it is finished'.

VIII/1 *After Jesus' death*   The Roman centurion, who has watched everything, is the first to confess: 'This is indeed the Son of God.' Accustomed as he is to scenes like this, he has obviously been so struck by our Lord's example, his patience, his love and his nobility, that he comes to believe. But many others, like him, recognized that our Lord had been unjustly condemned and crucified: 'They returned home

---

[32] 'And Herod and Pilate became friends with each other that very day, for before this they had been at enmity with each other' (Lk 23:12).

[33] A reference to the scornful reply of Pilate: 'What is truth?' (Jn 18:38).

[34] Cf Jn 19:28: 'After this Jesus, knowing that all was now finished, said (to fulfil the scriptures), "I thirst." '

beating their breasts'.[35] Many of them will receive the faith on the occasion of St Peter's first sermon [cf Acts 2:41]. Joseph of Arimathea and Nicodemus also gain courage now and openly confess their belief in him [Jn 19:38 f]. All these are the first fruits of the death on the cross, and they are followed in the course of the centuries by countless others, through the graces which our Lord won on the cross, and through his example. 'Peace to those who love him and salvation to those who turn in sorrow from their sins'[36] is what Jesus' heart became for those and everyone else, when it was opened by the soldier's lance. And in this Heart I lay all my retreat resolutions with confidence.

VIII/2 *Easter Day* For our Lord this is the beginning of his great work, the 'kingdom'; on this day he is the 'victorious king'[37] and will remain so until he has laid the kingdom at his Father's feet.[38] On Easter Day he takes care to give unassailable proof of his resurrection. The apostles are as sceptical as they can be; it is only when he convinces them 'palpably' as it were, that they accept it. They are not convinced by the appearances to the holy women: these are related only to show us how everything happened. But he uses this day too to give the Church instructions on the interpretation of scripture, 'he interpreted to them in all the scriptures the things concerning himself' [cf Lk 24:27]. And then in the evening he gives them the great Easter gift of the sacrament of penance [cf Jn 20:21 f]: 'who can forgive sins but God only?'[39] But the Father has sent him and 'I send you'. This is the great fruit of the redemptive passion, in which we all share, and I have a share in its application. When he appeared to Mary he must have given her to the Church as mother and patroness. 'Queen of heaven rejoice.'

VIII/3 *The last appearances and the Ascension* Now our Lord gives his Church its essential shape. He gives Peter full power over the whole flock [cf Jn 21:15 ff]. There is only one flock and it is this that Peter feeds: unity and primacy. But the flock is not Peter's property; he is to feed it in Christ's place, out of love for Christ and for the flock entrusted to him by our Lord. On the mountain he gives to the apostles (and only to them) the power of teaching, sanctifying and governing, and his all-embracing fullness of power. And to the end of time [cf Mt 28:16–20]: hence the hierarchy in apostolic succession,

---

[35] In Lk 23:48 we read: 'And all the multitude who assembled to see the sight, when they saw what had taken place, returned home beating their breasts.'
[36] From the Sacred Heart Preface, ICEL translation.
[37] From the Sequence of the Easter Mass.
[38] St Paul says, in his description of the final consummation of God's kingdom (with reference to Ps 110:1): 'For Christ must reign until he [God] has put all his enemies under his feet' (1 Cor 15:25).
[39] The Pharisees and scribes think this to themselves when Christ says to the palsied man: 'Man, your sins are forgiven you' (Lk 5:20; cf Mk 2:7): they consider the words blasphemous.

and again over the whole world: the catholicity of the Church. And finally he promises them 'the power from on high', 'promised by the Father', the Holy Spirit, so that they may be his witnesses to the ends of the earth [cf Apoc 1:4-8]. And 'lifting up his hands, he blessed them' and left them in order to be with them from heaven [cf Jn 14:18 ff].

VIII/4 *Love* The main thing for me is that I should live much more than before in a 'supernatural atmosphere', and should see in everything that happens to me, pleasant or unpleasant, in nature and in grace, in the world and in the Church, the hand of God, a reminder of God. I do not need to give up any of my work or activities; on the contrary I should really intensify them; but all the time I must be aware that I am cooperating with God, with the powers that he has given me and for the ends that he has decided for me. I must become more and more conscious of his presence in everything: and let creatures lead me to God. And whatever I see in the world and among men that is noble, beautiful and meaningful, I must tell myself that he is nobler, much more beautiful, much more powerful, in fact he is greatness, beauty, power and wisdom itself, and the source of all that is great in the world. I must keep on saying with St Augustine: 'If these are so great, how great God must be!' In a word: 'In all things let me seek God, see God and love God!'[40] That is the best way I can thank him for 'all his bounty to me' [Ps 115:12], and the best way I can practise the recollection and union with God that I have resolved on. Give me your love and grace: these are enough for me [cf Exercises 234].

1.VII.62

Neuhausen, 23 August 1961

FROM THE MONTHLY RECOLLECTIONS

8.X.1961
1) Earnest pursuit of sanctity.
2) Must not interrupt [?] my spiritual exercises; patience: not irritable; caution in what I say.
3) Careful and practical examination of conscience.
4) Kind, considerate, sympathetic to all.
5) Two visits to the Blessed Sacrament.

I/1 Guidance and direction!—special zeal, because of special grace; must not be self-seeking.

I/2 Complete devotion to God's will: deeds!

3.XII.1961
Every day carry out God's will with complete devotion. Avoid distractions or superficiality in spiritual exercises. Unkind criticism; judge

---
[40] For the source and explanation of this text cf 1959/VIII/4, p. 42, note 48.

natural principles too[41]—Examination of conscience. Understanding towards all, trust and kindness. 'Set on the lampstand.'

II/1 Recollection and union with God.
II/2 'The kingdom of God is at hand': eighty-one years old!
Love that makes sacrifices!—trusting, believing and loving devotion to God.
II/3 Efforts to avoid venial sin.
II/4 Last will and testament.

7.I.1962
Strive after perfection and sanctity, in accordance with my position. Full examination of conscience, according to the five points. Visits to the Blessed Sacrament: 10.30 and 17.30. Like a father, kind but true to principles. Not irritable. Work with devotion, in a supernatural spirit, in such a way that the Father who is in heaven may be glorified [cf Mt 5:16].

III/2 To keep my soul pure and holy; to distinguish myself: that is what following our Lord means.
III/3 Mary says little but keeps all these things in her heart.—The will of God, so fiat!
III/4 Glory to God and peace to men: only through effort and sacrifice! —unpleasantness—the spirit of sacrifice and love! 'Let me follow thee . . .'

4.III.1962
Spiritual exercises, impatience, lack of reverence, unkind criticism.— Examination of conscience; Visits to the Blessed Sacrament. Supernatural approach to my mission.

IV/1 He chose the cross, Lo. I come.
IV/2 Set out to be unknown—make progress in God's favour.
IV/3 My Father's business: never according to a whim.
IV/4 My mission: with the authority of God and in the fullness of the Spirit.
V/1 Vocation: a merited grace.
V/2 A light set on a lampstand in order to shine.
V/3 Do what I have to do: leave all the rest to the others.
V/4 Must not work, relying on dignity and position, but work indefatigably.

1.IV.1962
1) A zeal corresponding to the greater graces. Distractions and superficiality—spiritual duties.—Examination of conscience. Recollection

---

[41] At this point, the shorthand experts disagreed. The alternative reading is: 'judge calmly according to ecclesiastical principles'. It is probably a reference to what he has written in I/3: 'I can make use of everything that comes my way, every day, from morning to evening . . . but I must be in control . . . not live through it all without a thought. So there must be reflection . . .'

in teaching [?]—work in a spirit of devotion and in a supernatural frame of mind.

VI/1 Friendliness, kindness, love of order, humility.

VI/2 The hours like those on Tabor are soon over; but I must be united with God even in my work. According to the picture of the transfigured Lord in everyday life.[42]

VI/3 Must not allow myself to be prevented from doing good by negative considerations.[43]

VI/4 'Unity': my vocation to work for it.

3.VI.1962

Sanctity corresponding to my status as a cardinal and a bishop. Unkind criticism—recollection and union with God all day long. Supernatural understanding of my mission. No irritability. Precise examination of conscience. Two visits to the Blessed Sacrament.

VII/1 Pray: not what I will. Prayer: not mechanical but from the heart.

VII/2 Spirit of strength.

1.VII.1962

Full and loving devotion to the will of God at this particular moment. Strive after perfection and sanctity. 'Venial sins. . . .' [cf 1961/II/3]. Recollection and union with God. Judge according to supernatural principles. Like a father, kind, sympathetic, considerate towards all. Not seeking publicity, but not avoiding it either. 'Set on a lampstand.'

VIII/1 A haven for the pious and a saving refuge for the repentant.

VIII/2 Resurrection: beginning of the 'kingdom', in which I must cooperate and also suffer. 'If he follows me in suffering he will assuredly follow me in glory' [Exercises 95].

VIII/3 If you love me, feed my sheep—'I am with you'—'power from on high'–'he blesses them.'

VIII/4 Work with God, for God, through God. 'If these are so great—how great must he be!' Augustine.

---

[42] Cf the corresponding meditation: 'The picture of the transfigured Christ must go with me too into everyday life' (VI/2).

[43] I.e. by the anticipation of difficulties, just as our Lord did not allow such anticipation to prevent him from instituting the Eucharist (cf VI/3).

CHAPTER 6

In sight of the Council
1962

We have now reached the year before the opening of the Council, and the activity of the new cardinal, engaged in direct preparation for it and in lecturing, becomes almost hectic. A few days after his 1961 retreat, he presided over another plenary session of the Secretariat for the Promotion of Christian Unity in Bühl/Baden (26–31 August). On 2 September in St Odile near Strasbourg, he addressed the Congress of French Seminarists, on the subject of 'The Priest as the Servant of Unity'. This was followed by two courses of lectures in Switzerland, arising out of the one given in Lugano six months before, both devoted to the theme 'Council and Unity'; on 21 and 23 September in Bern and Basle respectively, on 14 November in the University town of Fribourg and on 17 November in Zürich. Two days before the Zürich lecture, he also spoke on the theme 'Academic Research and Teaching in the Service of Christian Unity' at the University of Fribourg, at the Dies Academicus.

Another full session of the Unity Secretariat (again held in Ariccia and lasting six days from 27 November to 2 December), the various duties connected with the feasts of Christmas and New Year, and the world octave of prayer for unity were again followed by very busy months: on 23 January there was an important lecture in the Palais de la Mutualité in Paris before an audience of about four thousand. This stay in Paris, as always, naturally also involved interviews, visits etc. In February another series of lectures began, always on the burning topic 'Council and Unity', mainly for various universities: on 9 February in the Aula Magna of Heidelberg University, on 11 February at Tübingen University. This lecture series was continued in May: on the 22nd at Munich University, on the 24th at Vienna University and on the 26th at Innsbruck University.

But in between these University lectures there were other tasks and happenings: from 6–10 March another full session at the Unity Secretariat; on 9 April a lecture in the Ruhr town of Essen to an audience of about four thousand: on 11 and 12 April lectures in East and West Berlin; on 30 April a lecture in Padua.

In this period came a quite different but great and important event in the cardinal's life: his consecration as a bishop. Up to that time the cardinal-deacons were not bishops but simply priests. Pope John XXIII decreed that from then on all cardinals should be consecrated. And on Maundy Thursday, 19 April 1962, in a very impressive and solemn ceremony, he personally consecrated the cardinal-deacons (there were twelve at that time) in his cathedral, the Lateran Basilica. So Cardinal Bea received the fullness of the priesthood and became one of the successors of the apostles and a member of the College of Bishops.

Not even the summer holidays were free of strenuous engagements. The main one was the journey to England, where the cardinal attended various meetings and gave various interviews in London, and attended an ecumenical gathering for priests from all the English dioceses in Heythrop College near Oxford. At this meeting he gave two lectures on the position and task of the priest in ecumenical work. One of these lectures was in English: at the age of 81 the cardinal managed to deliver his first lecture, lasting more than three-quarters of an hour, in English.

During his stay in London he paid a visit to Dr Michael Ramsey, the Archbishop of Canterbury and Primate of all England; the archbishop himself described this as an historic moment, since no Roman cardinal had crossed the threshold of Lambeth Palace for four hundred years.

In this account of the cardinal's work in these months, we have had to leave many things out—for example the ordinary sessions of the Roman congregations and especially the sessions of the Central Preparatory Commission of the Council. On 7 November 1961 this Commission began its consideration of more than seventy drafts prepared by the various Preparatory Commissions, a task that was not completed until June 1962. And during this last session of the Central Preparatory Commission (June 1962) political pressure caused the removal of the draft relating to the Church's relationship to the Jews. This had been prepared on Pope John's instructions by the Unity Secretariat. Cardinal Bea could do nothing but accept this decision with patience.

Apart from the work of the Central Preparatory Commission there was another very important task in the Unity Secretariat, the preparation of the invitations to the non-Catholic Churches, ecclesial communities or other Church groups to send observer-delegates. Since the pope had solemnly summoned the Council at Christmas 1961 and had announced on 2 February that it should open on 11 October, there was really not much time left and it was necessary to press on with the necessary negotiations patiently and circumspectly but also with the greatest energy, to decide who wished to be invited and how the invitations were to be made.

In spite of all this hectic work, the cardinal retired in August to the noviciate of his Province to make his retreat, as he had done in previous years. This retreat gave him the opportunity to review the intensive work of the previous months, but in particular it was made in the shadow of the opening and development of the Council, which produced not a few unknown quantities and problems.[1]

RETREAT 1962

Neuhausen, 12–19 August

Preparation: *Grace*—Faith; *Mercy*—Confidence; Peace: Generosity.

I/1 *Man has been created* [Exercises 23] 'Created.' This means that nothing that I have (apart from sin) is from me: everything that I have comes from God. My bodily life with its physical and spiritual powers. The measure according to which he has given them to me depends entirely on his will. And the fact that he has preserved them in me to this day is again a gift from him. Then the opportunities for development: how could I have had them if I had been left to myself—to this extent and with this perfection. It was he who guided and directed everything right up to the present. In this he must have had and must still have his plans, which can clearly only be that I should use all this for his honour; in practice this means in the service of the Church and souls. For this reason and only for this reason he has put me in the place that I have occupied for fifty years.—I could add all that I have received as a child of God, as a priest, religious and Jesuit. What return shall I make? (Ps 115:12.) Gratitude certainly, but not so much in words as in deeds— by the correct and most perfect possible use of all that he has given me. 'It is your gift to me, I now return it to you. It is all yours, to be used simply as you wish' [Exercises 234]. Amen.

I/2 *To praise, reverence and serve him* [Exercises 23] This is my job far more than it is for most other people. I have had thousands of greater opportunities to recognize God's greatness and continue to have them: in meditation, reading, study, in the history of mankind and above all of the saints, in his wonderful providence and guidance. So in the first place I must make specially good and faithful use of these opportunities. I can never learn enough and I must derive more and more benefit for my work from what I have learnt.—But then I have also greater opportunities for advancing the honour of God, more than thousands of others. In my lectures, sermons and speeches people see a special authority, which they attribute to me because of my experience, studies and knowledge. This greater authority, however, means a greater responsibility for me, and I must always try to live up to this in my position.

---

[1] A page in his retreat notebook gives his 'order for the day': 4.30 rise: 5.00 Lauds and Prime: 5.25–6.25 meditation: 6.25–6.55 Mass: 6.55–7.10 thanksgiving. None and rosary after breakfast: the times for the other meditations are not given: 12.45 examination of conscience. Vespers, Compline, Matins: after the siesta; 17.30–18.40 reception of his priest-secretary: 21–21, 30 points of meditation and examination of conscience.

If this is true in general, it is particularly so now in the year of the Council, when countless eyes are fixed on me expecting me to do something that will increase the knowledge and honour of God and the Church's influence on souls and therefore on the world. This task of advancing the greater glory of God and the salvation of souls is more important for me this year than any other year of my long life. Fiat, fiat! 25.VIII.62

I/3 *Thereby saving his soul* [Exercises 23] The meaning of this is a mystery, which even revelation can only explain to us in pictures and similes. It means a share in the life of the blessed Trinity, and thus infinite happiness and eternal blessedness. This shows me that it is worth the trouble to do everything and to suffer and work in every way for it. Everything else is worthless in comparison with this. The saints knew this and especially the martyrs, but also the great apostles, who worked and sacrificed their whole life long to give the chance of achieving this great immeasurable happiness to as many as possible. Thus my own mission now becomes clear too; to save my own soul and the souls of as many as possible. This is the meaning of all my work and labour, of all my sacrifices and suffering. This was also the meaning of the lives of the saints. Is this task worth the sacrifice? To ask the question is to answer 'Yes'. 'The sufferings of this present time are not worth comparing with the glory that is to be revealed us' [Rom 8:18], and, I may add, to many others.—This gives me a new incentive and new energy to say with the apostle: 'I will most gladly spend and be spent for your souls' [2 Cor 12:15] and at the same time for my own.

I/4 *Creatures—indifference* [Exercises 23] Of special importance for my present life.

1) *To see God's hand in everything*. In my life, from my childhood onwards, I have the clearest proofs of this, of how he guides and directs everything, often enough against the will and intentions of man.

2) *In all things let me seek God* and nothing else. In my present life I must put up with so much that is 'pleasant': receptions, visits, banquets, special attention, honours and so on. In all these I must seek God and not myself.—But even in all things that are burdensome and unpleasant, whatever they may be, I must see nothing but God's wise dispositions and providence, and bear everything in this spirit with patience and love.

3) As for my dealings with people: 'I shall love God in all his works and all his works in him'[2]

II/1 *The triple sin* [Exercises 45–54] God created 'everything good'; evil comes from creatures, either by the refusal of the mind or the weakness of the will, especially under the influence of the things that attract

---

[2] Cf 1959/VIII/4, chap. 3, note 48.

our senses. So the sin is all the greater when the intellect is more mature in religious matters and the will has been more strengthened by 'asceticism', self-control and mortification. This is why the sins of a priest or a religious are greater and more serious than those of ordinary Christians. Apart from this the grace of the priestly state and of the religious state is for them a stronger protection and a greater help than other people usually have. And yet I notice that often priests and religious do fail. This must make me very humble, very distrustful of myself and very grateful. It is a grace of God that I have not been devoured.[3]

23.IX.62

II/2 *My own sins* I can forget my earlier sins and failings: they rest in the bosom of God's mercy. What is important is that I should put my present life in order and do it in accordance with the 16th rule:[4] 'Integrity and virtue, and above all charity, a pure intention of serving God, familiarity with him in the performance of spiritual duties.' Much of this does not strike me as difficult. But what is lacking is precisely this familiarity with God. All my work is outwardly exact: but it should be filled with the spirit of recollection, with constant reference to God and frequent union with him. So I must take care to make this spirit part of my life, especially through meditation. In all my work this is almost the only source left for this spirit of recollection and union with God, and I will see to it that I do make my meditations wholly and completely. So I must order and arrange my time. (See the plan!)

And I must examine myself on this point in my examination of conscience and give an account to myself in the monthly recollection (first Sunday of the month).

That is the outward framework; it is important because it gives me the means of increasing this interior spirit.

II/3 *Laziness* It does not have to affect everything at the same time; things are bad enough if it affects one area. Then there is a danger that it will spread and gradually the spiritual man will become a worldly man, as history so often shows. And precisely in the position I occupy at the moment there is no place for worldliness. So it is absolutely necessary that my spiritual life should be sound, if only because I must draw strength from it for everything else. I have already considered meditation, but the examination of conscience is also important: firstly that I should make it: then that I should make it in such a way that it does me some good: shedding light on the past and present: hence investigation: grace: hence prayer. So once again make the examination methodically

---

[3] This sentence is a free version of Lamentations, according to the Vulgate text: 'misericordiae Domini quia non sumus consumpti . . .' (Jer 3:22), which the author often uses in these notes.

[4] The reference is to Rule 16 in the Summary, i.e. a short summary of the rules of the Society of Jesus. But the text quoted is not in fact to be found there, but in the Constitutions of the Society (X, 2).

(5 points!)⁵ Then union with God: recollection and a spirit of faith in all that I do. I have much to do; but I must not allow myself to be too wrapped up in material concerns; on the contrary I must make them spiritual, divinize them so to speak. 28.X.62

II/4 *Death* The thought of my death, which can really not be far off now, does not disturb me any longer. 'My desire is to depart and to be with Christ'—'Let us go to the house of the Lord' [cf Phil 1:20–24; Ps 122:2]. I must be prepared for death by having a clear conscience and concentrating on the fulfilment of the task that God has given me: the dying prayer of our Lord: 'Father . . . glorify thy Son. . . . I have manifested thy name to the men whom thou gavest me . . . having accomplished the work which thou gavest me to do' [cf Jn 17:1, 4, 6]. I must, then, look towards death with great confidence, indifferent as to when, how and where it comes. But I must daily 1) ask myself in the examination of conscience whether I am prepared; 2) pray in the examination of conscience and after Mass that I may be prepared.⁶—In the meantime, however, I do my work and do it as if I had to do it for a long time yet and so perfectly and exactly that there is no difficulty in someone else continuing it. God does not need me especially; but as long as he uses me I shall do my part until I can no longer do it. Work while there is light [cf Jn 12:35; 9:4].

The thought of death should also make me kind, not to win men's affection for myself but to distribute all the gifts that God has placed in my hands.—My will.⁷

III/1 *Judgment* 'Severe judgment falls on those in high places' (Wis 6:6).—I must apply these words to myself as well. For almost the whole of my life as a religious and a priest I have been in a position of responsibility and today more than ever. Hence 'severe judgment'— certainly much more severe than for an ordinary man, who simply carries out his domestic duties. When I am dead a great deal will be said and written about me. This is of no importance, but what is of

---

⁵ The Exercises give instructions about the general examination of conscience. '1) Give thanks to our Lord God for favours received. 2) Ask for grace to know and to root out your sins. 3) Demand of your conscience an hourly or periodic account, beginning with the moment of getting up until this examination, first as to thoughts, then words and then actions, in the way described in the Particular Examination. 4) Ask pardon of our Lord God for these faults. 5) Resolve, with the grace of God, to do better. An *Our Father*' (43).

⁶ Some years earlier the author had composed a prayer for this purpose which he used to say at the end of his thanksgiving after Mass. The yellowed piece of paper was found in his personal prayer-book after his death. It reads: 'Preparation for death. Lord, my God, even now I accept death from thy hands and willingly, however it may come to me according to thy will, together with all its fears, pains and sufferings' [cf Exercises 187]; then he adds: 'To advance daily in virtue until death!'

⁷ So long as the author was a simple religious the question of making a will did not arise. Now that he was a cardinal, he must do so, and the thought kept recurring to him during the retreat.

importance is the judgment the divine judge passes on me. How shall then my life appear? Who the saint my prayer to hear, when the just himself shall fear?[8] This retreat must definitely help me, in spite of all exterior activity and success, to do everything in a truly supernatural spirit, a spirit of recollection and union with God, in a spirit of deep faith. Then my judgment, on which all depends, will be such that I can face my heavenly judge. But only then! Mere outward activity and external success, even in religious matters, is not the decisive thing for 'those in high places'.

III/2 *The kingdom of Christ* [Exercises 91–98] It is not now a matter of 'making my choice'. For more than sixty years I have been following the heavenly King and I have bound myself to him more closely and he has drawn me more fully into his service. What I have to do now is to make myself ever more fit and ready to follow him and work for him, even to follow him 'in suffering' [Exercises 95]. Even if it costs something: even if I have to take a lower place, to humble myself, to make real sacrifices. He has given me the capability and the task: what matters is that I should do everything on my part to ensure that my work for him and his kingdom has the greatest possible success. 'To bring under my control the whole world and all my enemies'[9] becomes for me an absolutely concrete mission, which I can only accomplish properly if I really 'show greater enthusiasm' [Exercises 97] for Christ the King and work for him with this greater enthusiasm. But this is only present and effective if I am very closely bound to him by a real interior life, by constant union with him, by a spirit of recollection and of faith. This must be the great fruit of this retreat. 2.XII.62

III/3 *The annunciation and incarnation* [Lk 1:26–38] Here I see how God works through his instruments. His work is the greatest that he has ever done in the world, a real 'opus Dei'; and yet those who cooperate are, humanly speaking, so unimportant: 1) the angel, one of the many standing before God's throne. He has to announce the fulfilment of what brought Satan and his followers to their revolt—the incarnation of the World[10]—and this to a creature who is far below him—but he has been 'sent' by his master and that is enough; his personal thoughts do not count. I too am 'sent' by God in my position and my job and I must not be anything else but that. My own wishes do not count. 2) Mary, a poor unknown girl, humanly speaking quite 'unsuitable' for the task, but prepared by God. She hears things that are really tremendous. But she does not pay attention to that, but only to the

---

[8] From the liturgical hymn 'Dies Irae', used in Masses for the Dead.

[9] A phrase from the Exercises which links various biblical ideas: e.g. Ps 110:1 f; 1 Cor 15:25–28.

[10] St Thomas Aquinas and others held that the sin of the angels consisted in their rejection of the Incarnation of the Second Person of the Blessed Trinity, and their refusal to worship the Son of God made man.

question whether this is the will of God and does not contradict another will of God—that she should remain a virgin. When she is sure of that she has only one word to say, 'fiat'; for she is nothing but a 'handmaid of the Lord'. This is the great model for my cooperation in God's work. 'I am thy servant, the son of thy handmaid' [Ps 116:16].

III/4 *The Visitation* [Lk 1:39-56] Mary has not received any instructions: it is her motherly heart that has brought her to Elizabeth's house. With her she brings a blessing for mother and child but also receives in return, under the inspiration of the Holy Spirit,[11] the first confirmation of her dignity as the mother of God: 'the Mother of my Lord'. And what is her answer? She admits it: 'he has done great things for me . . . all generations shall call me blessed' (as you, Elizabeth, have done). But she realizes and admits too that all this is not her doing but the result of the omnipotence, the holiness and the mercy of God. This power, holiness and mercy God has now placed in her hands, and the whole history of the Church, of the saints, of those in need of help and of sinners is a proof of this. I too can say: he 'has done great things for me'. Whatever I do, whatever success I have, whatever people do in my honour, it is not to be attributed to me but to him who 'has done great things for me'.

6.I.63

IV/1 *The nativity* I must not forget that the unpleasant circumstances (poverty, contempt, travelling at a most unsuitable time) [Lk 2:1-7] have all been willed and arranged by our Lord, so that he might be 'born in utter destitution' [Exercises 116] and so that a start should be made with his sorrowful life on earth.—And we, even in our apostolic work, are always looking for easier conditions, we avoid unpleasantness and seek comfort. And as long as these things help and further the apostolate and our work, this is good; but never should mere comfort or love decide the issue. 'Tantum-quantum'—'as far as they help his purpose'! [Exercises 23]. 'Glory to God and on earth peace' (Lk 2:14): fundamentally and initially this has already been achieved in the incarnation and birth of our Lord: but effectively, in its application and exercise, it must be achieved in each individual case through our apostolic work. There is no other way to achieve it except the way our Lord went about it from the beginning: 'in utter destitution. After all his labours, after suffering from hunger and thirst, heat and cold, being treated with injustice and insulted, he is to die on the cross' [Exercises 116]. This is the apostolic programme that our Lord had in Bethlehem; it must be mine too.

IV/2 *The presentation in the temple* [Lk 2:22-40] Our Lord and our Lady are both anxious 'that justice should be fulfilled'.[12] They do not

---

[11] Elizabeth spoke after she 'was filled with the Holy Spirit' (Lk 1:41).

[12] Cf Christ's words to the Baptist at his baptism: 'Let it be so now; for thus it is fitting for us to fulfil all righteousness' (Mt 3:15).

waste time asking themselves whether they are really obliged to do this. So I too must be exact in everything that is prescribed, whether rubrics, or protocol or convention—and in a spirit of faith. In anticipation of Gethsemane and Golgotha our Lord repeats in the temple what he said 'when he came into the world . . . sacrifices and offerings . . .' [cf Heb 10:5 ff]. *To fulfil thy will* is the golden rule of my life, whatever form this will of God may take. What it means for our Lord and Mary is expressed by Simeon, inspired by the Holy Ghost: 'for the fall and rising of many in Israel—for a sign that is spoken against (and a sword will pierce through your own soul also)'. In this way the fate of Jesus and Mary is described—my fate too, in so far as God allows me to share in it.

IV/3 *The hidden life of Jesus* However busy my life seems now, still the greater part of it is a 'hidden life' in my own home. And I must love this quiet life more than anything. My model is our Lord who spent two-thirds of his life in quiet Nazareth.
1) A life of prayer, in which I receive exactly what I recognized as so important in II/2, familiarity with God. And to 'preach what I have meditated upon'. So I must have a fixed time-table for my whole prayer life and keep to it as far as possible (cf order of the day). This prayer life must make me 'increase . . . in favour with God'.
2) A life of work, quiet and organized work: work for the preparation of the sessions, for vota, lectures and correspondence. I must keep up with my correspondence (and so, when possible, get others to help me): half an hour every day at a convenient time.
3) A life of neighbourly love: he advanced in favour with men. The model is our Lord: they 'wondered at the gracious words' (Lk 4:22): they 'were amazed at his understanding (insight) and his answers' (Lk 2:47). Love of my neighbour (a) towards all who work with me: show confidence in them, prove my love for them whenever I can, be patient with them—making allowances for the character of each individual—and make sure that it is a joy to work with me. Pay tribute to the work they do: (b) towards all visitors: always friendly, even towards tiresome visitors: listen to them patiently and give them a clear answer, even when I cannot say yes. And take leave of everyone with a kind word: (c) towards my colleagues: show myself a colleague, not stressing the 'Prince of the Church': help them where I can. This is my apostolate of the 'hidden life'. 3.XI.64
13.XII.64

IV/4 *The twelve year old Jesus in the temple* [Lk 2: 41–50] The quiet work at home is interrupted by activity in public, but this must still be 'in the temple': divine service and work for souls: liturgy and pastoral work. Even recreation must come under the heading of the apostolate. And of course as a Jesuit I must always aim at the greater glory of God, this means trying to do the best by study and preparation.

'They found him in the temple, sitting amongst the teachers, listening to them and asking them questions.' This is true for me at all times but will be especially so at the Council. I must listen even to those, and especially to those, who have different ideas. Our Lord sat amongst 'the scribes and pharisees', and we know their views from later discussions. But he listened to them quietly and objectively, and where something was not clear he asked a question. Later he expressed his opinion and gave his teaching, but only what he had 'heard from the Father' [cf Jn 8:26; 15:15 etc], what the Father had given him. I too may give my view, in fact I must: the Church expects it of me because of my position, my previous experience and work. But it must always be what the Father teaches me, not my own wilfulness or any tendency to assert myself. I must be 'about my Father's business'.

V/1 *The baptism* [Mt 3:13-17] Our Lord does not want to begin his public life with 'a big bang', but with an act of the greatest humility and self-abasement, and when John wants to refuse he says quite simply: 'Let it be so now; for thus it is fitting for us to fulfil all righteousness' (Mt 3:15). But the Father rewards him for it: 'He saw the Spirit of God descending . . . and alighting on him'—and the Father's voice saying 'This is my beloved Son, with whom I am well pleased.' Thus his activity is, so to speak, authorized, and he is introduced by the Father himself. In my case too every work must begin with humility. 'I do not seek myself but my Father's business.'[13] And it must be accompanied by sacrifice, which includes misunderstandings, misrepresentations, failure, false judgments etc. Humility and sacrifice must accompany my work.

V/2 *The temptations* [Mt 4:1-11 and parallels] This meditation is important for me and for my work in the present world situation. For me: in my high position too, I must be lonely, must not mix with the 'world', must not seek things of this world, but must give an example of simplicity and modesty. This means too that I must avoid all pomp: I will let people give the liturgical honours that belong to my position and keep to protocol in my dealings with people, but no more. No mere formality! For my work: particularly at the Council it will have to be a matter of opposing the materialism of the age, of reminding the faithful of the need for a spiritual and supernatural life, and warning them against the manifold temptations to attachment to the goods and honours of this world. 'It is written': make sure that the teaching of the Gospel is preached clearly and understandably and that all pastoral work has a practical but supernatural direction. The Spirit

---

[13] A linking of Christ's words from the previous meditation 'I must be about my Father's business' (Lk 2:49) with similar texts from John: 'I can do nothing on my own authority . . . because I seek not my own will but the will of him who sent me' (Jn 5:30): 'Yet I do not seek my own glory; there is One who seeks it and he will be the judge' (Jn 8:50).

of Christ against the spirit of the prince of this world: if ever the struggle was necessary, then it is today—under the leadership of Christ.

V/3 *The call of the apostles* It is an extraordinary and unique thing that tewelve men without education or power should receive the mission: 'Go, therefore, and make disciples of all nations . . .' [Mt 28:19], that they should set about carrying it out without hesitation and without fear, and that they should in fact carry it out. It is clear that the decisive thing is certainly not human ability; but there is still a human element in all this, which drives and urges these men, and this is love for the Master: the love of Christ controls us. This love is so great that it makes them completely one with the Master; his inclinations, his plans and wishes become theirs, and these alone are decisive. Nothing else can explain this extraordinary phenomenon.—But for me this means that I must cultivate in myself an ever-increasing love for our Lord. I can now look back on fifty years as a priest. These prove that he loved me. He has become for me all that he became for his apostles. But I have not yet achieved that, I might almost call it, 'blind' love for our Lord, which places itself unreservedly and exclusively in his service and seeks and desires nothing else than to be his instrument, an instrument in the sense of Rule 16.[14] In my meditation and reading I must aim at this frame of mind and strengthen it more and more. O God I love thee—thou knowest all things, thou knowest that I love thee (cf Jn 21:17).   3.III.63

V/4 *The Sermon on the Mount* The demands of the eight Beatitudes [Mt 5:1–12] apply to me now more than ever. They must be my programme as a cardinal, and not just in a general sort of way, for I must be an exemplary cardinal, like Charles Borromeo, Bellarmine and Barbarigo (so their lives too as spiritual reading!). A further obligation is laid on me by the fact that in forty-seven of my fifty years as a priest,[15] I have been specially prepared by God in the Society, far more than can usually be the case with those who reach this position as part of their 'career'. This divine generosity in pouring graces upon me means a very special obligation for me. A light of the world [Mt 5–14]: I must not be blind to the fact that in a short time I have achieved

---

[14] The idea of the apostle as an 'instrument' in the hands of God (or of Christ) is not mentioned explicitly in Rule 16 of the Summary, but is to be found in Constitutions (X, 2). It might be useful to recall here what Vatican II has to say of the authors of scripture as the 'instruments' of the Holy Spirit: 'In composing the sacred books, God chose men and while employed by him they made use of their powers and abilities, so that with him acting in them and through them, they, as true authors, consigned to writing everything and only those things which he wanted' (Divine Revelation, 11). Obviously the priest in his apostolic activity is not used by God in exactly the same way as the authors of the books of scripture. But they have one thing in common—when he is used by Christ the priest retains full and free use of his capabilities and powers.

[15] The years spent in the Society of Jesus before he became cardinal.

a world-wide reputation, but it makes it more essential than ever that I should be 'a light of the world' by my words and example. Set on a lampstand!

VI/1 *The apostles are sent to preach* [cf Mt 10:5–23] 'I send you'. My mission also comes from him and only from him, through his representative here on earth. So I must carry it out according to his will and only according to his will. He gave the apostles the power but also the mandate: 'heal . . .',[16] and he also gives me the mandate to practise the works of spiritual mercy: love, friendliness, kindness and help in the needs and concerns of souls. And with it he gives me the power too. Preach the Kingdom of God: my preaching and my message must be of an altogether supernatural nature and not be concerned with earthly things.—In all my appearances in public there must be modesty and restraint, but in such a way that I can say in every house: Peace be on this house [Mt 10:12], supernatural peace. And where this greeting of peace is not accepted and answered, I must withdraw: leaving the house. Everything else I can safely leave to the Master who sent me.

14.IV.63

VI/2 *The multiplication of loaves* [Mk 6:30–56 and parallels] In the first place I see here our Lord's kindness to his apostles: he sent them out but he wants to give them the chance to rest as well, in a deserted place, apart. Of course the crowd never lets them get that far and our Lord in his kindness cannot bring himself to turn the poor people away. But he takes the main burden on himself: 'he had compassion on them and healed their sick' [Mt 14:14], and 'he began to teach them many things' [Mk 6:34]. There is often this clash between duty and kindness in my life too. In any case I must have the same care for the people who work with me as our Lord had for his apostles. In this mystery the apostles are a model for me as priest and bishop. For it is here that they emerge as Christ's instruments of goodness and power. Not 'domineering over those in your charge', but stewards of the mysteries of God:[17] of doctrine, of divine order and of divine graces. Everything passes through their hands. Our Lord blesses but they give it out and in their hands the miracle takes place. This is especially true of the eucharistic bread. So my motto must be: a minister of Christ and a steward of his mysteries, nothing else, not even as a cardinal!

VI/3 *The transfiguration* [Mt 17:1–19] Before the transfiguration comes the teaching about the cross. First our Lord announces the cross about himself, and when Peter takes him to task he applies it to all

---

[16] Cf Mt 10:8: 'heal the sick'.
[17] Cf Peter, in his old age, addressing the elders: '. . . not as domineering over those in your charge, but being examples to the flock' (1 Pet 5:3); and Paul's definition of the apostle: 'This is how one should regard us, as servants of Christ and stewards of the mysteries of God' (1 Cor 4:1).

[Mt 16:21 f]: let him take up his cross and follow me. The closer anyone is to our Lord, the more this talk about the cross refers to him—and so to me also, and particularly to me in my special task, which is bound to involve a great deal of effort, of failure and misrepresentation. In these situations I must draw courage and strength from the 'transfiguration', from the transfiguration that comes to me through prayer, 'as he was praying' [Lk 9:28]. This 'transfiguration' does not need to be a mystical phenomenon, but it is a state of soul that means peace, love and daily readiness, and so an atmosphere of supernatural approach to my whole life and work. If this state of mind is present, sacrifices are no longer sacrifices but acts of love, love of God and love of neighbour. Now once again I see how important the interior life is for me and the means to it, my spiritual duties, and all the more important now that my work is more significant and my position higher—Peter, James and John!

VI/4 *Palm Sunday* [Mt 21:1–17] This is a triumphant procession for our Lord and he, 'gentle and lowly in heart' [Mt 11:29], accepts it because this is his Father's will as he expressed it long ago through the prophet. Often enough I am in a similar position, having to put up with festive processions and celebrations. I do it because I see God's will in it and can hope that some good will come out of it. But for our Lord it is not only a triumph, it is also an occasion of sadness. He sees better than I ever can what is really genuine in this procession and how many join it just because it is a feast. He sees too that this procession will only irritate his opponents more and make them more implacable. But his only response is sympathy: he has tears in his eyes, but he does not forget to cure the blind and the lame in the temple, and he comes to the defence of the children who are shouting out 'Hosanna' in the temple, with the words of Psalm 8. He is inwardly detached from all outward pomp and all outward opposition. Here is a great model for me: in all the outward things I have to put up with, I must stay inwardly free and only think of carrying out, to the best of my ability, the task God has given me.

VII/1 *The last supper* [cf Lk 22:7 ff; Jn 13; and parallels] Our Lord is wonderfully calm as he goes in to the last supper and fulfils all that is prescribed and he seems to overlook the rather mean argument of the apostles over who should have the first places. He tries once again to influence the heart of the traitor, washes the feet of the disciples like a slave and then institutes the sacrament of life 'in remembrance of me' as his legacy to those for whose sake he is now going to his death. Only the God-Man could enjoy such a state of heavenly tranquillity. But I must make an effort even in this to be like him in all the situations of my life. Jesus, meek and humble of heart, make my heart like thine. Nor must I forget that I can achieve more through humility than through indignation and arrogance.—And finally the Blessed Sacrament must give me special power and strength to be more and more like him.

VII/2 *The holy Eucharist* The 50th anniversary of my ordination should be the occasion of renewing and deepening my devotion to the holy Eucharist. The day of my ordination was the fulfilment of my great wish. But it must live on in every new day the Lord gives me. Above all the Mass should be the centre and the climax of every day: carefully prepared, celebrated with the greatest recollection, devotion and correctness, followed by a good thanksgiving; every day it should give me life, counsel, strength and consolation in the faithful performance of my duties. During the day too by visits, not only the 'official ones', but some voluntary ones, an hour here and there in front of the Blessed Sacrament; and great devotion when I give benediction. Our Lord in the Eucharist should be my great model: of sacrifice, of humility, of patience and love. I must lead a eucharistic life by a fervent love for our Lord in the Eucharist, by a real devotion to the Blessed Sacrament, by great confidence in our eucharistic Lord, a real 'familiarity' with Jesus in the Blessed Sacrament, so that in me the words may be fulfilled: 'I live because of the Father, so he who eats me will live because of me' (Jn 6:57). 5.V.63

VII/3 *The Garden of Olives, the arrest and Annas* Once again I marvel at this extreme, overpowering tranquillity.—Even in the Garden of Olives, when he is deprived of all consolation and help, he prays calmly: 'Father, if . . . not my will but thine' [Lk 22:42]. He meets the officers of the law with deliberate calm: for the last time Judas experiences the extent of his goodness,[18] and Peter is reminded of the supernatural considerations: 'shall I not drink the cup which my Father has given me?' [Jn 18:11]. But above all when he meets Annas, the unmitigated scoundrel, who is responsible for the whole campaign against him [Jn 18:19–24]. No one could be calmer, colder, more objective than our Lord. What is it that gives him this tranquillity that so many martyrs have imitated? The closest union with his Father's will: this is, so to speak, the rock on which everything rests. No human consideration or goals, only: let thy will be done!

VII/4 *Before Caiphas and Pilate* Our Lord has simply become a mere plaything and no one is bothered about his rights. Caiphas and the Sanhedrin have only one thought: 'away with him. Crucify him' [Jn 19:15]. Pilate is not interested in religion, but political considerations demand after all that he should condemn him.—This is the picture of the extension of Christ, the Church, and of its leaders and servants. Not the same at all times: not always and everywhere with the same

---

[18] Cf Mt 26:50: 'Jesus said to him (Judas), "Friend why are you here?" '

means, sometimes with the weapons of the mind and then again sometimes with brute force. 'If they have persecuted the Master, then they will persecute you too' [cf Jn 15:20]. I must always remember that I am in the service of this persecuted Church and so have nothing to expect but what the founder prophesied for it and experienced in his own life. But I must not be afraid like Peter. He trusted in himself too much: even if all the rest do, I shall not [cf Mt 26:33]. And now our Lord makes him realize that he is only strong in him, in his divine Master. And since he never lost his love he finds his way back at once: he 'wept bitterly'. Later he confesses: 'Lord, you know that I love you.' Hence a love that knows no fear!

VIII/1 *The condemnation, way of the cross and crucifixion* The reason for the condemnation is hate in the case of the Jews, and political self-interest in the case of Pilate, but in the case of the heavenly Father the heavy burden of all our sins. I myself must first beat my own breast; for I too played my part in the cry 'he deserves death' (Mt 26:66). Now I must make sure that our Lord's death on the cross is not wasted on me and on all those entrusted to my care. On the other hand I must be crucified with our Lord: with Christ I am fixed to the cross [cf Gal 2:19 f]: I shall crucify my flesh with all its passions and desires [cf Gal 5:24].—Of all who accompanied our Lord on the way and stood by the cross, Mary is the greatest: the queen of martyrs. Here the prophecy is fulfilled: 'a sword will pierce through your own soul also'; but the sorrowful mother stood by the cross of her Son, and so she has become for us all the unrivalled model in carrying the cross, but in every cross and suffering she has also become our powerful mother and mediatrix.

VIII/2 *Our Lord as comforter* First of all he himself, his sacred humanity, is consoled: body and soul bound together in glory, made blessed by the vision of God . . . for which cause God has exalted him . . . [Phil 2:7–11]. So he has become the model for all who share his suffering and cross: if we have died with him we shall be glorified with him [cf 2 Tim 2:10 ff]. But after that he goes on to console those who stood nearest the cross, especially his holy Mother. She is raised to a real heavenly ecstasy, united with her Son with a love that is beyond all human understanding.[19] Now she is not only the mother of Jesus; she is also the spouse of Christ, of his Mystical Body.—The other holy women are also made happy and comforted, and Mary Magdalene too [Mt 16:1–11 and parallels]. And Peter stops crying: he 'has appeared to Simon' [Lk 24:34]. In fact he had long since recovered and had

---

[19] In the Exercises, St Ignatius says in connection with the appearance of Christ to his mother: 'First. He appeared to his virgin mother: it is true that this is not explicitly mentioned in scripture, but it is implied in the passage which says that he appeared to so many others. For scripture presumes that we possess understanding, in the words: "Are you too still lacking in understanding?" ' (299.)

hurried with John to the tomb. And at the Lake of Genesareth he can claim: 'you know that I love you' [Jn 21:15 ff].—And finally the two on the way to Emmaus [Lk 24:13–33], and in the evening all the apostles (except Thomas) in the Upper Room: 'Peace be with you' [Lk 24:36–43; Jn 20:19–23].

VIII/3 *The risen Jesus and the Church* During these forty days the Church takes shape: in Peter it receives its head [Jn 21:15 ff]; its mission is to preach the Gospel in the whole world and this mission is given to the eleven, to the apostles [Mt 28:16–20]. He puts the means of grace in their hands: the interpretation of scripture, baptism, the forgiveness of sins [Jn 20:21 ff], and earlier he had given them the Eucharist; he gives them also the task of seeing that the commandments are observed, and they receive the Holy Spirit, the 'power from on high' [Lk 24:49], and our Lord's assurance that he will stay with them to the end of time [Mt 28:20]. A Church, then, that will stand until the end. And I have the honour of serving this Church in a prominent position!

VIII/4 *As a conclusion to this retreat* I have prayed about my 'decision' before the all-holy one, and have renewed all my resolutions once again. The retreat has been a particularly great grace and the important thing now is for me to cooperate with this grace faithfully. In this the Eucharist must be my main help, as I resolved in VII/2, and as I summed up in my 'decision'. In everything our Lord must be my living model: the goodness and loving kindness of our God has appeared to me [Tit 3:4], on every occasion, especially in meditation and examination of conscience, I will ask how our Lord would have done it and how I should do it. Every morning Mass should remind me again that I too must be a victim, pure, innocent and undefiled,[20] and that every time I say the words of consecration it should also mean a transubstantiation of myself into Christ, into his spirit and his thoughts. So I hope and pray that the grace of this retreat will be a great union with our Lord in the Eucharist, from which I can draw light and strength for my whole life. 2.VI.63
19.VIII.1962

FROM THE MONTHLY RECOLLECTIONS

23.IX.1962
Must be exemplary, set upon a lampstand. Intensive spiritual life.— Recollection. Frequent union with God. Do my work as perfectly as possible. Accept pleasant and unpleasant things in humility and a spirit of sacrifice. Patience with all.

[20] From the first Eucharistic Prayer of the Mass.

I/1 Gratitude through action, most perfect use.[21]
2) Opportunity to further God's honour—greater responsibility! greater glory of God.
3) To save as many souls as possible.
4) Seek God in all things—love all in God and God in all—be exemplary: aim at the highest; spiritual duties.

Feast of Christ the King
Basic frame of mind: familiarity with God: seek God and only him. 'The love of Christ controls me.' More frequent recollection and union with God—Mass with special devotion—tranquillity and patience in my work—objectivity and moderation in my judgments—full of confidence in cooperating with others—set upon a lampstand, that I may give light.
II/2 Not just external activity—recollection, union with God, meditation!
II/3 Not a man of the world, but a spiritual man: no 'worldliness'.

2.XII.1962
II/4 I have manifested thy name ... examination of conscience—God does not need me especially: but as long as he uses me, I must do all that I can.
III/1 'Severe judgment falls on those in high places' (Wis 6:6)—everything in a really supernatural spirit in recollection and union with God, with the Holy Spirit: it is not success that is the decisive thing.
III/2 Make myself ever more fit and ready!

6.I.1963
Be exemplary: seek God and only him—recollection, union with God: work as an instrument of God in tranquillity and love, dignity, simplicity and modesty.
III/3 'Sent': that is all that counts, not my own wishes: 'fiat'—nothing but a servant of God.
III/4 The holiness, mercy, power of God, lie in Mary's arms; he has done great things for me—not I but God.

3.II.1963
Familiarity with God: seek God in all things and only him. Recollection and union with God—Work: look upon myself as an instrument of God, tranquil and objective in everything, do my work as perfectly as possible—set upon a lampstand, that I may give light.

[21] This passage is difficult to decipher. Probably the author is referring to the following words from the meditation he is thinking about: 'Thanks ... by the correct and most perfect possible use of all that he has given me.'

IV/1 That he may be 'born in utter destitution' . . . never must I let mere comfort, self-love or self-seeking be my motives—that he may 'die on the cross': must practise self-discipline . . .

IV/2 All in a spirit of faith: the smallest and the greatest things! Lo I come to do thy will . . . even if it is a sign that is contradicted!

3.III.1963

Intensive spiritual life: meditation, examination of conscience, recollection with God, spiritual reading. Work: tranquillity, readiness, love. Accept failure, misrepresentation, difficulties in a spirit of love and humility and sacrifice; calm, objective, kind in judgment and dealings with people.

IV/4 Everything in an apostolic spirit: try to do the best! Listening, asking questions, giving wise answers; teach what 'I have heard from the Father', not self-willed!

V/1 No pomp and ceremony, but humility and love: 'it is fitting for us to fulfil all righteousness': I must not seek my own ends but 'the things that are my Father's . . .'.

V/2 Simplicity and modesty, without external pomp.

V/3 One with the Master—love for our Lord, which puts itself at his service unreservedly and exclusively.

14.IV.1963

Exemplary in every respect; seek God and only him: everything and everywhere. In all things an instrument of God; do my work as perfectly as possible. Set upon a lampstand.

V/4 The abundance of divine grace means a very special responsibility for me.

5.V.1963

Spiritual life: meditation, examination of conscience; recollection and frequent union with God.—Work in tranquillity, love, readiness—exact preparation in everything; good example in everything.

VI/2 Concern for the people who work with me, a steward of the mysteries of God. Doctrine, graces, help 'through my hands'—accept misrepresentation and distrust patiently.

VI/3 Atmosphere of a supernatural approach to things.

VI/4 Accept recognition in a supernatural spirit: inwardly detached and free for my work.

VII/1 Interior peace in all situations!

VII/2 Place of the Mass in the day's work, eucharistic life: familiarity with Christ in the Eucharist. Holy Mass.

2.VI.1963

1) The love of Christ controls me: and only that love.
2) An instrument of God and a servant of Christ.

3) Never seek my own ends or human praise.
4) Tranquil, objective, loving towards all.
5) Modesty, humility and kindness even when being firm.

VII/3 In all things a deliberate tranquillity: closest union with God's will. No human considerations or goals.

VIII/2 If we die with Christ we shall be glorified with him.

VIII/3 To serve the Church in a prominent position!

VIII/4 How would our Lord do this?

CHAPTER 7

The first session of the Council
The death of Pope John
1963

The weeks after the 1962 retreat, the last before the opening of the Council, were also full of tension, activity and work. The quietness of the retreat was followed immediately by the German Catholic Congress in Hanover. Here on 23 August, the Cardinal described the right ecumenical attitude, using the life of the Danish scholar and convert, Niels Stensen (1638–86) as an example. At the congress itself, and afterwards in his home town, on 25 August, the Cardinal celebrated the golden jubilee of his priesthood.

In connection with the invitation of non-Catholic observer-delegates, the first direct contacts with the Patriarchate of Moscow had been in progress since the end of September, and on 4 October, a week before the Council opened, the cardinal gave a talk at the Institute for the Study of International Politics in Milan on the international aspects of the Council. Besides the strenuous work of the first session of the Council, there was no lack of other duties. On 8 November he gave a press conference in the Council pressroom. He took advantage of the occasion to announce to the press the collection of his lectures and interviews that had just been published under the title *The Unity of Christians*; it was also an opportunity to shed some light on the various questions that had arisen with regard to the presence of non-Catholic observer-delegates at the Council. On 19 November, at the invitation of the Patriarch of Venice, Cardinal Urbani, he spoke in Venice on the importance for Christian unity of the Council.

Naturally his main concern was the Council and to this he devoted most of his energy: in practice that meant the General Congregation, the usual plenary session of the Council, on all working day mornings lasting for three to three and a half hours and then, in the afternoon, there were often meetings of the Unity Secretariat. Apart from this there were the extremely important contacts with the non-Catholic observer-delegates, not to mention the many social engagements.

From this period, only two events, which concerned the secretariat for Unity, need to be mentioned: on 22 October at the plenary session of the Council, it was announced that Pope John had decided that the Secretariat, in spite of its different name and structure, should be equal to the Council commissions in the discussion of the drafts: it was empowered to present to the Council the drafts it had prepared and also to work together with the other Commissions in the Mixed Commission for the revision of the drafts. Cardinal Bea announced, in the Council that two sections were to be set up within the Secretariat: one for Eastern Churches and the other for reformed Churches or ecclesial communities; this was put into effect in January 1963.

During this first session of the Council the cardinal spoke seven times in his own right as a Council Father: firstly in the general discussion on the liturgy; then in the debate on the eucharistic sacrifice and in the debate on the office; he called for the thorough revision of the draft decree 'on the Sources of Revelation' and later also of the draft Constitution on the Church; he intervened in the discussion on the means of social communications; and finally he took part in the discussion on a text on the problem of unity, prepared by the Commission for Oriental Churches.

Soon after the end of the first session of the Council the cardinal had the pleasure of hearing that Pope John XXIII, in a letter of 13 December, had decisively restored to the programme the question of the relationship of the Church with the Jews, which, as we mentioned above, had been removed from the Council programme six months earlier for political reasons.

Even after this very strenuous session his work went on: firstly the work of the Secretariat: there were two plenary sessions each lasting about a week (25 February–2 March and 12–19 May), then his personal work as president: during the octave of world prayer the cardinal was in Denmark where he spoke on 25 January, in one of the most important theatres of the capital, on the theme 'The Second Council and the Non-Catholic Christians'; he accepted the invitation of the Mission Conference of the Christian Student Movement of Denmark to speak at their congress in Roskilde (26 January) on the theme 'The Missions and Ecumenical Aims'.

The main lecture tour of this year was in the United States of America. At the invitation of Harvard University he took part in the Catholic-Protestant Colloquium. On 22 March he addressed the faculty and the students on the opportunities offered by research and teaching activities in work for Christian Unity. On the next two days he gave two lectures to the general public on the theme 'Vatican II and the Non-Catholic Christians: an account of the first session and the prospects'. Following this there was a great 'Agape-Meeting' in New York: a meeting of the representatives of the various confessions and religions in which very prominent people took part, beginning with the President of the General Assembly of the United Nations and its General Secretary. The Cardinal spoke on the theme 'Unity in Freedom and the Sovereignty of God'.

There were two more ecumenical lectures in Baltimore and finally one at the Catholic University in Washington, where an honorary doctorate of theology was conferred on the Cardinal. Altogether on this tour the Cardinal made ten major speeches, all in English; and of course there were many other conversations and contacts.

Just before the conclave for the election of a new pope, he managed to complete the manuscript of a new book, which was published in September 1964 under the title *Unity in Freedom*. Basically this dealt with the theme that the Cardinal had treated in the Agape-Meeting in New York.

The death of Pope John and all its consequences, the conclave and the election of his successor, prevented another series of lectures that had been planned.

The annual retreat was made in the shadow of the great loss the Church had suffered in the death of Pope John and at the threshhold of a new pontificate. But it meant also a review of the experiences of the first Council session and a preparation for the next session, the opening of which Pope Paul, only ten days after his election, had fixed for 29 September.

RETREAT 1963

21–28 July

I/1 *God and I* 'Not that we are sufficient of ourselves to claim anything as coming from us; our sufficiency is from God' [2 Cor 3:5 f]. The older I become, the more my physical weakness shows itself, but the greater and the more world-wide my mission becomes, the more I see that I am not sufficient of myself to claim anything as coming from myself, but that in everything I need help and support. My fellow men and those who work with me can of course be a great help to me, but they too are limited in their powers, and in the last resort they cannot be my support. Only one person can be that: God. He is the almighty, the all-wise, the all-good; he is strength and life, and above all he is infinite love. He is also my help and support in all things. So in return I must do everything for him and only for him. For in his prayer, reverence and service [Exercises 23] lies the whole point of my work. My whole life and work, all that I say and all that I suffer, must be 'praise' for God; day after day and hour after hour. Whatever length of life I have left belongs to him and to him alone. What I get out of my work is of no importance, to God alone the honour and glory [cf 1 Tim 1:17].

I/2 *Christ and the fundamental principle* When I say: 'Man has been created' [Exercises 23], that also indicates, ontologically, my relationship with Christ, the 'Word'; 'all things were made through him'

[Jn 1:3], and so, according to his divine nature, he is the source and the foundation of my whole being. I owe everything to him: hence: everything belongs to him, to the last atom of my body, to the last particle of my soul. So in practice my service of God is service for Christ, for his interests, his Church, his Kingdom. 'You are Christ's; and Christ is God's [cf 1 Cor 3:21 ff]. By his word he teaches me how I should perform this service of God: 'in spirit and in truth' [Jn 4:23 f]—not just materially but with all my mind, my heart, really and truly.—And at the same time he is the infinite model for this service. 'I have come to do thy will [cf Heb 10:7]; for this was I born, to do the will of him who sent me' [cf Jn 6:38]. My spiritual life and all that I do must, then, be centred on Christ: Christ in all!

I/3 *Everything else on earth* [Exercises 23]   In the first place I must remind myself once again that the things of this world are there to raise me to God, both the good things and the bad things. So I must not face them with stoic resignation, on the contrary I must want to learn something from everything for my own interior life and for my apostolate. So must not go through the world thoughtlessly but 'always ready to be taught'. On the other hand I must not use things selfishly to achieve my own ends: to play a part, to 'push through' some views, to make too many demands on myself without regard to my strength, a certain tendency to want to 'please everyone'—all these things are rocks on which my spiritual life and my apostolic mission can, if not founder, at least suffer damage. I must take careful note of these 'more refined' movements and tendencies of the soul and make an effort to overcome them positively. This will not be possible without a great gift 'for distinguishing between different spiritual influences'.[1] If necessary I must allow myself to be restricted even in doing good: so in all enthusiasm I must preserve my freedom and make my decisions in freedom.   3/VII/64

I/4 *Indifference—what is 'more likely'* [Exercises 23]   This meditation tells me that I should do everything with deliberation, not with prejudice and bias, moods, considerations of convenience, selfish aims etc. I must maintain a certain detachment from things and not allow myself to be carried along by them with further ado, as worldly people do in so many cases. Things have their own value and a certain value as far as the end is concerned. Where I have the choice, I shall prefer what is of more value in itself, but I shall always have to have the concrete goal before my eyes, the natural one and the supernatural one, where that comes into the question. And even where it is a question of

---

[1] This idea of the 'discernment of spirits' is one of the characteristic ideas of the Exercises. It is a question of paying careful attention to the various 'movements and tendencies of the soul', as our author puts it. St Ignatius considers the matter so important that he gives the retreat-giver, and through him the retreatant, two sets of rules, entitled: 'Rules for distinguishing between different spiritual influences, so that only good ones may be admitted, evil ones being rejected' (313).

the supernatural goal, what is 'better' is not always identical with what is best in the concrete situation. 'What is more likely' is right, but what is 'more likely' is dependent on the will of God, which must be revealed to me through an inspiration or through the circumstances. So I must maintain a detachment from things and from myself, in order to be able to comply as perfectly as possible with God's will. To recognize the will of God is a grace and grace has to be prayed for.

These thoughts show me that in my actions I must seek God's will concretely, must recognize it joyfully and generously and carry it out faithfully, even more than I have done in the past. So I must not 'live for the moment' but must deliberate and choose. That is what the daily examination of conscience is for and I must really take it seriously and perform it faithfully: to know the will of God and do it generously.

6.X.63

II/1 *The mystery of sin*[2] is present throughout the world and throughout time. Essentially it is based on the freedom of creatures endowed with reason and their quest for 'more and more'. Where these two things are not ordered and connected sin necessarily arises. The danger is all the greater since the sin of our first parents introduced concupiscence into the world.[3] I should not be surprised, then, that sin has reached such proportions among men at all times. In this matter I must leave the judgment of the individual to God, who searches the heart. The conquest of sin is only possible through Christ, who won the grace for us on the cross. Even in my life I am never safe from sin: but I know that I too can overcome it precisely through our Lord and his grace, which is at my disposal in such abundance. 'I can do all things in him who strengthens me' (Phil 4:3).

II/2 *The essence of sin* It is not easy to define this philosophically. It is not just an offence against the prescribed order, as for example one can offend against the rules of a society. Nor is it enough to say: against the order 'prescribed by God'. In that case it would still remain in the material order of things. In reality it is an offence against God himself, my Creator, Lord and Father, to whom as a man, and even more as a Christian, I am most closely bound. How the Lord judges this offence is taught me by revelation, beginning with the first page of Genesis, and throughout the Old Testament, and by our Lord especially in the New Testament, in his teaching and his attitude to sinners, but particularly through his death on the cross on which the immaculate Lamb of God

---

[2] This expression is based on St Paul in 2 Thess 2:3 f, where he speaks of the final battle between good and evil, between Christ and his adversary 'the man of lawlessness . . . the son of perdition, who opposes and exalts himself against every so-called god or object of worship, so that he takes his seat in the temple of God, proclaiming himself to be God'. Paul stresses that the adversary—usually called the 'Anti-Christ'—has not yet appeared, although 'the mystery of lawlessness is already at work' (v. 7).

[3] Cf 1959/I/3, chap 3 note 6, for the idea of 'nature' and its corruption.

[cf 1 Pet 1:9; Eph 5:2 etc] took upon himself the sins of the world. So I should not be surprised that the world, which does not know or recognize Christ, has the wrong idea about sin—or even no idea at all—and particularly if it does not look to the cross for strength to avoid sin. This is the reason for missionary work and Catholic ecumenism.

II/3 *The triple sin* This meditation tells me firstly how every (serious) sin is the same in its essence and consequences, whether it is committed by an angel or our first parents or anyone: it is a rebellion against God,[4] the Creator and Lord, and thus, on the part of the sinner, it means a separation from him. No man, no matter who he is, can undo this separation. God can, but he only does so in view of what Christ the redeemer did. Anyone who rejects Christ, as the sinful angels did, is lost forever. God can give the grace; but he does not have to. If he gives it, he does so in view of the merits won for us by Christ on the cross. Thus it is right in the colloquy I should turn to my crucified saviour who is my only real help. Gratitude, trust, supplication.[5]

II/4 *My own sins* If I look back on my earliest years, I can only thank the Lord for my education and religious formation at home and at school. And yet there were still signs here and there of the effects of sensuality and other inclinations, if not in any serious way. Still I must thank the Lord not only for preserving me from worse but also for making the seeds of a vocation grow within me in spite of everything and in circumstances where no one would have expected. The best way I can show my gratitude is by living up to my vocation faithfully.

III/1 *Venial sin and the 'world'* Venial sin is the 'irregularity' in my life [cf Exercises 63] and now in this retreat I must restore order, both with regard to conscious or deliberate venial sins and also the failings that spring from my character, which I must try to perfect more and more.   3.XI.63

III/2 *My spiritual life* There is no need for any special new practices here nor for any special new self-denial and sacrifice, but I must not only

---

[4] Compare the way God speaks to Israel through Jeremiah: 'For long ago you broke your yoke and burst your bonds; and you said, "I will not serve".' So it is inevitable that sin should make man an 'adversary' of God: 'For, if while we were enemies we were reconciled to God by the death of his Son. . . .' (Rom 5:10); 'For the mind that is set on the flesh is hostile to God; it does not submit to God's law, indeed it cannot' (Rom 8:7; cf. also James 4:4).

[5] At the end of the first meditation on sin the Exercises suggest that the retreatant should pray to the crucified Lord in the following colloquy: 'Let me picture Christ our Lord hanging on the Cross before me, and speak to him in this way: how has he, the Creator, come to be man? Knowing eternal life, how has he come to this temporal death, this death for my sins? Then, turning to myself, I will ask: What have I done **for Christ? What am I doing for Christ?** What must I do for Christ? Seeing the state Christ is in, nailed to the Cross, let me dwell on such thoughts as present themselves' (53).

perform outwardly the practices I have had for years, but the spirit in which I do them must be very fervent. As far as externals are concerned there is nothing lacking; in fact I shall have to see whether it may not really be necessary to make reductions in these external practices, especially in certain external works. But there will still be many external practices left, beginning with the daily spiritual exercises (meditation, Mass, breviary, examination of conscience etc). I must not do all this just materially, mechanically, but with God and with my mind on God. Otherwise I am a worker who does his work faithfully and exactly, whatever his motives may be (sense of duty, sense of order, natural inclinations etc), but whose relationship with his boss is not deep, so that he would work just as well with anyone else. So what I must do is to keep up the faithful and exact performance of my duties but to do everything in a conscious, reflex union with God, for his intentions and, finally, out of love for him, whether it is something pleasant, that I like, or something disagreeable, tiresome and difficult. It is only this loving union with God that will give my daily life all its supernatural value.

III/3 *My life as a priest and religious* There is scarcely anything left of my vows apart from chastity[6] but I must guard this carefully, not as though any danger threatened but in order to make the sacrifice that is involved to the utmost. So modesty in my looks and my whole behaviour! But I must cultivate the spiritual life of a priest and a Jesuit all the more, and in the spirit of the rules and regulations of the Society. This means in the first place, a full hour of meditation, well prepared and faithfully performed. The content: the life of Jesus and scripture, liturgy, the saints. The same goes for the two examinations of conscience: I must make them thoroughly and completely; but on these occasions I must pray especially and provide for the next period of time. All this, as well as spiritual reading, is important if I am going to be a spiritual man and act as such in my dealings with people, my discussions and conversations, and so that everyone may leave my presence with some spiritual gain.[7]

III/4 *Death, judgment, last decision* 'Who will deliver me from this body of death?' [Rom 7:24]. 'My desire is to depart and to be with Christ' [cf Phil 1:23]. This is the frame of mind in which I want to meet my

[6] If a religious becomes a cardinal, he is dependent only on the pope, as far as the vow of obedience is concerned. As for the vow of poverty, he can own property and dispose of it in his lifetime and in his will—in accordance, of course, with other ecclesiastical regulations.

[7] Cf 1 Cor 2:12-15: 'Now we have received not the spirit of the world, but the Spirit which is from God, that we might understand the gifts bestowed on us by God. And we impart this in words not taught by human wisdom but taught by the Spirit, interpreting spiritual truths to those who possess the Spirit. The unspiritual man does not receive the gifts of the Spirit of God, for they are folly to him, and he is not able to understand them because they are spiritually discerned. The spiritual man judges all things, but he himself is judged by no one.'

death, whenever and however it may come. In my case every year, every month brings it nearer to me. How many of those close to me have died in this past year. But they are with God! Death does not mean a separation for me. I have already given up everything that could involve a separation. The little bit of money that is left is destined for poor nuns, so that they may pray for me and the Church. The great thing about death is that it brings the last decision. At the moment I must still work out my salvation in fear and trembling [cf Phil 2:12]; but then I shall be able to say 'who shall separate me from the love of Christ?' [Rom 8:35–39]—the judgment is only the confirmation of all this. But I must keep these words before my eyes: 'if we judge ourselves truly, we should not be judged' [1 Cor 11:31]. So no illusions about myself, gratefully accepting every well-meaning criticism from others and seeing what is true in the criticism of ill-wishers. But judging myself in my examination of conscience and confession! 8.XII.63

IV/1 *The kingdom of Christ* If this idea of 'greater enthusiasm' [Exercises 97] applies to anyone, then surely it applies especially to me, as I have received so very many graces and marks of favour from the Lord. So I must make more effort than anyone to 'distinguish' myself in my loyalty to our Lord and to model myself on him as much as possible.[8] The more I achieve this the more I shall be able to do his apostolic service. For the more I am free of 'natural weakness, and love of the world and of the flesh', the more I can be of use and help in Christ's army.

IV/2 *The Annunciation* [Lk 1:26–38] The greatest event in the history of the world, the incarnation, begins in as unlikely a way as may be imagined: in Nazareth, a young girl, an angelic apparition . . . But in reality it is all immeasurably great. The Virgin is full of grace, and by her fiat she brings divinity and humanity together: hypostatically in her blessed body and mystically in the Church. The angel is one of the very great ones who stand at the throne of God, Gabriel the messenger of the incarnation. And little Nazareth becomes this day the centre of the world. Indeed 'he who is mighty has done great things'! The most important thing for me is to let myself be used, however God wants to use me, in practice the unreserved fiat of my heart and my will.

General Confession (Father Schmitt).

IV/3 *The Nativity* No man can determine when, how and where he is to be born; he is simply placed in the world and must accept the situation. It is no merit to be born in a royal palace and no disgrace to be born in a poor negro hut. Only one person was able to choose, and that was our Lord. And he chose the crib, rejection and obscurity,

[8] Cf Rom 8:29: 'For those whom he foreknew he also predestined to be conformed to the image of his Son . . .'

although he was the richest, the mightiest and the noblest of all men. Why? Obviously because even here he wanted to choose the folly of the cross, for our sake and for our salvation [cf 1 Cor 1:21–25]. But this also shows me the proper way to work with him, no desire for influence or striving after riches, honour and recognition, but the hard way of the cross.

IV/4 *The hidden life* also has much to tell me. Firstly the loneliness of being a priest. I must not look for any 'substitute' for family life, neither at home nor outside. I am alone with Christ: a hidden life with Christ in God![9] However, still open to everything that goes on outside and that comes to me from outside, but from the religious point of view. I must not always be 'in the centre of things'—not a 'worldly' cardinal!

The second thing is progress: always ready to be taught, whatever the source of the wisdom, so long as it is wisdom. On the other hand he increased 'in favour with God and man': I must not lost the good will and sympathy of my fellow-men, nor of those who work with me, through harshness, hardness or prejudice, especially now during the Council. There are higher interests at stake and I must take care of them with love.

Finally work. For me this is a special part of my vocation. But this means proper organization; leaving the purely material side to others. On the other hand making the work part of my spiritual life, making it a prayer, without letting it take the place of the real prayer or restrict it.

5.I.64

V/1 *Jesus in the temple* [Lk 2:41–52] The Lord goes to the temple, although the Father is far more truly present in him than in the temple. He wants to show that religion is also an external practice. I can imagine how reverently he moved about in the temple: 'the house of my Father!' I must perform liturgical functions in the same way; not merely an external performance, but a deep interior spirit. He stays in the temple without saying anything to his mother: this is a moment of tension, for which neither of them is responsible: it is a duty that the Father has imposed on him to show his mother that her maternal rights are limited and that the day will come when the Father will claim him altogether. 'About my Father's business!'

V/2 *The call of the apostles* This story of the call of the apostles is to a great extent the story of mine too. 1) humble in origin: who would ever have expected that a little peasant cottage would produce a priest, a religious, a bishop and cardinal? Yet it all came so unexpectedly, so much 'from above', without being planned by anyone, indeed contrary to men's plans. But this means I have a special obligation to be com-

---

[9] The author here applies to himself what Paul says of the life of the Christian in general: 'For you have died, and your life is hid with Christ in God' (Col 3:3).

pletely true to my vocation now as well and to be a real apostle in the task for which he has especially called and prepared me throughout a long life. It is not so much a question here of dignities and honours—a greater external dignity is scarcely possible now; but of solid work in the service of the Church and of souls. 'To be with him always':[10] on my part this means being united with him in my work and not doing it merely materially and externally but in his spirit, in his grace and strength. Being with Christ, then, is the thing: 'I offer nothing but a share in my hardships!' [Exercises 95.]

V/3 *The Sermon on the Mount* [Mt 5:1–16] The meditation on the 'hidden life' has already shown me that I must take up a position of opposition to the world. I must belong wholly to God; then the eight 'blessed are those' will apply to me too. I shall be 'light of the world' and 'salt of the earth' all the more, if I am a truly interior man. I must perform the externals faithfully; but these actions must come from an interior spirit and be informed by it, so to speak. If our Lord says in Mt 5:48: 'You, therefore, must be perfect, as your heavenly Father is perfect', then this is the highest ideal; and I must at least aim at it.

V/4 *The mission of the apostles* [cf Mt 10:16–19, 24 f] Our Lord does not make any idyllic promises to the apostles: they are not to be any better off than he. But they can have confidence in the Holy Spirit: he will give them light and strength. For their part they must be prudent and wise; but that will not prevent persecution. They are just like lambs in the midst of wolves. And yet he tells me 'I . . . appointed you that you should go and bear fruit and that your fruit should abide' [Jn 15:16]. This is what has happened throughout the history of the Church. The final reason is: 'I chose you and appointed you.' But for Christ: 'Christ must reign' [cf 1 Cor 15:25].

VI/1 *The multiplication of the loaves* Our Lord wants to get away but he does not succeed. As always he is besieged by the crowds and cannot bring himself to turn them away. So the day passes. This is an image of my day's work too. It is after all God's will and I must bear the burden, in whatever way and as long as he wants me to. In Nomine Domini Jesu![11] I have no right to a 'peaceful' life: 'I offer nothing but a share in my hardships' [Exercises 95]—in this great miracle our Lord acts with tranquillity, impartiality and kindness as if it was all something very ordinary. He acts with a consciousness of his power and dignity. I too, when I am acting officially, must speak as objectively, calmly and kindly as possible, make decisions and act and do everything with dignity, but not ostentatiously, especially the ceremonies of holy

---

[10] Cf Mk 3:13 f: 'And Christ went up into the hills, and called to him those whom he desired; and they came to him.'
[11] This was Cardinal Bea's motto.

Church. Jesus is my great model in this and I must imitate him more and more.

VI/2 *The two standards* [Exercises 136–147] It is also important for me never to lose sight of the workings of the evil spirit, even in myself.[12] In so very many cases, it is up to me to make the right decision, right not only for me but for the Church and for souls. Although I make my decisions under the inspiration of the Holy Ghost, it is also possible for the evil spirit to influence me.[13] And so I must be cautious in everything and always keep the principles of the faith in mind, when I judge my 'first movements' and have to decide for or against, in this way or that. So I must consider things carefully in the examination of conscience as well, discuss them with others and make every effort myself to see things clearly, so that I may not fall 'into the snare of the devil' [cf 1 Tim 3:7 f].
9.XI.64

VI/3 *The transfiguration* There is no abiding city on Mount Tabor. And the great mystics show us this too: St Bernard, St Ignatius, and St Teresa. It is here that the apostolate finds its source of strength and energy. And even if it is not mysticism, there must at least be a solid interior life of union with God, of prayer, or self-denial and mortification, from which my apostolate whatever form it may take, draws its strength, drive and content. And as he was praying, he was transfigured [cf Lk 9:29 and parallels]. God only gives his graces to souls that pray and to pray properly I must be 'alone', alone with the Lord, or at least with those with whom I am united in the same spirit. 'Listen to him' (Mt 17:5): this is finally the most essential fruit of every prayer and of this rather curtailed retreat.[14]

VI/4 *My priesthood* is essentially a share in Christ's priesthood. It is his nature to be the mediator between God and man; and by his grace I have a share in his mediator's office. This means that I am under an obligation to men.[15] I can never be a priest just for my own sake; it is

---

[12] Compare the admonition from I Peter: 'Be sober, be watchful. Your adversary the devil prowls around like a roaring lion, seeking someone to devour. Resist him, firm in your faith . . .' (I Pet 5:8 f); and again, the parable of the sower: 'The ones along the path are those who have heard; then the devil comes and takes away the word from their hearts, that they may not believe and be saved' (Lk 8:12): and also what Christ says to Peter at the Last Supper: 'Simon, Simon, behold, Satan demanded to have you, that he might sift you like wheat, but I have prayed for you that your faith may not fail . . .' (Lk 22:31 f).

[13] Cf St Paul's warning: 'And no wonder, for even Satan disguises himself as an angel of light' (2 Cor 11:14).

[14] During this retreat the author had some difficulties with his health.

[15] Cf Heb 5:1 ff (also 8:3 : 'For every high priest chosen from among men is appointed to act on behalf of men in relation to God, to offer gifts and sacrifices for sins. He can deal gently with the ignorant and wayward, since he himself is beset with weakness. Because of this he is bound to offer sacrifice for his own sins as well as for those of the people.'

essential that I should be a priest for the sake of all and, if it is no longer possible in any other way, at least through the Mass and the sacrifice of sickness and suffering. This is important for me as cardinal; people must never get the impression that I am too wrapped up in matters of protocol and in external pomp etc. Necessary as these things may be, there must always be a genuinely priestly life behind them.

As a priest and a bishop I share in the very special way in the holiness of the Church. I must also try to make my life as faithful an image as possible of Christ the High Priest. If that is true for everyone, then it is especially true for a bishop and a cardinal. 5.IV.64

VII/1 *The institution of the holy Eucharist* He has left us 'a memorial of his wonderful works' in the holy Eucharist. When I think that I am the instrument for the distribution of all these wonderful works, I have to marvel at this and at the power I have to hand on these powers to others. But in all this I must not forget the consequences for myself: 'he who eats my flesh and drinks my blood, abides in me, and I in him' [Jn 6:56]. Already this is almost an anticipation of eternal life, at any rate it is a pledge of future glory'. So once again I must develop a fervent devotion to the holy Eucharist: Mass with great recollection, holy communion with a good preparation, and daily visits of devotion. Our Lord is so near me: so I must make use of the grace.

VII/2 *In the Garden of Olives* The 'agony' (not so much the physical one, as the spiritual one) in the garden is a mystery that I shall never be able to penetrate and one that could hardly happen to me with the same intensity, since basically it is connected with the hypostatic union, with a knowledge of sin and suffering that only the redeemer can have. But a part of it can be my lot too. Then I know that the strength to overcome the agony can only come from the firm unshakable intention of doing the will of the Father, and that this firmness is a grace I get from God through prayer, however lacking in shape and style that prayer may be—as our Lord's was, after all [cf Mt 26:39–44]. But his brave 'rise, let us be going' was the result of his prayer. And I must be quite clear what he meant by this 'let us be going': to judgment, to the way of the cross and to the cross! Passion of Christ, strengthen me!

VII/3 *From the garden to the cross* What makes this journey so hard for our Lord is the attitude of those in authority, in the spiritual sphere and in the temporal. In the spiritual sphere: they have fashioned for themselves a Messiah, according to their own ideas. This is no objective norm, but the triumph of subjective plans and wishes. That is why they allow no discussion. It is a 'council' in which one man lays down the law according to his own whims and not one of the seventy 'councillors' raises even one objection [cf Mt 26:65 f]. And the two who have different ideas are not present.¹⁶ The important thing for me is to make my judgment on the basis of clear and objective criteria, and always and everywhere to have the courage to stand by this judgment. It is only in this way that our Lord in his Church will be preserved from pain. The temporal authority, Pilate, shows me that in everything I must consider what is right and not my own personal interests. It is only in this way that I can really be a help to the Church, where I belong in some sort to 'those in authority', and can advance its cause in the right spirit.

VII/4 *On the cross* The essence of the cross is love: the love of the Blessed Trinity for men and the love of the incarnate Son of God for each of us: he 'loved me and gave his life for me'. This love is at the same time the obedience of the Son of Man towards God: he 'became obedient unto death, even death on a cross' [Phil 2:8]. God wanted to go to extremes: the redeemer was not to be spared anything. Even on the cross, as in the garden, he sees himself abandoned by God. Only after he had drained the 'cup of salvation' to the last drop was he able to say 'it is finished' [Jn 19:30] and once again use the dear name 'Father'. What there is left to me of life should be inspired and sustained more and more by this self-sacrificing and self-surrendering love. My God I love thee because thou hast loved me:¹⁷ not just with words, however, but in spirit and truth.

VIII/1 *The life of the risen Jesus* It is not just a repetition of his early life on earth but a completely new and special sort of activity: for his Church and for the apostles, whom he has destined to be the leaders of the Church and whom he strengthens particularly in faith. The apostle is able to say emphatically: 'if Christ has not risen, our faith is vain' [1 Cor 15:14]. The resurrection is a unique unparalleled miracle: he had died on the cross, shed the last drop of his blood and had his heart pierced. And now he raises himself up again on the third day to a new life,¹⁸ and apart from the five wounds, which have been kept deliberately, his body is once again completely undamaged and shining with the heavenly brightness. In this new life he teaches the apostles, gives the Church Peter as its head [Jn 21:15 ff], gives it the sacraments, and decrees that the whole world should be its proper sphere. So the Church is not just a pious society, but the continuation of Christ himself

---

¹⁶ Joseph of Arimathea and Nicodemus (cf Jn 19:38 ff).
¹⁷ From a hymn attributed to St Francis Xavier.
¹⁸ In the New Testament Christ's resurrection is normally attributed to the 'power of the Father' (Rom 4:24; 8:11; 10:9; 1 Cor 6:14; 15:15; 2 Cor 4:14; Col 2:12 etc). In these passages Christ is seen in his human nature. He himself can say: 'The Father is greater than I' (Jn 14:28). But when Christ emphasizes his divine dignity, he also stresses his power to raise himself (i.e. his human nature) from the dead: 'For this reason the Father loves me, because I lay down my life, that I may take it up again. No one takes it from me, but I lay it down of my own accord. I have power to lay it down, and I have power to take it up again' (Jn 10:17 f).

with all his gifts and graces.[19] No wonder that it cannot go under in all the storms: 'I am with you always, to the close of the age' [Mt 28:20].

VIII/2 *The Holy Spirit as the fruit of the redemption* I will cultivate devotion to the Holy Spirit in a very special way. He is the life of my soul, my light, and my strength and every day I need his help urgently.[20] But I must not forget that others have the Holy Spirit as well and that he works in a different way in the different members of the Mystical Body, in each according to his function. This can also be seen in the history of the Church: in the last centuries he has guided the Church in very different ways and led it to interior renewal, and he will also continue to do so. So I must see where and how he is working and then cooperate generously, even if I do not feel naturally inclined that way. The Spirit breathes where he will! [cf Jn 3:7.] If I tread the path of humility, of self-conquest, of patience in suffering and unpleasantness, in short the way of the imitation of Christ and work on myself so that I keep ever closer to this path, then I may be certain that the Holy Spirit is living and working in me, even if I have no subjective experience of this. But I must pray too that this influence of the Spirit within me may become stronger and more effective.   31.V.64

VIII/3 *'The decision'*[21]

VIII/4 *Love* When I say the Suscipe [Exercises 234] it always has a very special meaning. I have long since given myself and my freedom and powers to the Lord and I continue to do so. But now he has requisitioned me altogether, as it were; all my activity from morning to night belongs to him and is only for him. There is nothing else left on earth for me to do. My 'Suscipe' is not just an act of the will; it is a fact and must become more so every day. In my 'decision' I have confirmed this fact once again and all that matters now is that I should not take away the least thing from this fact. So I shall 'find God' in everything, either in his greatness and love or in his neglect. In this case it will be precisely

---

[19] Cf 1 Cor 12:12: 'For just as the (human) body is one and has many members, and all the members of the body, though many, are one body, so it is with Christ' (cf also 12:27).

[20] Bea was convinced of the need for a practical faith in the Holy Spirit. How thoroughly this idea is based on the New Testament may be seen from the following passages: the Holy Spirit as the *life of the soul*: 'But if Christ is in you, although your bodies are dead because of sin, your spirits are alive because of righteousness. If the spirit of him who raised Jesus from the dead dwells in you, he who raised Christ Jesus from the dead will give life to your mortal bodies also through his Spirit who dwells in you' (Rom 8:10 f). The Holy Spirit as *light*: 'When the Spirit of truth comes, he will guide you into all truth' (Jn 16:13). The Holy Spirit as *strength*: Christ promises the apostles: 'But you shall receive power when the Holy Spirit has come upon you; and you shall be my witnesses in Jerusalem and in all Judea and Samaria and to the end of the earth' (Acts 1:8).

[21] The brief summary of resolutions of the whole retreat, which the author set out on four pages. An example is to be found at the end of the 1968 retreat.

my task not just to find him myself, but to show him to others and lead them to him. My love for God, then, is not just a matter of feeling or words, but a fact and a truth.[22] If I have this frame of mind I can now return comforted to every day life, in order that in my prayers, work, suffering and enduring, I may find him whom my soul loves more and more, and help others to find him too. Amen, Amen! 3.VII.64

Neuhausen, 29.VII.63

FROM THE MONTHLY RECOLLECTIONS

6.X.1963

1) Make all my judgments according to supernatural principles.
2) Do everything in union with God (particularly examination of conscience).
3) Perform spiritual duties fully, in a spirit of recollection.
4) Edifying in my dealings with other people (some benefit for their souls).
5) Work in such a way that my spiritual life does not suffer.

To God alone be honour and glory.

I/2 You are of Christ: Christ in all things!
I/3 Everything must bring me closer to God: always learn something! Pay attention to the movements of my soul!
I/4 Proceed in all things with deliberation and seek the will of God in the concrete situation; must not waste my time! or 'live for the moment'.

3.XI.1963

1) In my work seek only God's will.
2) Union with God all day long (with God and directed towards God).
3) Edifying in all and to all.
4) Patience in all situations; always friendly, kind, loving.

II/1 More grace is at my disposal for overcoming sin than most others have; so use it to the full.
II/2 Every sin is directed against God, who is the author of order and the commandments.
II/4 Now bound to God all the more closely.

8.XII.1963

1) Solid interior life: union with God, spiritual duties, self-conquest.

[22] Cf 1 Jn 3:18: 'Little children, let us not love in word or speech but in deed and in truth'.

2) Holiness according to the example of the eternal High Priest.
3) Edifying in behaviour and conversation.
4) Kind, friendly and full of love to all.

III/2 In all my outward activity, with God and directed towards God; conscious reflex union with God, even in unpleasant situations.

III/3 Cultivate the spiritual life of a Jesuit.

Examination of conscience: look to the future!

5.I.1964

Make all my decisions according to supernatural principles; and so familiarity with God is a duty; recollected in God. Edifying in dealings with people and in conversation.

IV/1 To distinguish myself, in my loyalty to our Lord.

IV/2 Allow myself to be used however he wants to use me—'fiat'!

IV/3 No looking for approval and honour, but service.

IV/4 To be alone with Christ!—'always ready to be taught'—no violence, harshness or prejudice; loving objectively.

IV/5 Try to understand other people's views too—argue my case with love; work in a supernatural frame of mind.

9.II.1964

1) Love as the highest motive: the greatest of these is charity [1 Cor. 13:13].
2) Perform my spiritual duties as fully and perfectly as possible.
3) Aim at a sanctity and perfection in keeping with my status.
4) Always edifying in my dealings with people, especially layfolk.
5) Consideration and understanding for the people who work with me, full of love.

V/1 'About my Father's business.'

V/2 Gratitude for my vocation! Live up to it wholly and fully; 'to be with him' always; with Christ.

V/3 Confidence in God, but also work and prudence on my part: 'I have appointed you.'

VI/1 Bear the burden of the day's work; no 'life of leisure'!—objective, tranquil, kind in my dealings with people and in my official capacity.

VI/2 Examination of conscience.

5.IV.1964

A solid interior life, recollection; recollected in God; all day long union with God. Faithfulness in my spiritual duties (examination of conscience!); edifying in my speech and behaviour; when working with others patient and with a really supernatural love.

VI/3 On Tabor strength and energy for the apostolate; praying; 'alone'.

VI/4 As a priest I am under an obligation to men: a priest for all!

3.V.1964

1) Perform my spiritual duties faithfully and in a spirit of recollection.
2) All day long do everything well and conscientiously.
3) Everything with God and directed towards God.
4) Make all judgments according to supernatural principles.
5) Edify my fellow men and be of benefit to their souls.

31.V.1964

1) Make all decisions according to supernatural principles.
2) Listen to the people who work with me readily and in a kindly way; and be grateful to God.
3) Recollection and union with God.
4) Examination of conscience and spiritual reading.
5) Edifying in behaviour and speech.

VII/1 Daily visits; always good; and twice (morning and afternoon).
VII/2 My will (not feelings!) must be firmer and more unshakable—pray for this.
VII/3 Attitude of 'those in authority' during the Passion! Judgments on the basis of objective and clear criteria; I too belong to 'those in authority'; so!
VII/4 Self-sacrificing, self-surrendering love; not in words and speech but in deed and in truth (cf I John 3:18).
VIII/2 Devotion to the Holy Ghost; his influence in the Church.

3.VII.1964

Think, will and work supernaturally; recollected in God, even in the holidays. Edifying to all who have anything to do with me—judge without bias, calmly and objectively.

VIII/4 My 'suscipe' is a fact, everyday; not just a matter of feeling and words; find God in prayer, speech and work.
I/1 All my sufficiency is from God; God my support and help; not looking for success; for God alone.
I/2 My life must be centred on Jesus: in the name of the Lord Jesus.
I/3 Learn something for myself and my apostolate from everything that happens. No selfish aims! amidst all enthusiasm must preserve my interior freedom and make decisions in freedom!

CHAPTER 8

The first year of the new pontificate 1964

The second session of the Council opened on 29 September and was dominated by the long and extremely laborious discussion of episcopal collegiality and the first general vote on the question. It was very important for the Secretariat because of the discussion on the schemata on ecumenism, religious freedom and the Church's relationship with the Jews. Cardinal Bea, as President, presented the official report on this last schema and although the drafts on religious freedom and the Jews did not reach the stage of a preliminary vote, at least they had the great pleasure of seeing the schema on ecumenism put to the vote and accepted as the basis for further discussion, by a very large majority (only 86 votes against, out of 2,052).

The cardinal spoke five times in the Council: twice on the draft Constitution on the Church, once on the draft on the bishops and the government of dioceses, and twice on the schema on ecumenism.

The beginning of 1964 saw Pope Paul VI's pilgrimage to the Holy Land. From the ecumenical point of view this was the decisive breakthrough in the improvement of relations between Rome and the Orthodox Church.

Since the autumn of 1963 a new and heavy burden had been added to the cardinal's personal work: he became a member of the Holy Office, which meant very demanding meetings every week.

After the plenary session of the Secretariat for Unity, (24 February–6 March) the lecture tours began again. On 15 March the cardinal spoke in Cologne at the end of the 'Week of Brotherhood' on the theme 'The Council and Brotherhood Among Men'. A month later, on 16 April, he spoke at the Catholic University in Milan on the theme 'Christian Unity and the Laity'. This visit to Milan was also the occasion of a confidential meeting with the representatives of the World Council of Churches, and here the foundations were laid for further cooperation between the Catholic Church and the World Council of Churches.

Another important and strenuous journey followed: first of all the cardinal was to preside at the great May Pilgrimage at Fatima (13 May) which was dedicated amongst other things to the intentions of Unity. He gave short greetings in four languages and preached in Portuguese the main sermon, lasting more than twenty minutes, to about three quarters of a million pilgrims. On the way back he was invited by the recently appointed Bishop of Madrid, Morcillo Gonzalez, to visit Madrid where he gave a talk on the theme 'What does Christian Unity demand of the Laity?' This year's series of journeys ended with his third American tour: Harvard University had invited him to receive an honorary doctorate of law on 11 June in recognition of his ecumenical work.

The outlook for the third session of the Council was clouded by many problems. In the first place a general feeling of uncertainty prevailed; for some the Council had been going on too long already, while others were afraid that discussion would be curtailed at the expense of freedom and thoroughness in order to bring the Council to a conclusion this session. The concerns of the Secretariat itself were also causing a certain amount of unrest; for, even though the ecumenical schema had made good progress and the prospects were good, this was not the case with what were perhaps the two most controversial schemata in the Council; religious freedom, and the relationship with the Jews.

RETREAT 1964

Neuhausen, 2–9 August

I/1 *'Servant of God'* I must remember that I am nothing but a servant[1] of God, not acquired by him in some way, nor given to him by my free will, but created out of nothing, so that all I have, I have through him and from him and nothing is my own. What have you got that you did not receive? [cf 1 Cor 4:7]. So I must not use anything for myself, neither for my own convenience nor for my own honour, but everything for him alone and everything as he wants. Nor must I be extravagant with my powers; they belong to him and I must keep them for him as far as I can without on the one hand being fearful and scrupulous, but also without making too many demands on them without sufficient reason. They belong wholly to God and only to him. And I must not be under any illusions about my talents or my success, and certainly not about my titles and dignities. All these are also from him and for him. Nor must I let myself be discouraged by failure. I must simply ask myself whether it is my fault or whether it has been willed by God and permitted by him. 'It is all yours and I am wholly and completely yours' [cf Exercises 234].

I/2 *My privilege* is not to have honours and titles and dignities but the call to a definite mission and the greater recognition and the greater

---

[1] Some weeks before his death the German edition of Cardinal Bea's study, *We who serve* (English translation, Chapman, London, 1969), was published. The fourth chapter of this work bears the title: 'What does the service of God mean?' It gives a

grace that is connected with it, and the greater reward in heaven, if I have given faithful service. So I must not look at others to see what they are doing or thinking: nor have I to give an account of my actions to anyone but God alone and his representatives. Hence spiritual independence! But I do owe God a special debt of gratitude for all that he has done for me and for all the special graces that he has given me, not because I deserved them but simply and solely because he wanted me to be a special instrument of his saving will.[2] He has placed the realization of his will to redeem the world in my hands in a very special way. Therefore I must enter into this plan wholeheartedly, devote myself wholly to it and only to it and must not seek to do anything but work for it, and on the other hand I can expect everything I need for it from him. 'O Lord, I am thy servant . . . and the son of thy handmaid' [Ps 116:16]. Be it done unto me according to thy will [cf Lk 3:8], and I shall act in accordance with that same will!

I/3 *'We need to train ourselves to be impartial'* [Exercises 23] This means that I must have a great aim in life and let nothing, except the clearly recognized will of God, turn me from it. I have this great goal: to serve God and only him, always, everywhere and in everything. And what I have to do now is to protect this ideal from every hindrance which can come from me or my environment or from outside. I must be 'indifferent' to all this, that is without any inclination or preference. But the influences of the world and my environment can also be a possible help to me. So my task is to find the right path and keep to it. And this is no easy task. To do it I need first of all light and strength from God: so I must pray especially to the Holy Spirit, to the Virgin most prudent, the Seat of Wisdom,[3] to St Ignatius and my special patron. Then I must reflect: and for this I have meditation and the examination of conscience. Finally discussion with such people as can help me. In this way I shall constantly find the right path and not only remain true to my ideal but become evermore faithful to it. And then inordinate concern for others or the desire for approval and so on will not occur to hinder me. This is what is meant by 'training myself to be impartial'!

I/4 *'Thereby saving his soul'* [Exercises 23] This does not simply mean keeping myself safe from hell, but making sure that I received the fullest share in this 'salvation of soul' that a human being can have. For our Lord has not called me to do the minimum; the graces that he has given me show that he has destined me for a high degree of

---

number of New Testament passages dealing with the idea of the Christian as the 'servant of God' (Mt 6:4; 1 Thess 1:9; Rom 6:13, 17 f, 22; 7:6, 25; 12:11; Eph 6:6 f; 1 Pet 2:16; Rev 2:20; 7:3; 19:5 etc).

[2] Cf Constitutions X, 2. This idea is developed also in *The Decree on the Renewal of the Religious Life*, 14.

[3] These titles are given to Mary in the litany of Loretto.

blessedness. So for my part I must not offer him just the bare essentials in my life; on the contrary I must strive to achieve the ideal of the most perfect possible service of God, as I resolved in the first meditation. The sacrifices that this involves will be rewarded more richly: 'the sufferings of this present time are not worth comparing with the glory that is to be revealed to us' [Rom 8:18]. God will not be outdone in generosity[4] and he does not give his rewards mechanically but according to the merits of each individual [cf Rom 2:6 f; Mt 16:27; 2 Cor 5:10]. Then all our powers, our senses, understanding, heart and will come into their own. The greater the number of those whom I have influenced by my apostolic work and whom I have helped to achieve their eternal goal, the greater will be my joy and happiness.

II/1   *Concern for small things*   This must be a sign of my love of God and of our divine Lord. It is not just a matter of expressions of sentiment and so on—even if I had these feelings. Nor is it enough for me to avoid sin, both serious sin and deliberate venial sin; this is a matter of obligation and, in the end, of self-love. I must show my love by pleasing our Lord in things that are not prescribed by law, by imitating the example of consideration and love that he showed in the house in Nazareth and towards his apostles and so many others in his public life. I too must go beyond what is strict obligation and show my love by thoughtfulness in all my actions. This is a complete plan of action for my life every day and in every situation.   13.IX.64

II/2   *Sin* is a force in the life of man, of the Church and of the individual. The original sin of our first parents brought a great deal of pain and misery into the world, but it also brought a great deal of evil and wickedness. A glance at history shows this. But then in his mercy God provided a means of salvation, first in the Old Testament, then in the Church with its many avenues of salvation and grace, and God the Son died for the sin of mankind. But even this could not wipe sin out: even amongst the apostles there was a Judas, and how many there have been in the Church itself: priests, religious, bishops and cardinals, and even popes! The power of sin is just as great today and so the struggle of the Church against sin is just as necessary. It is also a force in my own heart. If I look back on my past I see how strong the inclination to evil was in me too, and how often I was in danger of giving way. It is only by God's mercy that I have not been devoured [cf Lam 3:22]. This look at my own life teaches me to be humble but also grateful to God. I can show this gratitude best by fighting against sin in the world now and by taking care that the means of grace that are in the Church are made available to as many as possible. God has called me now to this position and in it I can do so much good, and in this way make up for my own sins.

[4] Cf chap. 3, note 12, for the Ignatian principle of generosity towards God.

II/3 *Self-knowledge* 'One of the greatest graces we can receive from our Lord is the knowledge of what we are in whatever way that may come' (St Francis de Sales, *Vrais Entretiens* VI, 4). This self-knowledge is particularly important for me, since people usually over-estimate me and so I am in danger of over-estimating myself, whether it is with regard to my talents or successes or my personal life. I do not need to make little of what there really is; but I must also see what is lacking. My talents are not mine; God has given them to me and, more than that, he has given me the chance of developing them and using them. In this respect I am totally God's handiwork. And do I always make full use of them? Then as regards my successes; they are due mainly to God's grace; and secondly to the active and skilled cooperation of the people who work with me. Finally there is fame, and it is increasing. For I must know what to make of this and remain humble. And lastly my private life; I know quite well that I am no saint and that even today there is still a great deal lacking in my spiritual life. It must be one of the main resolutions of this retreat to pay more attention to my spiritual exercises. I must not live as a 'clerical pensioner'! I have critics too. I must be grateful to them and derive some benefit from their criticisms. But kind and full of charity towards all.

II/4 *My personal vocation* I really can speak of such a thing. It is due to the goodness and love of God not to me that I have become a priest, a Jesuit, a cardinal and a bishop. But while this is the case, God also expects something special from me. A maximum of effort for the honour of God must correspond to the maximum of grace. It is not hard to find what this maximum involves: the generous carrying out of the rules of the Society, so far as they still apply to me, and the total devotion to the tasks which Christ's Vicar has entrusted to me and continues to entrust to me. Obstacles and difficulties must not count in doing this. Our Lord so often said 'Follow me' and he says it to me in this retreat so urgently. And I shall only live up to my special vocation if I make this 'Follow me' a fact and do it wholeheartedly. In saying this to me our Lord has also given me a guarantee that he will help me with his grace. 'By the grace of God I am what I am' [1 Cor 15:10], but that presupposes that I use all the means of grace and supernatural help faithfully and generously.

III/1 *The incarnation* 'Go therefore and make disciples of all nations' (Mt 28:18). Today one-third of mankind is still far from the Gospel of Christ. This commission to 'Go therefore' still applies to us and in the fullest measure. So I too, even though I have no direct missionary work to do, must do all I can to help the missions. The Church must not be content with what it now has. Just as the Blessed Trinity wants to share the riches of its life with all mankind, so too must the Church. It does not exist to give comfortable livings, palaces and pomp, but to spread the kingdom of Christ. And it can only bring this about if it is poor and humble like our Lord and his holy mother.[5]

7.XI.63

III/2 *Bethlehem* teaches me total, unreserved and unswerving devotion to the will of God. The child in the crib knows all the details of the fulfilment of this will of God and knowing all this he says: 'Lo, I have come to do thy will,' and at the end of his life he can say: 'I have finished the work that thou gavest me to do' [Jn 17:4]. Mary and Joseph probably have a general idea what it is all about but no detailed knowledge of what it will bring them and mean for them. Yet Mary says: 'Behold I am the handmaid of the Lord; let it be to me according to your word,' and with that she accepts everything that is to come, including the separation from her Son and his cross. And St Joseph is simply the faithful servant to whom our Lord entrusts himself as long as he is alive. At the crib in Bethlehem there are no outbursts of sentiment, no signs of softness, just the stern and strict will of God, which demands devotion without qualification and without drawing back: this must now be my plan of action more and more consciously: 'I want what you want: when you want: as you want; I want it because you want it.' 'Give me your love and your grace; it is all I need' [Exercises 234].

General confession (Father Schmitt).

III/3 *The presentation in the temple* [Lk 2:22–38] 'To serve God' it is not just something that concerns the interior life, it means also the external fulfilment of the commandments of God. Outwardly too I must be 'righteous and devout'. Our Lord comes to his temple: every house of God with a tabernacle is in a special way his temple. The sacrifice is offered for him, but *he* is the victim that puts an end to all other sacrifices.[6] 'The cross and the eucharistic sacrifice. Even before this event our Lord had been the centre of old Simeon's life: he had been 'looking for the consolation of Israel'; and now he sees with the eyes of faith, and he becomes a means of revelation for Mary and Joseph

---

[5] Cf the *Constitution on the Church*, promulgated a few months after this retreat: 'Just as Christ carried out the work of redemption in poverty and under oppression, so the Church is called to follow the same path in communicating to men the fruits of salvation. Christ Jesus, "though he was by nature God . . . emptied himself, taking the nature of a slave" (Phil 2:6), and "being rich, he became poor" (2 Cor 8:9) for our sakes. Thus, although the Church needs human resources to carry out her mission, she is not set up to seek earthly glory, but to proclaim humility and self-sacrifice, even by her own example' (8).

[6] By Christ's sacrifice the old way of sacrificing has been abolished: 'When he [Christ, the High Priest] said above, "Thou hast neither desired nor taken pleasure in sacrifices and offerings and burnt offerings and sin offerings" (these are offered according to the law), then he added, "Lo, I have come to do thy will." He abolishes the first in order to establish the second. And by that will we have been sanctified through the offering of the body of Jesus Christ once for all' (Heb 10:8 ff).

as well. Mary has always said yes, but the extent of it all is revealed to her more and more: the birth in the stable, the flight into Egypt and now a glimpse of our Lord's passion and death and her own share in his suffering: 'A sword will pierce through your own soul also'; she is to share in the contradiction that her child will meet. She is not merely a passive onlooker. Anna: here too we see our Lord the redeemer as the centre of a life of self-denial and prayer. Christ the centre of our spiritual life. Only when he is present are outward works of any value—the works of those who are just 'doctors of the law' are of no value. 4.X.64

III/4 *Nazareth* [Lk 2:51 f]: *life at home*   This takes up a great part of my time and is important for my soul and for my apostolic work. It includes prayer, work, daily contacts and relaxation.

1) *Prayer:* About three and a half hours every day. What a treasure! But I must do it well and better. For me it means energy, light and strength: and it gives my work a purpose and a depth. I must be a 'praying cardinal'. Especially the Mass and breviary; but also visits and examination of conscience.

2) *Work:* As it comes—I have not much choice; preparation for meetings, lectures, correspondence. In God's eyes it has all the same value. But I must do everything conscientiously, thoroughly and as perfectly as possible, conscious of the responsibility that is mine.

3) *Visitors:* Kind, friendly but also clear and firm. Everyone should be edified by the meeting with me [cf 1 Thess 5:11].

4) *Relaxation:* This is also a duty, recreation, sleep, walks, exercise.

This is a short plan of action for when I am at home. Here too people should be able to say of me: he 'increased in wisdom . . . and favour': Wisdom, 'always ready to learn', even from people younger than myself, from the experience of others, from reading and observation. 'In favour with God and man': with God and by virtue and the use of the means of grace; with man: my actions should flow from my interior life. Fiat, fiat! 12.XII.65

IV/1 *The baptism and the desert* [Mt 3:13–17 and parallels]   What happened to our Lord at the baptism in the Jordan happens to us to a greater degree in the sacrament of baptism. He was already the Son of God: by baptism we are made 'adopted sons of God'. He already possessed the fullness of the Holy Spirit, and this is indicated by the appearance of the dove; at baptism the Holy Spirit comes to take up his abode in us and he remains with us, as long as we do not drive him away by sin [cf Jn 3:5; Gal 4:4–7 etc]. So I must have a particularly high regard for the sacrament of baptism, both for myself and in my preaching. I must allow myself to be guided and directed by the Holy Spirit: 'For all who are led by the Spirit of God are sons of God' [Rom 8:14]. I must then, listen to the voice of the Holy Spirit when he speaks to me, even if he asks me to make sacrifices and bear crosses.[7] He also led our Lord into the wilderness [Mt 4:1]. And it is said of him: 'The blood of Christ, who through the eternal spirit offered himself . . . to God' (Heb 9:14). So I must also let myself be guided and led by the Holy Spirit and listen to his voice faithfully. Hence I must pay particular attention to devotion to the Holy Spirit.[8]   8.XI.64; 13.XII.64

IV/2 *The call of the apostles* This call has also come to me, and a call to the highest degree of participation in Christ's office as teacher, shepherd and priest. But I must remember that I cannot do all this through my own strength but only through him who said to his apostles and also to me: 'I am with you.' I can labour, plant and water; but it is he who gives the increase [cf 1 Cor 3:5 ff]. In fact not even the planting and watering can be done without him but only with his grace. As a successor of the apostles I have the highest dignity in the Church. But this is not for myself but for the Church, the faithful, the whole world. And to match this highest dignity there is also the highest obligation: 'I will most gladly spend and be spent for your souls' [2 Cor 12:15]. I must put my whole heart into this and not grow tired; as long as the Lord gives me strength I shall do it by work; and when my powers are no longer sufficient, then through apostolic prayer and suffering. There is no higher task in the Church; so I must also try to achieve the highest; not for the greater glory of God, but the greatest! In the power of the Holy Spirit I can do this. Come, Holy Ghost!

IV/3 *The miracle of Cana* [Jn 2:1–11] This is a great lesson for me. In the first place I have often to take part in functions etc, not because I like them but for higher supernatural reasons. 2) I must be quick to notice the needs and predicaments and so on of my fellow-men, especially those around me. 3) I must do it from love or other higher motives; so I must not be stiff! 4) What great power our Lady has over the heart of our Lord! and this is an unimportant matter; I have often far greater and more important requests. Why do I not approach Mary with unlimited trust and through her Jesus? 5) But in this act of kindness our Lord has another and far greater intention: he 'manifested his glory and his disciples believed in him'. Even in ordinary actions I must not lose sight of the great apostolic intentions.

[7] Cf Gal 5:16 f, 24 f: 'But I say, walk by the Spirit, and do not gratify the desires of the flesh. For the desires of the flesh are against the Spirit, and the desires of the Spirit are against the flesh; for these are opposed to each other, to prevent you from doing what you would . . . And those who belong to Christ Jesus have crucified the flesh with its passions and desires. If we live by the Spirit, let us also walk by the Spirit.'
[8] That the Holy Spirit has a decisive role to play in Christ's sacrifice is an important concept to which unfortunately too little attention is paid.

IV/4 *The Sermon on the Mount* [Mt 5:1–16] Contains a great many thoughts that are of importance, especially for my present position. 1) I must be 'poor in spirit', not, like the Pharisees, ostentatious but offering the simple and straightforward teaching of the Gospel in a simple and straightforward manner—I must 'hunger and thirst for righteousness' and not be slack and lazy in my spiritual life and apostolic work; so I must be anxious and eager for an intensive spiritual life. I must be a 'peace-maker' and a reconciling and mediating influence, without abandoning any principles. 2) Salt of the earth: putting forward the doctrine of the Church without any falsification and without any abridgement, but also in such a way that it may be 'tasty', that it may appeal and take hold of mind and heart. I am preaching the 'good news' not a code of law!

I must be a light by my example. I am now in the public eye and cannot escape it. And so I must act and talk in such a way that people may 'give glory to (the) Father who is in heaven'. This must be my intention: to be a source of edification in all things out of love for God and souls. 3) 'Perfect righteousness':[9] I must practise what I preach not just outwardly but in spirit and in truth, from the depth of my heart.

6.I.65

V/1 *The transfiguration* [Mt 17:1–6] The deeper I penetrate into the depths, into the heart of our Lord, the better and more effectively I shall be able to preach him to men. The two apostles, Peter and John, and St Paul are the best proofs of that. For this I do not need a sensible experience like theirs: I have his word and his example in the Gospel and also in the life of the Church. In my meditation I have the opportunity of understanding him more and more and of impressing upon myself his divine-human image. By prayer and in prayer I must bind myself more closely to him, I must really 'make booths' in order to live with him and by self-conquest I must make myself more and more worthy of his grace. In this way an intensive spiritual life can mean a 'transfiguration' for me too.

V/2 *Walking on the waters* The Church is always exposed to storms, even when, like the apostles, it is where (and how) our Lord wants it. The disciples are not to be better off than their Master. The history of the Church confirms this: there has not been a century without difficulties and struggles. But time and time again it emerges from them victoriously. So it was in the last century. The Kulturkampf; Modernism; World War I; Fascism and Nazism . . . and yet it has never been more powerful in any century. Why is this? Our Lord is always praying for it, always living to make intercession for us [cf Heb 7:24]. He guides it invisibly and visibly and comes to its aid at the right moment. But

---

[9] Probably a reference to Mt 5:20: 'Unless your righteousness exceeds that of the scribes and Pharisees, you will never enter the kingdom of heaven.'

the disciples must row hard, do their duty, and even if sometimes they make a mistake, our Lord overlooks it, if only they mean well. Our Lord, praying and watching, is our strength and salvation.

V/3 *The mission of the apostles* This is the model and norm for my mission. St Ignatius speaks of the 'beloved disciples' [Exercises 281]. It was a proof of his love that he sent them out [cf Jn 15:9] and it is also a proof of his very special love that he sends me out to the various tasks ('Missiones') that I have had to do in my life and especially to the task to which I can now devote the last years of my life. This task is also a matter of preaching the 'kingdom of God' and leading back the 'lost sheep' to the fold, the Church of Christ. It is a task that calls for a great deal of prudence, supernatural prudence, but also for much simplicity, straightforwardness and honesty. It is a task for Christ the good shepherd, not for me. I must be modest, simple, unassuming, humble as our Lord was, not a 'grand prince of the Church' standing on his dignity but the image of the good shepherd simply going after the lost sheep.

V/4 *The multiplication of the loaves* 1) The people are tireless: they are eager to hear the words of our Lord and even forget earthly concerns [Mk 8:1]. There is still this demand among men today, if only they are approached in the right way: if they are shown the value and beauty and fruit of Christ's teaching and not just addressed in terms of doctrine and law. As far as lies in my power I must cooperate in making the Church 'come into the world'. 2) Our Lord: he is tireless too: his 'day of rest' has come to nothing. His rest is prayer.[10] This must be my rest too. Mediation, Mass, office, when I really withdraw from my occupation and devote myself wholly to God. 3) *The disciples:* for them this is a great day: it shows them that they are the dispensers of our Lord's gifts. And it is not just a question of earthly bread, but, as our Lord says next day in Capharnaum, of the 'bread of Life' that comes down from heaven, of doctrine, of the sacraments and of the holy Eucharist [cf Jn 6:22–60]. They are to be dispensers of all this. It is in this that the greatness and the dignity of the priesthood lie, especially of its highest degree, the bishop.

VI/1 *The raising of Lazarus* [Jn 11:1–44] Our Lord is very friendly with Lazarus' family; but his friendship is always subject to the higher will of the Father; it is supernaturally ruled. All my human connections must be like this too. 'I am the resurrection and the life.' He is Lord of life and death and so he raises the dead to life again and will raise us all on the last day [Jn 6:39 f]. He raises Lazarus to life, although he knows that this means the death sentence for himself.[11] But the Jews are to have

---

[10] After he had sent the crowds and his disciples away, Jesus 'went into the hills to pray' (Mk 6:46).
[11] After the account of the raising of Lazarus, John tells us: 'But some of them went to the Pharisees and told them what Jesus had done. So the chief priests and the

an irrefutable proof of his divine mission and power, and therefore he makes a sacrifice of himself by performing this act of kindness in their presence. 'Obedient unto death'! Our Lord weeps: because of the sufferings of Lazarus and of his sisters: here we see the human kindness of his heart: the priest who is able to 'sympathize with our weaknesses' [cf Heb 4:15].

VI/2 *The meal in Bethany* There is so much generosity to be seen here: in Lazarus, who appears although they want to kill him: in Simon who openly expresses his belief in our Lord [Mt 26:6]; in Mary, who anoints our Lord without counting the cost. Because our Lord sees this frame of mind, he accepts it; not because he is looking for something for himself. This must be my criterion in accepting invitations!—but I can also see the great ingratitude of Judas. Love has grown cold in him. Instead of rejoicing at these signs of honour, paid to the Master, he becomes excited and criticizes, not only inwardly but publicly—without love and without truth. An apostle who criticizes, and criticizes the Master himself to some extent, is a public scandal. When I criticize, even if it is justified and well meant, I always give scandal. So I must keep to Rule 10 in this matter of being in sympathy with the mind of the Church.[12] In all this I see how kind, gentle and tender our Lord is in public.   7.III.65

VI/3 *The entry into Jerusalem on Palm Sunday* [Lk 19:28–44] The crowds are indeed enthusiastic, but their enthusiasm has no really solid foundation. They are only thinking of the Messiah and the kingdom of David, not of the kingdom of God, the kingdom of heaven, which our Lord preached so often. No wonder that he weeps over Jerusalem because it has not recognized the 'time of the visitation' For his part he has quite a different kingdom in mind, the kingdom of truth [cf Jn 18:36 f], of that truth that leads to peace and conquers hearts. This is the Church. It must not work with worldly means. We must become more and more aware that our task is 'go therefore and make disciples' [Mt 28:19], that we must fight and conquer with the weapons of truth

---

Pharisees gathered the council, and said, "What are we to do? For this man performs many signs. If we let him go on thus, everyone will believe in him, and the Romans will come and destroy both our holy place and our nation." But one of them, Caiphas, who was high priest that year, said to them, "You know nothing at all; you do not understand that it is expedient for you that one man should die for the people, and that the whole nation should not perish" ' (Jn 11:46–50).

[12] 'We should be more inclined to approve and speak well of the regulations and instructions as well as the personal conduct of our superiors. It may well be that these are not or have not been always praiseworthy; but to criticize them, whether in public utterances or in dealing with ordinary people, is likely to give rise to complaint and scandal rather than to do good. This would arouse popular hostility towards authority both temporal and spiritual. Of course, whilst it does harm to speak ill of superiors behind their backs in the hearing of ordinary people, it can do good to point out their failings to these superiors themselves, who can correct them' (Rule 10, Exercises 362).

and only with these.[13] This is also true of the task that I have been given; I must appeal to men's minds and conquer by exposition of the truth. This is not achieved by outward show and the enthusiasm of the crowds but only by patient work in small things, renouncing all ostentation. It is only grace and the insights won by grace that lead to the 'kingdom of God', the true kingdom of God.

VI/4 *The holy Eucharist* What I need now more than anything is a really living faith in our Lord in the holy Eucharist. A faith that shows itself whenever I have anything to do with our Lord in the Blessed Sacrament. 'He gave himself to me', not just 'for me'. And above all I must remember that he is a source of strength and grace for me everywhere, but especially in the Mass. Every morning I must pray that this Mass may give me the strength and grace for a generous imitation of Jesus, for a love for him that shows itself in deeds and for faithful devotion in his service for the good of souls and of the Church. So the Mass should not be simply for the benefit of others but for my own good too. Nor must I ever forget that I can come to our Lord at any time with all my problems and worries. He lives together with me under the same roof, I can and I must tell him about everything that concerns me and worries me.

VII/1 *The prayer in the Garden of Olives* The divinity leaves the human nature of Jesus. So it is not surprising that the human nature should recoil from the thought of the unspeakable suffering: 'He began to be afraid and to be sorrowful and troubled,' and that he should plead for release from these things. But this prayer is not heard, and this is in the best interests of our Lord himself and in our best interests. Our Lord is to earn his infinite glory fully, 'therefore God has highly exalted him and bestowed on him the name which is above every name' [Phil 2:9]. But also for our good: for our Lord's terrible sufferings were to be a model for all of us in every situation, from which we could draw courage and strength, from the terrible suffering of the martyrs down to the little difficulties and illnesses of everyday life. And what are these when compared with the terrible suffering and agony of our crucified redeemer! But in all things I must say 'not as I will, but as thou wilt'.

VII/2 *The flight of the apostles* 'Then all the disciples forsook him and fled' [Mt 26:56]. They have not yet got the Master's great example of suffering, the 'power from on high' [cf Acts 1:8]. Later they give up everything for our Lord, even their lives. I have none of these excuses. And I also have the great example of the martyrs, especially those from our Society. Passion of Christ strengthen me! St Paul would say: 'Who shall separate us . . . ?' [Rom 8:35]. Mary, who was already full of the

---

[13] This is basically the same idea as that expressed by Vatican II in the *Decree on Religious Freedom*, para. 11, promulgated eighteen months later.

Holy Spirit,[14] comes of her own accord to Calvary without thinking of the insults that she may have to face; she is ready even to die for him and with him. For my part, I too am one of Jesus' favourite disciples, therefore a disciple of the crucified Lord! So I must not allow myself to be put off or disturbed in my loyalty and devotion to our Lord and to my task by any little difficulties and sufferings, by fear of criticism and disapproval and so on. 16.IV.65

VII/3 *Jesus before his judges* Jesus' judges are either hypocrites or worldlings (like Herod) or men interested only in their own careers (like Pilate). Our Lord could have defended himself quite adequately before each of these, but he is silent, where higher motives do not make it necessary for him to speak. Only before Pilate is he more explicit, because he must explain the situation to this judge. So our Lord's *silence* is well-calculated. And this in circumstances where his honour and his life are at stake! And yet the occasions when I feel I have to justify and defend myself are often matters of such little importance. So often it doesn't matter at all whether I am right or wrong! This will be particularly important in the Council, where I must be completely objective and unbiased and kind and friendly to everyone, as our Lord would be, even to those who have different opinions. So there must be no suggestion of taking offence or being sensitive, but 'he was silent' [cf Mt 26:63]. Apart from that I must not forget that I have promised our Lord so often to practise the third way of subjection: 'I desire and I choose . . . to be insulted along with Christ so grossly insulted, rather than to be well thought of: I would rather be thought a helpless fool for the sake of Christ who was so treated' [Exercises 167].

VII/4 *Jesus on the cross* What the cross meant in terms of suffering is clear already from the fact that, in the garden, Christ sweats blood at the mere thought of it [cf Lk 22:44]. The cross was not really necessary for our redemption but our Lord *chose* to die on the cross.[15] Out of love for us. What would the Christian religion be without the cross! It shows us all the great value of the sacrifice that our Lord made for us, and helps everyone to carry his own cross in imitation of the cross of Christ. And what great things the history of the Church (martyrs and apostles, unobtrusive men and women all bearing their crosses) has to tell us about this. Our Lord foresaw all this and so he chose the cross out of love for us. So I must also choose the cross out of love for him. In comparison with his, my cross is infinitely small. And yet it was a consolation for him on the cross that so many were to take up their crosses and carry them out of love for him—even that I should be ready and willing to carry it with

---

[14] Since she was 'full of grace' (Lk 1:25).
[15] Cf Heb 12:1 f: 'Let us run with perseverance the race that is set before us, looking to Jesus the pioneer and perfecter of our faith, who for the joy that was set before him endured the cross, despising the shame.'

him whatever form it might take, great or small. 'I have been crucified with Christ' [Gal 2:19]. 9.V.65

VIII/1 *Heart of Jesus pierced by the lance*[16] The essential thing in our Lord's life and passion is not the outward side but the depths from which it comes, his heart, the frame of mind in which he did it all, love. 'He loved me . . .'; 'greater love has no man . . .' With me too it must not remain an external matter, everything must come from the heart. As the wound in Jesus' side is never closed again (the opened Heart),[17] so too my love must never grow faint. When I approach the heart of our Lord I can do so not as a servant but as a friend to whom our Lord opens his heart.[18] And it must be true of me too: 'he loved them to the end' [Jn 13:1], to the very end, till all my powers have been used up in work, effort, suffering and the cross. I will most gladly spend everything and be spent for souls [2 Cor 12:15]. This is genuine, effective love for our Lord.

VIII/2 *The appearance and the Church* After our Lord's resurrection he sets to work founding his Church. It is to be universal: 'all nations . . .' throughout the whole world; it is the Church of the gospel [Mk 16:15]. Peter is its head: he feeds the sheep and the lambs, the whole flock, out of love for our Lord ('do you love me?') [cf Jn 21:15 ff]. And at his side stand the other ten apostles. Into their hands he commits the sacraments: penance [Jn 20:21 ff] and baptism [Mt 28:19], just as earlier he had entrusted the Eucharist to them. And he gives them all a very wide range of miraculous powers [cf Mk 16:17 f]. In this way the risen Lord ensures the success of his work. But he will not leave it: 'I am with you always, to the close of the age' [Mt 28:20]. And so he also gives it divine assistance in every way, in doctrine, in government and in sanctification. This is the Church according to the will of its founder, Christ. It is my great privilege to be able to preach this Church and lead as many as possible to it and give them a share in what it has to offer.

VIII/3 *The ascension* The mood of our Lord and the apostles as they go to Mount Olivet is now quite different from what it was on the Maundy Thursday. Not as though everything had already been achieved. On the contrary; their work is only just beginning. Our Lord sees in front of him the world still lying in darkness. It must be enlightened by the faith and warmed by love. That is now the task of the disciples. But he can hand it over to them with one great consolation. The Holy

---

[16] An invocation from the Litany of the Sacred Heart.

[17] A reference to the preface for the Feast of the Sacred Heart. For the full text, see chap. 3, note 44.

[18] Cf Jn 15:14 f: 'You are my friends if you do what I command you. No longer do I call you servants, for the servant does not know what his master is doing; but I have called you friends, for all that I have heard from my Father I have made known to you.'

Spirit will come upon them, the 'power from on high' (Lk 24:49), and he himself will be with them to the end of the world [cf Mt 28:20]. And I must help in carrying out this task: this is my vocation, already as a Jesuit and a priest and now in my very special position. The Holy Spirit has enlightened me in this retreat on this precise point and my 'decision' lays special emphasis on this. Through Mary I put my resolution into the hands and heart of our Lord, for him to bless them as he blessed the disciples and their work before his ascension [cf Lk 24:50 f].

VIII/4 *Love* [Exercises 230–237] This meditation sums up everything that these days of grace have given me, my special vocation and also my special obligations. I must always be aware of the presence of God, and see God in everything that is true, great and beautiful, but above all work for God. I am so fortunate that all my work is only for God: I exist only for this, and if God continues to give me strength, then it is only to enable me to go on working for him.

2.VIII.65

FROM THE MONTHLY RECOLLECTIONS

13.IX.1964
All my powers belong to God: an instrument of God's saving will (I/2): a solid spiritual life: faithfulness in my spiritual exercises; gaining new light and strength from them every day. Faithful, calm, patient in work; simple, uncomplicated, unassuming, humble.

I/1 Must not tax my powers unnecessarily. Everything from him and for him.
I/2 My privilege is my task; spiritual independence.
I/3 Without any false inclinations or aversions; no inordinate considerations or search for approval.
I/4 No minimalism—a maximum of grace, a maximum of effort.
II/1 Show love in my daily contacts; in my work and judgments; think of God in all my actions.

4.X.1964
A spirit of faith: following in all things the model of our Lord (a life of virtue, of apostolic work). Light and strength from my spiritual exercises, supernatural prudence and love in everything: good example for all.

II/2 Struggle against sin in the world.
II/3 No over-estimation of myself: everything is from God and everything is for God—remain humble—make use of criticism.
II/4 Maximum of grace—maximum of effort!
III/1 'Follow me'—poor and humble like our Lord!

III/2 Devotion without drawing back and without reservation!
III/3 Christ the centre of my spiritual life and work!

8.IX.1964
Maximum of grace—maximum of effort—prayer and a solid spiritual life: every day derive light and strength from my spiritual life—care over little things—do faithfully, patiently and calmly what every day brings—simple, straightforward, unassuming, humble.

III/4 My personal responsibility—always ready to learn—even from younger people!

12.XII.1964
1) Generous and faithful in carrying out my religious duties.
2) Prayer and a solid spiritual life in imitation of the divine Lord.
3) Supernatural wisdom, prudence, straightforwardness, simplicity, patience, even in unimportant work.

IV/1 (1962)[19] In order to be 'born in utter destitution'—not always on the look-out for the easiest way—not for the sake of convenience—in order 'after all his labours' to 'die on the cross'.
IV/2 (1962) Exact in everything out of a spirit of faith—'to do thy will'—'a sign that is spoken against'.
IV/3 (1962) The hidden life: love!—patient, ordered work;—visitors: always friendly!

6.I.1965
1) All my powers for God and only for him.
2) An instrument of God's saving will (I/2) for as many as possible.
3) As a 'praying cardinal' I must draw strength and light daily from my spiritual life.
4) Do faithfully and calmly what every day demands.
5) Be an example to all with whom I have to deal.

IV/2 My position is not for me, but for the Church and souls; put all my heart into it.
IV/3 Functions: not for my benefit; from supernatural considerations; unlimited trust in Mary. Always and everywhere I must have the great apostolic interests at heart, even in my ordinary work.
IV/4 Eager (hunger and thirst) in my search for an intensive spiritual life; reconciling and mediating . . .; a light by my example!

5.II.1965
1) Doing and teaching[20]—be an example to all!—a 'praying cardinal'; total devotion to the task . . .—a solid spiritual life; doing faithfully, patiently and calmly what every day brings, and not letting myself be

---

[19] The references here are to the 1962 retreat not, as usual, to the retreat just past.
[20] Cf Acts 1:1: 'In the first book, O Theophilus, I have dealt with all that Jesus began to do and to teach. . . .'

influenced by moods. Work: supernatural prudence, honesty, simplicity, patient work even in small things.

V/1 Unite myself more closely with him by prayer and in prayer; an intensive spiritual life.

V/2 Storms do not harm the Church! but there must be hard rowing, do my duty! our Lord praying and watching!

V/3 The beloved disciples are sent—'mission': my task!—modest, simple, unassuming, straightforward.

V/4 Help the Church to come to the world.

7.III.1965

1) 'We put no obstacle in anyone's way' (2 Cor 6:3)[21]—an example for all.

2) Strength from my spiritual life (meditation examination of conscience), light.

3) In all things I must show myself a minister of God . . . 'in honour and dishonour' (2 Cor 6:8).

4) Simple, unassuming, humble.

VI/1 All friendship must be ruled by supernatural considerations; a heart full of human kindness: a priest who can 'sympathize with our weaknesses'.

VI/2 Invitations accepted in order to do good. Not an apostle who criticizes—such a one is a scandal—in public: kindness, gentleness, tenderness!

16.IV.1965

1) All my powers for God.
2) Fulfilment of God's will, down to the last detail.
3) True to the inspirations of the Holy Ghost.
4) Spiritual exercises—faithfully and fully.

VI/3 Fight with the weapons of truth, but in love, not human respect.

VI/4 Visits to the Blessed Sacrament.

VII/1 Courage and strength from Christ's passion in all difficulties, even in the small daily difficulties.

VII/2 For this I have the example of Christ's passion and the 'power from on high' (Holy Spirit).

Passion of Christ strengthen me . . .; faithful devotion to my work.

9.V.1965

Maximum of grace—maximum of effort!; all my powers for God. An

---

[21] 2 Cor 6:2–10 was a passage from which Bea obviously drew inspiration at this time. It was also the inspiration of the prologue to the first edition of the Constitutions of the Society of Jesus, known today as the *Summa et scopus nostrarum Constitutionum*.

instrument of the saving will of God (I/2). Imitate our Lord's life of virtue. Success rests on God's grace—do faithfully, patiently and calmly what every day brings.

VII/3 'Silent': must not defend myself for the sake of unimportant matters. How often it does not matter whether I am right or wrong—objective, unbiased, kind, friendly.

VI/4 Christ chose the cross for himself! And out of love for me, for me!

VIII/1 Must not confine myself to the externals, but do things from the heart: 'opened his side'!

13.VI.1965
1) Faithfulness in carrying out my religious duties (a 'praying cardinal').
2) Imitate the apostolic virtues of our Lord.
3) Do each day's work faithfully, patiently and calmly.
4) Simple, straightforward, unassuming, humble.

VIII/1 An attitude of love (the Heart of Jesus!)—all must come from the heart—I shall love to the end: to the very end!—no miserliness or bargaining . . .'I shall be completely spent for souls'.

VIII/2 I shall be with you till the end of time—my privilege to serve the Church!

VIII/3 I have the 'power from on high'.

VIII/4 All my work only for God and the interests of God.

3.X.1965
Gratitude for the great graces—total devotion to my work—doing faithfully, patiently and tranquilly what every day brings.—Straightforwardness, simplicity, patient work in small things—edify by my example.

I/1 Everything from him and through him, not from myself! Everything only for him!

I/2 Spiritually independent—very special graces and vocation!

I/3 The 'world' should be a positive help for me: knowledge, culture . . . must not reject anything that can help me, for my health and strength as well! Everything can be a means of leading in to God.

7.XI.1965
Carrying out religious duties (examination of conscience, rosary); every day new strength and new light.—Total devotion to my work. Imitation of our Lord's life of virtue.

I/4 The ideal of the most perfect possible service of God.

II/1 Please our Lord in things which are not prescribed by law.

Our Lord's example of consideration and love.

II/2 The power of sin today.

II/3 Have a correct estimation of myself and be humble. Criticism: learn from this!

II/4 'Follow me', even where there are difficulties and obstacles!

12.XII.1965

1) All my power only for God and souls.
2) Imitate the apostolic virtues of our Lord.
3) Humble in success and recognition.
4) Faithful, patient, calm, kind to all.

III/1 Poor and humble, like Jesus and Mary.

III/2 'Lo, I have come to do thy will'—'I have finished . . .'—'let it be done to me according to your word'; the strict and uncompromising will of God without reservation.

III/3 Christ the centre of my spiritual life.

CHAPTER 9

'Let us run with perseverance the race that is set before us'

1965

Throughout July and August 1965 the cardinal was seriously ill. For this reason he was unable to make his annual retreat in the summer holidays as usual and had to put it off until after the end of the Council, January 1966. Therefore this chapter covers the period up to the end of the Council. There is a variety of reasons why the passage from Hebrews, taken as the title of this chapter, is so apt. It is an admonition to the reader: 'therefore, since we are surrounded by so great a crowd of witnesses . . . let us run with perseverance the race that is set before us' (Heb 12:1). This period was indeed in many respects like a race: there were stormy developments, great and decisive events followed one another, and the amount of work done by the cardinal himself, after the strenuous years of the Council was, purely from the physical point of view, really astounding.

The beginning of the third session was notable for the return of the relic of St Andrew's head to the Orthodox Archdiocese of Patras, an event that was historically very important. After the veneration of the relic by the whole Council assembly in a unique ceremony, the cardinal, as the head of the special papal mission, flew to Patras where the relic was received with great religious enthusiasm. The impression made on the Orthodox Church was also great. Pope Paul VI and the third Pan-orthodox Conference, which was meeting in the island of Rhodes in November, exchanged friendly messages. At the end of the Conference nearly all the participants made a pilgrimage to Patras to venerate the relic. Apart from the two official reports on the relationship of the Church to Non-Christian religions (the former schema on the relationship with the Jews), the cardinal also intervened five times in the discussion in his own right, as a father of the Council. In the first place he suggested various ecumenical considerations in the schema on the Mother of God: in the discussion on divine revelation he spoke of the importance of the scriptures, both Old and New Testaments, for the Church; and his other contributions were to the Constitution on the Church in the Modern World, to the decree on the Church's Missionary

Activity and to the decree on the Appropriate Renewal of the Religious Life.

At the end of this session he had the great joy of seeing the Decree on Ecumenism accepted with what amounted to a unanimous vote (of 2,137 votes only 11 were opposed!). His lecturing activity which began with the world octave of prayer in 1965, was devoted principally to the theme: 'The Course of the Council and Christian Unity'. On this subject he spoke in Munich (18 January)—and here again the biggest halls were not big enough to hold all the audience—then at Wurzburg (20 January) and Cologne (8 February) Universities.

Lecture tours, however, were not all that he was engaged in. On 18 February he paid an official visit to the headquarters of the World Council of Churches in Geneva. The climax of this visit was his announcement that the Catholic Church accepted the proposal made by the Central Committee of the World Council of Churches, announced a month before, to set up a joint committee of representatives from both sides. The committee's job was to investigate the possibilities and methods of dialogue and cooperation, and to put them to the competent groups for confirmation. This event was important enough in itself but it was reinforced by another: an official meeting between the cardinal and the Ex-President of the World Council of Churches, Pastor M. Boegner. It was significant that this meeting took place in the 'Reformation Room'.

No less important was the cardinal's official journey to Constantinople at the head of a special papal delegation (2–5 April). An official delegation from the Ecumenical Patriarch of Constantinople, in the name of the third Pan-Orthodox Conference, had informed the pope of the decisions of that Conference in February. The visit of the cardinal was meant as a sort of reply to this important visit. It represented a real milestone in the development of mutual relations between Rome and Constantinople. In fact it was the first time since the schism in the eleventh century that such a high representative of the Holy Father had visited the Ecumenical Patriarch in an official capacity.

The delegation handed the patriarch a personal message from the pope, and its president had discussions on the further development of the relations between the two groups. One particularly moving scene occurred when the cardinal, after taking part in the Orthodox liturgy, came out of the church with the Ecumenical Patriarch Athenagoras and walked through the crowd of faithful from various Churches. The patriarch repeatedly invited him to give the assembled crowd his blessing which was received by the faithful with indescribable enthusiasm.

In the meantime, before and after this journey, there were long plenary sessions of the Secretariat for Unity (28 February–6 March; 9–15 May. The object was definitive editing and despatch of the remaining Council schemata on religious freedom and the relationship of the Church with the Non-Christian religions. At the end of April the cardinal made his second American tour, in order to receive the International Brotherhood's Prize in Philadelphia. But all this was really too much for his strength. At the end of June he fell ill, and in spite of every effort the cause could not be identified although over-work was certainly a factor. When the usual medical help and care had proved of no avail, he spent about a month (20 July– 17 August) in a hospital in Zurich. Finally he tried to regain his strength near his home, by Lake Constance.

He returned in a slightly better state of health and took a strenuous part in the last session of the Council. Apart from the official report introducing for the last time the declaration on the relationship of the Church to Christian religions, he spoke on two other occasions; once on *The Church in the World of Today*, and once on the schema on the ministry and life of priests: in this latter speech he wished to draw special attention to the respect due to the special tradition in the East with regard to celibacy.

The end of the Council brought him great joy, in the first place the acceptance and publication of the two hotly debated declarations, 'On Religious Freedom' and 'The Relationship of the Church to Non-Christian Religions'. In the final vote on these documents there had still been respectively 249 and 250 votes against, but in a secret vote at the public final session these sank surprisingly to seventy and eighty (of about 2,300 votes) respectively. Nor, happily, was there any sign of a repetition of the unpleasant reaction against the Jews that the declaration on the Jews had caused in Arab countries the previous year. Another really great joy was the lifting of the mutual excommunication between Rome and Constantinople, which was historically and psychologically so important.

But it must be admitted that he had come to the limit of his endurance. On the urgent advice of his doctor he did not take part in the solemn conclusion of the Council in the square of St Peter's. The notes, written a few weeks later in his retreat, are significant from various points of view. In the meditation on the hidden life of our Lord he said: 'Now the time has come when I can really imitate our Lord's hidden life. The will of God is making itself known in the decline of my powers. He could have called me away altogether. And if he has not done that it shows that I have still work to do for his kingdom, even in the hidden life. So it is not a time of inactivity, but of intensive work, inwardly and outwardly' (III/2). And again; 'Now that I have not so much work to do outside, I must be all the more active in prayer: and I must really be a "praying cardinal" ' (III/3).

RETREAT 1965

Rome Brazilian College, 14–19 January 1966

I/1 *This is the whole duty of man*[1] I have nothing else to do except to honour God and keep his commandments. Everything else is 'vanity': St Augustine: 'he is not reformed according to the image of truth, but remains still in the shape of vanity' (*City of God* 20, 3). I exist to reflect in myself the 'image of God'. For this he created me in a wonderful way and equipped me both with physical powers and especially with spiritual qualities. But there is more than that: there is the whole position—and with it the destiny—that God has given me. The most unlikely circumstances produced first the student, then the priest, the professor and scholar, then the bishop and cardinal. But none of this is due to me, it is God who has given me one after the other. And why? Clearly so that I may be more like him, my model; a reflection of his image. 'This is the whole duty of man.' In other words I must become holy, as he is holy, and make others like him in holiness. Everything else: reputation, influence, success—or even the opposite—mean nothing: 'This is the whole duty of man.'

I/2 *The way of sanctity* Holiness is already a necessity for me as a man, but still more as a priest and apostle: 'Take heed to yourself', first 'to yourself' then 'to all the flock' [cf 1 Tim 4:16; Acts 20:28]. If I am not holy, then I shall not be able to win others and give them a longing for holiness. My first step must, then, be to attend to my own holiness and to awaken and foster in myself the ideal of sanctity. For this I have meditation, prayer and reading, and I must not neglect these. But then my vocation itself and my practice of it are a source of holiness. *Esto de te habentibus unus* (St Bernard).[2] In the first place by the instructions and advice I give to others and the influence they have on me. But: *quidquid recipitur ad modum recipientis.*[3] So it is always presupposed that I am holy myself and therefore receptive! In that case unpleasantness, difficulties, disappointments, lack of appreciation and so on can be a help to me. They will only confirm and encourage me and so make me holier. In this way everything is a means of holiness for me: '. . . in everything God works for good with those who love him'— 'those who love him' [cf Rom 8:28].

I/3 *To the eternal home* [cf Eccl 12:5] An eternity depends on this life. But the thought of this should not frighten me, it should rather

---

[1] 'Fear God, and keep his commandments; for this is the whole duty of man' (Eccl 12:13).
[2] 'Put yourself in the place of one of those entrusted to your care, and take care of yourself in the same way.'
[3] An axiom of scholastic philosophy: a man is not passive under external influences but assimilates them according to his character.

encourage and strengthen me. If God has guided me for eighty-five years with special love, then this is a sign that he also intends to give me a happy eternity. But I must cooperate. It is precisely this guidance and love which show that God does not expect small things from me, and that I must live up to this guidance. So it is not enough for me to avoid sin, both serious and venial; nor is it enough for me to pay attention to the small and even the smallest matters. God has given me a great task. And I must do it as he wants it done. Praise or blame have no part to play in this: they are just 'concomitant phenomena': the essential thing is the matter in hand. Nor must I be afraid of difficulties; they are the 'slight momentary affliction'; and in contrast there is the 'eternal weight of glory' [cf 2 Cor 4:17]. So I must do all that my position demands without regard to men, and do everything well so that, as far as depends on me, it may have a lasting value for the kingdom of God and souls; then it will also have lasting value for my eternity. 20.II.66

I/4 *Recollection* Recollection is not as easy for me as for those who have simple work to do that only occupies their outward attention. But for this very reason I must concentrate on it especially. And I do have many opportunities for this: at the beginning of work, during breaks in my work, while travelling, at the start of conversations and meetings and so on. Often there is a prayer beforehand—but how distractedly and, so to speak, absently, it is said! In all things I shall seek—I shall find—God:[4] that is after all my goal.
a. In prayer—(meditation, examination of conscience, breviary): beforehand: during (by avoiding distractions): and at the end. The result: 'worthily, attentively, and devoutly'.[5]
b. In work: St Paul 'the care of all the Churches'—and yet a man with such an interior life! St Ignatius! Before work, during pauses, in difficulties. Not a 'busyness', no 'activism': God's company in everything.
c. In daily contacts (visits, consultations etc). Beforehand recollection. With whom? How? What to avoid? What to encourage? and so on.

So I must be a man with an interior life in spite of all outward activity. Then in everything that I do I shall also be faithful, calm, objective and kind, balanced, even tempered: in God!

II/1 *The spiritual exercises*[6] They take up a considerable part of my day and so I must take care that these hours are not lost but made fruitful for my soul and for its main purpose: the honour and glory of God. It is not enough to seek this through my work: God also demands the 'sacrifice of the lips'.[7] And my soul is in need of these spiritual

---

[4] A constantly recurring idea, from the Constitutions of the Society of Jesus.
[5] From a prayer said before beginning the office.
[6] Referring not to the annual retreat, but the daily practice of prayer in all its forms.
[7] Cf Ps 50:23: 'He who brings thanksgiving as his sacrifice honours me.' Cf also Heb 13:15: 'Through Christ then let us continually offer up a sacrifice of praise to God, that is, the fruit of the lips that acknowledge his name.'

exercises: they should give it light and strength and perseverance in doing what is right. Without them I should soon become an automaton and my life would become simply a matter of external activity. But for a priest this means a real corruption and destroys his influence on souls.

So I must
1.) do conscientiously all that I can do in my situation: especially meditation and examination of conscience, then;
2.) do everything well and in a spirit of recollection: this means avoiding distractions and struggling against involuntary ones and driving them away as soon as I notice them.
3.) And ask for the grace always to pray well, recollectively and devoutly. Lord teach me how to pray [Lk 11:1].

I 'must ask for the grace of devotion with earnestness, must seek it with desire . . . and keep it with humility' (cf *Imit.* IV, 15).

II/2 *Purity of soul* Free me from all vain, perverse and wrong thoughts, words, actions[8]—that covers the whole area of the purity of soul. So it is not just a matter of keeping free from serious sin, but of warding off anything that can stain my soul. This is important for me, not only because of my human dignity but above all for me as a priest, as an apostle, as a prominent member of the hierarchy, very much in the public eye. History teaches us the truth of the saying: 'corruptio optimi pessima': so many schisms would never have happened if only the clergy, especially the higher clergy, had given good example, if they had not sought their own ends in their words and deeds, but God and souls. A word from me carries far more weight than one from any ordinary priest. Apart from that I am a religious and must be mindful of the example of so many holy religious and try to be worthy of them. The means of achieving this purity of soul: 1) pray for it; 2) watchfulness in my dealings with people, and 3) especially the examination of conscience, both the general examination, and, where necessary, the particular examination too. And it is especially in this examination that I can review the opportunities that are likely to come my way for good and also for mistakes. But the most important thing is the will to work seriously on myself (cf *Imit.* IV, 11).[9]

II/3 *The kingdom of Christ* Our Lord is a king: but he has still to conquer his kingdom [cf 1 Cor 15:25]. During his life on earth he began this conquest and sacrificed everything for it: possessions, family, honour and finally his life. Comfort and convenience and so on never played any part in his life. But for the complete conquest of the kingdom he needs

---

[8] From the prayer said before beginning the office.
[9] Chapter IV of the *Imitation* is a long one; the cardinal is probably thinking of what it has to say on the purity necessary for the priest as minister of the holy Eucharist.

fellow-workers, ready to sacrifice themselves for it as he sacrificed himself, without looking for anything for themselves. These helpers differ according to their disposition and according to the destiny and grace that he gives them. The history of the Church knows so many of them. Different as they are, they are all one in devoting themselves to their task wholeheartedly and in spite of all of the sacrifices that it involves, without regard to their own wishes. And I am one of those whom he has chosen himself, whom he has prepared and guided, not through any merits of mine but simply through his grace. Therefore I must sacrifice myself unreservedly for the task that he has given me in his army, and in all my actions follow his example, without thinking of my earthly wishes in doing this. It is clear that this must involve sacrifice. But it is precisely here that faithfulness in my ministry lies. Therefore my solution can only be: 'Take, Lord, into your possession, all my freedom of action . . . all that I have, all that I own:—it is your gift to me, I now return it to you' [Exercises 234]. So an instrument devoted to him at all times and in all things—according to his own example.

13.III.66

II/4 *Blessed are the poor* The birth of our Lord in Bethlehem in the utter destitution of the cave has been willed and brought about by him [cf 2 Cor 8:9]. From the beginning he wants to show the role of poverty in his kingdom. It is the Gospel of poverty that he preaches; even the rich must be 'poor in spirit' [Mt 5:3]. His missionaries are also poor in the material sense and for this reason they have access to the poorest of people in this world. And Christ's apostles addressed themselves to the poor; 'for theirs is the kingdom of heaven'. But they also take care of them: the charitable activity of the Church is the result of our Lord's poverty.[10] The poverty of the crib also attracts the children, the children of the poor, and teaches the faithful to bear material poverty in the spirit of our Lord, who, though he was rich, yet for our sake . . . became poor, so that by his poverty we might become rich [2 Cor 8:9]. This poverty must also go with me in my position in the Church, all the more so as I took the vow of poverty in the Society. As far as I can I too must be the friend of the poor and show myself to be such. (General confession: Father Danti).

III/1 *The presentation in the temple* [Lk 2:22–35] The first visit of our Lord to the temple is also the occasion of the announcement of his passion. A sacrifice has been offered for him; but it is himself that he

---

[10] Cf Vatican II, in the Constitution on the Church: 'Christ was sent by the Father "to bring good news to the poor, to heal the contrite of heart" (Lk 4:18), "to seek and to save what was lost" (Lk 19:10). Similarly, the Church encompasses with love all those who are afflicted with human weakness.

Indeed, she recognizes in the poor and the suffering the likeness of her poor and suffering Founder. She does all she can to relieve their need and in them she strives to serve Christ' (8).

offers in the first place: 'Lo, I have come to do thy will.' This will of the Father is his cross. While Simeon is proclaiming his great mission: 'a light for revelation to the Gentiles, and for glory to thy people Israel', he prophesies at once the struggle that he will have: 'for the fall and rising of many'. Men's true characters are revealed when they meet Christ: 'he came to his home, and his own people received him not' [Jn 1:11]. This is the first picture in the meditation on the kingdom. And Mary, who is nearest to him, is immediately drawn into the struggle: a sword of sorrow will pierce her soul—she is altogether innocent; but she must suffer with him because she stands by him. This is the destiny and the programme of those who want to show great enthusiasm for him [cf Exercises 97]. It is also my great programme. Fiat! Fiat!

III/2 *The hidden life* Now the time has come when I can really imitate our Lord's hidden life. The will of God is making itself known in the decline of my powers. He could have called me away altogether. And if he has not done that, it shows that I have still work to do for his kingdom, even in the hidden life. So it is not a time of inactivity but of intensive work, inwardly and outwardly: and now I can also work on my own perfection more than in past years—so a perfect spiritual life; prayer, patience and suffering in an apostolic spirit, efforts to advance in virtue which, as a religious, a priest, a bishop and a cardinal, I must develop by meditation, reading and examination. Outward work: I am not dispensed from apostolic activity by my retirement. I can and I must do it not only by prayer and sacrifice but also by active help; advice, planning, consultations. Especially in this respect I have a great deal to do in the many tasks that I still have; in study, reports and also by publishing books.[11] So for the time being I am far from having nothing to do. I can and I must still do a good deal for my own spiritual progress and for the kingdom of God, just as our Lord did during the long years of his hidden life.   17.IV.66

III/3 *'When Jesus also had been baptized and was praying'* [Lk 3:21]. Our Lord offers thanks after his baptism: but he also thinks of the millions and millions who will receive the grace of baptism, and prays for them, just as he also prays for the apostles before choosing them [cf Lk 6:12 f]. Our Lord at prayer must be my model. I have the opportunity—and the duty—of praying so often during the day. My daily life is, as it were, framed by prayer, prayer of supplication and of thanksgiving (cf II/1). I must use all these opportunities faithfully. Now that I have not so much work to do outside, I must be all the more active

---

[11] Between this time and his death the author published various radio talks and articles etc, and the following books: *The Way to Unity after the Council* (Chapman, 1967), *The Church and Mankind* (Chapman, 1967), *The Word of God and Mankind* (Chapman, 1968), *Ecumenism in Focus* (Chapman, 1969), *We who serve* (Chapman, 1969).

in prayer: I must really be a 'praying cardinal'. I have enough intentions to pray for, not only personal ones but above all apostolic ones for myself and for the others. I must seize these opportunities like our Lord on the eve of important occasions (cf the choice of the apostles). But I must also offer thanks for all that God does for me and the Church. Today especially, after the Council, I have special reasons for deep gratitude.

III/4 *'I chose you'—my apostolate* [cf Jn 15:16] As a bishop, a successor of the apostles, I share this apostolate in the full sense, and its duties and fruits. But this is through no merit of mine: 'You did not choose me.' The results are due neither to my talents nor to my work: 'I chose you . . . that you should go and bear fruit.' Of course I could refuse his call; and it is another of his special graces that I have not done so. In the deepest sense it is true 'I chose you'. To what end? He is the 'apostle of our confession' (Heb 3:1). Sent by the Father to save men. And we apostles are 'servants (of Christ) and stewards of the mysteries of God' [cf 1 Cor 4:1]; so we are ambassadors for Christ [2 Cor 5:20]. We must then bring his light: he enlightens every man by coming into the world [cf Jn 1:9]. And we must make the most of his strength: salt of the earth [Mt 5:13]. So our task as apostles is quite fixed. How I do it depends again on him, all that is required of me is that I should do it, as he wants. This also determines the present form of my apostolate. But, as always: if I have the will to do it properly he helps me; I have appointed you that you should go. The apostolate, then, is not left to my whim; I am an apostle to my last breath—but the manner of it is determined by him and revealed to me by the circumstances.

IV/1 *The Sermon on the Mount* This sermon is not just addressed to Israel but to the whole world, to the whole human family. From the beginning our Lord is thinking of the whole of mankind, to which he wants to bring salvation. 'A light for revelation to the Gentiles' [Lk 2:32]. Today the Church has become more conscious of this task and has regained the spirit of the apostle of the Gentiles. I too must cultivate this world-embracing attitude in myself and in others, far removed from all narrowness. For this reason in my meditations and reading I must get to know the whole world with its needs, sufferings, faults and errors, and try to bring it to our Lord, through my prayers and sacrifices at least. This is also the spirit of our Society, which numbers among its members men like St Robert Bellarmine as well as a man like St Francis Xavier, the great apostle to the heathen.

15.V.66

IV/2 *I am the good shepherd* [Jn 10:14 ff] Even though I have no direct jurisdiction, I do have many opportunities, indeed I have the positive duty to follow the example of the 'good shepherd'. In all the congregations and commissions and so on I must be active in his spirit, 'he knows his sheep': so I must study all situations thoroughly, people as well as things. He comes 'to seek what was lost' [cf Lk 10:10], but not by force, instead 'he takes it upon his shoulders' and brings it lovingly back to the flock. For this no effort must be too great, even when the way lies through thorns and thistles. Sacrifices and difficulties are also a means of bringing all to the one fold. 'He leads them to pasture': as far as I am able I must see to it that everyone finds good and sufficient spiritual nourishment. All this is a great undertaking. But even now in my old age I can live up to it and God has prepared me for it and gives me light and strength. Christ's flock needs work like this and every worker must do his best. 'Tend the flock of God that is your charge . . . being examples to the flock' (1 Pet 5:2).

IV/3 *The holy Eucharist* In this sacrament our Lord gives us the greatest gift that he can give us: himself. It is the fulfilment of everything that religions strive after: we have the sacrifice, we have the union of the God-Man with us, and we have 'God with us'.[12] This is not mere speculation, it is the word of our Lord himself. To prove this it is enough to read and meditate on John 6 and the words of institution [Mt 26:36 ff and parallels]. But all this applies to me in a very special way: every day it is my privilege to offer Mass, every day to receive the Lord in holy communion and unite myself with him; I have him present all the time only a few yards away in my chapel. Would it not be the height of ingratitude if I did not make the right use of all these graces? And not only the 'right' use but the most zealous and pious use? I must let all my day's work be penetrated by this presence and union, and find in this my greatest devotion. So to cultivate a very special love for the holy Eucharist and develop it must be my aim. 'A sacrament of piety— a sign of unity—the bond of charity'.[13] 'A pledge of glory.'[14]

IV/4 *The farewell address—the sermon on unity* In the light of the farewell address Christianity is seen to be something quite different from a list of do's and don'ts: it is the living image of the unity of the Trinity. The observance of the commandments is simply a proof that one is imitating this model.[15] This frame of mind penetrates every part of our life, in our love for Christ. He is not just a model of the virtues: he is himself for us a realization of the unity and love between the Persons of the Trinity, so much so that we have grown with him like

---

[12] Cf Mt 1:22 f: 'And his name shall be called Emmanuel (which means, God with us) (Is 7:14).'

[13] Augustine, in his *Johannis Evangelium Tractatus* XXVI, chap. VI, 13, PL 35, 1613.

[14] From the Roman breviary, the antiphon to the Magnificat from Second Vespers of the feast of Corpus Christi: 'O sacrum Convivium'.

[15] Cf Jn 15:9 f: 'As the Father has loved me, so have I loved you; abide in my love. If you keep my commandments, you will abide in my love, just as I have kept my Father's commandments and abide in his love.'

F

the branches with the vine, and all our 'fruits' are simply the result and the product of this profound unity [cf Jn 15:1 f]. The Eucharist, the 'sign of unity', is the thing that nourishes this fruitful unity [cf Jn 6:56 f]. Even love of neighbour is not just a 'sense of family' or 'friendship' or sympathy, but once again the image of this union between the Persons of the Trinity and of our union with Christ.[16] This is why it is a 'new' commandment, 'my commandment', the proof of our love for him and the image of this love [cf Jn 13:34]. Where this is missing there is no real Christianity. Therefore I must practise it and encourage it everywhere, apart from and beyond all natural motives. The heathen could have friendship: but there was no genuine love of neighbour in their case and there is none today either, away from Christ. 'By this all men will know that you are my disciples, if you have love for one another' (Jn 13:35).

V/1 *In the garden of olives* I can see the effectiveness of prayer when I look at our Lord: earlier he was filled with fear, anxiety and reluctance [Lk 14:33 f]. Now he advances to meet his enemies with remarkable firmness: 'Whom do you seek?' (Jn 18:47). And all the time not one harsh word, not one sign of hostility, neither towards the guards nor towards the apostles, whose flight and lack of loyalty he foresees, nor towards Peter, who is going to deny him in not many hours' time, nor even towards the traitor Judas: 'friend' [Mt 26:50]. In every situation I too must look for strength in prayer, but in prayer which is serious, fervent and concrete, like our Lord's prayer in the Garden: full of trust but at the same time completely resigned: 'Not my will but thine!' God is always the 'Father': 'Father, if thou art willing' [Lk 22:42].

V/2 *The cross* is the height of shame and of pain, but also the height of love. The love shows itself already in the choice of the cross as the instrument of salvation. Our Lord carrying his cross has become for countless people a source of comfort and strength. The death on the cross shows the love more clearly and impressively than any other martyrdom that is quickly over and leaves no lasting impression. But here we read: 'they looked on him whom they pierced'. The cross has become the sign of Christ's religion and even children are taught about the love of our Lord through the picture of the cross. If Jesus' enemies insisted on the crucifixion: 'let us condemn him to a shameful death',[17] then they achieved precisely the opposite effect: the cross has become the sign of love, of power and of honour. This is why our Lord did not defend himself—'but Jesus was silent' [Mt 26:63]—and, as St Andrew

---

[16] Cf Jn 15:12 ff: 'This is my commandment, that you love one another as I have loved you.'

[17] Cf Wisdom 2:19 f: 'Let us test him (the righteous one) with insult and torture, that we may find out how gentle he is, and make trial of his forbearance. Let us condemn him to a shameful death, for, according to what he says, he will be protected.'

is said to have done, welcomes the cross: 'Hail, Holy Cross',[18] I too, then, must welcome every cross that our Lord asks me to carry.   19.VI.66

V/3 *Speaking of the kingdom of God* [Acts 1:3]   The forty days after the resurrection are the time when our Lord teaches them about the Church, in fact the time of the foundation of the Church. Our Lord gives them firm faith [Lk 24:44 ff]; he also gives the sacraments, he sets up the organization of the Church and determines its nature [Jn 20:21 f]. It is his Church: 'feed my sheep'; Peter and the other apostles are only the 'ambassadors of Christ' and 'the stewards of the mysteries of God'[1 Cor 4:1]. They have no dictatorial powers, but are to feed the flock lovingly. The unity of the flock is guaranteed through Peter, who is given care of the 'lambs and sheep'. But Peter is not going to live for ever, either: so someone else must step into his position. The other apostles share his teaching office and his pastoral office and his priesthood: '... make disciples ... baptizing them ... teaching them' (Mt 28:18 f). The Church is not confined to one land or to one people: 'all nations'. Our Lord has complete power over the Church; he remains with it for ever [Mt 28:20]. But he exercises this power through the Holy Spirit whom he sends [cf Jn 16:8 ff]. The Church, then, is our Lord's masterpiece, the fruit of his life and suffering and of his resurrection. It is my privilege to serve it.

V/4 *Love*   My love for God cannot consist in feelings, it must be a matter of deeds. There must be progress in my spiritual life, even if I feel nothing. It must be a matter of the will and of deeds: deeds, wherever the actual circumstances make it possible, will, to do even more, if the chance is given to me and in whatever form it is given to me.

God has given me much, extraordinarily much. I can only repay him by making everything bear fruit for myself and for the kingdom of God, as I have just now resolved once again in my 'decision'.

The presence of God in everything teaches me to see him in everything. More frequent recollection should help me to walk more and more in the presence of God, to see him in everyone and everything. To see him also in all that he does. Whatever happens to me does not happen without him. Everything comes from his loving providence for me. For this reason I must also derive benefit for my soul and my apostolate from everything, both pleasant and unpleasant. 'In everything God works for good with those who love him' [cf Rom 8:28]. And finally whenever I see something great and beautiful I should rejoice and remember that everything in God is greater and more beautiful. 'To ascend to God the Creator from creatures' (St Robert Bellarmine).

Now I thank our Lord for the great graces of this retreat which has indeed been short but blessed, to him be honour and glory!   18.I.66

---

[18] Cf Roman breviary, on the feast of St Andrew (Nov. 30).

FROM THE MONTHLY RECOLLECTIONS

18.II.1966
1) Recollection and walking in the presence of God (in detail) at every moment.
2) In the midst of all outward activity, remain a man of interior life.
3) Sacrifice—an apostolic spirit.
4) The apostolate of example.

I/1 I must become holy, as he is holy: 'this is the whole duty of man'.
I/2 'Take heed to yourself': so examination of conscience! Esto de te habentibus unus (St Bernard).
I/3 God has given me a great task and I must perform it well.

13.III.1966
1) Obligation to aim high: holy—apostolic.
2) Recollection and walking in the presence of God.
3) Do everything in the spirit of the Good Shepherd.
4) Meditation and examination conscientiously.

I/4 Recollection: renew this again and again!
II/1 No exterior 'busyness'.
II/2 In the public eye. The will to work seriously on myself.

17.IV.1966
1) Recollection frequently during the day.
2) Raising the mind to God before the various activities.
3) Amidst all outward activity remain an interior recollected man.
4) Be patient, calm, objective, kind.
5) Quiet but intensive work.

II/3 (Christ needs) helpers who sacrifice themselves entirely and do not pursue their own interests!
II/4 The importance of poverty for apostolic activity.
III/2 Work in seclusion for Christ's kingdom and work on my sanctification.

15.V.1966
1) Special obligation to holiness.
2) Before every important act a minute of recollection [cf below: 19.VI.1966], and also for my dealings with others.
3) Faithful, balanced, objective, kind, patient.
4) Spirit of sacrifice (modest).

III/3 My day's work framed by prayer; work through prayer!
III/4 My share in the apostolate!—to bring our Lord!
IV/1 Concern for the world: a world-embracing interest.

19.VI.1966

1) A man with an interior life, recollected in God.
2) Walk in God's presence (recollection before all important actions).
3) Work in the spirit of the Good Shepherd (prayer, devotion, sacrifice).
4) The apostolate of example.

IV/2 Work in the spirit of the Good Shepherd (I know—I bring—I take)—Prayer, devotion, sacrifice.

IV/3 A visit to the Blessed Sacrament morning and afternoon.

IV/4 Grown up with Christ: you in me and I in you!—love of neighbour—the realization of the unity in Christ.

V/1 Prayers as a means of love and unity.

V/2 The cross always before my eyes as a sign of love 'to the end' [cf John 13:1].

CHAPTER 10

'Now the time for a hidden life has come for me'

1966

Since 1959 the author has been stressing in his notes the meaning and the value of the hidden life: 'As far as it depends on me, I must work quietly and unobtrusively and not look for sensational and remarkable events'. But there is now a decidedly more actual note: 'after the busy years a time of seclusion has come for me too' (V/3). The visits of the cardinal to Geneva and Constantinople did form a sort of ideal conclusion to his travels. Naturally he continued to receive invitations to give lectures in various places and in various countries, but in practice he hardly ever accepted them, so that many people, concerned for his health, asked why. There were various reasons. In the first place the condition of his health now made it advisable for him to husband his powers, after the long and serious illness of July and August 1965. But there were other considerations that were more important and more decisive for him. After the end of the Council there were many things in Rome waiting for his attention: apart from being the president of the Secretariat for Christian Unity he had also been chairman since December 1965 of the commission for the new edition of the Vulgate; and he was also a member of two other post-conciliar bodies—the Consilium for the implementation of the reforms in the liturgy and the Commission for the reform of Canon Law—and of six bodies concerned with the ordinary central government of the Church besides. In all these spheres his object was to safeguard the aims of the Council, especially the ecumenical aims, and gradually to see them translated into practical measures. The cardinal also felt it important to explain and publicize the documents presented to the Council by the Secretariat, and others that were of importance for the ecumenical movement, in order to determine the path to unity in the future more and more clearly.

There were plenty of striking events during this period. The most important was the solemn and official visit that the Anglican Archbishop of Canterbury, Primate of all England, Dr Michael Ramsey, paid Pope Paul VI in March 1966, with the backing of all the Anglican

Metropolitans and so in the name of the whole Anglican community. Two particularly moving moments were the solemn welcome in the Sistine Chapel and the communal service of the word in St Paul's Basilica. The visit had several practical results: firstly the 'common declaration' drawing a line under the past and deciding on a fresh start on mutual relations; next the decision to set up a mixed committee for the study and encouragement of mutual relations; and finally the foundation of an Anglican centre in Rome.

Unobtrusive work was devoted on the one hand to the establishment of ecumenism within Catholicism and on the other hand to the development and fostering of contacts with the various non-Catholic Churches, ecclesial communities or groups. As for Catholic ecumenism, work had been going on since the last years of the Council to produce an 'Ecumenical Directory', which would offer bishops guidelines to help them in their ecumenical work, without prejudice to their own legitimate responsibility. And the plenary session of the Secretariat this year 6–15 June was devoted mainly to the re-examination of the first part of this Directory. As for the furthering of contacts with non-Catholic Churches or ecclesial communities, this was done in the East by an exchange of visits and information, and in the West mainly by the setting up of the joint committees, of which mention has already been made. The committee associated with the World Council of Churches had already met twice in 1965, and by February 1966 was able to offer its first provisional report to the authorities on both sides and then to publish it. At the same time there had been a very practical step forward in this area: in February 1966 it was unanimously decided that the section of the World Council of Churches concerned with mutual help among Churches, together with the federation of charitable Catholic organizations, Caritas Internationalis, should make a joint appeal for the starving people in India. A special committee was appointed to continue to deal with this project. Another practical step in the same field was the presence of eight Catholic observers at the International Congress for Church and Community Problems, organized by the World Council of Churches at the end of July 1966: in fact one of them, Charles Möller, Under-Secretary of the Roman Congregation of Sacred Doctrine, delivered one of the main lectures.

In the course of 1965 a joint committee with the Lutheran World Federation had been set up; this had met for the first time in August 1965 and for the second time in April 1966; and it too produced a provisional report, which was published in July 1966, with the agreement of both sides.

Not many days after the visit of the Archbishop of Canterbury to Rome, on 4 April 1966, another very important decision was made: Pope Paul commissioned the Secretariat for Unity to study the question of world-wide cooperation with non-Catholic biblical societies, to work out guidelines for this purpose and to star putting them into practice.

One special aspect of the cardinal's own personal activity was his concern to publicize and explain the documents presented to the Council by the Secretariat, as well as others of ecumenical importance. In his notes the author writes on this point: 'today after the Council this teaching is especially important and particularly coming from me (in my position and with my influence)' (V/2). Three studies appeared in quick succession; in December, *The Church and the Jewish people* was ready; by the beginning of Spring *The Way to Unity after the Council* had been finished, and in July of the same year also, *The Church and Mankind*. All these works were published in the course of 1966 and 1967, in about five languages.

RETREAT 1966

Notre Dame de la Route, 1–8 August 1966

I/1 *The foundation* of everything concerned with religion is God the infinite. We know him by reason, but only imperfectly. Even this imperfect picture, however, is enough to make us aware of our duty to honour and serve God. Then comes the fuller revelation through the Son of God and the inspiration of the Holy Spirit of God, to let us penetrate more deeply into the essence of God.

On the other hand when I compare myself with God I see that of myself I am nothing, absolutely nothing—and that my whole existence depends on God, my Creator. I can only thank him for this by my complete devotion to him with all my powers and talents: intellect, will and actions. This is the result of the knowledge of God. A further consequence is love, which is increased by the knowledge of God's supernatural gifts. Therefore I must come to know and love God more and more in all his greatness: 'this is the whole duty of Man';[1] of myself I am nothing and less than nothing.

I/2 *Creatures* I must not forget that all created reality, apart from sin, is from God. So there is no room for a negative, a merely negative attitude to the 'world'. In fact I can use everything for the service of God. I have the freedom for this, but it must be the freedom of the child of God. I must, then, be in control of everything. Of sin too. It is only towards sin that I must not have a positive attitude. But even this has a positive value for me: through self-denial, through the 'cross'. Avoiding sin is not just a burden; through the cross of Christ and by my self-denial it becomes an instrument in the service of God and a source of grace. In everything the only thing that matters is for me to find out what God wants, and then do it in freedom and love. 'We know that in everything God works for good with those who love him' [cf Rom 8:28]. It is my main aim in this retreat to find out prayerfully what God wants of me

---

[1] Cf Eccles 12:13 and 1965/66, note 1, p. 145.

in the different circumstances of life, and how I can carry out this will of God in practice. 'Take, Lord, into your possession my complete freedom of action!' [Exercises 234.]

I/3 *Tantum—quantum; indifference; what is more likely*[2] These three things are very closely connected. I can reduce them all to the common denominator: to act in all things according to supernatural principles: not according to (perhaps only half-conscious) pre-judgments, nor whim; not according to worldly principles. How this works out in detail will be decided by practical consideration of the actual circumstances, either in the individual case or in general. For this I have need of meditation and the examination of conscience. It is, then, important that these should have a direct and practical application. In general it will be possible to say that whatever is naturally more difficult, that is mortification and self-conquest, will be 'more likely to achieve the purpose' [Exercises 23]. But even this must be considered according to supernatural principles. The positive values contained in 'created reality' can often suggest the opposite. Taking all in all, then, I must proceed with deliberation and let myself be guided on every occasion by supernatural principles. 'Speak, Lord, for thy servant hears' [1 Sam 3:9].

I/4 *Our Lord and the fundamental principle* I can only pick out a few points here. Everything else will be dealt with later, mainly in the second week. 1) To give glory to God: this was the main point of his life and death. He did everything for the glory of his Father; not for his own glory [cf Jn 5:30 etc]: he attributes nothing to himself and everything to the Father: 'what the Father has taught'. I too, then, must attribute all honour to God and claim nothing for myself. 2) Creatures: he sees what is positive in them and makes use of all that is positive in them. And he does not do this automatically but with supernatural consideration. He is not, then, opposed to the world, but rather uses the world and tries to make it more and more useful. He does not hide his light under a bushel: he speaks as one with power [Mt 7:28 f]; he uses his eloquence in the service of the Father and of men. He is also familiar with human feelings. And he pays tribute to the good that he sees in his opponents and enemies. He has favourites among his disciples but not at the expense of truth and love.[3] In everything, then, he is a glorious model, which I must learn to know and love more and more. And this retreat must really help me to do this. Fiat! 11.IX.66

II/2 *The triple sin* [Exercises 45–54] In my life sin is also a real possibility. The angels, pure spirits, could sin in spite of their clear under-

---
[2] The essential elements of the 'fundamental principle' relating to men's attitude to creatures (Exercises 23).

[3] Consider for instance the gentle answer he gave the mother of the sons of Zebedee, although one of them was his beloved disciple: (Mt 20:23).

standing.⁴ This is why their sin was final and their punishment eternal. Our first parents sinned though God had bestowed on them such privileges and graces. And redeemed man is even more in a position to sin, since he carries within himself the consequences of original sin and is subject to moods and feelings. And if he commits a serious sin he is subject to God's justice, which can punish him eternally. I must, then, regard sin as a reality in myself and in others and therefore do everything to preserve myself and others from it. There is no place for any utopian and feeble asceticism.⁵ In this too I must think realistically and take serious steps.

II/2 *My own sins* I can leave my past sins now to God's mercy, which I must value all the more highly and praise all the more fervently, because he has led me along the paths by which my life has been determined in spite of my sins. Now the main thing is to look at my present condition. Every week my weekly confession shows me that I am still far from being what I could be with God's grace, far from what people must rightly expect of me, considering my position and my job. And this is true in spite of all the resolutions that I keep on making. This shows me that from now on all the time that God gives me I must work more seriously and consistently on myself, in order to achieve the state corresponding to God's grace and demanded by my position. There is still time for this, and God's grace will not fail me. In my spiritual exercises, especially in my examination of conscience, I must renew my resolution repeatedly and pray for strength and grace to do this.

II/3 *The triple colloquy* Sin, irregularity, world.⁶ I am thinking mainly of the venial sins and all the irregularities in my life. These two things are for the most part the same or connected. Unkind criticism, defects and failure in my spiritual duties, lack of charity, impatience and so on, all this comes eventually from a lack of order in my nature and in my character. If I want to avoid failings, I must fight this lack of order. This calls for mortification and self-conquest. So the thing to do is to attack irregularities and failings at the root and not to wait until they show themselves. Asceticism is even in my old age a task from which I cannot excuse myself. There is one consideration that must give me strength in this: I am in the public eye. It must not be said of me: 'he sinned and made Israel to sin' [cf 1 Kgs 14:16]. There is a double respon-

---

⁴ 'And the angels that did not keep their own position but left their proper dwelling have been kept by God in eternal chains in the nether gloom until the judgment of the great day' (Jude v. 6); cf also what Jesus says about the devil: 'He (the devil) was a murderer from the beginning, and has nothing to do with the truth, because there is no truth in him. When he lies, he speaks according to his own nature, for he is a liar and the father of lies' (Jn 8:44).
⁵ Cf Mt 5:29 f: 'If your right eye causes you to sin, pluck it out and throw it away; it is better that you lose one of your members than that your whole body be thrown into hell. . . .'
⁶ Cf chap. 4, note 14, and Exercises 63.

sibility here for a cardinal who is a religious, a Jesuit. Things to which people pay less attention in others take on a greater importance in my case.

II/4 *Death* Death can no longer be far off for anyone in his 86th year, so I must prepare myself in order to be able to die 'with joy and satisfaction' (the second way of making a decision).[7] I must make death real even during my life: every day must see my old self die a little, a 'dying to myself' by self-denial, mortification and self-conquest [cf Rom 6:6, 8; Col 3:5 etc]. And the other way of bringing this about is increasing familiarity with the idea of heaven, so that this may become my real home even now (Phil 3:20). So my time on earth must also be a time of laying up treasure for myself in heaven (Mt 6:20). My real heavenly treasure is not the honour that I receive from men nor my reputation nor all the titles and decorations, but the deeds which will follow me (cf Rev 14:13). So now I must labour with Christ and for Christ, as long as he gives me strength for it.[8] This is the best way I can prepare for death. Nor will my death be lonely: 'Go forth, O Christian soul; may the angels and saints and our Lord himself welcome you'.[9] Every holy Communion should be a Viaticum, so that I shall not die without Viaticum even if I die suddenly: 'May the Lord himself protect me from the evil enemy and lead me to eternal life!'[9] If I live like this I shall be able to die 'with joy and satisfaction'.

III/1 *The ascetical life of a priest and religious* Just doing without things does not mean that one is leading an ascetical life. A sportsman denies himself all sorts of things but by itself that does not make him an ascetic. This self-denial only becomes asceticism if it is practised for supernatural reasons, 'for the sake of the kingdom of heaven' [Mt 19:12]. This also makes the evangelical counsels[10] and every day sacrifices into 'asceticism'. But this ascetical life is necessary for me as a priest and religious and in a special way for a man in my position. It is this position that demands all sorts of sacrifices from me that the ordinary priest does not have to make; but I must not do it from human and earthly considerations (for the sake of 'protocol') but for the sake of the kingdom of God. This means paying greater attention to the externals, it involves many restrictions on my freedom, much thought for others, many rules in my dealings with people and my correspondence. Much of this is the same for a man of the world as well; but I can sanctify it all by the

---

[7] Cf Exercises 187, on making a good choice in important matters: 'Let me ask myself how I would like to stand on the day of judgment. What decision would I then like to have made about this business? Knowing what rule I would then like to have kept, I will now observe it, so that then I may be filled with joy and satisfaction.' This can be extended to apply to death itself, when judgment occurs.

[8] Exercises, at the end of the meditation on the 'triple sin', asks 'What have I done for Christ? What am I doing for Christ? What must I do for Christ?' (53.)

[9] From prayers for the Dying, in the Roman Ritual.

[10] Of chastity, poverty and obedience.

constant intention of doing it all 'for God'. In this way I place it in the realm of grace and so received supernatural strength and energy. So, I must do both: do it faithfully and do it for supernatural reasons.

2.X.66
7.V.67

III/2 *The sacrament of penance* Our Lord placed the power of forgiveness in the hands of the Church, which is himself, his Mystical Body. For we have sinned against him and so we must receive forgiveness through him. The acts of sorrow and purpose of amendment by themselves, and the mere confession of failure: all these are a matter of preparation and disposition: while the forgiveness itself comes from our Lord and his Church. This can be seen by contrasting Peter and Judas. Judas also admitted his fault; he regretted it and did penance; but he did not go back to our Lord. He despairs and ends in despair. By contrast Peter caught one look from our Lord and went out and wept bitterly. All his sorrow is directed towards our Lord. He goes to him—into the group of the apostles. And so he receives from him forgiveness, which is greater even than his guilt.

Therefore I must value the sacrament of penance highly. It is the means of forgiveness because it binds me to Christ. But I must value it for this reason, not just as an institution of Canon Law or rule of the Society. It is Christ the Redeemer whom I meet in every confession and from whom I seek forgiveness. It is his love and his power, which apply to me the fruit of his cross.

III/3. *The imitation of Christ* The imitation of Christ is a law for all of us. But this cannot simply mean copying Christ's life—not for anyone. I must see what is fundamental in this life and then decide in my own case how I am to imitate this fundamental aspect in each concrete situation. This application is also a matter of obedience; it does not depend entirely on my judgment. In many cases our Lord has showed the way himself: I am thinking of the way he treated the individual apostles and in different situations, always remaining true to his principle: 'I always do what is pleasing to him (the Father)' [cf Jn 8:29]. It is not easy to see how this applies to my situation and it needs much light and strength to find the right course in each individual case. To help me I have meditation, examination of conscience, the example of the saints and also my own worldly knowledge, my experience. And then to all this must be added prayer and—honesty with myself.

III/4 *The kingdom of Christ* [Exercises 91–98] This is a question of sharing in the saving work of Christ, which he achieved by effort, pain and death. All men are called to this work, but I am called in a very special way; this is shown by my position. It is not now a case of living up to this call 'somehow or other', Christ has shown me so many favours that for my part I can do nothing but distinguish myself [Exercises 97] in his service. Where and how—as in the past that is up to him to decide and to show me clearly, revealing his plans to me from within or from without. There is no choice for me to make in this matter; I have only to keep myself open for any call and free from any sort of internal or external ties. There is no room here for thoughts of success, reputation or recognition, or men's praise or even of personal inclinations or inhibitions: I must be free from all 'natural weakness, love of the world and of the flesh' [id]. Then I am wholly and unreservedly at his service. And I must work at this anew in this retreat as far as I can. Then I shall also be ready to put up with all injustice, all abuse and all poverty [id 98], in other words ready to share in the hardships of Christ the King himself [id 95].

IV/1   *The incarnation and annunciation* (Lk 1:26–38)   The incarnation is a proof of the goodness and mercy of the Blessed Trinity. Not even all the evil of men prevents God from thinking of their salvation, and the most extreme means, the incarnation of the Second Person of the Blessed Trinity, is not too difficult for him. He still sees the basic goodness in men and wants to make it bear fruit. 'The mercies of the Lord that we are not consumed'! [Lamentations 3:22.] This shows me that not even the greatest sacrifices should be allowed to stop us working for the salvation of our neighbour; in spite of all sin he is worth it. But Mary only thinks of one thing: 'let it be to me according to your word', obedience to the will of God. This is the centre of her heart. Nothing else concerns her, neither honour nor position. But with all this she is still prudent. What does God want of me in these concrete circumstances? 'How can this be?' This is an example of the application of the will of God in the concrete situation.

IV/2   *The nativity*   When a man is born he has no idea of the situation into which he is being born. He cannot choose his future; he is simply there. Everything else follows in due course. It is not so with our Lord. He knows everything that lies ahead of him, from the crib to the cross. And he chooses it: 'A body hast thou prepared for me. . . . I have come to do thy will [cf Heb 10: 5, 7]. Neither do I know what the future holds for me. But I state it once again in this retreat: 'Lo, I have come to do thy will', in every possible situation.—Then what the angels said will become true through me and in me: 'peace among men with whom he is pleased' [Lk 2:14]. And the birth of our Lord is the guarantee of this: 'The goodness and loving kindness of God our Saviour appeared' [Tit 3:4]. It has appeared for me too as long as I do God's will faithfully. Already in the crib he won for me the grace to do this.—Mary was able to lift the child from the crib and pray: 'through him, with him and in him . . . all honour and glory. . . .'[11]

[11] Roman Missal, at the end of the eucharistic prayers.

IV/3 *The hidden life of Jesus*   After the busy years a time of seclusion has now come for me too. But it must be a 'life hidden in Christ', based on and inspired by the supernatural [Col 3:1–4]. As far as it depends on me I must avoid everything that is sensational, striking, extraordinary, and simply work for the Church and its interests, but work in a way that does not allow any influence from egoism, self-seeking, ambition or any other earthly motives. Nor must I fall into the rut of a life of ease, mediocrity and self-sufficiency. My work must always be the result of sharing in the life and the fate of the Church; the Church must be the norm. 'I always do what is pleasing to him' [Jn 8:29]. I must set to work and even take the initiative, in whatever way God calls me, and follow this call faithfully and conscientiously. In this way this hidden life of mine will also be of use to the Church and to souls.

IV/4 *The twelve year old Jesus in the temple* [Lk 2: 41–50] He was not obliged to do this, nor did he have to do it for his own sake; but he wanted to give a good example. People expect this of me too; as far as my age and position allow I must do everything that law and custom require. What would the people in Nazareth have said if he had stayed at home?

His action in staying behind (in the temple) led to a conflict between parents and son. There is the possibility of such clashes even between faithful servants of God, and both are right 'from their point of view'. And in such cases I must not immediately think in terms of malice, stupidity and stubbornness and so on, and I must preserve charity at all costs. 'I must be about my Father's business.' This obedience towards the Father calls for sacrifices from our Lord and from his parents. But these sacrifices demanded by obedience are not wasted. How many faithful servants of the Church would not have become what they were, if it had not been for such mutual sacrifices! Where I have to do the will of God I have to make sacrifices too, and also impose them on others in certain circumstances.

V/1 *The Sermon on the Mount I* [Mt 5:3–12]   The eight beatitudes are diametrically opposed to the spirit of the world. They only make sense in the light of the cross of Christ and of a share in his cross. He himself has gone before me in putting this beatitude into practice: 'Learn from me; for I am gentle and lowly in heart' [Mt 11:29]. He does not promise me happiness here on earth in all these ways. Complete fulfilment will be mine in the 'kingdom of God'. But St Paul could still say: 'with all our affliction I am overjoyed' [cf 2 Cor 7:4]. So I must and I will take up the cross, in whatever form our Lord offers it to me. Then I am certain of having a share in the true happiness as well. Even here on earth the cross will bring me joy and consolation. Hail, holy cross.

V/2 *The Sermon on the Mount II* [Mt 5:13–16] The Sermon on the Mount is a programme given me by God to guide my thoughts and desires and my whole life's work. I must follow it as if I was hearing it for the first time and had still many years ahead of me in which to put it all into practice. Firstly the basic frame of mind: a really interior and supernatural attitude, seeking only God's honour and not thinking of self. From this will flow what I teach ('Light', 'Salt'). Today, after the Council, this teaching is especially important and particularly coming from me (in my position and with my influence). Then there is my life: 'a city set on a hill', with all eyes upon it. The city has its effect by its very existence; there should be nothing affected or precious, no search for sensation, but the simple straightforward expression of the interior spirit. And this in everything: in prayer and the religious life (simply devout!): honest and not diplomatic, honourable and straightforward; above all in conversation and dealings with people: working through the wisdom and strength of Christ and so on.

But this is all a narrow gate and a hard way [Mt 7:13 f]: it presupposes sacrifice, self-control and self-conquest. But it is the way our Lord went and so it must be my way too. 12.XII.66

V/3 *Three groups of men* [Exercises 150–156]¹² By the grace of God I have come to recognize my task and its demands better, and all that remains is for me to set about putting it into practice at once. Many points are quite obvious. And where I still have some doubt how to proceed in the concrete circumstances, I have my spiritual exercises and my prayer as a source of enlightenment and strength. But I must begin at once without any delay or hesitation. My 'decision' should help me in this.

V/4 *The sending of the apostles* [cf Mt 10:16, 18 ff] My sense of mission: the manner of my call and mission have been quite out of the ordinary; and therefore our Lord expects more than the usual of me. The object of my mission: the 'kingdom of God', not literature, aesthetics, art etc. Now after the Council: preaching about the Council decrees, interpretations, applications, especially in those areas for which I am responsible). Execution: 'go', active not just waiting, passive etc.— Difficulties: there will be no shortage of these, whatever their origin.— But I must not cause them by lack of prudence or truthfulness; I must preach the kingdom of God simply, straightforwardly and faithfully. And in all this unassuming, not looking for honour, recognition or praise from people. In the midst of difficulties my trust is our Lord. He has sent me and sends the Holy Spirit as well: 'What you are to say will be given to you in that hour.' And I shall bear difficulties that come from without in imitation of our Lord: 'if they persecuted me, they will persecute you' [Jn 15:20]. 'By your endurance you will gain your lives' [Lk 21:19].

¹² This meditation is intended to find out how far the retreatant is determined to follow to the end the path recognized as the will of God.

VI/1 *The transfiguration* [Mt 17:1-8] If our Lord asks for great sacrifices, he also prepares a person for them. For the apostles the mere announcement of the passion is a shock and Peter even vigorously opposes the idea [Mt 16:22]. When it actually happened it was going to throw them into complete confusion. So our Lord prepares them by the Transfiguration. And when it came about in fact, it was still difficult enough; but on the whole they passed the test. I should not expect any extraordinary preparation like this. I have God's word ('listen to him') and all the wonderful confirmation offered by the history of the Church. This must be enough for me to take upon myself and bear even more difficult things.

VI/2 *The multiplication of the loaves* [Mk 6:31-46] Here our Lord shows his heart: in the first place in the way he treats his disciples. After their work he wants to give them a rest and time to recover. Holiday time and daily recreation are also in accordance with our Lord's will. 'Come away . . . and rest awhile!' [Mk 6:31.] In the way he treats the crowds: first of all he gives thousands of them the bread of doctrine, all day long until sunset, but also wants to provide the bread for the body. Not, it is true, personally but through his apostles: '*you* give them something to eat!' The early Church understood what this meant in the apostles' day (the deacons; St Paul's collections) [Acts 6:1 ff; Rom 15:26 f; 1 Cor 16:2 etc]; and it understands it to this day; the social concern of the Church. This too flows from our Lord's heart. But he works through us, his priests and faithful. Now, just as then, he remains as it were in the background, even when he gives the supernatural bread of life, the holy Eucharist. He gives it through us, his representatives. He wants no earthly reward for this kindness. When they want to acclaim him king he forces his disciples to go into the boat and 'withdrew again to the hills by himself' (Jn 6:15). Everything must remain on the level of the supernatural; even the social welfare work of the Church should help souls.

VI/3 *The washing of the feet and the institution of the Blessed Sacrament* [Jn 13:1-17] The solemn words with which John introduces this scene refer in the first place to the washing of the feet, but even more to the institution and first celebration of the Holy Eucharist. This is love to the last degree, but also a proof of the power of the one into whose hands the Father has put everything. In these days of liturgical renewal I want to renew my great appreciation of this gift. The frame of mind displayed by Peter must be mine too with regard to the Holy Eucharist: above all the feeling of unworthiness (Lord, I am not worthy . . . Lord, do you give me yourself as food?);[13] but then a great love that would like to have everything from our Lord: 'hands and

---

[13] The first text is taken from the liturgy of the Mass; the second is based on Peter's words: 'Lord, do you wash my feet?' and applied to the Eucharist.

head'. The celebration of the Holy Eucharist must not become a matter of routine for me, on the contrary every Mass and every Holy Communion should find me in that festive mood that prevailed at the Last Supper, when our Lord performed this sacred action for the first time and gave the disciples a share in it. 15.I.67

VI/4. *The high-priestly prayer* (Jn 17) This is the evening prayer of our Lord's life. A glance at his life: he can sum it all up in a word: 'I glorified thee on earth'. But first through the cross. To glorify the Father through the cross is the great objective of the sacrifice. At every Mass that I offer this is the 'first intention' and I should always remember this.[14] I can only pray that I shall also be able to say on my deathbed: 'I glorified thee on earth,' and not only by individual acts but by my whole life and above all by my whole life and work as a priest.—Here I have also our Lord's farewell prayer for his disciples. This was not just a friendly gathering. They have been given to him by the Father and therefore they should be one as he and the Father are one, one with the Father through him. This is the mystical bond that holds them together, even when they are dispersed all over the world. And this bond also holds together everyone who is going to believe through them. Unity is not just the material fact of being united; it has a trinitarian character, so to speak.

VII/1 *In the Garden of Olives* [Mt 26:36–46] The spiritual sufferings of our Lord in the garden are a great mystery. For me the most important thing is not to fathom this mystery but to see how deeply our Lord wanted to descend into the abyss of the suffering of the human soul. Sadness, fear, disgust, horror: all this floods into his soul and forces him to cry out: 'My soul is very sorrowful, even to death,' and brings on the sweat of blood [cf Lk 22:44]. Surely the soul cannot possibly suffer more than this. He bore it for our sake; it is, so to speak, an anticipation of his death on the cross. He bore it in expiation of all the disorder in our souls, but also to show me how to behave in all suffering, inward and outward. And above all he points to the main means: prayer, urgent, humble and trusting prayer. In such a situation men cannot offer consolation; only God can do this, as he showed in our Lord's case, for his spiritual suffering ends in a brave: 'Rise, let us be going'!

VII/2 *From the garden to Annas* Our Lord's conduct at this hour is full of dignity and courage, but also full of love and kindness to all. He stands up for his cause against his enemies, especially against Annas: 'I am he,' he says to all who accuse him, but he is gentle and kind, even to someone like Judas. How often the enemies of the Church are led by

---

[14] Priests usually have one or two special intentions for which they offer the Mass. The author is stressing that the main purpose and intention of every Mass, the glory of God, should not give way to these special intentions.

unfaithful priests and bishops. 'Friends'; in spite of all their hostility he treats them with love and patience. With his 'I am he' he commits himself wholly to his mission. But he can also claim: 'I have spoken openly to the world... I have said nothing secretly' [Jn 18:20]; openly he admits and stands by what he has said and taught, both in public and in private conversation. The crowds are not loyal to him; their enthusiasm was not based on conviction but on passing impressions; but he did not let himself be deceived by this; he wants loyalty based on conviction. And this he finds in the apostles, even if they abandon him for a time or even, like Peter, deny him.

VII/3 *Caiaphas, Pilate, Herod* There are three groups involved in our Lord's death: religious fanatics, a weak official, who is concerned with his own career more than anything else, and a worldling and libertine, who takes nothing seriously. It is the same people who condemn the Church today. And the Church's answer can only be to confess Christ clearly, to be silent, where people will not listen to the truth, and to put up with it all patiently. I have a share in the fate of the Church and I must act as it acts or as our Lord acted. In my position too it is often better to be silent, unless bound to speak by an objective obligation. But when this is the case, I must confess to the truth clearly and distinctly, although without hurting or offending the other person.

12.II.67

VII/4 *The scourging, crowning with thorns and condemnation* The scourging and crowning with thorns are not a necessary part of the judicial procedure. Our Lord accepts them out of special love for us and one could say especially: for priests and religious. I know only too well how many of them come to grief because of sensuality and ambition. And I myself have still to work seriously on myself in these matters. As regards sensuality I must not make any concessions, neither in the way of looks or of feelings. And as for ambition: 'A life hidden in Christ' [cf Col 3:3]. I cannot avoid men's esteem; but it must never in any circumstances be the driving force behind my action: I may admit it, but not desire it or seek it. May our Lord, crowned with thorns, give me the grace for this. O God I love thee, as thou hast loved me!

VIII/1 *The mysteries of the cross* What happened on the cross takes place in an unbloody manner over and over again in the eucharistic sacrifice. Like the cross the eucharistic sacrifice is a source of reconciliation, of grace, of devotion to the heavenly Father and of the completion of the redemption. And so I will offer this sacrifice every day with great devotion and recollection, and in doing this as an instrument of the crucified Lord I will imitate the frame of mind that our Lord had and showed on the Cross.[15] In this way daily Mass will be for me

[15] Cf Vatican II, Decree on the Life and Ministry of Priests: 'By the sacrament

and countless others a lasting source of grace and blessing. Our Lord could not have left his Church and me a greater grace and gift, when he uttered his 'it is finished'.

VIII/2 *The risen Lord* It is an historical fact that our Lord rose. But the risen Lord is no longer the same as he was before. He is no longer visible and yet he can appear at any moment; he knows everything, even if he does not appear to be present [cf Jn 20:25-27]; there is nothing that can restrain or hinder him, not even closed doors. His Spirit, who lives in us through his grace, is the Spirit of the risen Lord [cf Jn 16:7]. As such he sees into the depths of our hearts and prays in us and for us 'with sighs too deep for words' [Rom 8:26]. He is in us with his victorious power: nothing can withstand him, 'neither death, nor life . . . nor anything else in all creation, will be able to separate us from the love of God' (Rom 8:37-39). I must keep all of this in mind at all times and with the help of God's grace try to penetrate it and understand it more and more, in order that the risen Jesus may take hold of me completely and fill my whole being and that I should no longer live in myself but in Christ, the risen and glorified Lord.

VIII/3 *The Spirit as the fruit of the redemption* The source of the Holy Spirit is the pierced heart of our Lord on the cross.[16] Before this the Spirit was not yet active as he is now.[17] But today, as his different name shows, he pervades all 'spiritual' life. When I speak of 'grace' I must not think only of the accident of which the theologians speak: grace is the Holy Spirit living and working in my soul.[18] He is my light and my strength [1 Cor 2:10 f]. He lets me take part in his search into the depths of the God head [cf 1 Cor 2:9-11]; it is through him that I know what I do know about God, in theology and contemplative prayer. But I must be open to his influence. And it is not only the 'flesh' that can put obstacles in his way, but lack of mortification, self-denial, in short the denial or neglect of the cross.[19] Therefore this 'cross' is so important for me. The works of the 'flesh' 'opera carnis' (Gal 5:19-21) are where the cross is not; while the 'fruit

---

of orders priests are configured to Christ the Priest so that as ministers of the Head and co-workers of the episcopal order they can build up and establish his whole Body which is the Church . . . (12)'

[16] See above, chap. 3, note 44.

[17] Cf Jn 7:37 ff: 'On the last day of the feast, the great day, Jesus stood up and proclaimed, "If any one thirst, let him come to me and drink. He who believes in me, as the scripture has said, 'out of his heart shall flow rivers of living water.'" Now this he said about the (Holy) Spirit, which those who believed in him were to receive; for as yet the Spirit had not been given, because Jesus was not yet glorified.'

[18] In philosophical and theological language, an 'accident' is that which further determines a substance, which already has a certain degree of being (cf Rahner: *Concise Theological Dictionary*).

[19] Cf Gal 5:17, 19: 'For the desires of the flesh are against the Spirit, and the desires of the Spirit are against the flesh.'

of the Spirit' exists where I 'crucify the flesh'. 'If I live by the Spirit, let me also walk by the Spirit' [cf Gal 5:22, 25].

VIII/4 *To achieve spiritual love* [Exercises 230–237] God has been infinitely generous to me, more than to many others. For my part I cannot give him anything that does not belong to him already. But I can and must use all this only for him and at the same time be ready to give it back to him at any time in whole or in part, if he wants to take it back. So many people have received similar generosity or more; but they use it for themselves and do not think of the one who gave it to them. In my 'decision' I have drawn up the programme: 'to do everything according to God's will and for him'. This is my 'Suscipe' [Exercises 234] and I will live up to it with greater faithfulness than ever.—If God is present in everything, then I must also see him and find him in everything. I must not look on the world with profane eyes but find God everywhere in it, that is I must see everything in a spirit of faith. For this also gives me the opportunity to make use of all the good that is in the world and in things for God. This is also the 'redemption of the world' for which it is groaning [Rom 8:19–22]. God works for me; I work for him, as I have just resolved in my 'decision'. And finally I see in all the good and beauty that exists in persons and in things a ray, a reflection from God. This is the way in which the world can help me to know and love God more and more in everything, until one day I see him 'face to face' [1 Cor 13:12], when he calls me. 5.III.67
8.VIII.66

FROM THE MONTHLY RECOLLECTIONS

11.IX.1966
Supernatural approach to everything; an intensive spiritual life; carrying out my duties every day quietly and without fuss; setting a good example in behaviour and teaching.

I/1 Complete devotion to God with all my powers. Get to know God more and more.
I/2 Make use of everything in God's service.
I/3 Examination of conscience: practical!—make full use of the positive values that exist in 'created reality'.
I/4 Attitude to the 'world'; put all my powers at God's service.

2.X.1966
1) Intensive spiritual life alongside all my outside work.
2) Meditation and examination of conscience; visits morning and afternoon—ejaculatory prayers before important actions.

3) Faithfulness in my external work, carrying out my duties without fuss and human considerations—a life hidden in Christ.

II/1 Sin is a reality!
II/2 Work on myself seriously and consistently—in accordance with my status—a holy cardinal.
II/3 Irregularities in my character: control and asceticism—in the public eye.
II/4 Die 'with joy and satisfaction'. Preparation.
III/1 Constant intention: 'for God', not just a matter of protocol!

6.XI.1966
1) 'Our commonwealth is a heaven' (II/4): supernatural approach to everything.
2) Examination of conscience, but not mechanically.
3) Teaching and example; in the public eye.
4) In everything carry out my duties without fuss.
5) To distinguish myself in the service of the King.
III/1 Confession: a meeting with Christ.
III/2 'I always do what is pleasing to the Father': imitating Christ as a matter of principle; in everything, and everywhere! No thoughtlessness!
III/4 Keep myself open for any call.

11.XII.1966
The Lord is near:[20]
1) in my spiritual exercises: Mass, examination of conscience!
2) in my work: order and energy.
3) in unpleasant situations: patience and love.
4) in my dealings with others: good example, love, reverence.
IV/2 I shall do your will in every situation.
IV/3 A life hidden in Christ; work only for the Church and for souls!—Work with devotion, initiative, with my eyes on the goal: the things that are pleasing to him!
IV/4 Good example in everything!—in a spirit of love towards others; and a spirit of sacrifice in my work.
VI/1 'Blessed'—but only in the 'kingdom of God'—and through the cross. A real interior supernatural approach; only God! Everything should be a genuine expression of my interior spirit.

15.I.1967
1) An intensive spiritual life (cf General Congregation).[21]

[20] This recollection was made in Advent, and its emphasis is on the nearness of the Lord in all things, not just in spiritual exercises (cf Phil 4:4).
[21] In spring 1965 and summer 1966 the Society of Jesus held its 'General Congregation' (which corresponds to the General Chapter in other orders). Cardinal Bea—always loyal to his Society—read its decisions carefully and used them for his meditations.

2) Carry out my daily work faithfully.
3) Exemplary in my teaching and behaviour.
4) Unassuming and modest.

V/4 Sense of mission; active; straightforward, simple, faithful, unassuming.
VI/2 Concern for souls in all that I do.
VI/3 'Celebration' of Mass—visits!

12.II.1967

Supernatural approach to everything. Sacrifice: exercises in mortification. Share in the cross of Christ.

2) Carrying out daily duties quietly and without fuss.
3) To distinguish myself in the service of my King (III/4).
4) Genuine brotherly love.

VI/4 'I glorified thee on earth': and I?—by my whole life!
VII/1 Garden of olives: our Lord plumbs the depths of the suffering of a human soul. But with it all—prayer.
VII/2 Love and patience even towards enemies and renegades.

'I have spoken openly'. Loyalty based on conviction.

VII/3 The three classes: fanatics, weak officials, worldlings.
VII/3 It is often better to be silent, where I am not duty-bound to speak.

5.III.1967

1) Always and everywhere the will of God.
2) In meditation and examination. Practical.
3) Edify by teaching and example.
4) Quiet and selfless work for the Church.
5) Genuine brotherly love towards all.

VII/4 No concessions to sensuality or ambition. A life hidden in Christ.
VIII/1 Mass: devotion and recollection!—the frame of mind that our Lord had on the cross!
VIII/3 The Holy Ghost in my soul! Open to the influence of the Holy Ghost! Not 'the works of the flesh' but 'the fruit of the Spirit'.
VIII/3 Look on everything in a spirit of faith.

2.IV.1967

1) Carry out my daily work faithfully, calmly, patiently.
2) With my eyes on God.
3) Edifying in teaching and example.
4) And at the same time quiet and unobtrusive: a life hidden in Christ (VII/4).
I/1 All that I am is from God; hence, complete devotion to him.

I/2 Be in control of everything.

I/3 Proceed according to supernatural principles, with deliberation.

2.V.1967

Everyday die to myself: exposed to the view of all. Quietly and faithfully carrying out my duties; my work must be something special!

II/1 A serious sin is particularly serious for me, as I have received so many graces from God.

II/2 Still far from what I could be with God's grace (must work earnestly and constantly on myself)! Confession alone is not enough, I must improve!

II/3 Work earnestly on myself; what attracts less attention in others is more noticable in me (a cardinal and a religious and a priest).

II/4 My real treasure in heaven is not my fame etc, but my work for God and the Church.

III/1 Self-conquest not for the sake of 'protocol' but for the sake of the kingdom of God.

11.VI.1967

1) Use everything that God gives me well.
2) Selfless and modest.
3) Kind to all.

III/4 Keep myself open for every call.

CHAPTER 11

'Accept everything with tranquillity and energy'

1967

'I can make use of everything to serve God generously: old age, busy life, physical weakness. All this and everything else can be for me a means of serving him' (I/2). I will and I must 'use fully, actively and decisively the extraordinary graces that I have received and continue to receive from God, in order to become what God wants me to become with his grace' (I/4). These remarks from the 1967 retreat are significant for the attitude of the author throughout the whole of this year. The decline of his powers made it advisable for him to take life more gently; I must try 'as long as possible, to conserve my strength for my work, and not be unreasonable!' (II1–2; these resolutions really were necessary since there was certainly no lack of work. But in spite of all this he still approached and carried out the work as energetically as ever.

Nor was this period lacking in unusual happenings. The cardinal even undertook one or two journeys. From 12–15 September he took an active part in the Youth Congress at Taizé. This was the realization of a long-entertained wish to pay well-deserved tribute to the ecumenical work of this community. On this occasion he spoke—gently but at the same time very firmly and clearly—on the question of intercommunion. The young people were not at all happy with the current situation but were quite ready to accept his explanations.

At the end of September he was in Frankfurt, where an extraordinary ecumenical event took place at the Book Fair: on the 25th, he and Dr Wilhelm Visser 't Hooft received the peace prize of the German book industry. That evening there was an impressive Liturgy of the Word in the Lutheran Church of St Peter, presided over by the two peace prize winners. The whole service was televised. 'I should never have dreamed that one day Cardinal Bea and I should together be giving the blessing to a congregation,' said Pastor Visser 't Hooft.

But such events were the exception. Most of his time was spent in quiet but still strenuous work: the daily 'anxiety for all the Churches' for our non-Catholic brethren, which he had to bear in the Secretariat for Unity. Then there were the regular sessions of the commission for the new Vulgate translation of scripture. There were two meetings of the Congregation dealing with the beatification and canonization processes, which can entail the perusal of whole volumes of documents. And, above all, there were the weekly meetings of the Congregation for the Doctrine of Faith, where the issues were all important and by no means easily settled.

At the same time his literary activity was as intensive as ever: in March 1967, he completed *The Word of God and Mankind,* an extensive commentary on the *Constitution on Divine Revelation*—as co-president of the mixed commission responsible for it, the author had played a very active part in the composition of this document. Almost immediately after that another work was undertaken: *Ecumenism in the Council,* an account of ecumenical events from the pontificate of John XXIII up to the time of writing, illustrated from the relevant documents. This book, too, was completed before the summer holidays.

The plenary session of the Secretariat for Unity took place from 19–28 April 1967. Its object was to review the ecumenical situation and above all to examine the proposals for the second part of the Ecumenical Directory: it closed with a solemn audience with Pope Paul VI. In his detailed address the Pope sketched in broad outlines the ecumenical events of the past years, paying generous tribute to the work of the Secretariat and solemnly announcing the papal approval for the first part of the Ecumenical Directory.

Two weeks later (9–11 May) Rome received the Armenian-Orthodox Patriarch Khoren I of Silicia. This was the first time that the head of an eastern Church had paid an official visit to Rome.

During the preparations for Pope Paul's visit to Constantinople, the cardinal fell ill and was forced to ask to be relieved of his duty of accompanying the pope on this very important journey. On 16 July he was present in his native village at the transfer of his parents' remains to the vault which had been prepared in the parish church, where they now rest alongside their son. In a moving speech, he spoke of all that he owed his parents. On this occasion also he gave his approval to the artist's design for the inscription for his gravestone, which he had composed himself.

He returned to the noviciate at Neuhausen for a rest and for his annual retreat. The following sentences from his notes show his frame of mind in those days: 'Old age is making its presence felt more and more —so I must bear this in the spirit of faith and love; and not complain but accept everything with tranquillity and energy and regard it as part of the service of God . . . I look forward to death with tranquillity and confidence' (II/1–2). In the meditation of our Lord asleep in the boat during the storm we read: 'The fact that he is asleep on the boat shows how often he is tired. If I am tired now, it was certainly not in vain. But I must not use this as an excuse for taking life easy: I can only be happy that our Lord has made use of me and pray that I may labour for him to the end. This will be a special grace from God' (V/3).

RETREAT 1967

Noviciate, Neuhausen, 1–8 August

I/1 I must live up to my vocation as perfectly as possible and make no compromises that could harm it in any way. I do not just mean my 'vocation' in general but my actual daily work. All self-sufficiency, all stubbornness, any lack of love or trust is opposed to this. And in this matter I must not look at the example of others. Everyone has his own views and opinions according to the conditions in which God has placed him and the way he has directed him. He has shown me an unusual amount of favour, almost without limit or reserve. And so I must use the same measure in my dealings with him and must not be content with the minimum, but must rather try in all things to seek the greater glory of God, the greater service, because he has given me so much help and the grace to know him so well.

I/2 *No mediocrity* There have been no half-measures in the way God has treated me, in fact he has been exceedingly generous. Therefore I must act in the same way towards him, not primarily looking for a reward but rather thinking of his goodness. Nothing can dispense me from my duty to be generous towards him; and I can make use of everything to serve him generously: old age, busy life, physical weakness. All this and everything else can be for me a means of serving him. And looking at it the other way round, every event and every experience can be an incentive: how many examples, stimuli (especially in my present position!), reminders and so on there are! All this is an incentive and at the same time a means of serving God generously and a response to the abundance of his goodness. The decisive thing for me is the basic attitude: no 'half measures'! 10.III.68

I/3 *The way to perfection* This is not the way of nature: 'for all who are led by the spirit are sons of God' [Rom 8:14]. So I must be guided by the Holy Spirit. This means: 1) listening to him (meditation, spiritual reading, examination of conscience, instructions etc); 2) cooperating with him positively; so avoiding obstacles. 'Nature' is an obstacle: my inclinations, preferences, attachments: 'I need to train myself to be impartial' [cf Exercises 23] so look out for obstacles and exclude them). This means a continual and earnest struggle against myself. Finally I must cooperate: by faithful use of the means of grace (especially prayer, Mass, meditation and so on). Therefore I must allow myself to be guided and keep myself free from anything that could disturb the activity of the Holy Spirit in me [cf Gal 5:17]. In short I must live in a supernatural atmosphere and cultivate it more and more.

I/4 *I confess to Almighty God, to all the saints and to you, brethren...*[1]
What a picture this is! In my position I have the duty to be what my fellow-men think of me, to be what they must take me for and what I make myself out to be! I teach, I guide others—and myself? I should be an example to others, but am I really? Or am I a 'hypocrite'? [cf Mt 6:5.] Have people (popes, cardinals, superiors etc.) been mistaken in me? What does a man like Pius XII or John XXIII think of me today? And all those whose superior, teacher and guide I have been? My parents? My friends? I will and I must make a great effort really to be what they rightly expect of me and take me for. And I must make use fully, actively and decisively of the extraordinary graces that I have received and continue to receive from God, in order to become what God wants me to become with his grace.

II/1–2 *The thought of death* I cannot prepare death like a lecture or a talk, but I must always be ready for it. And I can and I must make an indirect preparation by my life: my work, my prayer, my sufferings. How shall I think of these three things on my deathbed? In the face of death? There has been no lack of work, it is true; but it must always be directed towards God. Prayer (spiritual life): too little faithfulness—too much time spent in externals (interruptions, visits, rosary!). Old age is making its presence felt more and more—so I must just bear this in the spirit of faith and love; and not complain but accept everything with tranquillity and energy and regard it as part of the service of God; but at the same time try, as long as possible, to conserve my strength for my work and not be unreasonable!

I look upon the approach of death with tranquillity and confidence: God has given me so many graces and he will not abandon me then. But now more than ever I must realize that the rest of my life is a (or the) preparation for death. 'Therefore you must also be ready: for the Son of Man is coming at an hour (and in a way) you do not expect' [cf Mt 24:44]. 17.IX.67
7.IV.68

II/3 *The avoidance of sin, irregularity and the spirit of the world*[2]
I shall only avoid sin, even the smallest sin, if I learn to avoid all irregularity inwardly and outwardly and refuse to flirt with the principles of the world. As for irregularity: 'nature' has never really been

---

[1] From the prayers at the foot of the altar in the Tridentine Mass.
[2] Cf Exercises, colloquy after the meditation on sin. The retreatant is advised to ask for three graces: 'a deep felt consciousness of my sins and a profound disgust with them; an appreciation of the irregularity of what I have done, so that, by hating that, I may lead a better and more regular life; a knowledge of the world such that I may come to hate it and so give up all worldliness and folly' (63).

completely dead in me; sensuality, selfishness and laziness keep on appearing, even if it is only in small things, and they easily lead to irregularities, if not sin. I cannot afford to make any concessions in this respect but must observe order in all things. The world shows its influence in the shrill clamour of its principles and its half-truths, which then automatically lead on to irregularities and sin. They are for the most part half true and so can easily deceive.

All this is so for me even after sixty-five years in the Society. So I must always keep a check on myself, daily through a carefully made examination of conscience, weekly through confession and monthly through the recollection. Only by using these means shall I be able to keep myself free from faults.

II/4 *The choice of me in particular* Out of countless millions the Lord has chosen me for his special service, not for any merit of mine but by a decree of his love: 'for those whom he foreknew he also predestined to be conformed to the image of his Son' (cf Rom 8:29). My goal is to be conformed to the image of his Son. Christ, then, is my model. It is not for me to make the first move: 'the men whom thou gavest me' [Jn 17:6]—indeed even our Lord as man had no choice to make: I have been given to him. And my task is clear—to be conformed to Christ—that means to live and work according to his example. In this I must not let myself be held back: 'by my own natural weakness and love of the world and of the flesh' [cf Exercises 97]. The way is clear and I have now only to consider how I am to proceed along it in spite of these obstacles. Our Lord says: 'Follow me' [cf Mk 2:16]. I must make a serious renewal on this point. Fiat, fiat!

III/1 *God's decree to redeem the world* The Blessed Trinity wanted to share its glory and happiness with others for its own honour and the salvation of these its creatures. They were all meant to ratify the decree of God by their free will. But as they misused their free will and so failed in their vocation, God helps them by the decision that his Son should become man.[3]

III/2 *The Annunciation* (Lk 1:26–38) The greatest happening (of all time) with the simplest means. An unknown virgin—but full of grace; at the announcement of the greatest dignity: the handmaid of the Lord. And she remained the handmaid of the Lord throughout her life right up to the time when she stood beneath the cross. Therefore he who is mighty has done great things for her [Lk 1:49]! I must also be a servant

---

[3] Cf Vatican II: '(The Father) did not abandon men after they had fallen in Adam, but ceaselessly offered them helps to salvation, in anticipation of Christ the redeemer, "who is the image of the invisible God, the first-born of every creature" (Col 1:15). All the elect, before time began, the Father "foreknew and predestined to become conformed to the image of his Son, that he should be the first-born among many brethren" (Rom 8:29)' (*Constit. on the Church*, 2).

of the Lord in all things and at all times, as our Lord himself was the Servant of the Lord.

III/3 *The Nativity* (Lk 2:1–7) The birth in Bethlehem meant an unusual amount of sacrifice for our Lord: but he arranged it all like this himself and refused to avoid any of it: this was how he began to put into effect the plan of salvation, his task as the redeemer. This is what sharing in the realization of the plan of salvation means for me too. I must not avoid any sacrifice. Mary and Joseph also had to share in it.

Mary gave our Lord his human body, through which he was able to suffer for us. She was fully conscious of what she was doing ('fiat') and so by this was already cooperator.[4]

Joseph offers himself for God's service as a virgin: and he too does so voluntarily. Celibacy!
15.X.67
5.V.68

III/4 *The presentation in the temple* [Lk 2:22–35] Everything here is a story of sacrifice: not so much material sacrifices, such as were made for other children as well, but principally sacrifices for God's work of salvation, which our Lord and his holy mother are already making in their hearts and which they are later to complete by the cross and by suffering. This is cooperation in God's saving work, absolutely essential and predetermined in God's eternal decree. These sacrifices can be for the salvation of all for the 'rising' of all; but in fact they are only so for those who accept the grace by their own free choice.

This scene must be a model for all the work I have still to do: sacrifice on my part for the salvation of souls; success does not depend on me; but I can pray and suffer for this. Fiat.

IV/2 *Nazareth* [cf Lk 2: 40, 52] I can learn a lot from Nazareth.
1) Work: hundreds of little 'unimportant' matters, but they are part of my position and so part of God's will; so I must do them with precision, joy and love, everything with apostolic intentions.
2) Love in daily contacts: always try to make others happy by taking interest in them, talking to them with no trace of criticism or negative attitude.
3) Prayer must be joined to work and never be allowed to be disturbed by busyness.
4) Progress: even in my old age I must try to make progress—in wisdom and grace. So always be willing to learn!

[4] In describing the role of the Blessed Virgin Mary in the economy of salvation, the Council says: 'Rightly therefore the holy Fathers see her as used by God not merely in a passive way, but as cooperating in the work of human salvation through free faith and obedience. For, as St Irenaeus says, she, "being obedient, became the cause of salvation for herself and for the whole human race". Hence in their preaching not a few of the early Fathers gladly assert with him: "The knot of Eve's disobedience was untied by Mary's obedience. What the virgin Eve bound through her unbelief, Mary loosened by her faith." Comparing Mary with Eve, they call her "the mother of the living", and still more often they say: "death through Eve, life through Mary" ' (*Const. on the Church*, 56).

IV/3 *The call of the apostles* Our Lord has put his work into the hands of men, whom he chooses himself. They have, therefore, an uncommonly heavy responsibility: the welfare or the downfall of Christ's foundation depends on them.

Everyone's task is not at once clear; it evolves gradually and can often only be recognized at the end of life. And at any moment there may be a fresh call. The genuineness of the call will be clear through obedience, and sometimes also through the circumstances, if understood correctly. If it is clear, then I can and must follow it.

But those who are called do not call one another as in a commercial company; by their call they are led to one another and so must deal with one another in harmony and unanimity. But they also supplement one another's work and in so doing promote the cause of Christ. I must remember all this as I carry out my task.

IV/4 *The marriage feast of Cana* [Jn 2:1–11] This episode has more than a material significance; this is the beginning of the revaluation of the primary cell of human society,[5] which had become so devalued in paganism (and Judaism). Our Lord goes there to show what an important thing the family is and how concerned he is about it, and this in the company of his holy mother, from whose virginal marriage he himself comes. This is why he is so quick and ready to listen to her intercession, for she knows how important this moment is. Clearly all this has been arranged by providence.

But the main thing is that here on this occasion, which is so fundamentally human, we see the importance, the symbolism as it were, of the mother's role. From the cradle of society Mary takes this role to herself (cf Church and Modern World 47–49). This is, however, at the same time an occasion for strengthening the Church ('and his disciples believed in him'). 13.VI.68

V/1 *The Sermon on the Mount* [Mt 5:1–16] This is addressed principally to the disciples—and so in a special way to me as well. It tells me I must be free from all selfishness, from all laziness, all irritability, from everything that can cloud the purity of the soul. In all these ways I must be a light and a model; I must be like salt that makes the others resistant and tasty—and again not for my sake or my honour, but that they may glorify the Father who is in heaven. In this way even my interior life has an apostolic aim. And this is particularly true of me in my exposed position. 12.XI.67

V/2 *The mission of the apostles* Our Lord sends his 'beloved' disciples out. Love for them does not make him selfish, wanting to have them always at his side. It is an act of love for him to send them and in such a way that they are not only to work for him but also to suffer for

---

[5] The family.

him. He leaves no doubt in their minds on that score [cf Mt 10:16 ff]. The apostolate is always a cross. Our Lord does not want comfortable apostles [cf Mk 6:7 ff]. Of course he always gives them his grace but this must find a soul that is inwardly cleansed and ready to receive it. So our Lord also speaks of the cross, of his example and of following him [cf Mt 16:21–26]. Only then will the apostolate be fruitful [cf Jn 12:24 f]. The true apostle must be a saint.

V/3 *The multiplication of the loaves* [Mk 6:30–44] Our Lord attracts the crowds because they are looking for a shepherd who is not like the Pharisees. It is his noble love that has this effect. Thus he cannot send them away, even when he and the disciples are tired. How often he is tired is shown by the fact that he goes to sleep on the boat [Mk 4:37]. If I am tired now, it was certainly not in vain. But I must not use this as an excuse for taking life easy: I can only be happy that our Lord has made use of me and pray that I may labour for him to the end. This will be a special grace from God!

Our Lord's example: he does not force himself into the foreground and yet he is the one from whom everything comes. We are only the instruments he uses and nothing else. Am I always a good instrument? I will make an effort to be so more and more. But I must not force myself into the foreground either; I must let my helpers do their work and allow them the credit that comes from it. Hence, modesty and selflessness. Our Lord is at work in everything and everyone.

V/4 *I am the good shepherd* [Jn 10: 11–18] Our Lord puts this into practice to the extreme: he gave his life for his sheep. The principle, the basic principle, is the realization of God's decree of salvation. This is why he is the good shepherd not only for one nation or one class but for all men. All are called to salvation. And so I must not restrict my pastoral concern either: I must always, at least in my intentions, regard all men as my objective and be concerned in some way for all, at least through prayer and sacrifice. For me, then, there must not just be a Secretariat for Christians but also for the non-Christians and also for the non-believers: 'he wants all men to be saved and come to the knowledge of truth' [1 Tim 2:4]. Therefore I must have a world-wide apostolic zeal. Even if I have a definite task, my interest must be for all, and show itself, as far as possible, mainly in prayer (intentions in Mass, prayer after Mass, examination of conscience, visits etc).

VI/1 & 2 *The transfiguration* This mystery made a profound impression on the apostles. Peter sees it as the confirmation of his preaching of the 'power and coming of our Lord' [2 Pet 1:16 f]. He was an 'eye witness' of his majesty; for him it is a confirmation of the 'prophetic word', a 'lamp shining in a dark place'. For him it is the great event he still carries in his memory before the 'putting off of my body'. In the transfiguration

John sees the evidence of his 'glory', of the glory of 'the only Son of God', ('this is my beloved son'), in a way the confirmation of his whole gospel of the 'Word' [cf Jn 1:14]. For me too this mystery is very important: it shows me how meaningful my teaching is and how important my life. This is not the quiet summit of Mount Tabor, where I can build lasting arbours: but it is the foundation on which, like the apostles, I must build, 'as long as I am in this body'. For I too belong to those favourites to whom the Lord gave this deeper insight into his glory, and so I too must preach this till the 'putting off of my body', as well and as faithfully as I can. But I must not forget to speak of his 'departure in Jerusalem' (Lk 9:31) of the cross, which is my lot too and perhaps from now on more than ever.

V/3 *Palm Sunday* [Jn 12:12–36] Our Lord celebrates this triumph because the Father wants it this way. But it is a sad procession. It reminds our Lord that the town that is celebrating does not believe in him or receive him. On the other hand he does see good will among the 'heathen':[6] but their time has not yet come. First the grain of wheat must fall into the ground and die; but then it will bear 'much' fruit. Imagine all that our Lord may have seen at this moment in spirit! Here once again we have the world-wide view, corresponding to God's universal plan of salvation. But the only way it can be put into effect is still the cross, this 'dying'. It is this that our Lord stresses once again here. I too must keep this spiritual element always present in all that I do. It is the basic condition for fruitfulness. 17.XII.67

VI/4 *The holy Eucharist* I must keep myself free from any 'half-heartedness'. If this applies to anything, it applies to love for the holy Eucharist. Every day I celebrate my Mass but it must never become an 'everyday affair' for me. And my visits? Preparation for Mass? Thanksgiving? Once again I have seen what a great thing this sacrament of union is,[7]—but I must put it into practice! Many saints have perhaps, or certainly, had less understanding—but they had greater devotion and love. This resolution must be one of the main resolutions of this retreat and in my recollections it must be renewed again and again and perfected.

VII/1 & 2 *The Garden of Olives and the flight of the disciples* (Mt 26:33–41) The behaviour of the disciples was a great blow to our Lord. Even the most favoured of them cannot watch 'one hour' with him. They all protested their loyalty but what a gap there is between resolution and reality. 'Though they all fall away . . . I will never fall away'—and it is precisely he who denies him three times [Mt 26:69–75].

[6] A reference to the Greeks, who had also come to the feast and wanted to see Christ (cf Jn 12:20 ff).

[7] 'A memorial of his death and resurrection; a sacrament of love, a sign of unity, a bond of charity' (*Constit. on the Liturgy*, 47).

Are my retreat resolutions to be as ineffectual as the protestations of the disciples? I must remember our Lord's warning: 'watch and pray that you may not enter into temptation'—that you may be preserved from the danger. This lack of loyalty is a bitter blow to our Lord; but in spite of all this he does not grow tired of the disciples but showers new graces on them; for they have been given to him by the Father [cf Jn 17:6]. But the disciples should have spared him these disappointments, as I too should spare him such things. Would that I could say to him, like Peter after the resurrection: 'Lord, you know everything; you know that I love you' [Jn 21:17].

VII/3 *Our Lord on the cross* He is really a king in the way he bears it all. He shows no sign of his cruel suffering but he does show his noble patience and his truly divine love. We can see this mainly in his words: they are the words of someone in complete control, as if he had nothing at all to suffer himself. It can hardly ever have happened that a dying man resembled him in this way. And his love goes out above all to his enemies, who have brought him to the cross; to the men crucified with him and only then to his mother and the beloved disciple, who has followed him right to the foot of the cross. He gives only a hint of his inward suffering. Happy the dying man who can be even a little like him!

VIII/1 & 2 *The resurrection* Our Lord's victory begins with his death: the removal of his body from the cross by Joseph of Arimathea: the anointing by Nicodemus, the watching soldiers as witnesses of his resurrection [Mt 28:11–14], his appearance in 'hell':[8] all these things are a sign of the power of the crucified Lord over his enemies and his love for his friends. And then come the appearances as proofs of the resurrection and evidence of his love. And this now goes on through the centuries and happens to millions of people; great is the Lord, great his power and great his love! [cf Ps 147:5.]

VIII/3 *The days after the resurrection* are an important time for the Church.[9] Our Lord gives the faith a firm foundation; he does all he can to confirm his disciples' faith. It is also a time of love: he has comfort to offer everywhere—to Peter, the disciples, the women.[10] And lastly a time of power and of the handing over of power: the sacrament of penance, the primacy and the power of teaching. And lastly a time of hope: 'I am with you always, to the close of the age' [Mt 28:20]. Gratitude and love!

VIII/4 *Love* [Exercises 230–237] This meditation is only a confirmation and development of all that this retreat has shown me and all that I

---

[8] Cf 1 Pet 3:18–19; also Apostles' Creed.   [9] Cf 1965 and 66/V/3.
[10] In the meditation on the mysteries of the risen Christ, Exercises suggest among other things that one should 'see Christ our Lord doing the work of consolation, comparing it with the way friends are accustomed to console one another' (224).

have put down in my 'decision'. It tells me that all the gifts that I have received from God are for God and only for God, and that I must perfect and develop them more and more for God's sake. I must be conscious of his presence at all times and in all things, but especially too of his presence in my soul through grace [cf Jn 14:23]. So I must see him in my colleagues and in general in all my fellow-men, indeed in all creatures. Then I shall keep him constantly present—that I am working for him is clear; but I must not forget that all inspirations, all illuminations etc are his 'work' for me personally.—So the thing is to recognize him more and more and use all the means to this end (meditation, reading) more and more faithfully. Make me love thee more and more.

13.VI.68

FROM THE MONTHLY RECOLLECTIONS

17.IX.1967
1) A universal apostolic interest. Prayer and sacrifice.
2) No half-measures in the religious life, in work and behaviour.
3) Must not become too wrapped up in work (visits).
4) Make everyone happy and encourage them.

I/1 Must not be content with the minimum.
I/2 Make use of everything to serve God generously; everything is a means to that end and an incentive.
I/3 Supernatural atmosphere!
I/4 I must be what people rightly expect me to be. My position is a special responsibility.
II/1 Prayer, work and suffering as a preparation for death.

15.X.1967
1) Magnanimous and open. Correspond with grace.
2) 'A model to the flock' [cf 1 Pet 5:3]—give everyone a good example in everything.
3) Have God present even in the midst of work.
4) Encourage everyone with love and patience. Ave M.

II/3 Nature—sensuality (looks etc). No concessions! take things seriously!
II/4 To be conformed to the image of Christ.
III/2 Handmaid of the Lord—servant of the Lord.
III/3 A conscious fiat!

12.XI.1967
1) Live up to my vocation without special intentions.[11]

---

[11] This phrase is not clear. The cardinal seems to be referring to I/1; the phrase could mean either that all *secondary* intentions should be excluded or that he should not follow the possibly different method of others.

2) A model for others in all my behaviour.
3) Must not become wrapped up in my work.
4) 'I shall not refuse to carry on working.'[12]

IV/3 Call to cooperation—must not insist on others sharing my views.

IV/4 Concern for the family is also a strengthening of the Church.

V/1 The apostolate of my interior life and of my conduct.

17.XII.1967
1) Make an effort to be a model for others.
2) Try to live in a deep and constant union with God.
3) The Lord is near: in my heart, in the Eucharist—only learn to know myself: in grace.[13]
4) Try to make everyone happy.

V/2 Not comfortable apostles! Cross!

V/3 Must labour to the end for our Lord as his instrument.

V/4 Apostolate for all: worldwide!—at least by prayer for all.

VI/2 Until the 'putting off of my body'.

14.I.1968
Must be a model for all at all times! Not too wrapped up in my work. 'That I may . . . be found in him' (Phil 3:9). Examination of conscience. In my old age I must still advance in virtue and perfection (IV/2). Love, obliging, advice, help, patience, no unkind criticism.

VII/4 Love for the holy Eucharist.

VII/1 Spare our Lord disappointment (Peter—they all fled [Mt 26:56]!).

11.II.1968
The many graces call for a special effort from me, a personal effort [?], but also for my work, precisely because of the many graces—no half-measures, an example to others! But not too wrapped up in my work: recollection—raising the mind to God [?]—visits. Try to make everyone happy and to encourage all. No [?] unkind criticism.

VI/4 Visits! Eucharist: a devotion corresponding to the grace and understanding given to me.

VII/1 Energetic loyalty to our Lord: 'and all fled'!! Do not disappoint our Lord! 'You know that I love you!'

VII/3 The Cross: as if he had nothing to suffer! Such majestic suffering. Do not look for sympathy!'

---

[12] From the liturgy: the office of St Martin of Tours (11 November). Martin fell ill and prayed that God might free him from this 'mortal prison'; but his disciples heard this and implored him not to leave them. So he changed his prayer and, inspired by St Paul in Phil 1:24 f, prayed 'O Lord, if I am still necessary to your people, I do not refuse to labour.' The author often used these words in conversation.

[13] Cf the monthly recollection of 11 December 1966.

10.III.1968
1) Live up to my vocation faithfully in everything; cooperate with God's grace.
2) Faithful to my spiritual exercises: examination of conscience, rosary, visits.
3) Faithfulness and order in my daily work.
4) Faithful in understanding love.

I/1 Everywhere seek the greater glory of God.
I/2 No half-measures, but generous in everything—everything is a means to his service: response to God's love.

12.IV.1968
An example for all at all times, try to spread happiness. The people who work with me—given to me by God as assistants.

I/3 Live in a supernatural atmosphere: led by the Spirit of God!
I/4 Make an effort to be what people take me for.

5.V.1968
Examination of conscience—you will see me again and you will rejoice [cf Jn 16:22]—to see: in revelation, (in the Church), in my neighbour, even in tribulations: to rejoice in Jesus—in Mass . . .

12.VI.1968
World-wide interests—an example for all: religious life; work, love, recollection and union with God.—Encourage all that is good—celebration of Mass.

VIII/4 Perfect the gifts that God has given me more and more—see God in everything—sacrifice for the kingdom of God and souls—not 'activism'.

CHAPTER 12

'A life of quiet humble faith'
1968

In the retreat notes for 1968 the author writes: 'In my old age I cannot make any plans or start any long term projects: it is God who makes plans for me and I have only to carry them out quietly and faithfully. Every situation that he sends me gives me an opportunity to sanctify myself and also to work for his Church and for souls, at least through patience and suffering, through love and good example' (I/3). In the meditation on the Presentation in the Temple we read: 'my life too must be a life of quiet humble faith, not making anything of itself but in all things standing by what is revealed, without being concerned with what people think' (IV/2). These words are very significant for the last period of the author's life. Apart from one or two unusual happenings, his life became more and more quiet; his work, however, continued to be intensive.

On 24 September 1967 he again flew to Germany to open the rebuilt grammar school in Rastatt, where he had matriculated in 1900. On this occasion he was the only speaker to speak without notes! On 29 September the synod of bishops began and in his capacity as president of the secretariat he took part. And at his advanced age the three-hour sessions, which were held nearly every day, were more than enough and very arduous. Twice he intervened in the discussion: once in the debate on the problem of mixed marriages and the other time on the draft proposal on modern problems in the field of doctrine. On this last occasion he stressed especially the duty of bishops or episcopal conferences to preach, and spoke in favour of the setting up of an international theological commission, to assist the Holy See's Congregation for the Doctrine of the Faith in the difficult questions of today.

During the last days of this bishops' Synod, Rome had the unique experience of an official visit by the Ecumenical Patriarch Athenagoras I. And the communal Liturgy of the Word that took place in St Peter's in the presence of all the members of the Synod was particularly impressive. At the end, when the old cardinal climbed up onto the platform in front of the Confession, where the Holy Father and the Patriarch were standing, to give the Patriarch the kiss of peace, Pope Paul put his hands on the shoulders of both of them as if he was trying to embrace them both at once. The applause with which those present greeted this surprising and deeply symbolic gesture was quite extraordinary. The results of this visit were drawn up in a far-sighted 'Common Declaration', which was read out at the farewell audience on 28 October.

One afternoon soon after the end of the synod the cardinal fell in his bedroom. Fortunately nothing was broken, but for some weeks he suffered considerable pain. The accident meant that the cardinal had to take an enforced holiday after all the strain of the bishops' synod. It was a relief that because of this he was automatically dispensed from the day-long sessions of the Consilium for Liturgical Reform. His literary activity continued however, with the result that *We Who Serve* was ready by the end of 1967: this book explains the Council's teaching on the concept of the ministry and its biblical basis.

Even in the first month of 1968 he pressed on with his writing. He was working on a book with the provisional title *Christ and Mankind*, whose aim was to arrange a systematic order, and give the exegesis and theological explanation of, the Pauline texts quoted in the Council documents. By the summer holidays it was rather more than half finished (seven chapters).

At the beginning of June the Secretatriat was able to publish the essential guidelines for cooperation with non-Catholic colleagues in the production of common translations of scripture—the preparation of this had been entrusted by the Holy Father to the Secretariat, and was of great importance.

In July a great ecumenical event took place at Uppsala—the fourth General Assembly of the World Council of Churches. Only five observers had been sent by the Catholics to the preceding assembly in New Delhi in 1961, and now there were three times as many—not counting the guests.

About the same time (20–24 July) the cardinal left his Swiss holiday resort to visit his home village—now almost an annual event—without any idea that this was to be the last visit he would make there. Then he returned to Switzerland for his annual retreat.

In his notebook there is a sheet with the order of the day which he had drawn up for this retreat: 5.30 rise: 6 o'clock Lauds/Terce; 6.30 to 7.30 first meditation; 7.30 to 8.15 Mass; 8.15 reflection etc; 8.30 breakfast; 8.45 to 9.15 rest; 10 to 11.30 second meditation; 12 to 1.30 lunch—rest; 1.30 Vespers, Compline, Rosary; 2.30 to 4 third meditation; 5 to 6.30 fourth meditation. And after this he had added 'post 11.30; 6.30'.

After the retreat, he celebrated the golden jubilee of his solemn vows, on 18 August. Ten days later he fell ill with a serious lung complaint. He never fully recovered from this.

RETREAT 1968

Menzingen, 1–8 August

I/1 *The will of God, my sanctification* [1 Thess 4:3; cf Const. on the Church, 5, 39] My sanctification is in a special way the will of God: the many unusual graces that he has given me from the beginning of my life are a proof of this. But this sanctification does not depend on my will: God shows me what it involves in the circumstances of life in which he has placed me. It is in these circumstances that I must sanctify myself and behave in a holy way. In this sense too my sanctification is the will of God. It is not, then, an abstract mechanical holiness; I must be a holy priest, Jesuit, cardinal in the concrete circumstances of my job. Holiness means doing the will of God in all circumstances, as I recognize it and as it comes to me, and not seeking my own ends in this but only God's will. The will of God my sanctification.

I/2 *The source of holiness* Holiness is not an obligation imposed on me by a law from outside; it comes from the innermost being of a Christian. Bound to God by faith and baptism I must share his inmost being. In this the great model is Christ, the Son of God, born of the Holy Spirit and filled with the Holy Spirit at baptism. I must let Christ 'make me his own'[1] and share his thoughts, actions and works. The 'imitation of Christ' is, then, the inner law of sanctity [cf Rom 8:29], but again it is not a merely mechanical imitation but imitation of his thoughts, will and love. These are his through the Spirit of God, who dwells in him, and they are mine too through the same Holy Spirit, who dwells in me too. The more I am inspired by these basic truths and the more I strive to put them into effect, the closer I shall be to sanctity.

I/3 *The way to holiness* In the first place: 1) Faithfulness in spiritual exercises, in which I get examples of holiness and at the same time pray for strength, perseverance and persistence. 2) Faithfulness in carrying out all my other duties, just as every day brings them. So every day must be ordered: daily examination of conscience: to arrange the day I must prepare myself for it; prayer for help and strength. 3) Interior peace (indifference!): the only thing that matters is the will of God. It is he who determines my progress, and so also my progress towards sanctity. In my old age I cannot make any plans or start any long term projects: it is God who makes plans for me and I have only to carry them out quietly and faithfully. Every situation that he sends me gives me an opportunity of sanctifying myself and also of working for his Church

---

[1] Cf Phil 3:12: '. . . I press on (towards the goal) to make it my own, because Christ Jesus has made me his own.' In 1966 Cardinal Bea had published a small book entitled *Von Christus erfasst*, which dealt with various aspects of the personality and theology of St Paul,' this was translated into various languages.

and for souls, at least by patience and suffering, by love and good example. 4) In all things I have our Lord's example before my eyes: 'that I may do your will always'.

I/4 *My sanctity in the Church* My position in the Church obliges me to aim at a special sanctity: 1) First of all my position as a member of the hierarchy.² As a cardinal I am set on the lampstand and in a very special way with my reputation. In all things I must be an outstanding model of sanctity—and also in the exercise of my office and my various functions. Never under any circumstances must I act according to worldly principles and rules. St Robert Bellarmine is my model!
2) I am a priest of the Church. The few priestly functions³ that I do carry out should be edifying and elevating; especially, however, the Mass.
3) I am a religious, and so consecrated and bound in a special way to God, to the Church and to souls.⁴ How much the Church owes to holy religious, especially priests. As a cardinal I do not cease to be a religious. So I must avoid all worldly and earthly pomp and give an example of true fervour.
4) And finally I am a Jesuit, and so in a special way an apostle. This apostolate should be a special task for me. 25.VIII.68

II/1 *The Sacred Heart: his love—my response?* What has Jesus' love done for me? Vocation, preservation and encouragement in my vocation. He has guided me, and without my having any inkling of it he has prepared me for my work, along ways that did not depend on me. I have not responded fully to this love. Not that there has been any lack of work but the work was too much a matter of 'activity', without any loving union and link with God, without any true and genuine fervour. This is what I must now aim at above all else, especially now that external work is less possible for me.

II/2 *The struggle against sin* The great heresy of our time is 'humanism'.⁵ In reality man is not simply good, and 'human' is not yet the same as 'good'. The whole of the history of the world shows this. So in my own life and in my work I must treat things with a certain suspicion, but not in a way that hinders me but one that guides me. In my own life: I must make faithful use of the means that are at my disposal as a protection and a help: spiritual exercises, meditation, reading and above all prayer.

² Cf *Const. on the Church*, 41.
³ The author means that he can have little part in *direct* pastoral or liturgical work.
⁴ Cf Vatican II, *Decree on the Appropriate Renewal of the Religious Life*, 1.
⁵ What follows shows that the author is not opposed to all humanism, but is on his guard against illusions; the fact of sin, together with all its consequences must be kept in mind (cf the remarks on the corruption of human nature in 1959/I/3, note 6). It is scarcely necessary to point out that the author's views are straight from the New Testament; cf Mt 7:13; Jn 7:7; Rom 5:12 etc.

Then there is the example and the strength of our Lord: the incarnation itself is a sign that our Lord wants to help the world, not only by expiation and satisfaction, but above all by his example and strength: an example by his life, strength through grace and especially through baptism, the Eucharist and the sacrament of penance. For this reason he founded the Church and for this reason too he made me a mediator. Thus I am myself involved in the struggle against sin and so must first avoid it myself and overcome it in myself. Cooperation with our Lord, then, encourages in the world as well a true and genuine 'humanism', assimilation to the God-man Christ.

II/3 *The will of God in our Society*[6] By the grace of God I am a member of the Society and therefore must put the will of God into practice according to its mind and its spirit. But, as expressed in St Ignatius, this spirit is the closest union with God: 'to find God in everything',[7] not in imagination but in reality. He is in all things: by his presence, his will and his essence. Therefore, I must also 'find' him, see him and recognize him in all things, all events, every happening. This will affect my whole conduct towards people and teach me to love even those who are opposed to me. I must 'serve' everyone in the Lord, and their souls in particular. This basic thought will and must overcome all obstacles and difficulties, because in all things I see only the will of God.

II/4 *The kingdom of Christ* [Exercises 91–98] The title could be misleading: it is not a question of a material kingdom but of the rule of the Spirit, of truth: 'that I may bear witness to the truth'. This 'witness' is not given with earthly weapons but by preaching [cf Jn 18:36 f]. It is, then, my task to preach the 'truth', that truth that is in the Word of God, the 'Gospel'. But in order to do this I must myself be thoroughly penetrated by it. Today this task is more important than ever. Today people resist the Word of God not with the force of weapons but with spiritual weapons, especially since the Council, which has done so much good. I must fight this spiritual battle loyally and with the 'armour of God' (Eph 6:11), but above all with prayer too: 'pray at all times in the Spirit, with all prayer and supplication, making supplication for all the saints', in order 'that utterance may be given' to the preachers of the Gospel and that they 'may declare it boldly as they ought' [Eph 6:18 f]. This is a major task today.

III/1 *The incarnation*—God could have left men to their fate, which they had freely chosen. But he wanted to lead them back to him in love

---

[6] i.e. the Society of Jesus.

[7] This meditation is based mainly on Exercises 230–237, on achieving love. The Constitutions describe the 'right intention', by which members of the Society are to be guided in all things: 'They should often be reminded to seek our Lord in all things and to put away love for all creatures as much as possible, so as to be able to bestow it on the Creator of all things. They should love him in all his creatures and all his creatures in him, according to his most holy and divine will' (III, 1, 26).

and because of love, and all of them, all races and all peoples. And this was the reason for the commission given to the apostles for all: 'go therefore and make disciples of *all* nations' (Mt 28:19). Therefore mankind should be one.[8] The Church is the means of salvation for all men and its mission is directed at all. And this is why he chooses all sorts, not only learned men and important ones, but poor fishermen, little people: me too, and I should never have a thought of such a mission. I must have the same world-wide approach as the one who chose me.

III/2 *The annunciation* [Lk 1:26–38]   The angel: his only concern is to pass on the message to Mary, to carry out God's orders. He has no thought for himself, for his dignity or position. He has no desire to be anything but God's servant. A glorious example for every member of the hierarchy and also for me! No seeking for honour, respect or possessions: to be nothing but God's delegates and servants of the Church and of souls.

And Mary too wants to be nothing but 'the hand-maid of the Lord'. All the great promises concerning her Son make no impression on her; she only wants to know how God's will can be fulfilled in her. She does not say: 'since I have not known my husband', but: how shall what is to happen in the future come about?[9] She knows that by God's will she is dedicated to virginity. Here we see the expression of all Mary's profound greatness. This consideration is a new incentive for me to honour Mary as my great model and to imitate her virtues faithfully.

III/3 *The visitation* [Lk 1:39–55]   (a) 'In haste': if I can be of assistance to someone, I will not hesitate. Will not make people keep on asking me. If I have to turn down the request, then I will do it with love and kindness.

'Into the hill country': I must help my neighbour even if it involves sacrifice.

'She greeted Elizabeth': although she knows what God has done to her she greets her relative before she is greeted herself: significant for me; in all things I must be obliging and not seek the limelight! And bring blessings wherever I go, even without being asked.

(b) 'Mother of my Lord': the *theotokos* announced by Elizabeth, filled with the Holy Spirit.

(c) Magnificat: Mary is quite aware of what God has done for her and rejoices over it, but 'in the Lord': she knows and admits that he is the great and holy one. Humility is truth. She also knows that these gifts of hers are for the benefit of Israel, for God's people. What the Lord gives me, too, is not for me but for the Church and for souls.

---

[8] Cf Vatican II, *Declaration on the Relationship of the Church to Non-Christian Religions*, 1.

[9] The author uses the Greek *syllempse*, used at the Annunciation by the Angel, to show that Mary's question 'how shall this be?' also refers to the whole future conduct of the Mother of God, and to her resolution of virginity for the future.

III/4 *The nativity* [Lk 2:1-7]

1) Everything is difficult for the Holy Family, but I cannot imagine that they had any thoughts or uttered any sound of complaint or criticism. This is an important point for me. I can certainly not agree with everything that happens, but I must avoid criticism. As a cardinal I must give good example and rather than criticize I should defend the authorities, especially the Holy Father, and explain their meaning, or at least be silent.[10] And as a Jesuit too I must be loyal and careful on this point, for the sake of good example and the reputation of the Society.

2) Mary and Joseph accepted all the unpleasantness, disappointment and disagreement in a spirit of faith. They have God's word through the angel and they know that their child is the Son of God. This is the basis of their faith, which nothing can shake but which on the other hand instils into them the greatest reverence in all that they see and suffer, just as faith gives me the greatest reverence towards our Lord in the Holy Eucharist, especially in the Mass.

3) All this for me [cf Exercises 116], for me a sinner, all that our Lord took upon himself. What shall I do for thee?

IV/1 *The shepherds* [Lk 2:8-18] It is significant that the first people called to the crib are poor shepherds and that after the well-attested information of the angel they go 'with haste' to the crib without taking offence at the news of the 'Saviour, Christ and Lord' so unknown, 'wrapped in swaddling clothes and lying in a manger'. This is a strong faith that does not rationalize and one that does lead to action as a result. And this faith is rewarded so that they returned home joyfully and praised God 'for all that they had heard and seen'. At the same time, however, they are also made apostles. Here I have the opposite of our rationalistic secularized world, which does not recognize the idea of 'mystery' any more but wants to grasp everything with the human mind. It is my task to oppose this spirit of the times and see that justic is done to the faith.

IV/2 *The presentation in the temple* [Lk 2:22-38] This episode is also a mystery of *faith*, of a living but quiet, almost hidden, faith, both in the case of our Lord and also of Mary and Joseph and finally of Simeon and Annas. They all know the nature and mission of our Lord, but they are all silent and behave as if they knew nothing of it. For Mary this is true of her whole life: in all things she is a quiet, humble, modestly retiring woman, who does not stand on her dignity: 'my secret to myself' [Is 24:16]. This is the sword that pierces her heart until she is taken up in glory into heaven. My life too must be a life of quiet, humble faith, not making anything of itself, but in all things standing by what is revealed to it, without being concerned with what people think.

---

[10] Cf Rule 10, quoted in 1964/VI/2, note 12: 'in order that we may hold the opinions we should hold in the Church militant' (Exercises 362).

IV/3 *The hidden life* [Lk 2:40, 52] 1) My life too must be a 'hidden life': I must not try to create a sensation, especially now that I have no further occasion to appear in public (journeys, lectures etc). In quietness and seclusion I must perform my daily and weekly tasks. But I must always try to advance in wisdom by the study of topical questions, informative reading, discussion with others, 'always ready to learn'.
2) But apart from this my life must be a life of progress in God's favour. And it will be, if I carry out faithfully my resolutions to grow in sanctity. The decrees of the Council on priestly and religious virtue should be a constant help to me in this.

IV/4 *The baptism* [Mt 3:13–17] With the baptism our Lord begins his active redemptive work. The hidden life was also important for that; but the real work of organizing the redemption begins with the sacrament of 'initiation'. St Ignatius is right to point out that he said 'goodbye' to his mother [Exercises 273], and indeed it is a fact that through baptism a new family is created, having no further connections with the earthly family.[11] Of course Mary felt all the sorrow of this parting but here too she says her 'fiat'. For the bishop and priest of God's family this fact is significant.

Baptism is not only a purification ('baptism of water') but above all the coming of the 'fire', the Holy Spirit.[12] At baptism he begins his great work of redemption: incorporation into Christ, and so a temple of God, like Christ a child of God with all the graces resulting for us from that. So I must continue zealously to cultivate devotion to the Holy Spirit, especially for the work of union, which after all depends on him in a very special way [cf 1 Cor 12:12 f; Eph 4:3–6].

V/1 *The choice of the apostles* [Mt 3:31–19] The apostles did not appoint themselves but were chosen individually by our Lord, and chosen not because of their capabilities but simply by God's decree [Jn 17:6]. But our Lord gives them proof of his power and authority, so that they can all say with St Paul: 'I know whom I have believed' [2 Tim 1:12]. Their capability will come from the Holy Spirit. So the whole of the apostolate is an entirely divine institution. For us too, the successors of the apostles, this is a source of strength and confidence.

V/2 *The mission and the attitude of the apostles* If our Lord, in his day, could say that the harvest to be brought in was great, this is very

---

[11] Remember Christ's words: 'Here are my mother and my brethren! For whoever does the will of my Father in heaven is my brother, and sister, and mother' (Mt 12:48, 50). The union of which he is thinking is the deep union of grace; just as the Father is in Christ and Christ in the Father, so also are these people one in the Father and in Christ (cf Jn 14:23; Jn 17:21).

[12] Cf the preaching of the Baptist: 'I baptize you with water for repentance, but he who is coming after me is mightier than I . . . he will baptize you with the Holy Spirit and with fire' (Mt 3:11).

true of today.¹³ All the more since he sends us not just to Israel but 'into the whole world'. The world of today is not without God, but to a great extent anti-God; it does not want to have him and maintains that it does not need him.¹⁴ And so our Lord, and we ourselves with him, must have compassion on the people, and where they are looking for an earthly 'kingdom', bring them the kingdom of God, but also show them that the kingdom of God really brings them what they are longing for. The 'diseases' which the apostles are to cure are today diseases of the spirit, of the soul. The Church must stand today as a sign of God's love for mankind, and so I too must represent and embody this love to the full.¹⁵ I must understand and sympathize with the needs of the world and do all that lies in my power to help and to encourage others to help,¹⁶ and this even though we are 'like sheep in the midst of wolves' [Mt 10:16]

V/3 *The multiplication of the loaves and the walking on the water* Today when there is so much hunger in the world the multiplication of the loaves is a very topical theme. And if I cannot play a direct part, at least in my various positions I can encourage cooperation and urge people to help.¹⁷

The walking on the water is preceded by our Lord's night prayers; 'he went into the hills alone to pray' until about the fourth watch of the night [cf Mk 6:46 ff]. This prayer is the ideal, the sort of 'dialogue with God' that the Holy Father wants priests to have. And indeed: how many intentions, personal and apostolic, I have to bring before the heavenly Father day after day, just as the Church does in the Mass—it must not be mechanical, however, but personal and from the heart (a dialogue!).

V/4 *The beatitudes and the duty of example* [Mt 5:1–16] The eight beatitudes are diametrically opposed to the spirit of the world and yet there are millions who put them into practice today, not only religious but also many many layfolk.¹⁸ This is the great miracle of Christianity.

Salt of the earth—light of the world—to be this is my special vocation. As salt I must prove myself by representing genuinely Christian principles clearly and decisively without curtailment, either in my own private life or in public. This does not stop me adapting myself to the times in form, expression and speech. As a light I am, more than most, set on a lampstand and must be conscious of this all the time, without working ostentatiously but quietly, as a flame burns, without making a fuss.

¹³ Cf Vatican II, *Decree on the Church's Missionary Activity*, 10.
¹⁴ Cf *Constitution on the Church in the Modern World*, 19.
¹⁵ Cf ibid, 45; *Constitution on the Church*, 8.
¹⁶ Cf *Constitution on the Church in the Modern World*, 1.
¹⁷ In the field of cooperation with the World Council of Churches, one of the first steps taken was cooperation between the Catholic organization Caritas Internationalis and the corresponding section of the WCC.
¹⁸ Cf *Decree on the Apostolate of the Laity*, 4.

VI/1 *The transfiguration* [Mt 17:1–8]   The asceticism that our Lord teaches is a realistic one: he teaches not only the cross but also the transfiguration and insists on the connection between the two. And as an illustration of this he offers his own example. So it is just as remote from the type of asceticism that only overpowers its own ego as it is from the ideal of self-satisfaction that sets itself no limit. In my spiritual life, then, I must practise both these things: faithfulness to the cross and hope in glorification. The disciple is not above his master [Mt 10:24] but it is also true that 'the sufferings of this present time are not worth comparing with the glory that is to be revealed to us' [Rom 8:18].

VI/2 *The raising of Lazarus* [Jn 11:1–44]   In this miracle our Lord allows me a deep insight into his divine-human heart. He is not without feelings. Anyone loving him is sure that he will also be loved by him, whether man or boy, woman or girl. But his love is supernatural, not of flesh and blood. What a beautiful model for me! For my everyday life! He loves his disciples too as they love him. They are afraid for his life; he is not; but he puts them to the test—out of supernatural love for them [cf Jn 15:15]. And they are ready to go with him even if they have to 'die with him'. But how kind he is in talking it over with them!— Here we see no conventional 'Heart of Jesus', but our Lord in his everyday contacts and life. Only a person like John who hangs on every word from the lips of his 'friend' and sees into his heart can draw this picture of his master and friend. For me this heart of our Lord is an inimitable model!

VI/3 *The holy Eucharist*   This is the greatest thing I have as a priest. In it our Lord becomes present and active in me, when I celebrate the eucharistic sacrifice, and at the same time he becomes present for all under the eucharistic forms. This is why Mass must not become just a 'function' for me, something to be done like a lesson, for example. It must take hold of and lay claim to the depths of my being. It is an action which fulfils the prophecy that from the rising of the sun to its setting a 'pure oblation' will be offered to the Lord [Mal 1:10 f]. For those who celebrate it with me it must be a source of grace and blessing, and through me, the sacrificing priest, they should be encouraged to derive from it all the graces they need. So once again I must practise devotion to the holy Eucharist in a special way, but particularly the 'dialogue with Christ in the Eucharist', in frequent and regular visits to the Blessed Sacrament!

VI/4 *The farewell address and the high-priestly prayer*   The farewell address also applies to coming out of retreat. Our Lord is not leaving me: he stays and keeps me united to him, like the vine and the branch. More than that, he gives me the Holy Spirit who is in me and remains in me and recalls to my mind [Jn 14:26] what our Lord has said to me in this of the spiritual life. Moreover our Lord leaves me the effective help of retreat: this means not only theological truths but the practical lessons 'prayer in his name', which the Father will always hear [Jn 14:13 f].

But there is a condition for all this: that I should do the 'will of the Father', not only in great things but in such a way that all my daily activity is a fulfilment of the divine will, so that in a way I can say with our Lord: I have 'accomplished the work which thou gavest me to do' [Jn 17:4]. This must be the quintessence of this year's 'decision'.

VII/1 *The Garden of Olives* [Mt 26:31-44] The conduct of his disciples must have hurt our Lord a great deal. In the first place their self-confidence, in the fact of all that the Lord had foretold would happen. But then particularly their lack of sympathy. Of course they were tired after all that had gone before, but so was Judas! And after the kind way the Lord treated the three apostles he might at least have expected that they would have asked him why he was so upset and how they could help him. 'But they slept.' They think only of themselves! And how much he had watched for them and prayed and cared! Our Lord is not without feelings, neither then nor now. This lack of sympathy must hurt him deeply.

VII/2 *The Decision 1968*[19]

VII/3 *Jesus before his judges* This is not just the personal suffering of our Lord but in a way a programme: his Church will face countless judges, undefended and unarmed ('the sword into its sheath'!) [Jn 18:11]; it will not be in a position to defend itself but will be condemned unheard. This is the fate of millions of martyrs—and yet the Church is victorious. Two thousand years are proof of this. History confirms this too. There is no capitulation, no compromise. Everyone must stand clearly by the truth: only then can he conquer, he personally, and the truth and the Church as well. This was our Lord's promise; at the end of all the struggles stands his victory. 'Do not be afraid; I have overcome the world' [Jn 16:33].

VII/4 *The cross* This is my model and my strength. Model: our Lord suffers all this shame and all the pain without a word of complaint coming from his lips. The seven words that have been handed down to us are not complaints but words of love. For how many millions is the cross of our Lord the model, helping them to bear all pain and suffering with patience and love. But it also gives them the strength. The crucified Lord won all these graces precisely by his cross; for in his case everything he suffers is of infinite value. And every day this strength is given to us

---

[19] The heading shows that even at this stage in the retreat the cardinal was beginning to concern himself with the details of the summary of his resolutions in the 'decision'. The actual text of the 'decision' follows the last day of the retreat.

again through the renewal of the sacrifice of the cross, the Mass. From this point of view as well I will treasure Mass especially and celebrate it as devoutly as possible, both for my own sake and for the sake of all who have commended themselves to my prayers or whom I must help. Hail Cross, our only hope![20]

VIII/1 *The resurrection* Our Lord's death had been confirmed beyond doubt; his resurrection is verified by many witnesses, and so it is the fundamental fact to which all preachers of Christianity from Peter onwards appeal [Acts 2:22–36], fundamental too, in so far as the risen Christ is the prototype for all of us [cf 1 Cor 15:20–23]. But it is important that our resurrection should be to life and not to condemnation.[21] Easter is the central feast of the Church, and so the centre of our liturgy and other spiritual life as well.

VIII/2 *The disciples on the way to Emmaus and the upper room* [Lk 24:36–48; Jn 20:19–23] Our Lord begins to organize his Church. First he appears to Peter. Obviously he confirmed his position among the disciples once again. Then he starts interpreting the scriptures and in such a way that the hearts of the disciples burned within them as he 'opened' the scriptures to them. He also allows himself to be recognized in 'the breaking of bread'—all these are part of the make-up of the Church. But in the Upper Room he gives them the proof of his resurrection and at the same time the great gift of the sacrament of the forgiveness of sin. But also at the same time he shows in both cases that he possesses a 'glorified body', which is no longer bound by the limits of material things and yet is identical with the material body. What a great deal of light was shed on the faith in those few hours of the first day of Easter!

VIII/3 *By Lake Genesareth* [Jn 21:1–23] This scene is another example of the familiar and loving way our Lord treated his disciples and also the way they treated one another. We see here an expression of all the Lord's care for his flock and of his provision for its whole future; but he wants to have this based on love and also confidence in his ultimate guidance: love for him but also a readiness to leave him to take care of the concerns of the individual. 'Do you love me?'—but also: 'what is that to you?' Hence, a sense of community and ready and charitable cooperation: all in all a glorious programme for pastoral work. And over everything is our Lord as the 'chief shepherd' [1 Pet 5:4], who gives the direction by his example and guides everything with his love.

[20] From the liturgy.
[21] An allusion to Christ's words: 'Do not marvel at this; for the hour is coming when all who are in the tombs will hear his voice, and come forth, those who have done good, to the resurrection of life, and those who have done evil, to the resurrection of judgment' (Jn 5:28 f).

VIII/4 *Love* [Exercises 230–237] 'Take, Lord, into your possession': I am entirely in God's hands and will behave accordingly. The clearly recognized will of God will be decisive for me. Not that I want to be passive. I must examine things, decide conscientiously and then—leave everything to God, that means a real indifference towards my own will! But in everything that God decrees I must see him: 'find God in all things'. And that of course presupposes grace from God, and for my part much prayer and a supernatural approach. This must be my objective, as I have resolved in my 'decision'. But this calls for an intensive interior life and therefore regular daily effort in this direction. 'Give me your love and your grace; it is all I need' [Exercises 234]. 8.VIII.68

Decision 1968
My main task is my sanctification, and I am bound to aim at this in a special way as a priest, a Jesuit and a cardinal. It should be my response to the special graces that the Lord has given me in my long life and continues to give me. It means doing the will of God faithfully in everything, as it comes to me in the concrete circumstances, with tranquillity, simplicity and devotion to God, following the example of our Lord and his holy mother, with true fervour and union with the omnipresent God: 'find God in all things'.

The main means to this end are the spiritual exercises: spiritual reading, the twice daily examination of conscience, the monthly recollection, but above all heartfelt personal prayer, especially at Mass and in visits to the Blessed Sacrament.

Towards my fellow men I will practise a true supernatural love, a love that is not stiff and unfeeling but one that shows and answers love with love. It must show itself above all in service, in selfless service, helping without being asked and without expecting anything in return. And in doing this I will not seek to attract attention to myself but will act quietly and without fuss. I will not criticize but, where it is possible, give positive encouragement. With the others I will cooperate selflessly, recognizing and encouraging their work. And in particular I will pray for others (the Holy Father, the bishops, the people who work with me etc.), so that 'utterance may be given' them [cf Eph 6:19] and they may 'declare it boldly, as they ought to speak' [id v. 20].

In my own work I will above all do my best for the faith, as the world and especially Christianity needs it today, not rationalizing but listening humbly to the Word of God, as it is given us in revelation and proposed by the Church. I will bear witness to the truth, even if this means sacrifices, and encourage everything that serves the truth. But in doing all this I will work quietly and in seclusion without making a fuss.

The devotions that I will practise especially:
1) To the Holy Spirit, who will above all enlighten and guide me as a successor of the apostles according to our Lord's promise;
2) to our Lord in the Eucharist: Mass with great recollection and

devotion (treating it not as a 'function' but as the centre of my day); faithful to my visits;

3) to Our Lady. And through her I offer this 'decision' to Our Lord.

26.VIII.68

29.IX.68

8.VIII.68
The last recollection

The entries in the booklet *Recollectio Mensilis* end with the 30.6.68. But it is certain that this was not the last day of recollection made by the author. In fact we find two more dates in the retreat notes of 1968: the first at the end of I/4 for 25 August 1968. This refers to the first date entered at the end of the 'decision'. On 25 August there were symptoms of the severe lung complaint that threatened the life of the author that evening and which made it very doubtful if he would recover. Not even in these circumstances did the author allow himself to be distracted from care for his spiritual life.[22]

While the author was convalescing from this serious illness, from which he never did fully recover, he made his last day of recollection: at the end of II/4 and the 'decision' we find the date 29/IX. After the cardinal's death a piece of paper was found in his personal prayer book, with the same date on it and clearly representing the result of this recollection. The text is:

1) Do the will of God, as the concrete circumstances demand.
2) Personal prayer from the heart (Mass, visits).
3) Selfless service for all.

[22] In fact the date noted at the end of the 'decision' is 26 August. But this must be a mistake, for on 26 August the author was seriously ill in hospital, had no retreat notes with him, and so was not in any position to make a day of recollection.

PART TWO
A Spiritual Profile of Cardinal Bea

Introduction

After finishing the notes, the reader needs to arrange his thoughts and impressions, to dwell at greater length on the main characteristics of this extraordinary retreatant and if possible to form a picture out of them. The following chapters are intended to help him to do this. We have no intention of attempting an analysis of the ethical or psychological character of our author. It is quite simply a matter of a few reflections—the sort of thing one does for example after a conversation with someone for whom one has esteem and affection—when one thinks over the main impressions and thoughts to let them sink in more deeply. Such reflections are the more called for here, since this is a 'conversation' spread over ten years and one that has repeatedly touched on the most varied and profound aspects of the interior life and activity of such an unusual person. These reflections make no claim to give a perfect picture, and considering the extraordinary variety and depth of the notes this would be quite impossible. It is just a case of drawing the attention of the reader to the many and varied traits of the religious character of the author as contained in the notes, of arranging them in some sort of order according to the main themes and so building up for him a picture of this retreat.

In accordance with the objective and psychological nature of these chapters we have allowed the author to speak for himself as much as possible. This will also help to keep things brief. Our main aim will be to try to bring together the scattered statements of each theme, while in the case of those points that the author has dealt with at length in the same context, a reference to the relevant passages will suffice. References to similar or parallel passages in the notes will be fairly copious, so that the reader may find out for himself that the point in question is not just a case of incidental remarks but of really fundamental traits, which appear again and again.

We hope that these chapters will give the reader the opportunity of experiencing what the editor himself experienced as he worked on them: the deeper he went into the notes from different points of view, the more he was compelled, to his own surprise, to recognize their depth and richness. Again and again very interesting and important points appeared that he had not noticed before in spite of his intensive work on the notes. These notes are similar to the really great works of art: because of their perfection they seem so natural and obvious that their real depth is not at first apparent and is only discovered gradually in the course of detailed study. Because of their simplicity these notes seem so obvious, and one does not notice the depth that is in them; but studied in greater detail they constantly reveal new and unsuspected depths and insights.

CHAPTER 13

God has been 'extraordinarily generous to me'

As we are dealing with the religious profile of a person, we must start with this person's attitude of God. This will be the starting point of each of these chapters.

From God, for God
The starting point is quite concretely given in the 'fundamental principle' of the Spiritual Exercises themselves; in biblical language and terse catechism form the doctrine is here stated, that man has been created to praise God, to show him reverence and to serve him, and so to save his soul (Exercises 23). The author expresses this thought in many different ways: 'The foundation of everything concerned with religion is God the infinite. We know him by reason, but only imperfectly. Even this imperfect picture, however, is enough to make us aware of our duty to honour and serve God' (1966/I/1). Or again: 'Created: this one word tells me everything: from me comes nothing and from God comes all that I am and all that I have' (1961/I/1). Then, already drawing the conclusions: 'The servant of God: I must remember that I am nothing but a servant of God, not acquired by him in some way, nor given to him by my free will, but created out of nothing, so that all that I have I have through him and from him, and nothing is my own' (1964/I/1). And in even greater detail: 'I only exist for him to the last moment of my life, and wherever he wants to have me. This is my duty but also my privilege and salvation for now and all eternity' (1961/I/1). Again: 'I am so happy that all my work is only for God: I exist only for this . . .' (1964/VIII/4). Then the goal is described more exactly: '. . . I must do everything for him and only for him. For in his praise, reverence and service lies the whole point of my work' (1963/I/1). 'I have nothing else to do except to honour God and keep his commandments (1965/I/1).

The truth that is expressed in the 'fundamental principle' about man's purpose and mission applies to everyone and is so essentially unchangeable that the God-Man himself is a model for us, in fact *the* model, in its realization. In a meditation headed 'Our Lord and the fundamental principle' Bea says: 'to give glory to God: this was the main point of his life and death. He did everything for the glory of his Father; not for his own glory: he attributes nothing to himself and everything to the Father: 'what the Father has taught'. I must, then, also attribute all honour to God and claim none for myself' (1966/I/4). The author draws a practical conclusion from this, seeing it in the light of the doctrine of the Mystical Body of Christ: 'I am a creature "in Christ", that is as part of him, one of his members, and so I share the task that God by his eternal decree have to him, the "Word made flesh". All praise, reverence and service is an image of his ministry, a share in his ministry, the work of his ministry' (1960/I/2).

By praising God, showing him reverence and serving him, man works out his salvation. The further explanation of this idea takes us deeper into the mystery of man's predestination and shows us at the same time how much this predestination also must be seen 'in Christ': the salvation of one's soul does not simply mean, he says: 'keeping myself safe from hell but making sure that I receive the fullest share in this "salvation of soul" that a human being can have' (1964/I/4). The author explains the content of this idea more precisely and fully in this way: 'God's real motive for creating me was not any desire to receive glory from me—his glory is not increased by anything I can do—it was his love' (1959/I/1). For if even among men good tries to spread itself and to give other beings a share in its goodness this is all the more so the case with God. The self-communication that he intends means 'a supernatural raising to a quasi-divine level. This is the share in the divine nature, the divine sonship, which means also a share in the divine happiness' (id). So man's salvation is 'a mystery, which even revelation can only explain to us in pictures and similes. It means a share in the life of the Blessed Trinity, and thus infinite happiness and eternal blessedness' (1962/I/3; cf also 1965/IV/4).

But this explanation points immediately to Christ. This share in God's inmost being and life, and so also in his blessedness, is given to us essentially and only in Christ. So the author says in a meditation on the pursuit of sanctity: 'Holiness is not an obligation imposed on me by a law from outside; it flows from the inmost being of a Christian. Bound to God by faith and baptism I must share his inmost being. In this the great model is Christ, the Son of God, born of the Holy Spirit and filled with the Holy Spirit at baptism. I must let Christ "make me his own" and share his thoughts, actions and works. The "imitation of Christ" is, then, the inner law of sanctity' (1968/I/2; cf also 1966/III/3). This puts the task of man as described above in a completely new light: it is 'not simply human, but "Christlike", in so far as this is at all possible for a finite creature. My praise too goes through Christ to the Father, but must be like the praise of God's Son. My reverence must be the reverence of Christ for his Father, as it appeared in his life and suffering (Garden of Olives). My ministry is like Christ's ministry: not simply fulfilling God's will but fulfilling it with sacrifice and suffering, in fact self-sacrifice, just as Christ offered himself . . .' (1960/I/2). From this is drawn the conclusion: 'Jesus is my great model in this, and I must imitate him more and more' (1963/VI/1); 'so my spiritual life and all that I do must, then, be centred on Christ. Christ in all!' (1963/I/2).¹

Sin and Guilt
Apart from the thought of creation and a share in God's own life, two other factors have an essential bearing on man's relationship with God, and they can be summed up in four ideas: sin and guilt, redemption and grace.

What are sin and what are its consequences? Sin is in reality 'an offence against God himself, my Creator, Lord and Father, to whom as a man and even more as a Christian I am most closely bound. How the Lord judges this offence is taught me by revelation, beginning with the first page of Genesis, and throughout the whole of the Old Testament, and by our Lord, especially in the New Testament in his teaching and his attitude to sinners, but particularly through his death on the cross, on which the immaculate Lamb of God took upon himself the sins of the world' (1963/II/2). Sin is also 'a rebellion against God, the Creator and Lord, and thus, on the part of the sinner, it means a separation from him. No man, no matter who he is, can undo this separation. God can, but he only does so in view of what Christ the redeemer did. Anyone who rejects Christ, as the sinful angels did, is lost for ever. God can give the grace; but he does not have to. If he gives it, he does so in view of the merits won for us by Christ on the cross' (1963/II/3). What do we mean when we say that, if God does not grant forgiveness, man is lost? We mean that he is condemned to hell: 'I think the most frightening thing about hell is not the pain of the senses but the pain of loss: to be separated for ever from God, who here on earth meant everything to me. After spending my whole life with him what would I be without him for all eternity!' (1960/III/1).

And indeed this sad and frightening reality of sin has penetrated deep into God's creation. The author regularly devotes a meditation to the 'triple sin', that is, the sin of the angels, the sin of our first

¹ Readers who have made the Spiritual Exercises of St Ignatius at some time may ask if this is still genuine 'Ignatian' spirituality, and whether the meditation on the Kingdom of Christ has not been anticipated and transferred to the 'fundamental principle'. In principle, the Exercises lead the person, even the beginner, step by step from the first beginnings of the spiritual life, the purification of the soul, to the love of God. And in principle the author's notes follow the same plan. But only in principle: this method is really only used fully in the thirty-day retreats, and in other cases is adapted to the state of the retreatant's spiritual life. The purpose of this chapter is essentially different: we are attempting to reveal the self-portrait of the cardinal as it exists in the notes—beginning with the fundamental traits. Hence, at this early point, we already offer the full picture of his relationship with God in all its depth and fullness, including, therefore, the supernatural characteristics; this is why we see it 'in Christ'.

parents and the sins of men in general. Talking about the sin of our first parents he says: 'The origin of sin of our first parents brought a great deal of pain and misery into the world but it also brought a great deal of evil and wickedness. A glance at history shows this' (1964/II/2). The consequences of the original sin of our first parents are described in still greater detail: 'The mystery of sin is present throughout the world and throughout time. Essentially it is based on the freedom of creatures endowed with reason ...' (1963/II/1; cf also 1964/II/2). From this an important and very definite conclusion can be drawn for a correct appreciation of man: 'In reality man is not simply good, and "human" is not yet the same as "good". The whole of the history of the world shows this. So in my own life and in my work I must treat things with a certain suspicion, but not in a way that hinders me but one that guides me' (1968/II/2). But the cardinal does not dwell for long on this general idea: he directs his attention very honestly to his own particular case: 'I must not forget the past: whatever it may have been like, it cannot have been pleasing to God, and like the Apostle I have to say: "I am the least of all" ' (1959/I/3). And even more clearly: sin 'is also a force in my own heart. If I look back on my past I see how strong the inclination to evil was in me too and how often I was in danger of giving way. It is only by God's mercy that I have not been devoured. This look at my own life teaches me to be humble but also grateful to God' (1964/II/2). Of course the author is aware of God's mercy and knows by faith that past sins have been forgiven: 'The "story of the sins" of my past life must not be a source of worry any more: "your sins are forgiven you", our Lord has said to me too, and I must believe his divine word' (1961/II/2).[2]

But forgiveness does not wipe out past facts as such. And the author is ready to draw conclusions from this: 'If I look back over my life, I can never thank God enough for his goodness in forgiving me my past sins, in preserving me from so many sins and in showering so many graces upon me. I am really "a sinner manqué" and I can repeat a thousand times with St Paul: "by the grace of God (and only by the grace of God) I am what I am" ' (1960/II/3). This consciousness of his own sins is also particularly noticeable in the meditation on Christ's passion. Referring to the condemnation of Christ he says: 'I myself must first beat my own breast; for I too played my part in the cry "he deserves death" ' (1962/VIII/1; cf also 1959/VIII/1).

Again: 'The sufferings of the Lord teach me to have a horror of sin, and of my own sins . . .' (1959/VII/3). And again: 'It is only thanks to the crucified Lord, if I am preserved from eternal damnation' (1960/III/1).

The fact of sin, however, is not just a matter of the past, but in various forms and repeatedly a matter of the present as well. The danger

[2] This confidence with regard to past sins is often expressed: cf 1959/II/1; 1961/III/1; 1962/II/2; 1966/II/2.

of sinning is always there: '. . . the Son of God died for the sins of mankind. But even this could not wipe sin out: even amongst the apostles there was a Judas, and how many there have been in the Church itself: priests, religious, bishops and cardinals, and even popes! The power of sin is just as great today and so the struggle of the Church against sin is just as necessary.—It is also a force in my own heart' (1964/II/2). The danger presented by sin is explained more fully: 'I must take this question of sin seriously. In the first place because sin still remains a possibility with me too. I must have no illusions on this score, on the other hand, however, there must be no over vivid imagination. The concupiscence of the flesh and the pride of life are still in me. And I have the free will that can refuse God's command. In every Mass I pray "take away from us our sins" ' (1960/II/1). From this the author concludes that he must have a certain 'distrust' with regard to himself (cf 1962/II/1; 1968/II/2). But it is not just a question of danger. In the retreats he admits openly that he is constantly giving way to this danger, in what he calls deliberate venial sins or sins of thoughtlessness. So in reference to religious exercises he says: 'Unpunctuality, distractions, superficiality and negligence are particularly serious in my case' (1961/II/3; cf also 1959/II/2; 1967/II/1–2). He also accuses himself in another respect: 'Hasty words, criticism of high dignitaries, fits of impatience, irritability, taking offence, carelessness in my attitude, thoughtless speech and so on; all this is of much more importance in my case than with anyone else . . .' (1961/II/3; cf also 1966/II/3; 1967/II/3). Elsewhere he says: 'My main thought is that I have not made full use of so many graces or that I have not won more grace by greater attention to my spiritual exercises nor have I always given the good example that a person of my age and position should give' (1959/II/1).

This strict and honest self-judgment leads him in a meditation entitled 'I confess to almighty God, to all the saints and to you, brethren . . .' to say: 'I teach, I guide others—and myself? I should be an example to others, but am I really? Or am I a "hypocrite"? Have people (popes, cardinals, superiors etc) been mistaken in me? What does a man like Pius XII or John XXIII think of me today? And all those whose superior, teacher and guide I have been? My parents? My friends? I will and I must make a great effort really to be what they rightly expect of me and take me for' (1967/I/4).

So the author tries to spur himself on to an energetic struggle against sin. Repeatedly in the meditations on venial sin he says 'It must be my concern to reduce the number of the venial sins all the time, especially deliberate venial sins' (1960/II/4). And the reason for this: 'These sins offend our Lord, wound his Sacred Heart and his love. They are an abomination to the heavenly Father. The heavens are not pure enough for him. They are ingratitude in response to the love that was so great that he gave us his only begotten Son' (id.) But what is more serious is that negligence in this struggle against more or less deliberate venial sins stifles love for God: 'Lack of care in avoiding these venial sins extinguishes the fire of love in me, prevents me from giving myself totally to God and his service, and makes me less pleasing to God' (1961/II/3). These thoughts also help one to understand the severe judgment of the author that venial sin leads to hell: "faults and defects", that is venial sins and giving in to evil desires, lead to hell' (1960/III/1), in so far as they hinder the action of grace and gradually make love grow cold, so that the person is also running the risk of falling into serious sin and thus being damned for ever.

As with sin in general the author also sees the social effects of venial sin in particular: 'In my position all eyes are on me. I can do a great deal of good by my actions but also a great deal of harm. People notice even the smallest things' (1960/II/2). And again: 'It is not just a matter of keeping free from serious sin, but of warding off anything that can stain my soul. This is important for me, not only because of my human dignity but above all for me as a priest, as an apostle, as a prominent member of a hierarchy, very much in the public eye' (1965/II/2).

In practice the author never tires of discussing the ways and means of carrying on this struggle: 'I must fight the sins of thoughtlessness constantly and perseveringly. To help me in this I have once again the examination of conscience and the monthly renewal, when I must come back to this point again and again' (1959/II/2). Elsewhere he also mentions weekly confession (cf 1959/VI/4). Its nature is explained in this way: 'I must value the sacrament of penance highly. It is the means of forgiveness because it binds me to Christ. But I must value it for this reason, not just as an institution of canon law or a rule of the Society. It is Christ the Redeemer whom I meet in every confession and from whom I seek forgiveness. It is his love and his power which apply to me the fruit of his cross' (1966/III/2). Very frequently he stresses mortification and self-conquest as a means to this end. And finally there is this positive and significant statement: 'In order to avoid sin I must aim at perfection by every means at my disposal' (1960/II/1).

The fact of guilt, running rather like a thread throughout a person's life, adds an entirely new dimension to his relationship with God: people know that by their sins they have offended and rebelled against God and so have placed themselves in opposition to God, and that they are thrown on the mercy and grace of God for forgiveness: 'God can give the grace; but he does not have to. If he gives it, he does so in view of the merits won for us by Christ on the cross' (1963/II/3). 'It is only thanks to the crucified Lord, if I am preserved from eternal damnation' (1960/III/1). All this—sin and forgiveness—is not something that happens just once: people are falling into sin repeatedly and so need mercy and forgiveness from God repeatedly. But there is more to it than this: because the lower nature and inclinations to evil are always lying in wait, people are in constant need of undeserved help from God in order to win through the battle, and therefore they must not only pray for their daily bread but also implore him: 'Lead us not into temptation' (cf Mt 6:13). Certainly God gives grace, 'but I must cooperate with grace ... I really cannot complain of lack of grace; indeed God showers his graces on me; but for that reason my obligation to cooperate is all the greater and also my responsibility to avoid even the slightest sin and aim at perfection' (1960/II/2). How often he has to reproach himself for not having cooperated sufficiently with grace (cf e.g. 1959/II/1).

But this consciousness of personal guilt and of forgiveness repeatedly granted by God also influences a man's relationship with God in another respect: this must not hold him back or make him give up the struggle, but on the contrary should be an incentive and a source of further progress: 'but this consideration (about past sins) must not depress me or paralyse my efforts, any more than it paralysed St Paul's, who, far from being faint-hearted, derived the greatest driving force from it to work tirelessly for God' (1969/II/3). And above all this consciousness of personal sinfulness is, as we have already seen, a source of great humility: 'I am the least of all' (1959/II/3: cf 1964/II/2). Nor are past sins any hindrance to apostolic work: 'Peter, Paul, Augustine all did great things in spite of their earlier sins' (1959/II/3). In fact the consciousness of sins forgiven is a source of greater love and an incentive to greater love: 'And now (that my sins have been forgiven) I must give him everything in love, as the sinful woman did, and the degree of loving devotion determines the degree of forgiveness: "her sins, which are many, are forgiven, for she loved much." Her love was generous: she made a sacrifice of everything that she had found her pleasure in before, and without a word put her trust in our Lord's love. The prodigal son, the repentant Peter, the good thief on the cross, all did the same. The main thing is to begin and to carry on a life of trust, believing, devoted love. "Late have I loved thee," but I have loved thee and do love thee!' (1961/II/2).

Believing, trusting, loving devotion to God

A man's relationship with God is, then, determined by the following fundamental facts: creation, the mysterious participation in the divine life itself, sin and guilt, redemption and grace. In discussing these basic factors we have already come across various expressions of this relationship: the obedience owed by a creature to God; then sorrow for sin and humility and grateful love for forgiveness received. There are still three more fundamental expressions to discuss: faith, hope and charity. For the unique relationship between man and God described above finds concrete expression and is put into effect in the surrender of the man to God, and this has three qualities: it is rooted in faith, sustained by trust and finds its perfection in active love.

If we now try to see what the notes have to say about faith, the first thing we notice is that not one meditation is devoted to the subject ex professo. Amongst the very many subjects that are repeatedly discussed we do not find the theme of faith. But that does not mean that he has lost sight of faith. It is repeatedly stressed in different forms; but briefly, almost in passing, like something taken for granted. This, then, shows that for the author the faith—unlike so many other points—was such a secure possession that he felt no need to devote special consideration to it, as he had to so many other essential points of the religious life. The notes show: he moves in God's world, that is, in everything that we have said up to now about creation, the self-communication of God, sin, redemption and grace—and also in all that we have to say about Christ, the Church etc—with the same matter-of-fact approach with which the average person moves in the world of the senses. This is all the more striking since it was precisely in this last period of his life that the author was very much aware how much so many people's faith is today attacked and endangered. In this context he writes in his last retreat notes, with reference to the simple faith of the shepherds: 'This is a strong faith that does not rationalize and one that leads to action as a result. And this faith is rewarded so that they returned home joyfully and praised God "for all that they had heard and seen". At the same time, however, they are also made apostles. Here I have the opposite of our rationalistic secularized world, which does not recognize the idea of "mystery" any more but wants to grasp everything with the human mind. It is my great task to oppose this spirit of the times and see that justice is done to the faith' (1968/IV/1). And in the same way in the 'decision' for 1968: 'in my own work I will above all do my best for the faith, as the world and especially Christianity need it today, not rationalizing but listening humbly to the Word of God, as it is given us in revelation and proposed by the Church. I will bear witness to the truth, even if this means sacrifices, and encourage everything that serves the truth.'

First of all some passages indicating the essential connection between faith and the union with God: in the meditation on 'spiritual laziness' the importance of 'union with God' is stressed and explained in this way: 'Recollection and a spirit of faith in all that I do. I have much to do; but I must not allow myself to be too wrapped up in material concerns, on the contrary I must make them spiritual, deify them so to speak' (1962/II/3). In a similar context the author writes: 'This retreat must definitely help me, in spite of all exterior activity and success, to do everything in a truly supernatural spirit, in a spirit of recollection and union with God, in a spirit of deep faith' (1962/III/1). Elsewhere we read that the Holy Spirit brings it about: that 'I keep the faith always before my eyes and so live from faith' (1959/VI/4). On the other hand he says of faith in the indwelling of the Holy Spirit in us: 'if I tread the path ... of the imitation of Christ ... then I may be certain that the

Holy Spirit is living and working in men, even if I have no subjective experience of this' (1963/VIII/2).³

After these fundamental explanations a few particular expressions of faith. Firm faith in the word of God. After establishing that by the mystery of the transfiguration our Lord was trying to prepare his disciples for his passion, the author makes the following reflection: 'I should not expect any extraordinary preparation like this. I have God's word ("listen to him") and all the wonderful confirmation offered by the history of the Church. This must be enough for me to take upon myself and bear even more difficult things' (1966/VI/1). We have already seen what he wrote with regard to the sins of his past life: 'The "story of the sins" of my past life must not be a source of worry any more: "your sins are forgiven you", our Lord has said to me too and I must believe his divine word' (1961/II/2). In the meditation on the mysteries of Christ's birth he sees in Mary and Joseph models of the genuine spirit of faith, with which a man must see God's providence in everyday events: 'Mary and Joseph accepted all the unpleasantness, disappointment and disagreement in a spirit of faith. They have God's word through the angel and they know that their child is the Son of God. This is the basis of their faith, which nothing can shake but which on the other hand instils into them the greatest reverence in all that they see and suffer, just as faith gives me the greatest reverence towards our Lord in the holy Eucharist, especially in the Mass' (1968/III/4; cf also 1959/III/3). He writes in a similar vein about the presentation in the temple: 'This episode is also a mystery of faith, of a living but quiet, almost hidden, faith, both in the case of our Lord and also of Mary and Joseph and finally of Simeon and Anna' (1968/IV/2). Then he applies this thought to himself: 'my life too must be quiet and a life of humble faith, not making anything of itself, but in all things standing by what is revealed to it, without being concerned with what people think' (id; cf also 1959/III/3).

In the meditation on achieving love these reflections are raised to the level of general principles for life, which are meant to govern the whole of life and determine its relationship to God. I must 'see him in everyone and everything. See him in all that he does also. Whatever happens to me does not happen without him. Everything comes from his loving providence for me' (1965/V/4). More general still: 'The main thing for me is that I . . . should see in everything that happens to me, pleasant or unpleasant, in nature and in grace, in the world and in the Church, the hand of God and a reminder of God' (1961/VIII/4). Further, 'I must be aware that I am cooperating with God, with the powers that he has given me and for the ends that he has decided for

---

³ In what follows we refer to texts speaking of faith in Christ. The faith is directed really and fundamentally towards God and therefore also to the God-Man. Hence it is possible to include at this point all that the notes have to say about faith—faith in Christ as well.

me' (id). A step further: 'I must become more and more conscious of his presence in everything, and let creatures lead me to God. And whatever I see in the world and among men that is noble, beautiful and meaningful, I must tell myself that he is nobler, much more beautiful, much more powerful, in fact he is greatness, beauty, power and wisdom itself, and the source of all that is great in the world' (id). All this is, then, 'the spirit of faith which enables me to see all things in a supernatural light' (1959/VIII/4).

This attitude of faith is very closely connected with that of trust. Consider for example some of the passages just quoted. For instance where the author is talking about past sins and says that they should not worry him, for 'our Lord has said to me too "your sins are forgiven you", and I must believe his divine word' (1961/II/2; cf also 1961/II/4). Similarly trust in God's guidance in and through the events of his own life is based on an attitude of faith: I must 'see him . . . in everything. See him also in all that he does. Whatever happens to me does not happen without him. Everything comes from his loving providence for me' (1965/V/4). This close connection with faith also explains the fact that the author regards trust, rather like faith, as a possession so safely assured that no special meditations are devoted to it. It is like the air that is breathed every day without a thought.

Trust is really based on God's promises and the love that he revealed to us in the incarnation and redemption. A continuation and concrete application of this will of God to love us is his providence shown in the life of every individual. In this way the graces already received are a motive for trust in the future: 'If God has guided me for eighty-five years with special love, then this is a sign that he also intends to give me a happy eternity' (1965/I/3). And in an allusion to a phrase from St Augustine the author says: 'Nor must I forget that God is going to give me this soon. The seventy-nine years that he has given me tell me that he will soon be calling me to eternity. So no hesitation in carrying out the programme, always keeping in sight the greater thing that he wants to give me, namely himself' (1959/I/3). Again: 'Our Lord has not called me to do the minimum: the graces that he has given me show that he has destined me for a high degree of blessedness' (1964/I/4).

This basic attitude of trust, then, finds its application in different areas of life. First, in carrying out the basic task of man: 'I really cannot complain of lack of grace (to enable me to serve God); indeed God showers his graces upon me' (1960/II/2). Also as regards faithfulness to one's own vocation: 'The vocation to be an apostle and to do apostolic work is an unmerited grace, the result of God's eternal decree. But I may be sure that if he gives me this grace he will also give me all the help I need to live up to this grace and cooperate with it. This is a great consolation and at the same time a powerful encouragement' (1961/V/1). 'He (God) has placed the realization of his will to redeem the world in my hands in a very special way. Therefore I must enter into this plan wholeheartedly, devote myself wholly to it and only to it, and must not seek to do anything but work for it, and on the other hand, can expect everything I need for it from him' 1964/I/2). Moreover this trust, for the individual and for the whole Church, has its rock-firm foundation in the assurance of Christ: 'Lo, I am with you always even to the close of the age. This divine guarantee also accompanies me as I go from this retreat back to the service of the Church and of the Mystical Body of our Lord' (1960/VIII/3).

Even when the last decision and test of death are near, this trusting devotion does not waver, for this is really the hour of its confirmation: 'I look upon the approach of death with tranquillity and confidence: God has given me so many graces and he will not abandon me then' (1967/II/1–2). It is in this light that death is seen, and indeed longed for, as a welcome guest and a guide to our Lord. Repeatedly this longing is expressed by the author in the famous words of St Paul: 'My desire is to depart and to be with Christ.' This is the frame of mind with which I want to meet my death, whenever and however it may come' (1963/III/4; cf also 1962/II/4).

As is to be expected in the spiritual life, the author's relationship with God reaches its climax in love. There is hardly any other subject that is dealt with so often and at such lengths in the notes. Not only does love form the regular conclusion to the retreats; it often appears already in the meditation on the 'fundamental principle' (cf e.g. 1959/I/1) or in the meditations of the so-called first week. In the meditation on venial sin he says: 'the ultimate and highest motive (for avoiding venial sin) here too is the love of God: for him and his honour and in gratitude to him I must aim at the highest, and should not ask: what I can do without actually sinning . . .' (1959/II/2; cf also 1959/II/4; 1963/III/2; 1964/II/1; 1968/II/3). Even in the meditation on hell we read: 'I think the most frightening thing about hell is not the pain of the senses but the pain of loss: to be separated for ever from God, who here on earth meant everything to me' (1960/III/1). Finally in the meditation on 'achieving love' the author writes: 'This meditation sums up everything that these days of grace have given me: my special vocation and also my special obligation' (1964/VIII/4). These words again give the impression, which is the general impression one gets from reading the notes, that love really is the sum of all the resolutions and the essence of the author's whole spiritual life.

Moving now to particular points: one of the first characteristics of the author's attitude to the love of God is that it rests entirely on an outlook on life and the world that comes from faith. The first series of facts on which love is based are the favours received from God: 'If anyone ever had reason to say with St Ignatius: all that I have, all that I own: it is your gift to me, I now return it to you . . . then it is I' (1960/VIII/4). The second fact on which love is based is his way of looking at creation: 'If

God is present in everything, then I must also see him and find him in everything. I must not look on the world with profane eyes, but find God everywhere in it, that is I must see everything in a spirit of faith' (1966/VIII/4). The third fact is God's activity in his creation. Creatures only exist 'because God has cooperated and because his activity is of an infinitely higher and greater order' (1959/VIII/4). 'I must not forget that all inspirations, all illuminations etc are his (God's) "work" for me personally' (1967/VIII/4).

The nature and essence of love itself correspond to this outlook based on faith. In contrast to the temptation to sentimentality which is so easily possible, in fact so close to love, the author emphasizes that love—in keeping with what the beloved disciple himself said—must be a matter of deed and truth: 'My love for God cannot consist in feelings but in deeds. There must be progress in my spiritual life, even if I feel nothing. It must be a matter of the will and of deeds: deeds, wherever the concrete circumstances make it possible, the will to do even more, if the chance is given to me and in whatever form it is given to me' (1965/V/4). 'My "suscipe" is not just an act of the will; it is a fact and must become more so every day' (1963/VIII/4). With regard to the favours received from God this means in practice: 'God has given me much, extraordinarily much. I can only repay him by making everything bear fruit for myself and for the kingdom of God, as I have just now resolved once again in my "decision"' (1965/V/4). 'The things I have decided on in this retreat are not just "resolutions": they form a programme of restitution, to which I am bound' (1960/VIII/4; cf also 1959/VIII/4).

But it is not just a case of making God's gifts bear fruit for God and in his service, but also of walking in God's presence and cooperating with him: in my work I must 'become more and more conscious of his presence in everything: and let creatures lead me to God' (1961/VIII/4). This is not just a matter of actions but is accompanied by the attitude of love: 'My love for God, then, is not just a matter of feeling or words but a fact and a truth. If I have this frame of mind I can now return comforted to everyday life, in order that in my prayers, work, suffering and enduring I may find him whom my soul loves more and more and help others to find him too' (1963/VIII/4). This idea of finding God in all things is described even more precisely: if God is present and active in everything, then everything great is 'nothing but a sign to me, a reflection, an image of the infinitely greater beauty, wisdom and power of God . . . This is the spirit of faith, which enables me to see all things in a supernatural light. And through this I must eventually be led to the final thing; to the love of God for the sake of his own infinite greatness. I do not need to "despise" the world, for it is a ladder that leads to God, and whatever greatness I see in the world, I see something still greater in God. May I arrive at this profound and exalted understanding of all things and thus at the perfect love of God!' (1959/VIII/4).

Later we read 'that the most important thing is that I should now seek him and see him in everything . . . that I should love him in everything and everyone, and love everything and everyone in him and only in him' (1960/VIII/4).

Summing up, we can say that to love God means to seek communion and union with God in a spirit of gratitude and reverence and so to be intent on living, working and suffering for him and with him.

'The basic attitude: no half-measures!'
There is still one last point about the author's relationship with God, his generosity. This is a quality which comes from a magnanimous character and is connected with love and influences all the forms of the relationship with God that we have already discussed. First of all a few general texts illustrating its nature and motives: God 'has shown me an unusual amount of favour, almost without limit or reserve. And so I must use the same measure in my dealings with him and must not be content with the minimum but must rather try in all things to seek the greater glory of God, the greater service, because he has given me so much help and the grace to know him so well' (1967/I/1). 'I could add all that I have received as a child of God, as a priest, religious and Jesuit. What return shall I make? Gratitude certainly but not so much in words as in deeds—by the correct and most perfect possible use of all that he has given me' (1962/I/1; cf also 1961/II/3). Again: 'There have been no half-measures in the way God has treated me, in fact he has been exceedingly generous. Therefore I must act in the same way towards him, not primarily looking for a reward but rather thinking of his goodness. Nothing can dispense me from my duty to be generous towards him' (1967/I/2). The motive for generosity can also be the greatness and holiness of God. My reverence for God 'must be more fervent, corresponding to my knowledge of the greatness, nobility and holiness of God. My "service" must not simply be a matter of avoiding sin, of doing what is essential; it must be the most perfect possible fulfilment of the vows and rules, all the duties of my position, all the daily work and tasks: by choosing what is more likely to achieve the purpose of my creation' (1959/I/2).

In the preceding quotations we have also indicated some ways in which this generosity towards God is expressed. At first they are more negative: 'No half-measures, half-heartedness, no slackness in his (Christ's) service, which is the service of the crucified Lord' (1960/III/1). More positively expressed: 'I can make use of everything to serve him (God) generously . . . The decisive thing for me is the basic attitude: no "half-measures"!' (1967/I/2). Or put another way: 'It is due to the goodness and love of God, not to me, that I have become a priest, a Jesuit, a cardinal and a bishop. But if this is the case, God also expects something special from me. A maximum of effort for the honour of God must correspond to the maximum of grace. It is not hard to find what this maximum involves: the generous carrying out of the rules of the Society, so far as they still apply to me, and total devotion to the tasks that Christ's Vicar has entrusted to me and still entrusts to me. Obstacles and difficulties must not count in doing this ... And I shall only live up to my special vocation if I make this "follow me" a fact and do it wholeheartedly' (1964/II/4).

But the most frequent expression of generosity occurs in the pursuit of 'perfection': 'The graces that he (God) has given me show that he has destined me for a high degree of blessedness. So for my part I must not offer him just the bare essentials in my life; on the contrary I must strive to achieve the ideal of the most perfect possible service of God as I resolved in the first meditation ... God will not be outdone in generosity' (1964/I/4). Even more explicit: 'The most important thing for me is to aim at perfection with all my strength. And the best way to do this is by love—to imitate the love of God who gave his Son for us, the love of our Lord who gave himself up for me. I must, therefore, refuse God nothing: whatever God wants, however he wants it, and as long as he wants. He has been so generous with me: I must not bargain with him' (1959/I/3). The pursuit of perfection is described as hunger for justice in the meditation on the eight beatitudes: 'The most important thing for me is to hunger and thirst, that is to have a great desire for "justice", for the perfection demanded by my vocation and position. Everything else follows from that' (1959/V/2; cf also 1964/IV/4).

But the author warns that perfection must not simply be a matter of 'external legality and regularity': after describing the eight beatitudes as *the* programme, he continues: 'So I must "embody" this plan, so to speak, not just by conforming to these rules outwardly but through a genuine interior spirit, out of which these externals can, so to speak, grow. My perfection must not just be a legal matter, it must flow from a deep interior, spiritual poverty, humility and self-sacrifice. Finally it must be the expression of a great and deep love of God and of neighbour' (1960/VI/1). More concretely, perfection means 'a perfect spiritual life; prayer, patience and suffering in an apostolic spirit, efforts to advance in virtue, which, as a religious, a priest, a bishop and a cardinal, I must develop by meditation, reading and study' (1965/III/2). As we have seen, preciseness was one of the main traits of the author's character. Now in this context he indicates the profound motive for this: 'The concern for small things: this must be a sign of my love of God and of our divine Lord ... I must show my love by pleasing our Lord in things that are not prescribed by law' (1964/II/1).

If we look back over this chapter we see that the relationship between the author and God is essentially determined by two facts attested by faith, the fact of creation and the fact that man is predestined to participate in a mysterious way in the innermost being and life of God himself; but apart from these there is the fact of sin, the consequences of the sin of our first parents and of the personal sins of the author on the one hand, and on the other the related ideas of the redemption and grace. Thus the author lives in a state of humble sorrow for his lack of devotion to God and of constant resolution to surrender himself to God in faith, trust and love, and to do this wholly, generously and perfectly.

CHAPTER 14

'*I must be a praying cardinal*'

The relationship of a person with God, as expressed in the attitude of believing, trusting and loving self-surrender to God, shows itself in practice most intensively in prayer in all its various forms, where it also finds strength and nourishment. The spirit of prayer and concern for the life of prayer—in all its different forms of expression—runs like a golden thread through the notes. In connection with Christ's prayer after his baptism we read: 'Our Lord at prayer must be my model. I have the opportunity—and the duty—of praying so often during the day. My daily life is, as it were, framed by prayer, prayer of supplication and of thanksgiving [cf II/1]. I must use all these opportunities faithfully. Now that I have not so much work to do outside, I must be all the more active in prayer: I must really be a "praying cardinal" ' (1965/III/3). Speaking of the necessity of prayer, he says: 'The Lord only gives his graces to souls which pray' (1963/VI/3); and in the meditation on the transfiguration: 'by prayer and in prayer I must bind myself more closely to him [our Lord], I must really "make booths" in order to live with him . . .' (1964/V/1). And again: 'If I do not share our Lord's prayer, I shall not share his transfiguration. Here too it is a case of "let him follow me!" ' (1959/VI/2). 'It must be one of the main resolutions of this retreat to pay more attention to my spiritual exercises' (1964/II/3).[1]

The first and most frequent thought that recurs again and again in the notes in this context of prayer concerns the 'deep spirit of fervour' with which one must pray! In the meditation on the boy Jesus in the temple: 'I can imagine how reverently he moved about in the temple: "in the house of my Father!" I must perform liturgical functions in the same way; not merely an external performance but a deep interior spirit' (1963/V/1). With regard to the 'daily spiritual exercises (meditation, Mass, breviary, examination of conscience etc)' he says: 'I must not do all this just materially, mechanically, but with God and with my mind on God' (1963/III/2). In the meditation on the 'night prayer of our Lord' we read: 'This prayer is the ideal, the sort of "dialogue with God", that the Holy Father wants priests to have. And indeed: how many intentions, personal and apostolic I have to bring before the heavenly Father,

[1] Since prayer is not only directed towards God but also towards Christ, the God-Man, we can say everything that needs to be said about prayer—prayer to Christ as well—in this chapter.

day after day, just as the Church does in the Mass—but it must not be mechanical, however, but personal and from the heart (dialogue!)' (1968/V/3). The phrase 'from the heart' must not make us think that this is only a matter of feeling. In fact the author is thinking more of the movements of the will: 'The will must control the mind; more attention must be paid to the affections (of the will) and to the interior appreciation. Very active prayer, precisely through the affections' (1959/IV/Consideration of Spiritual State).

Now in practice what does prayer mean in the life of the author? After contemplating the prayer of our Lord in the Garden he makes this basic point: 'in every situation I too must look for strength in prayer, but in prayer which is serious, fervent and concrete, like our Lord's prayer in the Garden: full of trust but at the same time completely resigned: "not my will, but thine!" God is always the "Father": "Father, if thou art willing" ' (1965/V/1). This general principle is applied in other places to different situations and so becomes clearer. Speaking of the daily examination of conscience he says: '. . . I must fight the sin of thoughtlessness constantly and perseveringly. To help me in this I have once again the examination of conscience . . .' (1959/II/2). Elsewhere, however, he says in general: 'But the examination of conscience is important too: firstly that I should make it: then that I should make it in such a way that it does me good: shedding light on the past and the present: hence investigation: grace: hence prayer. So once again make the examination methodically (five points!)' (1962/II/3). And again: 'and it is especially in this examination that I can review the opportunities that are likely to come my way for good and also for mistakes' (1965/II/2; cf also 1962/II/2; 1967/II/3).

In another passage he speaks of prayer pervading all the day's work: 'prayer before every important action; "in thy company, Lord, through thee, for thee!" ' (1959/IV/Consideration of Spiritual State). There are still two great tasks or rather fruits of prayer. The author declares that he has not sufficient 'familiarity with God' and so resolves: 'All my work . . . should be filled with a spirit of recollection, with constant reference to God and frequent union with him. So I must take care to make this spirit part of my life, especially through meditation. In all my work this is almost the only source left for this spirit of recollection and union with God and I will see to it that I make my meditations wholly and completely' (1962/II/2). Apart from this, prayer is and should be a source of strength for the apostolate. In the meditation on the transfiguration: 'There is no abiding city on Mount Tabor and the great mystics show us this too . . . It is here that the apostolate finds its source of strength and energy. And even if it is not mysticism, there must at least be a solid interior life of union with God, of prayer, of self-denial and mortification, from which my apostolate, whatever form it may take, draws its strength, drive and content' (1963/VI/3).

As this last passage shows, prayer for the author also means peace and 'relaxation'. Prayer in the retreats represents his 'Tabor hours'. He says explicitly: 'Hours like those on Mount Tabor are not lasting here on earth, particularly not in my position. As soon as the retreat is over, humdrum everyday life will begin again, as with our Lord and the three apostles when they had come down from the Mount' (1961/VI/2). Speaking of our Lord's prayer in the night he says (Christ's) 'rest is prayer. This must be my rest too: meditation, Mass, office, when I really withdraw from my occupations and devote myself wholly to God' (1964/V/4).

To what extent and why can prayer be a rest and relaxation? In answer to this we give just two significant suggestions: in the first place prayer is precisely an exercise in trust and so represents a strengthening. We are reminded that prayer of this sort is part of the consolation left for us by our Lord in his farewell address: 'Moreover our Lord leaves me the effective help of "prayer in his name", which the Father will always hear' (1968/VI/4). But the fruit of prayer is significantly more varied. On this point he speaks in a passage which also tells us a great deal about the depths of the author's own prayer. In the meditation on the transfiguration he speaks about the cross and particularly the cross that is connected with his 'special mission', that is, Christian unity, in so far as this 'is bound to involve a great deal of effort, of failure and of misrepresentation' (1962/VI/3). Then he indicates where the strength to carry this cross must be found: 'In these situations I must draw courage and strength from the "transfiguration", from the transfiguration that comes to me through prayer. "As he was praying." This "transfiguration" does not need to be a mystical phenomenon, but it is a state of soul that means peace, love and daily readiness, and so an atmosphere of a supernatural approach to my whole life and work. If this state of mind is present, sacrifices are no longer sacrifices but acts of love, love of God and love of neighbour' (id).

CHAPTER 15

'My life and work must be centred on Jesus'

It is clear that Cardinal Bea's relationship with Christ is deeply influenced by the factors which have already been discussed of his relationship with God. Christ, the incarnate Son of God, is also his God, Creator, redeemer and the one from whom he has sought forgiveness of his sins. Hence, the attitude described above of believing, trusting, loving and generous self-surrender to God, refers in its entirety to Christ, the God-Man, as well. But through the contemplation of the incarnate Son of God, as we meet him in the gospel, this attitude receives new and more obvious human nuances and shades. So it is in this sense we ask: what is the author's personal image of Christ, that is, what characteristics of the gospel portrait of Christ figure most largely in the notes, and in what way does this private and personal image of Christ influence the author's personal attitude to Christ?

The image of Christ
The first aspects of Christ's character, repeatedly stressed by the cardinal, are the kindness, the friendliness, the 'heart' of our Lord. We see this particularly in the meditation on the multiplication of the loaves: 'The goodness of our Lord is boundless: towards the disciples and towards the people. At all times gentle and thoughtful' (1959/V/4; cf also 1962/VI/2). Elsewhere this thought is explained more fully: 'Here (in this miracle) more than anywhere I can see all the consideration and kindness of our Lord: towards his weary apostles, but also towards the people, whom he does not want to send away and whom he teaches till late in the evening. Then his friendliness towards the disciples: he talks to them as if he was one of them. Then his concern for the material well-being of his audience' (1961/VI/1). Our Lord wanted to give the apostles a day off; but 'the crowd never let them get that far and our Lord in his kindness cannot bring himself to turn the poor people away. But he takes the main burden on himself: "he had compassion on them, and healed their sick" and "he began to teach them many things"' (1962/VI/2; cf also 1963/VI/1). Our Lord 'gives thousands of them the bread of doctrine all day long until sunset, but also wants to provide the

bread for the body. Not, it is true, personally but through his apostles . . .' (1966/VI/2). Similar thoughts are expressed by the author, when he meditates on the appearance of the risen Lord by the Lake of Genesareth: 'This scene is another example of the familiar and loving way our Lord treated his disciples and also the way they treated one another' (1968/VIII/3).

This idea of kindness is closely linked by the author to the 'heart' of our Lord. With regard to the raising of Lazarus he writes: 'In this miracle our Lord allows me a deep insight into his divine–human heart. He is not without feelings. Anyone loving him is sure that he will also be loved by him, whether man or boy, woman or girl. But his love is supernatural, not of flesh and blood' (1968/VI/2; cf also 1964/VI/1). Naturally this quality is particularly noticeable in our Lord's dealings with his apostles: 'Here our Lord shows his heart: in the first place in the way he treats his disciples. After their work he wants to give them a rest and time to recover' (1966/VI/2). In the meditation on Christ's conversation with his disciples before the raising of Lazarus we read: 'He loves his disciples too and they love him. They are afraid for his life; he is not; but he puts them to the test—out of supernatural love for them. And they are ready to go with him even if they have to "die with him". But how kind he is in talking it over with them!—here we see no conventional "heart of Jesus", but our Lord in his everyday contacts and life. Only a person like John, who hangs on every word from the lips of his "friend" and sees into his heart, can draw this picture of his master and friend. For me this heart of our Lord is an inimitable model!' (1968/VI/2). Speaking of the laborious rowing during the night on the Lake of Genesareth after the multiplication of the loaves he says our Lord 'does not spare them the burden of the night. In his great goodness he knows how to protect them and preserve them from dangers. Our Lord is not just kind-hearted, he is also powerful and wise' (1959/V/4).

This heart is sensitive as well. With regard to the attitude of the disciples in the Garden before the passion we read: 'the conduct of his disciples must have hurt our Lord a great deal. In the first place their self-confidence, in the face of all that the Lord had foretold would happen. But then particularly their lack of sympathy. Of course they were tired after all that had gone before . . . They think only of themselves! And how much he had watched for them and prayed and cared! Our Lord is not without feelings, neither then nor now. This lack of sympathy must hurt him deeply' (1968/VII/1). 'But in spite of this he does not grow tired of the disciples, but showers graces on them; for they have been given to him by the Father' (1967/VII/2). Similarly in the meditation on the appearances of the risen Christ we read: the appearances 'reveal the tender love and thoughtfulness of our Lord for all those who are unhappy and weak (Emmaus, Peter, Thomas)' (1960/VIII/3). 'The days after the resurrection are . . . also a time of love: he has comfort to offer everywhere—to Peter, the disciples, the women' (1967/VIII/3).

Christ's generosity is connected with his kindness of heart. The author meditates on this mainly from the personal point of view and thinks of it as it is revealed in the life and the redeeming death of Christ. Christ 'did and still does "distinguish" himself in serving me: vocation, special graces, special mercies. He did not confine himself to essentials; he could have redeemed the world with one divine–human act of the will; but he became a man like us, led a life of poverty and need, worked hard, suffered in body and soul' (1961/III/2). Christ 'has done far more than was necessary for me and to me; his graces and his help have really been showered on me. So it is only fitting that I should do more than what is absolutely necessary; that I should be outstanding in sharing his work for me' (1959/III/1).

Apart from this the author 'admires' especially the 'tranquillity' and 'objectivity' of Christ: 'In this great miracle [the multiplication of the loaves] our Lord acts with tranquillity, impartiality and kindness, as if it was all something very ordinary. He acts with a consciousness of his own power and dignity' (1963/VI/1). 'Our Lord is wonderfully tranquil as he goes into the Last Supper and fulfils all that is prescribed and seems to overlook the rather mean argument of the apostles over who should have the first place. He tries once again to influence the heart of the traitor, washes the feet of the disciples like a slave and then institutes the sacrament of life "in remembrance of me" as his legacy to those for whose sake he is now going to his death. Only the God-Man could enjoy such a state of heavenly tranquillity' (1962/VII/1). More remarkable than anything is the tranquillity shown by Christ during the passion. In the meditation on the mysteries of the Garden of Olives, of the arrest and of the trial before Annas we read: 'Once again I marvel at this extreme, overpowering tranquillity. Even in the Garden of Olives, when he is deprived of all consolation and help, he prays calmly: "Father, if . . . not my will but thine." He meets the officers of the law with deliberate calm; for the last time Judas experiences the extent of his goodness, and Peter is reminded of supernatural considerations. . . . But it is above all when he meets Annas, the unmitigated scoundrel who is responsible for the whole campaign against him. No one could be calmer, colder, more objective than our Lord' (1962/VII/3; cf also 1960/VII/3).

But all these qualities shine out in a unique way on the cross: '[Our Lord] is really a king in the way he bears it all. He shows no sign of his cruel sufferings, but he does show his noble patience and his truly divine love. We can see this mainly in his words: they are the words of someone in complete control, as if he had nothing at all to suffer himself. It can hardly ever have happened that a dying man resembled him in this way. And his love goes out above all to his enemies, who have brought him to the cross; to the men crucified with him, and only then to his mother and the beloved disciple, who has followed him right to the foot

of the cross. He only gives a hint of his inward suffering' (1967/VII/3).
'It is particularly noticeable how in the midst of all the pain and agony of the cross our Lord thinks of others and takes care of them, first of all his enemies and crucifiers...' (1961/VII/4; cf 1959/VII/4).

This helps us to understand the profound statement the author makes about the mystery of the cross: 'The essence of the cross is love: the love of the Blessed Trinity for men and the love of the incarnate Son of God for each of us: "he loved me and gave his life for me". This love is at the same time the obedience of the Son of Man towards God: he "became obedient unto death, even death on a cross". God wanted to go to extremes: the redeemer was not to be spared anything. Even on the cross, as in the Garden, he sees himself abandoned by God...' (1963/VII/4; cf 1964/VIII/1). And again: 'The cross is the height of shame and of pain, but also the height of love. The love shows itself already in the choice of the cross as the instrument of salvation. Our Lord carrying his cross has become for countless people a source of comfort and strength. The death on the cross shows the love more clearly and impressively than any other martyrdom, which is quickly over and leaves no lasting impression... even children are taught about the love of our Lord through the picture of the cross' (1965/V/2).

Relationship with Christ

In the light of what we have seen, how does the personal relationship of the author with Christ appear? In the meditation on the choice of the apostles the author also thinks of his own vocation: our Lord 'called me that I might be with him, and in fact there cannot even have been one month in my fifty-seven years in the Society that I have not lived under the same roof as our Lord. But being with him also means that I had his example always in front of me (meditation, reading) and heard his teaching—to a degree which few enjoy' (1959/IV/4). In the meditation on the crowd pressing round our Lord we read: 'From the people I can learn how to be eager to hear our Lord and be with him: in meditations, visits and spiritual reading. For me too he is the Good Shepherd, particularly where I cannot see my path clearly' (1959/V/4). 'Jesus is my great model in this, and I must imitate him more and more' (1963/VI/1). 'For me this heart of our Lord is an inimitable model!' (1968/VI/2). On the subject of the 'way to holiness' he says: 'In all things I have our Lord's example before my eyes: "that I may do your will always"' (1968/I/3; cf II/2). Similarly in the meditation on achieving love we read: 'In everything our Lord must be my living model: the goodness and loving-kindness of our God has appeared to me. On every occasion, especially in meditation and examination of conscience, I will ask how our Lord would have done it and how I should do it. Every morning Mass should remind me again that I too must be a victim, pure, innocent and undefiled, and that every time I say the words of consecration it should also mean a transubstantiation of myself into Christ, into his spirits and thoughts' (1962/VIII/4). 'My spiritual life and all that I do must, then, be centred on Christ: Christ in all!' (1963/I/2).

But the author is also fortunate to belong to Christ. In the meditation on the mystery of the opening of Jesus' side he explains: 'Since that moment how many graces have flowed into the world out of our Lord's heart, beginning with the Church, which was born out of his side as his pure bride . . . I belong to a kind, powerful and gracious master indeed!' (1960/VIII/1). The apostles have been called ' "to be with him always": on my part this means being united with him in my work and not doing it merely materially and externally but in his spirit, in his grace and strength' (1963/V/2).

It is not, however, merely a matter of imitation, of work for Christ and with Christ: our Lord, especially in the Eucharist, is also strength, support, refuge and friend. 'I must receive the Eucharist in such a way that the Eucharist may really nourish and strengthen my spiritual life. I shall need this strength especially now after this retreat so that I can really carry out and persevere in carrying out the programme and practical resolutions that the retreat has produced' (1959/VI/3). Again: 'So the Mass should not be simply for the benefit of others but for my own good too. Nor must I ever forget that I can come to our Lord at any time with all my problems and worries. He lives together with me under the same roof. I can and I must tell him about everything that concerns and worries me' (1964/VI/4; cf also 1962/VII/2; 1968/VI/3). 'I must let all my day's work be penetrated by this presence and union (with our Lord in the Eucharist) and find in this my greatest devotion. So to cultivate a very special love for the Holy Eucharist and develop it must be my aim' (1965/IV/3). The idea of union with Christ is summed up by the author the virtues: he is himself for us a realization of the unity and love between the Persons of the Trinity, so much so that we have grown with him like the branches with the vine, and all our "fruits" are nothing but the result and the product of this profound unity. The Eucharist, the "sign of unity", is the thing that nourishes this fruitful unity' (1965/IV/4).

The author responds to our Lord's generosity with a generous devotion to Christ and his kingdom: 'If this idea of "greater enthusiasm" applies to anyone, then surely it applies especially to me, as I have received so very many graces and marks of favour from the Lord. So I must make more effort than anyone to "distinguish" myself in my loyalty to our Lord and to model myself on him as much as possible. The more I achieve this, the more I shall be able to do in this apostolic service' (1963/IV/1; cf also 1959/III/1; 1960/III/2; 1961/III/2; 1966/III/4). 'I have the highest dignity in the Church . . . there is no higher task in the Church; so I must also try to achieve the highest: not for the greater glory of God, but for the greatest!' (1964/IV/2.) 'The years that I have left I must and I will spend energetically and with my eyes fixed on the goal, in apostolic work, apostolic prayer, apostolic example and apostolic suffering' (1959/IV/4).

Here too, as usual, this generous devotion must be translated into deed and truth: it is only fitting that 'I should want to "distinguish" myself in sharing his (Christ's) work for me: and so overcome by decisive effort all the obstacles that are in me—attack them—and make faithful use of all helps, especially his example, so that I may reach the end, for which he came, in the most perfect possible way—so once again aim at perfection in all things' (II/1).

But all this must be done in the closest union with Christ: 'The king and Lord of all things is now the only one who can, through his Vicar, give me orders. I am, then, his most direct and nearest instrument and exist only to offer him the most immediate and direct service' (1960/III/2). 'So an instrument devoted to him at all times and in everything—according to his own example' (1965/II/3). 'I can do nothing but distinguish myself in his service. Where and how—as in the past that is up to him to decide and to show me clearly, revealing his plans to me from within or from without. There is no choice for me to make in this matter; I have only to keep myself open for any call and free from any sort of internal or external ties. There is no room here for thoughts of success, honour or recognition, of men's praise, or even of personal inhibitions or inclinations: I must be free . . .' (1966/III/4).

The passages so far quoted show well enough that the ultimate source and motive of everything is love. In this regard and in all modesty and honesty the author makes the following claim, together with a resolution: 'I can now look back on fifty years as a priest. These prove that he loved me. He has become for me all that he became for his apostles. But I have not yet achieved that, I might almost call it "blind", love for our Lord which places itself unreservedly and exclusively in his service and seeks and desires nothing else than to be his instrument. . . . In my meditation and reading I must aim at this frame of mind and strengthen it more and more' (1962/V/3). 'With me too it must not remain an external matter, everything must come from the heart. As the wound in Jesus' side never closed again ("the opened heart") so too my love must never grow faint. When I approach the Heart of our Lord I can do so not as a servant but as a friend to whom our Lord opens his Heart. And it must be true of me too: "he loved them to the end", to the very end, till all my powers have been used up in work, effort, suffering and the cross' (1964/VIII/1).

These last words show how close is the connection between love and the spirit of sacrifice: this is repeatedly mentioned, especially in the meditation on the death of our Lord on the cross: Christ 'gives his life for me: I must sacrifice my life and give it up for him. This is the meaning of my decision' (1959/VII/4). 'What there is left to me of life should be inspired and sustained more and more by this self-sacrificing and self-surrendering love. My God I love thee because thou hast loved me: not just with words, however, but in spirit and truth' (1963/VII/4).

The attitude of the author to the love of Christ crucified is shown particularly in his devotion to the Heart of Jesus. The origin of this devotion is the mystery of the side of Jesus pierced by a soldier in the account of the fourth Gospel. In this painful episode God wants 'to give us in the pierced heart of our Lord and the blood and water that flows out an image of that inexhaustible love of our Lord, with which he gives up everything for us. Thus devotion to the Sacred Heart is above all devotion to the love of Jesus, this generous, kind, forgiving love' (1959/VIII/1). The author meditates on the mystery again and again, and in the light of the ancient tradition of the Church and of the liturgy, 'the opening of Jesus' side is already one of the fruits of the redemption: the opening of the way to the treasury of love, the streams of mercy and of grace: the place of rest for the good and of refuge for the repentant. Since that moment how many graces have flowed into the world out of our Lord's Heart . . .' (1960/VIII/1; cf also 1964/VIII/1). '. . . We have pierced the heart of our Lord ourselves, but we can look to him with confidence and hope. He is all things to all men: rest for the good—the contemplative souls—a refuge for sinners, but for us all, through the Church and the sacraments, a torrent of mercy (baptism, confession) and of grace (Eucharist etc)' (1959/VIII/1).

From this we can see why the devotion to the Heart of Jesus is 'of such great importance' (1959/VIII/1) to the author that he reveals various expressions of his personal relationship with Christ precisely in connection with this devotion: 'meditation on and the imitation of Jesus' Heart is, therefore, my special duty and task' (1959/VIII/1). For him this devotion is a source of strength and grace (cf 1960/VIII/1). 'Through Mary I put my resolution in the hands and Heart of our Lord, for him to bless them' (1964/VIII/3). The fact that these expressions are connected with the Heart of the redeemer means that they refer to the 'generous, kind, forgiving love' of the crucified Lord (1959/VIII/1). In this sense it can be said that the author sees devotion to the Sacred Heart as the essence and the climax of his personal relationship with Christ. The 'Sacred Heart', that is, precisely the generous, kind and forgiving love of Christ, sums up all the features of the author's personal picture of Christ: the kindness and friendliness, the love of Christ, who offers himself so generously. And his response to the generous and kind love is: imitation, union, unreserved devotion in 'blind' love, and all this in deed and truth, that is, in faithful, self-sacrificing cooperation in his work.

CHAPTER 16

'The Church must be the norm'

Bea's relationship with Christ was indeed completely spontaneous and extremely pastoral. But that does not mean that it was exclusively individual or individualistic. It is really in the Church that he meets Christ and to a great extent through the Church, through the Gospel of Christ that it preaches, through the sacraments that it offers, in fact through its whole life and history, precisely because Christ himself works and continues to live in it and work through it.

To begin with let us look at a few passages that give a general picture of this essential connection between Christ and the Church. In the meditation on the incarnation we read: 'The incarnation itself is a sign that our Lord wants to help the world, not only by expiation and satisfaction, but above all by his example and strength: an example by his life, strength through grace and especially through baptism, the Eucharist and the sacrament of penance.' Then the author adds: 'For this reason he founded the Church and for this reason too he makes me a mediator' (1968/II/2). God's plan of salvation is described in this way: 'Mankind has totally rejected God, but he does not condemn it and destroy it, he wants to save it. And to this end he decides to send his own Son: he is to become a man, teach men by word and example, suffer and die for them.' But that is not all the work of redemption means. He continues at once: 'and then set up an institution to make sure that the effects of his life and suffering reach men: the Church' (1960/III/3). In the meditation on the piercing of Jesus' side on the cross he says: our Lord 'is all things to all men: rest for the good—the contemplative souls—refuge for sinners, but for us all, through the Church and the sacraments, a torrent of mercy (baptism, confession) and of grace (the Eucharist etc)' (1959/VIII/1). Notice the words, 'through the Church and the sacraments'. It is clear and later will become even clearer that the sacraments are not a way to Christ independent of the Church, but that Christ has entrusted them to the Church, and men receive them from the Church and through the Church from Christ. In this sense the author says elsewhere, in the meditation on the same mystery—and altogether in keeping with the ancient tradition of the Church: 'Since that moment how many graces have flowed into the world out of our Lord's Heart, beginning with the Church, which was born out of his side as his pure bride' (1960/VIII/1). So the Church is the first thing to come from our Lord's Heart 'as his pure bride'.

As a consequence Bea also sees his own life in this same framework of the Church: 'The fact that I am myself a member of this Church is the great grace of my life, and the fact that I have the privilege of working for this Church—and in fact only for it—is the special calling that he has given me' (1959/VIII/3). And in this same framework he thinks of his own personal sanctification: he devotes a whole meditation to the subject of 'my holiness in the Church'. He views his work in the same way: after discussing God's plan of salvation up to the founding of the Church he continues: 'And he has placed me in this institution, not in an unimportant position but in an important position, with a great job to do, as one of his first helpers' (1960/III/3).

Let us look at this in greater detail. After the Church had been born out of the Heart of Christ 'as his pure bride' (1960/VIII/1), the risen Christ gradually reveals its nature in his appearances. For, if the appearances of the risen Christ show 'the tender love and consideration of our Lord for all the weak and those in need of consolation', they show 'above all his concern for the Church' (1960/VIII/3; cf especially the summaries in 1962/VIII/3 and 1964/VIII/2). By his redeeming death our Lord won all 'grace for us, but all this has to be applied to us and for this an instrument was needed, the Church founded on the apostles, and especially on Peter' (1959/VIII/2). In the course of his appearances 'our Lord gives the Church the precious gift of baptism, the consecration to the Blessed Trinity, and the sacrament of peace, the sacrament of penance' (1960/VIII/3). This last sacrament is described in more detail: on Easter day our Lord gives 'the great Easter gift of the sacrament of penance. "Who can forgive sins but God only?" But the Father has sent him and "I send you". This is the great fruit of the redemptive passion, in which we all share, and I have a share even in its application' (1961/VIII/2). He had already given them the Eucharist earlier (cf 1962/VIII/3).

Of course 'it is his Church: "Feed my sheep"; Peter and the other apostles are only the "ambassadors of Christ" and "stewards of the mysteries of God"' (1965/V/3). But as administrators and by his commission they have an important mission: 'on the mountain he (our Lord) gives the apostles (and only them) the power of teaching, sanctifying and governing, and this from his all-embracing fullness of power. And to the end of time: hence the hierarchy in apostolic succession, and again over the whole world: the catholicity of the Church' (1961/VIII/3; cf also 1965/V/3). He teaches the apostles how to interpret the scriptures: he spends Easter day giving 'the Church instructions on the interpretation of scripture: "he interpreted to them in all the scriptures the things concerning himself"' (1961/VIII/2; cf 1968/VIII/2).

By the Lake of Genesareth 'he gives Peter full power over the whole flock. There is only one flock and it is this that Peter feeds: unity and primacy. But the flock is not Peter's property; he is to feed it in Christ's place and in love for Christ and so also for the flock entrusted to him by our Lord' (1961/VIII/3). And again 'the link that holds everything together is Peter, the shepherd, and his successor, the primate, whose exercise of authority does not come from any lust for power or ambition but from a love that must be greater than the love of all the others. The closer I am to St Peter's successor, the more the question: "Do you love me? Do you love me more than these?" applies to me too, and in all humility I must be able to reply: "Lord, you know everything; you know that I love you"' (1960/VIII/3). 'And I have the honour of serving this Church in a prominent position!' (1962/VIII/3). 'I must consider it an honour and a joy to work for the successor of St Peter' (1959/VI/1).

'And finally he promises them (the apostles) "the power from on high", "promised by the Father", the Holy Spirit, so that they may be his witnesses to the end of the earth' (1961/VIII/3; cf also 1962/VIII/3). They also receive 'our Lord's assurance that he will stay with them to the end of time. A Church, then, that will stand until the end. And I have the honour of serving this Church in a prominent position' (1962/VIII/3).

To sum up: the Church 'is based on the handing over of "all power in heaven and on earth". That is, so to speak, the foundation stone of the building: unshakable and invincible' (1960/VIII/3). Our Lord himself will not abandon his Church: "I am with you always, to the close of the age." And so he gives it divine assistance in every way, in doctrine, in government and sanctification. This is the Church according to the will of its founder, Christ. It is my great privilege to be able to preach this Church and lead as many as possible to it and give them a share in what it has to offer' (1964/VIII/2).

What is more exactly the relationship of Christ to his Church? 'The Church, then, is our Lord's masterpiece, the fruit of his life and suffering, and of his resurrection' (1965/V/3). Christ is its chief shepherd: 'and over everything is our Lord as the "chief shepherd", who gives the direction by his example and guides everything with his love' (1969/VIII/3). What is more Christ himself lives in it: 'The feast of Pentecost is nothing but the completion of his (Christ's) life on earth and the beginning of his mystical life in the Church' (1959/VIII/2). The Church as the 'Mystical Body of Christ' keeps on recurring in the notes. The author shows how familiar he is with the idea by seeing even 'the fundamental principle' in this light: 'I am a creature "in Christ", that is as part of him, one of his members, and so I share the task that God by his eternal decree gave to him, the "Word made flesh". All praise, reverence and service is an image of his ministry, a share in his ministry, the work of his ministry. This gives all my actions, words and thoughts his dignity but also his stamp, his form and his character: not simply human, but "Christlike", in so far as this is at all possible for a finite creature' (1960/I/2). 'The Church is not just a pious society but the continuation of Christ himself with all his gifts and graces. No wonder that it cannot go under in all the storms' (1963/VIII/1).

Since the Church is sent by Christ and acts in his name, carrying on his mission in the world, so Christ and the Church share a common life and a common fate. It shares his lot on earth in every respect and must bear it as he did, in order to be able to share his final victory as well. We shall come across this community of life and fate again and again. At this point only one striking fact needs to be mentioned, that in the meditation on Christ's passion and his victory in the resurrection, Bea thinks almost exclusively of the Church and its fate, when he makes the 'application', and sees his own life and work only in this context. 'Our Lord went through all that his Church had to suffer later and still suffers today' (1960/VII/3). On the subject of 'Jesus before his judges' we read: 'This is not just the personal suffering of our Lord but in a way a programme: his Church will face countless judges, undefended and unarmed ("the sword into its sheath"!); it will not be in a position to defend itself, but will be condemned unheard.—This is the fate of millions of martyrs, and yet the Church is victorious. Two thousand years are a proof of that. History confirms this too' (1968/VII/3). And again: 'Our Lord has simply become a plaything and no one is bothered about his rights ... This is the picture of the extension of Christ, the Church, and of its leaders and servants. Not the same at all times; not always and everywhere with the same means, sometimes with the weapons of the mind and then again sometimes with brute force ...' (1962/VII/4). These general thoughts are developed in other scenes: 'What happens to it is only as much as the Father wills ...' (1961/VII/2). 'How often the enemies of the Church are led by unfaithful priests and bishops, "friends"; in spite of all their hostility he treats them with love and patience' (1966/VII/2).

What is the reaction of the Church on these occasions and what should it be? Before its judges 'the Church's answer can only be to confess Christ clearly, to be silent, where people will not listen to the truth, and to put up with it all patiently. I have a share in the fate of the Church and I must act as it acts or as our Lord acted. In my position too it is often better to be silent, unless bound to speak by an objective obligation. But when that is the case, I must confess to the truth clearly and distinctly, although without hurting or offending the other person' (1966/VII/3).

This sharing of fate is absolutely necessary: 'I should have to doubt the Church if it did not suffer this fate even today. In fact it suffers it today more than ever. While its reputation has grown in one part of the world and it is recognized in its greatness, attacks on it from the other side are all the more fierce and ruthless' (1960/VII/2). This sharing of life and fate is so certain that the author finds confirmation of his faith in Christ even in the history of the Church. By the transfiguration our Lord prepared the disciples for his passion: 'I should not expect any extraordinary preparation like this. I have God's Word ("Listen to him") and all the wonderful confirmation offered by the history of the Church. This must be enough for me to take upon myself and bear even more difficult things' (1966/VI/1). 'For this I do not need a sensible experience like theirs [the apostles]: I have his word and his example in the Gospel and also in the life of the Church' (1964/V/1). 'Our Lord's victory begins with his death ... and then come the appearances as proofs of the resurrection and evidence of his love' (1967/VIII/2).

In the passages that we have already quoted the author repeatedly protests that it is an honour, a joy and a piece of good fortune to belong to the Church and to work for it and in particular for the successor of Peter and Christ's representative on earth. We shall now quote at some length a few examples of this outlook of faith. In the meditation on the subject of 'my holiness in the Church', which we have already mentioned, the author writes: 'My position in the Church obliges me to aim at a special sanctity: 1) first of all my position as a member of the hierarchy. As a cardinal I am set on the lampstand and in a very special way with my reputation. In all things I must be an outstanding model of sanctity—and also in the exercise of my office and my various functions ... 2) I am a priest of the Church ... 3) I am a religious, and so consecrated and bound in a special way to God, to the Church and to souls' (1968/I/4).

The author sees his apostolic work and suffering in the same light: 'My job is the same as the one Christ gave the apostles: to work for his Church through teaching and the sacraments' (1959/VIII/3). 'The fact that I am called to work for this Church is a great grace, especially since I have the privilege of working directly for the Vicar of Christ. This calls for joyful and ungrudging cooperation in the work of the Church' (1959/VIII/2). In the first retreat after he became a cardinal he writes in the meditation on the kingdom of Christ: 'This meditation has an entirely new meaning for me now. The King ... is now the only one who can, through his Vicar, give me orders. I am, then, his most direct and nearest instrument and exist only to offer him the most immediate and direct service' (1960/III/2; cf also 1964/I/2). 'My work must always be the result of sharing in the life and fate of the Church; the Church must be the norm' (1966/IV/3). But it is not just a question of working for the Church but also of sharing its life and destiny and of suffering with it. In the meditation on the attitude of Christ before Caiphas and Pilate we read: 'I must always remember that I am in the service of this persecuted Church and so have nothing to expect but what the founder prophesied for it and experienced in his own life' (1962/VII/4).

This chapter shows us, then, a new side of Cardinal Bea. His spiritual life and his apostolic work are certainly influenced by his personal relationship with Christ. But this relationship itself has also a social-mystical dimension. This means that the author meets Christ not only in his physical person—in the Gospel, in the Eucharist, etc—but also in his mystical person, in the mystical Christ, the Church. Thus his believing, trusting, loving devotion in his work, suffering and sacrifices is directed to the physical and to the mystical Christ, the Church. So the Church is really 'the norm' in all his life and work.

CHAPTER 17

'The family of God'

Today we have a deep appreciation of the social side of human life and attach great importance to it. And as Christians we are in a special way open to the sign of Christ's disciples, brotherly love. Because of his age, Cardinal Bea belonged to another generation. But in spite of this it is true to say that in this, as in so much else, he was altogether in sympathy with the modern generation. But he does not regard brotherly love as a matter of social feeling. He sees his fellow-men and particularly his fellow-Christians and his own attitude to them in the light of his relationship with God and with Christ. By baptism a new family has been created, 'the family of God' (1968/IV/4), which is an 'image of this union between the Persons of the Trinity and of our union with Christ' (1965/IV/4). This is why the command to love one's neighbour is a new commandment (id).

Let us start with the author's sense of his social responsibility, with the fact that all that he does and does not do is bound to have an effect, good or bad, on his fellow-men. He often reproaches himself, because 'I have not always given the good example that a person of my age and position should give' (1959/II/1). 'My age, my position, my authority demand that I should in all things be exemplary and faithful' (1959/II/2). This responsibility is made even heavier by the priesthood and his position in general: 'The good example that a priest gives inspires people and encourages them to imitate him; while the sin of a priest, even if it is only a venial sin, has a corrupting effect. The life of a priest by itself, if it is good, is an encouragement but, if it is corrupted by sin, it is a temptation and a snare' (1960/II/1; cf 1965/II/2). 'I am in the public eye ... there is a double responsibility here for a cardinal who is a religious, a Jesuit. Things to which people pay less attention in others take on a greater importance in my case' (1966/II/3).

In this context it is significant and interesting that in the meditation on the salvation of souls the author does not think just of himself but also of his fellow-men; the meditation urges him on to new zeal for the salvation of men. Salvation means 'a share in the life of the Blessed Trinity, and thus infinite happiness and eternal blessedness. This shows me that it is worth the trouble to do everything and to suffer and work in every way for it. . . . The saints knew this . . . but also the great apostles, who worked and sacrificed their whole life long to give the chance of achieving this great immeasurable happiness to as many as possible. Thus my own mission now becomes clear too: to save my own soul and the souls of as many as possible. This is the meaning of my work and labour, of all my sacrifices and suffering' (1962/I/3). 'The greater the number of those whom I have influenced by my apostolic work and whom I have helped to achieve their eternal goal, the greater will be my joy and happiness (in heaven)' (1964/I/4).

If we go into this in more detail, the first thing we notice is the author's determined struggle against 'criticizing'. On the conduct of Judas at the meal in Bethany he writes: 'An apostle who criticizes, and criticizes the Master himself to some extent, is a public scandal. When I criticize, even if it is justified and well meant, I always give scandal. So I must keep to Rule 10 in this matter of being in sympathy with the mind of the Church' (1964/VI/2). And in connection with the meditation on the nativity of Jesus we read: 'Everything is difficult for the Holy Family, but I cannot imagine that they had any thoughts or uttered any sound of complaint or criticism. This is an important point for me. I can certainly not agree with everything that happens but I must avoid criticism. As a cardinal I must give good example and rather than criticize I should defend the authorities, especially the Holy Father, and explain their meaning or at least be silent. And as a Jesuit too I must be loyal and careful on this score, for the sake of good example and the reputation of the Society' (1968/III/4).

The notes frequently refer to his attitude to the people who work with him, either in the meditation on the hidden life in Nazareth or in the meditation on the multiplication of loaves: 'Towards the people who work with me kind, considerate, and like a father' (1960/IV/2). If we look for more detail it is interesting to note the following resolutions: 'Trusting cooperation with others, with consideration and patience.— The cardinal's household: fatherliness, kindness, patience, spiritual care. —Relations with others: 1) with cardinals: respectful, ready to help, modest, understanding, but also open and straightforward in all things' (1960/II/3). In the meditation on the call of the apostles we read: 'Our Lord knows so well how to adapt himself to the character of each of them . . . In the same way I must adapt myself with love and prudence to each of the people who work with me' (1961/V/1). 'I must have the same care for the people who work with me as the Lord had for his apostles' (1962/VI/2). 'Our Lord's example: he does not force himself into the foreground and yet he is the one from whom everything comes . . . but I must not force myself into the foreground either; I must let my helpers do their work and allow them the credit that comes from it. Hence, modesty and selflessness. Our Lord is at work in everything and everyone' (1967/V/3).

This special concern for his assistants does not, however, mean that his life is exclusively concentrated on them alone. With regard to the conduct of the child Jesus amongst the doctors of the law: 'Listening to them and asking them questions', we read: 'I must show understanding towards everything that I hear from others; I must not be stubborn and exclusive, unless that should be necessary for higher reasons' (1959/IV/2). In the meditation on the Sermon on the Mount—probably in a reference to the beatitudes concerning the meek and peace-loving—we read: 'Towards my fellow-men: kindness, gentleness, understanding, not in any artificial way for the sake of diplomacy, but the result of a genuine supernatural love of neighbour. In particular must do my best always to encourage peace and cooperation' (1959/V/2). He explains the mission given to the apostles to 'heal the sick' in this way: 'He also gives me the mandate to practise the works of spiritual mercy: love, friendliness, kindness and help in the needs and concerns of souls' (1962/VI/1). Meditating on the kindness of our Lord he writes: 'In my position I shall be in contact with all sorts of people either personally or by letter. I must always receive them and treat them with love and kindness . . .' (1960/IV/4). There are still two more points to note. In connection with Cana: 'I must be quick to notice the needs and predicaments and so on of my fellow-men, especially those around me. I must do it from love or other higher motives; so I must not be stiff!' (1964/IV/3). And noting the fact that Mary went 'in haste' to her cousin, he says: 'If I can be of assistance to someone, I will not hesitate, will not make people keep on asking me. If I have to turn down the request, then I will do it with love and kindness. "Into the hill country": must help my neighbour even if it involves sacrifices . . . I must be obliging and not seek the limelight! And bring blessings wherever I go, even without being asked' (1968/III/3).

Love, however, certainly does not mean weakness. It must not degenerate into 'human respect'. '[In the way I serve God] I must not look at the example of others. Everyone has his own views and opinions, according to the conditions in which God has placed him and the way he has directed him. He has shown me an unusual amount of favour, almost without limit or reserve. And so I must use the same measure in my dealings with him . . .' (1967/I/1). 'How others do this, is no concern of mine: I do not know how much grace they have—but I do know how much grace I have and I must make the most of it' (1959/I/2). In the meditation on the boy Jesus in the Temple we read: 'Where I have to do the will of God I have also to make sacrifices and also to impose them on others in certain circumstances' (1966/IV/4). Referring to the fact that the child Jesus stayed behind in the temple, Bea writes: 'As a rule I must be kind, obliging and considerate to all; but there are also times when I have to say a clear decisive no (or yes), whoever the person concerned may be. The deciding factor is the will of God: about my Father's business! And in my case too people will not always understand: "They did not understand the saying which he spoke to them." But that is not the point. The important thing is always that I should be quite clear in my mind that this is the will of God' (1961/IV/3). An example of this combination of strength, gentleness and kindness is our Lord's behaviour before his judges: 'Our Lord's conduct at this hour is full of dignity and courage, but also full of love and kindness to all. He stands up for his cause against his enemies, especially against Annas: "I am he," he says to all who accuse him, but he is gentle and kind, even to someone like Judas' (1966/VII/2).

Of course this is not just a matter of outward behaviour. It must come from a deep spirit, from principles of faith: 'Our Lord is very friendly with Lazarus' family; but his friendship is always subject to the higher will of the Father; it is supernaturally ruled. All my human connections must be like that too' (1964/VI/1; cf 1968/VI/2). But what precisely is this 'supernatural' attitude? It is described in various ways: in the first place as 'a love of service towards my fellow-men, for I wish to be of service to them in their apostolic work' (1959/V/1). Here the author also takes as his model the attitude of God in the incarnation. In spite of the grave fall of mankind God 'sees the basic goodness in men and wants to make it bear fruit. . . . This shows me that not even the greatest sacrifices should be allowed us to stop us working for the salvation of our neighbour; in spite of all sin he is worth it' (1966/IV/1). Another point of view: 'I must be conscious of [God's] presence at all times and in all things, but especially too of his presence in my soul through grace. So I must see him in my colleagues and in general in all my fellow-men . . .' (1967/VIII/4; cf 1961/I/3). And more profoundly still: 'the motive for love is the 'mystical bond' which binds us Christians together. So we read with regard to the apostles' familiarity with Christ: theirs 'was not just a friendly gathering. They have been given to him by the Father and therefore they should be one as he and the Father are one, one with the Father through him. This is the mystical bond that holds them together, even when they are dispersed all over the world. And this bond also holds together everyone who is going to believe through them. Unity is not just the material fact of being united; it has a trinitarian character . . .' (1966/VI/4). Such a bond is forged at every baptism: 'It is a fact that through baptism a new family is created, having no further connections with the earthly family' (1968/IV/4). In the same context the author speaks of the 'family of God' (id). Therefore in everyone I must see 'a child of God and also a member of the 'Mystical Body and treat them as such' (1960/IV/4). From this he concludes: 'Love of neighbour is not just a "sense of family" or "friendship", or sympathy, but once again the image of this union between the Persons of the Trinity and of our union with Christ. This is why it is a "new" commandment, "my commandment", the proof of our love for him and the image of this love. Where this is missing there is no real Christianity. Therefore I must practise it and encourage it everywhere, apart from and beyond all natural motives' (1965/IV/4).

In the last chapter we examined the cardinal's attitude to the Church as a whole; in this, we have looked at his attitude towards the individual members. We see in the first place that his approach is marked by a strong sense of his social responsibility—by the consciousness that his actions, good or bad, inevitably influence his brethren. He is concerned about love and consideration, help and understanding in cooperating with others—firstly his assistants and those with whom he normally lives and has contact; but at the same time with all the people he meets. He also makes sure that these qualities and tendencies do not degenerate into weakness and false human respect. The whole of his conduct is ultimately based on a deep spirit of faith, so that it becomes an image of Christ's own conduct, and so an image of the relationships that exist in the Blessed Trinity.

CHAPTER 18

'Servants of Christ and stewards of the mysteries of God'

Apostolic work is simply work in the name of Christ and in close union with him, in order gradually to realize his work in the world for the benefit of mankind until its completion at the end of time. With this in mind, Bea says: 'My motto must be: a minister of Christ and a steward of the mysteries of God' (1962/VI/2). When he speaks of carrying out his task, he is often thinking directly of his personal vocation and mission, since a retreat is precisely aimed at a renewal in the retreatant's personal spiritual life and apostolic work. Yet there is no doubt—and we have already seen this in our discussion of his relationship with the Church—that he also sees his vocation and mission in the framework of the general mission of the Church, as a fulfilment of the mission which he has received from Christ through the Church. ' "I send you': my mission also comes from him and only from him, through his representative here on earth' (1962/VI/1; cf also 1960/III/3; 1964/I/2). So his apostolic work means 'solid work in the service of the Church' (1963/V/2). 'As a successor of the apostles I have the highest dignity in the Church. But this is not for myself but for the Church, the faithful, the whole world' (1964/IV/2). Indeed we shall see that in considering the apostolate he speaks repeatedly of the mission and work of the *Church*. This is why we are turning now to ask what is his attitude towards the apostolate: its foundations, its nature, its aims and its means?

In the name of Christ—in the power of his grace
The first basic thought is that the apostolate is not exercised in one's own name or according to one's own whim, but in the name of *Christ*, on the strength of a special and absolutely unmerited call by Christ: 'The apostles did not appoint themselves but were chosen individually by our Lord, and chosen not because of their capabilities but simply by God's decree ... so the whole of the apostolate is an entirely divine institution. For us too, the successors of the apostles, this is a source of strength and confidence' (1968/V/I). The same is true of his personal vocation: 'In the vocation of the apostles I see my own vocation. You have not chosen

me, I have chosen you, not because of natural qualities—he could find these in a thousand others, not for my merits—I have none, but because "he wanted". The conditions in which I lived when he called me were unusual, so that I might appreciate better the gratuity of my vocation' (1959/IV/4; cf also 1965/III/4). In various ways the author returns to these simple and poor circumstances out of which he was called: 'This story of the call of the apostles is to a great extent the story of mine too; 1) humble in origin: who would ever have expected that a little peasant cottage would produce a priest, a religious, a bishop and cardinal? It all came so unexpectedly, so much "from above", without being planned by anyone, indeed contrary to men's plans' (1963/V/2).

'The vocation to be an apostle and to do apostolic work is an unmerited grace, the result of God's eternal decree' (1961/V/1; cf also 1968/V/I). Like every grace, indeed more than any grace, the call is a proof of our Lord's love: 'It was a proof of his love that he sent them out; and it is also a proof of his very special love that he sends me out to the various tasks that I have had to do in my life . . .' (1964/V/3; cf also 1967/V/2). He says simply and humbly of this sign of love: 'Now, as I near the end of my life, I must be especially grateful for this vocation and have only one thing to regret, that I have not cooperated with this vocation as much as he might have expected' (1959/IV/4).

Just as the apostolate is not exercised in one's own name, neither is it exercised with one's own strength, but in the power of Christ's grace. The vocation has given him a share 'in Christ's office as teacher, shepherd and priest. But I must remember that I cannot do all this by my own strength but only through him who said to his apostles and so also to me: "I am with you". I can labour, plant and water; but it is he who gives the increase. In fact not even the planting and watering can be done without him but only with his grace' (1964/IV/2). Of course after the first grace of vocation the next grace is assured: 'I may be sure that if he gives me this grace he will also give me all the help I need to live up to this grace and cooperate with it. That is a great consolation and at the same time a powerful encouragement. "I am praying for them . . . for those whom thou hast given me, for they are thine . . . keep them in thy name, which thou hast given me" (Jn 17:9, 11). Our Lord's prayer is for me too' (1961/V/1).

But as the vocation and the apostolic work depend on the grace of God and of Christ, so also does their fruit: 'The results are due neither to my talents nor my work: "I chose you . . . that you should go and bear fruit." Of course I could refuse his call; and it is another of his special graces that I have not done so. In the deepest sense it is true: "I chose you" ' (1965/III/4). And again: 'Only he knows how much fruit I have borne. I hope that there was some at least. And now I can only pray: "that my fruit may remain", the fruit deep inside me, but also whatever apostolic fruit my efforts may have produced' (1959/IV/4).

The task of Christ—in the Spirit of Christ

In what spirit is the mission to be carried out? First of all, with unselfishness and in love and service of one's fellow-men. The cardinal explains this by the example of the angel at the annunciation. The angel had to announce 'the fulfilment of the thing that brought Satan and his followers to their revolt: the incarnation of the Word, and this to a creature who is far below him—but he "has been sent" by his master and that is enough: his personal thoughts do not count' (1962/III/3). All selfishness must be excluded: 'It is a task for Christ the good Shepherd not for me. I must be modest, simple, unassuming' (1964/V/3; 1964/IV/2). What sustains it all must be 'a love of service towards my fellow-men, for I wish to be of service to them in their apostolic work ... that was the first thing the apostles had to learn, to overcome their ambition, their eagerness to have the first place, their impatience, in order to become genuine stewards of God's mysteries. The example of our Lord (meditation!) and his warnings trained them ...' (1959/V/1).

Moreover the apostolate must be marked by a world-embracing frame of mind, just as our Lord's heart and the mission of the Church embraced the whole world. In the meditation on the incarnation we read: 'I must have the same world-wide approach as the one who chose me' (1968/III/1). And again: ' "Go therefore and make disciples of all nations." Today one third of mankind is still far from the Gospel of Christ. This commission to "go therefore" still applies to us and in the fullest measure. So I too, even though I have no direct missionary work to do, must do all I can to help the missions. The Church must not be content with what it now has. Just as the Blessed Trinity wants to share the riches of its life with all mankind, so too must the Church' (1964/III/1). Speaking of the Sermon on the Mount he says: 'This sermon is not just addressed to Israel, but to the world, to the whole human family. From the beginning our Lord is thinking of the whole of mankind, to which he wants to bring salvation, "a light for revelation to the Gentiles". Today the Church has become more conscious of this and has regained the spirit of the Apostle of the Gentiles. I too must cultivate this world-embracing attitude in myself and in others, far removed from all narrowness. For this reason in my meditations and reading I must get to know the whole world with its needs, sufferings, faults and mistakes, and try to bring it to our Lord, through my prayers and sacrifices at least' (1965/IV/1). 'The cross is the most visible and the most striking symbol of Christ's religion. It spreads its arms over the whole world and calls all to itself, as it were' (1961/VII/4). 'I must always, at least in my intentions, regard all men as my objective and be concerned in some way for all, at least through prayer and sacrifice. For me, then, there must not just be a Secretariat for Christians but also for the non-Christians and also for the non-believers: "he wants all men to be saved and come to the knowledge of the truth". Therefore I must have a world-wide apostolic zeal' (1967/V/4; cf also 1968/V/3).

The preparation and training of the apostle must also correspond with the spirit of unselfishness and universality, by which the apostolate is sustained. In the meditation on the baptism of Christ we read: 'Our Lord prepares for his public life by cutting himself off completely from all that had gone before (his mother, his home, his occupation), by an infinite act of humility ("and they were baptized . . . confessing their sins"), and by prayer ("and when Jesus also had been baptized and was praying")' (1961/IV/4). And again: 'I must thank the Lord from the bottom of my heart for the example he has given me: 1) freedom from all earthly attachments, even from his holy mother, whom he loved so much: and all this in order to be able to carry out his task without any hindrance' (1959/IV/3; cf also 1959/IV/2). 'My own preparation and training: free from any attachment to money or possessions and earnestly striving after "justice" (sanctity and perfection in accordance with my position), clean of heart . . .' (1961/V/2). The Sermon on the Mount 'tells me I must be free from all selfishness, from all laziness, all irritability, from everything that can cloud the purity of the soul' (1967/V/1).

Apart from freedom from every attachment and purity of heart our Lord also gives an example of humility: 'Our Lord does not want to begin his public life with a "big bang", but with an act of the greatest humility and self-abasement . . .' (1962/V/1). 'Although he is the purest and the holiest, he stands in the midst of sinners and waits his turn. In this way it really comes true that he bore our sins . . .' (1959/IV/3). 'In my case too every work must begin with humility. "I do not seek myself but my Father's business." And it must be accompanied by sacrifice, which includes misunderstandings, misrepresentations, failure, false judgement etc. Humility and sacrifice must accompany my work' (1962/V/1).

The concrete and practical way in which the author looks upon the task of the Church and also his own task is significant. In the meditation on the 'mission and outlook of the apostles' we read: 'The world of today is not without God but to a great extent anti-God: it does not want to have him and maintains that it does not need him. And so our Lord, and we ourselves with him, must have compassion on the people, and where they are looking for an earthly "kingdom" bring them the kingdom of God, but also show them that the kingdom of God really brings them what they are longing for . . . The Church today must stand as a sign of God's love for mankind, and so I too must represent and embody this love to the full. I must understand and sympathize with the needs of the world and do all that lies in my power to help and to encourage others to help and this even though we are "like sheep in the midst of wolves"' (1968/V/2). 'We must preach the "kingdom of God", that is the Gospel with all that it contains, not philosophy or social science etc. We must "cast out devils"—but the devil dresses differently today: in scientific clothes, in the guise of false humanism, or all sorts of philosophic systems. We must unmask him. The diseases of our time are greed, desire for material prosperity, the lust of the senses in all its forms, among the youth and in married life, to the ruin of the family and of human society' (1961/V/4). 'The object of my mission: the "kingdom of God", not literature, aesthetics, art etc. Now after the Council: preaching about the Council (decrees, interpretations, application, especially in those areas for which I am responsible)' (1966/V/4). 'Preach the kingdom of God: my preaching and my message must be of an altogether supernatural nature, and not be concerned with earthly things' (1962/VI/1).

The manner of preaching the Gospel is also important. With reference to the multiplication of the loaves we read: 'The people are tireless; they are eager to hear the words of our Lord and even forget earthly concerns. There is still this demand among men today, if only they are approached in the right way: if they are shown the value and beauty and fruit of Christ's teaching and not just addressed in terms of doctrine and law. As far as lies in my power I must cooperate in making the Church "come into the world" ' (1964/V/4). How is this to be done? 'Salt of the earth: proposing the doctrine of the Church without any falsification and without any abridgement, but also in such a way that it may be "tasty", that it may appeal and take hold of mind and heart. I am preaching the "good news" not a code of law!' (1964/IV/4). But there is another way of looking at this idea of the salt of the earth: 'As salt I must prove myself by representing genuinely Christian principles clearly and decisively without curtailment, either in my own private life or in public. This does not stop me adapting myself to the times in form, expression and speech' (1968/V/4). 'Salt of the earth: I must try to give men a taste for Christ's teaching, and so always show the attractive and inspiring side of Christian truth and of scripture. But at the same time preserve them from corruption: teach and champion sound doctrine . . .' (1959/V/3).

The Gospel is to be preached attractively and without any curtailment and also in simple clear speech: 'The light of the world: I must enlighten by solid well-founded and clear teaching, expressed clearly, understandably and impressively' (1961/V/2; cf also 1967/V/1). The same idea is expressed in characteristic biblical language: 'I must be "poor in spirit", not, like the Pharisees, ostentatious, but offering the simple and straightforward teaching of the Gospel in a simple and straightforward manner' (1964/IV/4; cf also 1966/V/4).

Allied to the simple and straightforward approach that has just been mentioned is the exclusion of all use of force. To deal with the ills of modern man 'force is no use . . . the only answer is to work earnestly and unassumingly, not giving oneself airs and asserting oneself, but straightforwardly, simply content with everything, doing the work where it is accepted and leaving it where it is rejected, as Paul did with the Jews. Today too we often find ourselves in opposition to material power, against which we cannot defend ourselves with material means, but by being as cunning as serpents, trying to save what is essential and, like the simple doves, coming back again and again' (1961/V/4; cf also 1962/VII/1). 'Our Lord's example: he does not force himself into the foreground and yet he is the one from whom everything comes. We are only the instruments he uses and nothing else' (1967/V/3).

The apostles 'must be prudent and wise; but that will not prevent persecution. They are just like lambs in the midst of wolves' (1963/V/4). But simplicity and straightforwardness apply to everything: 'my life: "the city set on a hill", with all eyes upon it. The town has its effect by its very existence; there should be nothing affected or precious, no search for sensation, but the simple straightforward expression of the interior spirit. And this in everything: in prayer and the religious life (simply devout!), in my relations with my neighbour: honest, not diplomatic, and honourable and straightforward; above all in conversation and dealings with people: working through the wisdom and strength of Christ and so on' (1966/V/2). But significantly the author adds: 'This is all a narrow gate and a hard way: it presupposes sacrifice, self-control and self-conquest. But it is the way our Lord went and so it must be my way too' (id). As in other cases so here too Christ's example is the way and the light (cf 1959/V/2; VII/3).

In this context it is interesting to see how the author looks on his special work, Christian unity, and the methods to be used in it. In the meditation on the sending out of the apostles he writes: 'I look upon the task that I have been given as the real "mission" our Lord has now given me, which I must fulfil with utter devotion' (1960/VI/2). 'It is also a proof of his very special love that he sends me out to the various tasks ... and especially to the task to which I can now devote the last years of my life. This task is also a matter of preaching the "Kingdom of God" ...' (1964/V/3). The desired unity 'is not just the material fact of being united; it has a trinitarian character, so to speak' (1966/VI/4). 'The special task he has committed to me is very great indeed. But I know that I am working "with him" ... So I must approach it with courage and be on the look-out for anything and everything that has anything to do with it; I must listen, encourage, help and spare no effort in this task. Not thinking of myself' (1960/III/2).

As far as the method is concerned: 'We must become more and more aware that our task is: "Go therefore and make disciples", that we must fight and conquer with the weapons of truth and only with these. This is also true of the task that I have been given: I must appeal to men's minds and conquer by the exposition of truth' (1964/VI/3; cf also 1961/V/4). 'So I must do everything to make the quest for unity worth their [the separated Christians] while, and offer them every help to achieve this goal. But above all I must show my love: in my relations with people, in my conversation, correspondence and dealings with people. They should recognize that it is only the love of Christ that inspires me. And I will make every effort to instil this frame of mind into all the people who work with me. The work must be done with fervour (of spirit) and in the spirit of power: with supernatural strength. Everyone must see: here is no lust for power, no earthly interest, no mere busyness, no matter of routine, but the genuine spirit of Christ' (1960/VI/2). To these last words, he adds: 'If it is definitely entrusted to me I shall treat the Jewish question in this spirit too' (id).

The notes are full of indications as to the way apostolic work is to be done. We must remember of course that Bea is not attempting to draw up a full systematic list of the many means that are at the disposal of the apostle, and which his ingenuity can discover in the great variety of situations, as the occasion arises. It is a question of pointing out the possibilities that present themselves to him in his actual situation. In the first place he stresses that it is important not to be on the look-out for extraordinary means but to be aware of the everyday opportunities and to make full use of them. For him it is a question of using 'everyday opportunities of doing good and carrying out my work: audiences, meetings, correspondence and so on. No one should leave me without taking away something important for his soul, his spiritual life and his vocation. I must not forget those words of Pius XII: "it is always the Pope who speaks". So I must not look out for "great opportunities"!' (1960/IV/3).

In this framework of the ordinary day he very often insists on the apostolate of good example. 'The lamp set on the lampstand: good example for those around me and all who come into contact with me' (1961/V/2). 'As a light I am, more than most, set on a lampstand and must be conscious of this all the time, without working ostentatiously, but quietly, as a flame burns, without making a fuss' (1968/V/4; cf also 1962/V/4; 1966/V/2; 1967/V/1). 'I must be a light by my example. I am now in the public eye and cannot escape it. So I must act and talk in such a way that people may "give glory to the Father who is in heaven". That must be my intention: to be a source of edification in all things out of love for God and souls' (1964/IV/4).

The author often stresses means that are connected with the social side of human life and especially friendliness, love and cooperation: 'with subordinates: always friendly, patient, kind, but not familiar, firm and clear' (1960/II/3; cf also 1961/IV/2). 'Towards all visitors: always friendly, even towards tiresome visitors: listen to them patiently and give them a clear answer, even when I cannot say yes, and take leave of everyone with a kind word' (1962/IV/3; cf also 1961/IV/2; 1960/II/3; 1964/III/4). 'Towards all who work with me: show confidence in them, prove my love for them whenever I can, be patient with them—making allowances for the character of each individual—and make sure that it is a joy to work with me. Pay tribute to the work they do' (1962/IV/3; cf also 1967/V/3). Then in general: 'Trusting cooperation with others, with consideration and patience' (1960/II/3). In many ways the following reflection is significant: '. . . the multiplication of the loaves is a very topical theme. And if I cannot play a direct part, at least in my various positions I can encourage cooperation and urge people to help' (1968/V/3; cf also 1961/VI/1).

In the closest union with Christ

In the apostolate the essential means are 'prayer and work', and it is extremely important to strike a balance between the two, to keep them in mind and apply them in practice. Prayer as a means of apostolic work is mentioned mainly in connection with the world-embracing view: 'I must get to know the whole world with its needs, sufferings, faults and mistakes, and try to bring it to our Lord, through my prayers and sacrifices at least' (1965/IV/1). 'I must not restrict my pastoral concern either: I must always, at least in my intentions, regard all men as my objective and be concerned in some way for all, at least through prayer and sacrifice' (1967/V/4). Even when his powers decline this remains a possibility: he must work for souls, 'as long as the Lord gives me strength, I shall do it by work; and when my powers are no longer sufficient, then through apostolic prayer and suffering' (1964/IV/2). This is after all only a consequence of the idea, mentioned earlier, that the fulfilment of the mission depends essentially on the grace of God.

This emphasis on grace and the need for prayer does not, however, mean being passive: it must be joined to the energetic application of all one's abilities. Speaking of the execution of the apostolic mission he says: 'Execution: "go", active, not just waiting, passive etc' (1966/V/4). 'I must set to work and even take the initiative, in whatever way God calls me, and follow this call faithfully and concientiously' (1966/IV/3). As for himself, he says he is overwhelmed with business just as our Lord 'is besieged by the crowds and cannot bring himself to turn them away. So the day passes—this is an image of my day's work too. It is after all God's will, and I must bear the burden, in whatever way and as long as he wants me to. In the name of the Lord Jesus! I have no right to a "peaceful" life' (1963/VI/1). 'If I am tired now, it was certainly not in vain. But I must not use this as an excuse for taking life easy: I can only be happy that our Lord has made use of me, and pray that I may labour for him to the end. This will be a special grace from God' (1967/V/3).

The need for energetic action is illustrated and stressed particularly strongly in the meditation on the storm on the lake: 'In all storms in the Church and in the Society and in our own hearts two things must help us: our own work and fervent prayer. In order that my work may be successful God's help is needed. This is more powerful than any human effort, but as a rule God does not help unless I make a serious effort myself. Much that is harmful could have been avoided in the Church if people who were responsible and held positions of authority had intervened actively, energetically and promptly. So whenever I have to deal with difficulties, whether they are my own or the Church's or whether it is in some matter confided to my care, I must act with all my strength, but in all this I must not forget prayer' (1959/VI/1; cf

1964/V/2). 'Today all over the world there is a storm and a violent storm against God and the Church. This must not mislead me. The thing is to fight the storm and fight it with courage and confidence. Our Lord does not sleep but he wants us to work and fight for him. He could still all storms with one word, one sign of his power: peace! be still! and there was a great calm. But he does not do so, or rather he does it through the work of his apostles by strengthening their arm' (1961/V/3).

There is hardly any thought stressed so often in the notes as the absolute necessity for the apostolate to be founded on and to spring from a deep spiritual life: 'All my activity must come from within, from a religious supernatural foundation. Otherwise it is activism, pretence, without any real foundation and hence without lasting success, "a noisy gong or a clashing cymbal". And the final and deepest foundation must be love: a love of God striving to give him the greatest possible honour and glory, and a love of service towards my fellow-men' (1959/V/1). 'I shall be "light of the world" and "salt of the earth" all the more, if I am a truly interior man. I must perform the externals faithfully; but these actions must come from an interior spirit and be informed by it, so to speak' (1963/V/3; cf also 1960/VI/2).

These are some of the more profound reasons for this necessity. In the apostolate a man is an instrument of God: but 'God does not work by external means, but with men ready to serve and surrender themselves' (1960/III/3). On Tabor 'the apostolate finds its source of strength and energy. And even if it is not mysticism, there must at least be a solid interior life of union with God, of prayer, of self-denial and mortification, on which my apostolate, whatever form it may take, draws its strength, drive and content' (1963/VI/3; cf also 1967/VI/1–2). In the meditation on the transfiguration we read: 'The deeper I penetrate into the depths, into the Heart of our Lord, the better and more effectively I shall be able to preach him to men. The two apostles, Peter and John, and St Paul are the best proofs of that' (1964/V/1).

Close union with our Lord is emphasized in particular. In the meditation on the Kingdom of God we read: 'So I must make more effort than anyone to "distinguish" myself in my loyalty to our Lord and to model myself on him as much as possible. The more I achieve this, the more I shall be able to do in his apostolic service' (1963/IV/1). He can only carry out his task 'properly if I really "show greater enthusiasm" for Christ the King and work for him with this greater enthusiasm. But this is only present and effective if I am very closely bound to him by a real interior life, by constant union with him, by a spirit of recollection and of faith' (1962/III/2). In connection with the farewell address the author writes: ' "He remains in me and I in him": this is a constant and profound union with our Lord, not merely a moral union but an ontological one, as the branch is united to the vine. From this union I receive strength, power and joy. It makes it possible for me to bear fruit, and indeed, as our Lord said, much fruit' (1959/VI/4). The apostles are called 'to be with me [with our Lord] always': 'on my part that means being united with him in my work and not doing it merely materially and externally but in his spirit, in his grace and strength. Being with Christ, then, is the thing: "I offer nothing but a share in my hardships"!' (1963/V/2).

But this close union with Christ also means union in suffering and carrying the cross. Very often the cardinal insists on the apostolic fruitfulness of this. The theme will be discussed at greater length later. Here it will be enough to quote two basic explanations. In the meditation on the presentation in the temple we read: 'Everything here is a story of sacrifice: not so much material sacrifices, such as were made for other children as well, but principally sacrifices for God's work of salvation, which our Lord and his holy mother are already making in their hearts and which they are later to complete by the cross and by suffering. This is cooperation in God's saving work, absolutely essential and predetermined in God's eternal decree' (1967/III/4). Speaking of the mission of the apostles he writes: 'It is an act of love for him to send them and in such a way that they are not only to work for him but also to suffer for him. He leaves no doubt in their minds on that score. The apostolate is always a cross. Our Lord does not want comfortable apostles. Of course he always gives them his grace, but this must find a soul that is inwardly cleansed and ready to receive it. So our Lord also speaks of the cross, of his example and of following him. Only then will the apostolate be fruitful. The true apostle must be a saint' (1967/V/2).

Of his own special task, Christian unity, the cardinal writes that it is 'a proof of our Lord's special love' (1964/V/3), but 'the closer anyone is to our Lord, the more this talk about the cross refers to him—and so to me also, and particularly to me in my special task, which is bound to involve a great deal of effort, of failure, and of misrepresentation' (1962/VI/3).

The apostle is 'a servant of Christ and a steward of the mysteries of God', that is, he acts on the strength of a special and undeserved vocation, under the orders of Christ and in his name. Therefore his work depends essentially on grace, that is, on help and support given as a gift. In all things he must be a faithful ambassador of Christ, not seeking his own ends but serving Christ and his fellow-men in love. His spirit and his heart must be as world-embracing as those of Christ himself. His mission is the mission of Christ himself: to preach the Kingdom of God and to do it with the weapons of the Spirit and of truth. He must work in the closest union, love and cooperation with the other delegates of Christ, indeed with all members of his Mystical Body. The activity of the apostle receives its strength and fruitfulness from a deep interior life and especially from the closest and most complete union with Christ, especially in carrying the cross, just as Christ redeemed the world mainly by his cross.

CHAPTER 19

Servants of Christ in the holy Eucharist

In the extracts given in the last chapter, the author was not thinking of the apostolate in general, but of his apostolate as a priest, a bishop and a cardinal, an apostolate which St Paul defined as servant of Christ and stewards of the mysteries of God. In his writings, Cardinal Bea distinguished two functions in this office: the first he called 'ministers of the word' and the other 'ministers of the sacraments'. In fact both these functions are included in the Pauline definition 'stewards of the mysteries of God', in so far as the expression 'mysteries of God' includes the 'mysteries' both of doctrine and of the means of grace, and in both the priest is a servant of Christ, and it makes no difference whether he is a simple priest or enjoys the fullness of the priesthood, the episcopal office (cf 1964/V/4). Our last chapter was mainly concerned with the ministry of the Word; so in this we turn to the ministry of the sacraments. As the modern mind connects the idea of the priesthood especially with the Eucharist, we shall begin with the discussion of the author's view of the priesthood in general.

The essence of the priesthood
'My priesthood is essentially a share in Christ's priesthood. It is his nature to be the mediator between God and man; and by his grace I have a share in this mediator's office. That means that I am under an obligation to men. I can never be a priest just for my own sake; it is essential that I should be a priest for the sake of all' (1963/VI/4). In other words: 'he is a bishop and a priest of God's family' (1968/IV/4), that is, of the Church. What is the precise nature of this mediator's office? 'As a priest I also have the privilege of offering to the heavenly Father the sacrifice of all the others and even the sacrifice of our Lord himself' (1960/I/2). By his cruel death Christ wipes out sin: 'He allows me too a share in this expiation, after taking on himself the more difficult part: the load and sin and the suffering . . . I have a share in his powers of expiation and so I must share too his humility, his suffering and his self-immolation: I am his "servant" and nothing else' (1960/V/1). Some more general remarks, with regard to the multiplication of the loaves: 'In this mystery the apostles are a model for me

as priest and bishop. For it is here that they emerge as Christ's instruments of goodness and power. Not "domineering over those in your charge" but stewards of the mysteries of God: of doctrine, of divine order and of divine grace. Everything passes through their hands. Our Lord blesses but they give it out and in their hands the miracle occurs. This is especially true of the eucharistic bread. So my motto must be: a minister of Christ and a steward of his mysteries and nothing else . . .' (1962/VI/2). Still in the context of the multiplication of the loaves he repeats: this day means something special for the disciples: 'It shows them that they are the stewards of our Lord's gifts. And it is not just a question of earthly bread but, as our Lord says next day in Capernaum, of the "bread of life" that comes down from heaven, of doctrine, of the sacraments and of the holy Eucharist. They are to be dispensers of all this. It is in this that the greatness and the dignity of the priesthood lie, especially of its highest degree, the bishop' (1964/V/4). After describing his position in this way the author draws this conclusion: 'As a priest and a bishop I share in a very special way in the holiness of the Church. I must also try to make my life as faithful an image as possible of Christ the High Priest. If this is true for everyone, then it is especially true for a bishop and a cardinal' (1963/VI/4).

But now we come to what Bea has to say about the holy Eucharist in more detail: 'This is the greatest thing I have as a priest. In it our Lord becomes present and active in me, when I celebrate the eucharistic sacrifice, and at the same time he becomes present for all under the eucharistic forms' (1968/VI/3). 'He has left us "a memorial of his wonderful works" in the holy Eucharist. When I think that I am the instrument for the distribution of all these wonderful works I have to marvel at this and at the power I have to hand on these powers to others' (1963/VII/1). In his love Christ gives us the Eucharist as 'a parting gift, as a source of grace, as a constant renewal of his death on the cross and as the application of the fruits of that death. Having loved his own . . . he loved them to the end' (1961/VI/3; cf also 1966/VI/3; VIII/1). In the Eucharist 'our Lord gives the greatest gift that he can give us: himself. It is the fulfilment of everything that religions strive after: we have the sacrifice, we have the union of the God-Man with us, and we have "God with us" ' (1965/IV/3).

And the nature, the power and the fruits of the Eucharist? The Eucharist 'is the epitome of our divine Lord's whole life of love; everything that he did on earth for the poor, the sick, the blind, the lame, for children and for sinners, he continues here tirelessly and he does it through my hands. This is the sacrament of humble love and service, as he showed before he instituted the Blessed Sacrament by washing their feet' (1960/VI/4). How does the Eucharist mean all this? Because of its very essence, because in it the sacrifice of the cross becomes present and active: 'What happened on the cross takes place in an unbloody manner over and over again in the eucharistic sacrifice. Like the cross, the eucharistic sacrifice is a source of reconciliation, of grace, of devotion to the heavenly Father and of the completion of the redemption' (1966/VIII/1). So we must remember that in the Eucharist 'our Lord is present and active in me' (1968/VI/3), and 'that as our Lord's instrument I am renewing his sacrifice of praise, thanksgiving, supplication and expiation . . .' (1961/VI/3). In all this the first aim is God's glory. In the meditation on Christ's words in the sacerdotal prayer 'I have glorified thee on earth', Bea remarks that this only happened 'through the cross. To glorify the Father through the cross is the great objective of the sacrifice. At every Mass that I offer this is the 'first intention' and I should always remember this' (1966/VI/4).

The practical consequences: 'Mass is the hour when I can lay all my intentions, problems and needs on the altar, but also the intentions and problems of the Church and of each one of the faithful. Every day it is for me, for the Church, for the world the great hour of grace, and I must make fresh use of it every day. How many of our separated brethren envy us this grace!' (1960/VI/4). 'In this way daily Mass will become for me and countless others a lasting source of grace and blessing' (1966/VIII/1). 'For those who celebrate it with me it must be a source of grace and blessing, and through me, the sacrificing priest, they should be encouraged to derive from it all the graces they need' (1968/VI/3).

'The holy Eucharist should always be the centre and focal point of my interior life and of my apostolic work . . . This is the great hour of each day for me and for the life of the world. The moment of the consecration is the greatest in all my day's work' (1960/VI/4). Notice how he stresses the importance of the Eucharist as something done for others, for the Church, that is for his apostolic work. This aspect of the Eucharist is so uppermost in his mind that on another occasion he has reminded himself: 'But in all this I must not forget the consequences for myself: "he who eats my flesh and drinks my blood abides in me and I in him". Already this is almost an anticipation of eternal life, at any rate it is a "pledge of future glory"' (1963/VII/1; cf also 1961/VI/3). But it is not just a matter of the future and of future glory: 'I must remember that he (our Lord in the Eucharist) is a source of strength and grace for me everywhere, but especially in the Mass. Every morning I must pray that this Mass may give me the strength and grace for a generous imitation of Jesus, for a love for him that shows itself in deed and for faithful devotion in his service, for the good of souls and of the Church. So the Mass should not be simply for the benefit of others but for my own good too' (1964/VI/4).

Turning to more practical details we see that Bea makes special use of the retreat before the golden jubilee of his ordination (25 August 1962) to renew and deepen 'my devotion to the holy Eucharist. The day of my ordination was the fulfilment of my great wish. But it must live on in every new day the Lord gives me. Above all the Mass should be the centre and the climax of every day' (1962/VII/2). 'The Mass is the greatest thing that I do and can do every day. So I must celebrate it with the greatest devotion and care' (1961/VI/3).

But what does this care mean, more precisely? 'The celebration of the holy Eucharist must not become a matter of routine for me, on the contrary every Mass and every holy Communion should find me in that festive mood that prevailed at the Last Supper, when our Lord performed this sacred action for the first time and gave the apostles a share in it' (1966/VI/3). The struggle against this merely routine celebration of the Eucharist is a theme that often recurs: 'Mass must not become just a "function" for me, something to be done like a lesson, for example. It must take hold of and lay claim to the depths of my being' (1968/VI/3). 'I must keep myself free from any "half-heartedness". If this is true of anything, it is true of love for the holy Eucharist. Everyday I celebrate my Mass, but it must never become an "everyday affair" for me' (1967/VI/4; cf also 1959/VI/3; 1960/VI/4). 'And so I will offer this sacrifice every day with great devotion and recollection, and in doing this as an instrument of the crucified Lord I will imitate the frame of mind that our Lord had and expressed on the cross' (1966/VIII/1; cf also 1961/VI/3). 'What I need now more than anything is a really living faith in our Lord in the holy Eucharist, a faith that shows itself whenever I have anything to do with our Lord in the Blessed Sacrament' (1964/VI/4). In the meditation on the washing of the feet we read: 'The frame of mind displayed by Peter must be mine too with regard to the holy Eucharist: above all the feeling of unworthiness (Lord, I am not worthy . . . Lord, do you give me yourself as food?); but then a great love that would like to have everything from our Lord: "hands and head"' (1966/VI/3). 'Every morning Mass should remind me again that I too must be a victim, pure, innocent and undefiled and that every time I say the words of consecration it should also mean a transubstantiation of myself into Christ, into his spirit and thoughts' (1962/VIII/4).

Finally there are the daily visits to the Blessed Sacrament, mentioned over and over again: 'so once again I must practise devotion to the holy Eucharist in a special way, but particularly the "dialogue with Christ in the Eucharist" in frequent and regular visits to the Blessed Sacrament' (1968/VI/3). The Eucharist should 'give light, counsel, strength and comfort every day', 'during the day too by visits, not only the "official ones" but some voluntary ones, an hour here and there in front of the Blessed Sacrament' (1962/VII/2; cf also 1963/VII/3; 1967/VI/4).

To sum up: as a priest a man shares Christ's office as mediator and becomes a steward and dispenser of God's gifts to men. In so far as this office is a ministry of the sacraments it is exercised principally in the Eucharist. This is the greatest of our Lord's gifts to the Church, because in it, in the Mass, the sacrifice of the cross, Christ becames present and active again. Seen in this light the meaning of the following summary given by the author becomes clear in all its depth: 'So I must lead a eucharistic life by a fervent love for our Lord in the Eucharist, a real devotion to the Blessed Sacrament, by great confidence in our eucharistic Lord, a real "familiarity" with Jesus in the Blessed Sacrament, so that in me the words may be fulfilled: "I live because of the Father, so he who eats me will live because of me"' (Jn 6:57) (1962/VII/2).

CHAPTER 20

Creation, 'the world', the cross

A man, a Christian, and even more an apostle is every day brought face to face with the 'world'. It is in their attitude to the world that ideologies and religions part company. The world represents the concrete point at which we decide for or against God. It is the essential means of raising ourselves to God, of serving him and of doing apostolic work. But it can also be an obstacle to the service of God and even a temptation, and so lead to a fall and to a complete rejection of God. In the notes the whole complex idea is treated under the heading of two closely related phrases. The first is 'creation', that is, 'everything else on earth' (Exercises 23), as a means whereby man's end can be achieved. The second catchword is 'the world', in the pejorative sense of the word, a notion that we meet mainly in the New Testament; it stands for the world, above all the world of man, in so far as it is under the influence of sin and of the origin of sin, the 'prince of darkness'.

The diagnosis

The world as God's creation is good, not bad: 'I must not forget that all created reality, apart from sin, is from God. So there is no room for a negative, a merely negative, attitude to the "world". In fact I can use everything for the service of God' (1966/I/2). 'In the first place I must remind myself once again that the things of this world are there to raise me to God' (1963/I/3). 'Everything is a means of holiness for me: '... in everything God works for good with those who love him"—"those who love him"' (1965/I/2; cf also 1961/I/3). This approach is also based on Christ's attitude to creatures: 'He sees what is positive in them and makes use of all that is positive in them. And he does not do this automatically but with supernatural consideration. He is not, then, opposed to the world but rather uses the world and tries to make it more and more useful' (1966/I/4).

But now a further step: the world can become bad. How? 'The world I live in is not bad in itself: it is made by God and should lead me to God. It only becomes bad when it is untrue to this purpose for which it was created or is used by men or the devil for a bad purpose (irrational nature) or when I myself use it against its purpose' (1961/I/3). This leads—simply on the basis of experience—to the assertion that there is in man a certain disorder, and this can be the cause of disorder entering into the world of God. On this score the author is scrupulously honest with himself. In the meditation on 'Sin, disorder, world' we read: 'I am thinking mainly of the venial sins and all the irregularities in my life. These two things are for the most part the same or connected. Unkind criticism, defects and failures in my spiritual duties, lack of charity, impatience and so on, all this comes eventually from a lack of order in my nature and in my character' (1966/II/3). 'I shall only avoid sin, even the smallest sins, if I learn to avoid all irregularity inwardly and outwardly and refuse to flirt with the principles of the world. As for irregularities: "nature" has never really been completely dead in me: sensuality, selfishness and laziness keep on appearing, even if it is only in small things, and they easily lead to irregularities, if not sin' (1967/II/3). From the fact that creatures exist in order to lead me to God, this disorder can also take the following form: 'I must not use things selfishly to achieve my own ends: to play a part, to "push through" some views, to make too many demands on myself without regard to my strength, a certain tendency to want to "please everyone"—all these things are rocks on which my spiritual life and my apostolic mission can, if not founder, at least suffer damage' (1963/I/3; cf also 1960/II/4; 1962/II/3; 1964/I/3). In this connection the author also points to the consequences that such disorders have had in the Church: 'So many schisms would never have happened if only the clergy, especially the higher clergy, had given good example, if they had not sought their own ends in their words and deeds, but God and souls' (1965/II/2). In other places this disorder is described, with the help of the notion of freedom or of its absence, as loss of freedom: 'any dependence on creatures, any lack of self-control in my way of life and my relations with others, any love of ease or of self: anything of this sort holds me back in my pursuit of my goal, as my own experience and observation of others shows' (1959/I/3). 'Impatience, sensitivity, desire to make a name for myself, lack of recollection in prayer and in my spiritual exercises, lack of order in my work and so on: all this proves that I am not free deep down in my heart, as I should be. And behind these failings lie inclinations against which I do not struggle enough and so even now in my old age I must pay attention to these tendencies and fight them systematically ... I must fight the very urge to do my own will, every inclination to look for approval and recognition, every irregular desire to have and possess something, at its very beginning, at its root, so that I can face all things with inward freedom' (1961/I/4; cf 1960/I/4).

What is the origin of this disorder and what exactly does it mean? 'The mystery of sin is present throughout the world and throughout time. Essentially it is based on the freedom of creatures endowed with reason and their quest for "more and more". Where these two things are not ordered and connected, sin necessarily arises. The danger is all the greater since the sin of our first parents introduced concupiscence into the world. I should not be surprised, then, that sin has reached such proportions among men at all times' (1963/II/1). The author applies this thought in all honesty to the history of the Church and to himself: 'Even amongst the apostles there was a Judas, and how many there have been in the Church itself, priests, religious, bishops and cardinals, and even popes! The power of sin is just as great today . . . It is also a force in my own heart. If I look back on my past, I see how strong the inclination to evil was in me too and how often I was in danger of giving way. It is only by God's mercy that I have not been devoured' (1964/II/2).

This leads us to the New Testament notion of the 'world', in so far as it is under the influence, the control even, of sin and concupiscence: 'In reality man is not simply good, and "human" is not yet the same as "good". The whole of the history of the world shows this. So in my own life and in my own work I must treat things with a certain suspicion, but not in a way that hinders me but one that guides me' (1968/II/2). Our Lord 'never tires of warning against the world: the lust of the flesh and of the eyes and the pride of life. "The world hates me" ' (1960/II/4). 'If I live up to the eight beatitudes, I shall be blessed unlike the world, where the ideal is to be rich enough to be able to lead a life of luxury, to indulge one's passions and to have one's way in all things' (1960/VI/1). The author also looks at Christian unity in this light: 'The enemy of unity is the world: through its spirit and through its hate' (1961/VI/4). But here too the author also thinks immediately of himself: 'I must take this question of sin seriously. In the first place because sin still remains a possibility with me too. . . . The concupiscence of the flesh and the pride of life are still in me. And I have the free will that can refuse God's command. In every Mass I pray: take away from us our sins' (1960/II/1). After stressing the need to avoid 'flirtation' with the 'principles of the world' he continues: 'The world shows its influence in the shrill clamour of its principles and its half-truths, which then automatically lead on to irregularities and sin. They are for the most part half true and so can easily deceive. All this is true for me even after sixty-five years in the Society' (1967/II/3). And he finds it necessary to remind himself: 'Precisely in the position I occupy at the moment there is no place for worldliness' (1962/II/3).

Freedom of the spirit
What sort of attitude is needed? It is a case of using the world, as God's creation, only and exclusively as a means of achieving man's God-given ends, without disorder or lack of freedom, without becoming attached to it. So it means using these things, while maintaining a distance from all irregular attachments that already exist in man, in order to be able to dispose of oneself freely. '. . . I should do everything with deliberation; not with prejudice and bias, moods, considerations of convenience, selfish aims etc. I must maintain a certain detachment from things and not allow myself to be carried along by them without further ado, as

worldly people do in so many cases' (1963/I/4; cf 1966/I/3). And again: 'I can make use of everything that comes my way, every day from morning to evening, of the pleasant things and of the unpleasant things; but I must be in control, exercise a certain sovereignty over things, and not live through it all without thought' (1961/I/3). So indifference is not something 'for beginners; the more I want to advance in the spiritual life and the more I want to work for the Church and souls, the more I need it, to become free from myself, free from the hindrance of any regard for myself, carrying out what I recognize clearly as God's will. In this respect the great saints are my model: St Paul in his apostolate, St Ignatius in his foundation' (1959/I/4).

This interior freedom with regard to the surrounding world is a prerequisite for the prudent consideration which should lead to the actual choice of means to the end in any particular case: 'Indifference does not stop me advancing in wisdom and prudence. On the contrary it excludes whatever is merely emotion or a matter of feeling and in its place it puts considerations of faith and reason, which I can follow, unhampered by personal considerations' (1959/I/4; cf also 1963/I/3; 1966/I/3; V/3). 'Only the clearly recognized will of God will be decisive for me. Not that I want to be passive. I must examine things, decide conscientiously and then—leave everything to God, that means a real indifference towards my own will!' (1968/VIII/4). 'So my task is to find the right path and keep to it. And this is no easy task. To do it I need first of all light and strength from God: so I must pray' (1964/I/3).

The final result is complete self-surrender to God and to the goal he has set for man: 'I exist only for him and for his interests, and the consequences of this for me, whether recognition and praise or blame and scorn, are of no account. For God and God alone!' (1960/I/1); this is the 'freedom of the children of God' (1966/I/2), that is, 'the true freedom of spirit, independence of every influence that is not willed by God, and therefore energy and strength. The energy with which the saints pursued their goal would not have been possible without this interior freedom, that is without indifference. But indifference itself presupposes a great love of God, by which all self love is, so to speak, burnt up and supplanted. This love does not need to be a matter of feeling: it must be in the will, which wants to give itself up wholly to God' (1959/I/4).

In this chapter, apart from the idea of indifference, of detachment and inward freedom, we have come across another idea from time to time: the idea of self-denial, of mortification and self-conquest. In any particular case reflection must show what will help one to achieve the goal and what means are to be used, but 'in general it will be possible to say that whatever is naturally more difficult, that is, mortification and self-conquest, will be "more likely to achieve the purpose"' (1966/I/3). It is clear that this is a new idea. Up to now we have been discussing the preservation and creation of a state of detachment or interior freedom, that is in a way the defensive; now we are talking about a direct struggle against irregular tendencies, of behaviour and action in direct opposition to them. This is typical of the Gospel approach and of the tactics used by God and Christ himself in the work of redemption, and then entrusted to the Church in the Gospel as a mystery. In order to understand these tactics correctly, we must bear in mind the qualities of the 'world' in the pejorative sense of the word as described above, together with the 'concupiscence of the flesh, of the eyes and the pride of life' by which it is controlled and against which Christ warned (cf 1960/II/4); a world whose ideal it is 'to be rich enough to be able to lead a life of luxury, to indulge one's passions and have one's own way in all things' (1960/VI/1).

God's tactics
In this respect how does God himself act in his decree of salvation and in its execution? For man's redemption 'he decides to send his own Son: he is to become man, teach men by word and example, suffer and die for them...' (1960/III/3). In the incarnation we have 'the opposite of what the "world" seeks: instead of ambition he is the servant of the Lord; instead of riches we have poverty-stricken Nazareth; instead of self-satisfaction and pleasure we see work and self-denial' (1959/III/2). With regard to the birth of Christ 'God the Father arranged everything in a wonderful way: even the power of Rome had to serve him without realizing it that our Lord might be born in utter destitution, unknown, not famous, in a stable, with poor shepherds, not kings and princes, as his first worshippers' (1960/III/4). ' "Glory to God and peace among men" is the song at the birth of the Saviour. But all this will be achieved by means of unspeakable disappointment, opposition, discomfort, inconvenience, which Joseph and Mary and the Child himself will have to bear. Humanly speaking everything should have been quite different. But our Lord wanted it this way and chose to do it this way, but all this to give all of us, who are in the service of God's honour and want to bring peace to men, a model, a motto as it were' (1961/III/4; cf also 1959/III/3; 1962/IV/1–2; 1967/III/3).

The role of poverty as a source of humility remains to be mentioned. 'Externals do not count: Bethlehem not Jerusalem or Athens or Rome: a poor girl, wife of a manual labourer, a miserable little house in despised Nazareth' (1960/III/3). 'The birth of our Lord in Bethlehem in the utter destitution of the cave has been willed and brought about by him. From the beginning he wants to show the role of poverty in his kingdom. It is the Gospel of poverty that he preaches; even the rich must be "poor in spirit" ' (1965/II/4; cf also 1962/IV/1).

Naturally these tactics were also the will of Christ as God and quite deliberately chosen: 'No man can determine where, how and when he is to be born . . . only one person was able to choose, and that was our Lord. And he chose the crib, rejection and obscurity, although he was the richest, the mightiest and the noblest of all men. Why? Obviously because even here he wanted to choose the folly of the cross, for our sake and for our salvation. But that also shows me the proper way to work with him: no desire for influence or striving after riches, honour and recognition, but the hard way of the cross' (1963/IV/3). But this was the whole life of our Lord. It will be sufficient to give a brief quotation here summing up this idea: Christ 'could have redeemed the world with one divine-human act of the will; but he became a man like us, led a life of poverty and need, worked hard, suffered in body and soul. And in this way he became a model for me . . .' (1961/III/2).

The example Christ gave by his life is explicitly explained by Christ in his teaching and proposed for our imitation. The cardinal comes back to this thought particularly in the meditations on the Sermon on the Mount, on the transfiguration and on Christ's passion: 'The eight beatitudes are diametrically opposed to the spirit of the world, and yet there are millions who put them into practice today . . .' (1968/V/4; cf also 1960/VI/1). 'The eight beatitudes are diametrically opposed to the spirit of the world. They only make sense in the light of the cross of Christ and of a share in his cross. He himself has gone before me in putting this beatitude into practice: "Learn from me; for I am gentle and lowly in heart." He does not promise me happiness here on earth in all these ways. Complete fulfilment will be mine in the "kingdom of God". But St Paul could still say: "with all our affliction I am overjoyed" ' (1966/V/1).

The example Christ gave naturally reaches its climax in his passion: 'The spiritual sufferings of our Lord in the Garden are a great mystery. For me the most important thing is not to fathom this mystery but to see how deeply our Lord wanted to descend into the abyss of the suffering of the human soul. Sadness, fear, disgust, horror: all this floods into his soul and forces him to cry out: "my soul is very sorrowful, even to death", and brings on the sweat of blood. Surely the soul cannot suffer more than this. He bore it for our sake; it is so to speak an anticipation of his death on the cross. He bore it in expiation of all the disorders in our souls, but also to show me how to behave in suffering, inward and outward' (1966/VII/1; cf also 1964/VII/1). On the cross 'he gave himself up to the most painful and shameful death. He could go no further in generosity' (1960/VII/4). 'God wanted to go to extremes: the redeemer was not to be spared anything. Even on the cross, as in the Garden, he sees himself abandoned by God. It was only after he had drained the cup of salvation to the last drop that he was able . . . once again (to) use the dear name "Father" ' (1963/VII/4). 'Our Lord's pain is expiation for all the lust of the world, his poverty and nakedness the expiation for all the selfishness, his shame (quite concretely) the expiation for all ambition' (1959/VII/4). 'What the cross meant in terms of suffering is already clear from the fact that in the Garden Christ sweats blood at the mere thought of it' (1964/VII/4). 'The cross is the height of shame and of pain, but also the height of love' (1965/V/2).

Sharing Christ's cross

Christ's way, his programme, the means he chose for the redemption, all this applies to the Church too: in its path through history, its attitude to the world and its principles, in the continuation of Christ's work. But this also holds in a special way for those of its members who have prominent positions and tasks in the Church. In this context we should remember first what was said above about Christ continuing to live and work in the Church, so that as a consequence the closest community of life and suffering exists between him and the Church. Just one passage in particular may be quoted: 'Just as the Blessed Trinity wants to share the riches of its life with all mankind, so too must the Church. It does not exist to give comfortable livings, palaces and pomp, but to spread the kingdom of Christ. And it can only bring this about if it is poor and humble like our Lord, and his holy mother' (1964/III/1).

The author repeatedly reminds himself of this rule. In the meditation on the Sermon on the Mount he says: 'The meditation on the "hidden life" has already shown me that I must take up a position of opposition to the world. I must belong wholly to God; then the eight beatitudes will apply to me too' (1963/V/3). 'I must avoid all worldly and earthly pomp and give an example of true fervour' (1968/I/4). 'In my high position too I must be lonely, must not mix with the "world", must not seek the things of this world, but must give an example of simplicity and modesty. This means too that I must avoid all pomp: I will let people give me the liturgical honours that belong to my position and keep to protocol in my dealings with people, but no more. No mere formality!' (1962/V/2).

A particular application of this resolution is the love of poverty in all its forms. On the subject of 'preparation and training' for his apostolate Bea says he must 'be free from attachment to money and possessions' (1961/V/2). Elsewhere he speaks of the poverty practised in imitation of Christ: 'His missionaries are also poor in the material sense and for this reason they have access to the poorest people in this world. And Christ's apostles address themselves to the poor, "for theirs is the kingdom of heaven". But they also take care of them: the charitable activity of the Church is the result of our Lord's poverty . . . This poverty must also go with me in my position in the Church, all the more so as I took the vow of poverty in the Society. As far as I can I too must be the friend of the poor and show myself to be such' (1965/II/4).

Positively expressed: 'I must not forget that the unpleasant circumstances (poverty, contempt, travelling at a most unsuitable time) have been willed and arranged by our Lord . . . and we, even in our apostolic work, are always looking for easier conditions, we avoid unpleasantness and seek comfort. And as long as these things help and further the apostolate and our work, that is good; but never should mere comfort or self-love decide the issue' (1962/IV/1). ' "Glory to God and on earth peace" . . . there is no other way to achieve it except the way our Lord went about it from the beginning: "in utter destitution; after all his labours, after suffering from hunger and thirst, heat and cold, being treated with injustice and insulted, he is to die on the cross". This is the apostolic programme that our Lord had in Bethlehem; this must be mine too' (id). 'The birth in Bethlehem meant for our Lord an unusual amount of sacrifice; . . . this is what sharing in the realization of the plan of salvation means for me too. I must not avoid any sacrifice' (1967/III/3; cf also 1959/VII/4; 1963/VII/4). Our Lord has become 'a model for me; to imitate you in putting up with all injustice, all abuse, all poverty in reality no less than in spirit. To follow him is, even now in my present position, my duty and my task, which I must not forget or neglect for one day, even in the midst of all exterior pomp and ceremony' (1961/III/2).

We look now more closely at the idea of sharing Christ's cross. It has already been observed that the cardinal said that the eight beatitudes 'only make sense in the light of the cross of Christ and of a share in his cross' (1966/V/1). But now he writes: 'The demand of the eight beatitudes . . . must be my programme as cardinal and not just in a general sort of way, for I must be an exemplary cardinal' (1962/V/4). 'I must and I will take up the cross, in whatever form our Lord offers it to me. Then I am certain of having a share in the true happiness as well. Even here on earth the cross will bring me joy and consolation' (1966/V/1). From his contemplation of Christ on the cross he draws the following conclusion: 'There is nothing left for me to do but to copy this generosity (of our Lord) and generously to accept and bear the crosses that life brings me: to grow in faithful love for the crucified Christ and the cross, even if for love of our crucified Lord I must reach out for the cross (3rd way), as I have resolved, "granted an equal measure of praise to God" ' (1960/VII/4; cf also 1965/V/2). Our Lord 'chose the cross out of love for us. So I must also choose the cross out of love for him. In comparison with his my cross is infinitely small. And yet it was a consolation for him on the cross that so many were to take up their crosses and carry them out of love for him—even that I should be ready and willing to carry it with him, whatever form it might take, great or small' (1964/VII/4). This resolution, however, is not enough by itself: one must make oneself 'fit' to carry it out: 'What I have to do now is to make myself more and more fit and ready to follow him and work for him, even to follow him "in suffering"; even if it costs something, if I have to take a lower place, to humble myself, to make real sacrifices' (1962/III/2).

This general intention finds its daily application in mortification and self-conquest: in the meditation on the beatitude 'blessed are the mourners', we read: 'A life that is mortified, overcoming self, one that does not attract attention, spent quietly without any special comforts in my room and without anything special in the way of food and drink' (1959/V/2). Another interesting and significant point, which is often neglected, is the connection between mortification and the indwelling and action of the Holy Spirit in a person. 'I must be open to his [the Spirit's] influence. And it is not only the "flesh" that can put obstacles in his way, but lack of mortification, self-denial, in short the denial or neglect of the cross. Therefore this "cross" is so important for me. The works of the "flesh" . . . are where the cross is not; while the "fruit of the Spirit" exists where I "crucify the flesh" ' (1966/VIII/3).

This love of the cross together with the spirit of living faith gives Bea great insight, and enables him to look at so many everyday events in this light and so to accept and bear them. For example, ill-health: 'In any case infirmities, hardships, ill-health are also forms of suffering that I must bear in union with the suffering of our Lord. Must bear and can bear, for it is only a drop in the full overflowing cup of *his* suffering. Even if it is difficult: have faith—I have overcome (the world)' (1959/VI/4). In the meditation on the transfiguration he says: 'The transfiguration will affect the body as well, so the cross must also have its physical side, and also because the kingdom of God will not be spread without hard physical effort. Another reason is that our Lord himself suffered so much physically, to give us an example but also to give us strength. So I must bear physical discomfort, whatever its origin, not only with patience but in union with the physical sufferings of our Lord, and so for his intentions too and following his example (3rd degree of subjection)' (1959/VI/2). And in the same way every form of opposition and unpleasantness: 'I must make an effort to accept the unpleasantnesses and opposition that my work and my job bring me in the spirit of faithful imitation of our Lord' (1961/III/4). And again: 'I shall scarcely be called upon to face these [persecutions], but I must bear opposition and disagreements in a spirit of love and patience' (1959/V/2). Looking back over his life he says modestly: 'Really there has been little, almost too little,' of the cross and of difficulties in his apostolic activity (1959/IV/4). Then there are the difficulties caused by his fellow-men: he wants to be 'kind, sympathetic and merciful, peaceable and peace-making towards my neighbour.—And in all this: ready for hatred, scorn, calumny and detraction "for my sake". And not just "ready" but "rejoice and be glad" ' (1961/V/2). And when all this happens he resolves to bear it without a murmur, in patience and love (cf 1964/VII/3). 'I must always remember that I am in the service of this the persecuted Church and so have nothing to expect but what the founder prophesied for it and experienced in his own life' (1962/VII/4).

This love of the cross must also be preserved in the midst of storms and struggles: 'The Church is always exposed to storms, even when, like the apostles, it is where (and how) our Lord wants it. The disciples are not to be better off than their master. The history of the Church confirms this: there has not been a century without difficulties and struggles. But time and time again it emerges from them victorious' (1964/V/2). Finally comes what is perhaps the most difficult thing to bear: the spiritual sufferings, the share in the agony in the Garden: 'Hours like those our Lord experienced in the Garden of Olives can always come upon me either through interior dryness, lack of consolation and so on, or from without through failure, misunderstandings, misinterpretations, opposition, attacks and so on' (1960/VII/1). 'The "agony" (not so much the physical one as the spiritual one) in the Garden is a mystery that I shall never be able to penetrate and one that could hardly happen to me with the same intensity, since basically it is connected with the hypostatic union and with a knowledge of sin and suffering that only the redeemer can have. But a part of it can be my lot too' (1963/VII/2).

In the strength of Christ

We will devote a later chapter to some particular applications of this opposition to the world, this love of the cross and bearing of the cross, and especially with regard to honour and recognition. At this point there is only one further point to discuss and that is how the cross is to be borne and where the strength is to be found. Some indications have already been given in the passages quoted so far. A more systematic investigation leads to the following sources of strength and perseverance. First of all the Word of God. By the mystery of the transfiguration our Lord prepared the apostles for the passion: 'I should not expect any extraordinary preparation like this. I have God's word ("listen to him") and all the wonderful confirmation offered by the history of the Church. This must be enough for me to take upon myself and bear even more difficult things' (1966/VI/1).

Secondly our Lord's example: 'Through the shame and pain of the cross he (Christ) really did reform the world, and the cross will now give me once again strength and perseverance in following him' (1959/VII/4). Next there is love and union with our Lord. Meditating on Peter's denial he says: 'But I must not be afraid like Peter. He trusted in himself too much: even if all the rest do, I shall not. And now our Lord makes him realize that he is only strong in him, in his divine Master. And since he never lost his love he finds his way back at once: he "wept bitterly". Later he confesses: "Lord, you know that I love you." Hence a love that knows no fear!' (1962/VII/4).

Then there is the certainty of victory and the hope of future glory; 'The asceticism that our Lord teaches is a realistic one: he teaches not only the cross but also the transfiguration and insists on the connection between the two. And as an illustration of this he offers his own example. So it is just as remote from the type of asceticism that only overpowers its own ego as it is from the ideal of self-satisfaction that sets itself no limit. In my spiritual life then, I must practise both these things: faithfulness to the cross and hope in glorification' (1968/VI/1; cf also 1959/VI/4). Therefore 'the picture of the transfigured Lord must go with me too into everyday life, "if he follows him in suffering, he will assuredly follow him in glory"' (1961/VI/2; cf 1964/V/2). It is the same with the picture of the risen Christ. Our Lord's resurrection means his 'victory over his enemies, his exaltation (he exalted him), the reward for his sufferings and death (he gave him a name . . .). So he became a model for us all; and we will follow him along this way too, if we have followed the way of the cross with him' (1959/VIII/2; cf also 1962/VIII/2). 'Everyone must stand clearly by the truth: only then can he conquer, he personally but the truth and the Church as well. This was our Lord's promise; at the end of all the struggles stands his victory. "Do not be afraid; I have overcome the world" ' (1968/VII/3). But the victory also means that no persecution can destroy the lasting and eternal fruit of the apostolic work. The apostles 'must be prudent and wise; but that will not prevent persecution. They are just like lambs in the midst of wolves. And yet he tells them: "I appointed you that you should go and bear fruit and that your fruit should abide." And this is what has happened throughout the history of the Church. The final reason is: "I chose you and appointed you." But his destiny is: "Christ must reign" ' (1963/V/4).

There is still one final source of strength, which in a way includes all that has been mentioned above: prayer. For it is in prayer that a man asks for the grace that strengthens him, in prayer that faith and hope in the final victory and glory become deeper and more living: 'prayer is my strength too, whatever I have to bear. "Watch and pray" ' (1961/VII/1). Our Lord's attitude in the Garden is a model for him 'how to behave in all suffering, inward and outward. And above all he points to the main means: prayer, urgent, humble, trusting prayer. In such a situation man cannot offer consolation; only God can do this as he showed in our Lord's case (in the Garden), for his spiritual suffering ends in a brave "Rise, let us be going"!' (1966/VII/1; cf 1959/VII/2; 1960/VII/1.) So it is with our Lord in the Garden: 'the only help our Lord receives is from the Father. He sends him an angel to strengthen him, but not to tell him that the Father is going to relieve him of the suffering, but only that it is his will. And he repeats "not what I will, but what thou wilt" ' (1961/VII/1). If 'a part' of our Lord's agony becomes his lot, 'then I know that the strength to overcome the agony can only come from the firm, unshakeable intention of doing the will of the Father, and that this firmness is a grace I get from God through prayer, however lacking in shape and style that prayer may be, as our Lord's was in the end' (1963/VII/2).

What the author has to say about the 'world' in the pejorative sense and about the cross must not be misunderstood as a sort of Manicheism: the creation of God, as it left the hands of the Creator, was good; but sin brought disorder into mankind and into creation, so that now man is under the influence of the triple concupiscence, and through him creation is indirectly so too. There are two ways of reacting against this disorder: the defensive attitude, the effort to maintain a suitable detachment from things and from irregular tendencies and so to preserve one's own spiritual freedom. The radical way of acting against it, which is a direct attack on the irregular tendencies, is total self-denial, of which the cross of Christ is the revelation and striking symbol. God himself used these tactics in the incarnation; in his life and above all in his passion Christ lived them and entrusted them to the Church as *the* mystery of the cross. In fact as he lives and continues to be active in the Church in other ways, so he continues to tread the way of the cross in the Church and its members and is active in and through it, above all with the means that he used to bring about the redemption, that is the cross in the widest and most comprehensive sense of the word. The strength to follow this way with Christ, a way that is certainly not an easy one, is found by the Church, and so also by its members, in his word, in his example, in the certainty of victory, that is, in the belief that if they share his suffering and cross they will also share his glory.

CHAPTER 21

Eyes fixed firmly on the goal and on the cross

In this chapter we bring together what the notes have to say about the 'religious life', by which we mean not that consecration to God proper to the religious orders, but the means they use in the pursuit of perfection: the practice of the evangelical counsels. The essence of the religious life is given by Vatican II in the following passage: 'The faithful of Christ can bind themselves to the three counsels either by vows or by other sacred bonds which are like vows in their purpose. Through such a bond a person is totally dedicated to God by an act of supreme love, and is committed to the honour and service of God under a new and special title '(*Constitution on the Church*, 44).

Devotion to God and the pursuit of perfection have already been discussed in chapter 13. Here we shall deal with the evangelical counsels, which represent the fundamental opposition of Christ, and so of the Christian, to the 'world' and to the threefold concupiscence; the vow of poverty represents opposition to the concupiscence of the eyes for earthly goods; the vow of chastity with its renunciation of marriage and family represents opposition to the concupiscence of the flesh; and opposition to the pride of life (or inordinate pride) is represented by the vow of obedience. In the light of what was said in the last chapter it is clear that the practice of the evangelical counsels does not mean the condemnation of the good things they renounce, but only the adoption of a radical position in face of the disorder that exists in men with regard to these good things. In this chapter we want to give some indication of Bea's understanding of his status as a religious and of the obligations that go with it. And he is very conscious of these. His membership of the Society, the training he received in it and the religious life he lived in it were the decisive factors in his devotion to God, to Christ and the Church.

Firstly, he is very conscious that he is a religious: not only does he mention the fact repeatedly in various contexts, but he devotes whole meditations to the subject: 'The religious life and the fundamental principle' (1961/II/1); 'My priesthood and the religious life' (1963/III/3); 'The ascetical life of the priest and of the religious' (1966/III/1); 'The will of God and our Society' (1968/II/3). In the meditation on 'My holiness in the Church' he writes: 'I am a religious, and so consecrated and bound in a special way to God, to the Church and to souls' (1968/I/4).

True, he states that, since he became a cardinal 'there is scarcely anything left of my vows apart from chastity' (1963/III/3). But on the other hand he insists that he must practise poverty—as far as his position allows—and therefore try to be free 'from attachment to money and goods' (1961/V/2). He writes: 'This poverty (preached, lived and insisted upon by Christ) must also go with me in my position in the Church, all the more so as I took the vow of poverty in the Society' (1965/II/4). He returns repeatedly to the subject of chastity: 'I must guard this (vow of chastity) carefully, not as though any danger threatened but in order to make the sacrifice that it involves to the utmost' (1963/III/3). 'As regards sensuality I must not make any concessions, neither in the way of looks or feelings' (1966/VII/4). 'The hidden life (in Nazareth) also has much to tell me. Firstly the loneliness of being a priest. I must not look for any "substitute" for family life, neither at home nor outside. I am alone with Christ' (1963/IV/4).

In the retreat made before he became a cardinal he stressed the dependence on superiors and authorities demanded by the vow of obedience: 'I can recognize the will of God clearly through the instructions of my superiors . . .' (1959/I/4). Later he stresses his dependence on the representative of Christ on earth and the close relationship that this creates between him and Christ the King. In the meditation on the kingdom of Christ we read: 'The King and Lord of all things is now the only one who can, through his Vicar, give me orders. I am, then, his most direct and nearest instrument and exist only to offer him the most immediate and direct service' (1960/III/2).

He also insists again and again on the observance of the rules of the Society: 'I must cultivate the spiritual life of a priest and a Jesuit all the more, and in the spirit of the rules and regulations of the Society' (1963/III/3). In response to God's generosity and in the context of his efforts to respond to this generosity with 'the maximum of effort for God's honour' he resolves on whole-hearted obedience to 'the rules of the Society, in so far as they still apply to me, and total devotion to the task that Christ's Vicar has entrusted to me and still entrusts to me' (1964/II/4).

These few indications are enough to show how completely Bea regards himself as a religious, and accepts all that this means.

It remains to explain some applications of the principles we looked at in the last chapter in certain special areas: work, concern for health and lastly (a subject which is so important to men) reputation.[1]

---

[1] We are not discussing the cardinal as a 'Jesuit'. It will have been apparent throughout how closely he lived in the spirit of St Ignatius, and the Rules and Constitutions of his Society. It does not seem necessary to devote special attention to this point.

1) Considering the enormous amount of work the author did in the course of his very varied life, it is certainly of interest to understand his basic attitude, what could be termed the work-ethos, the principles governing the various aspects of his whole complex of activities. 'My life is devoted to work for the Church, in whatever way I am needed—just as our Lord did the things that were required of him' (1959/IV/1). What exactly is this work? It is 'quiet organized work . . . for the preparation of the sessions, for vota, lectures and correspondence. I must keep up to date with my correspondence (and so, where possible, get the others to help me): half an hour every day at a convenient time' (1962/IV/3). It is 'intensive work': 'advice, planning, consultations. Especially in this respect I have a great deal to do in the many tasks that I still have: in study, reports and also by publishing books. So for the time being I am far from having nothing to do' (1965/III/2). 'Work: as it comes—I have not much choice: preparation for meetings, lectures, correspondence. In God's eyes it has all the same value' (1964/III/4).

The manner: 'I must do everything conscientiously, thoroughly and as perfectly as possible, conscious of the responsibility that is mine' (1964/III/4). 'Work: calm, method, care, no haste. At the same time preserve recollection' (1960/II/3). Again: 'Work systematically, calmly, constantly, with a definite programme for the day' (1961/IV/2). Everything shows the author's characteristic love of order. He even insists on this characteristic in our Lord himself, in the meditation on the multiplication of the loaves: '[Our Lord's] love of order: "make them sit down in companies, about fifty each", and the gathering up of the remnants' (1961/VI/1). 'Nor should there be any slovenliness, shabbiness or anything slipshod in my life. And not just for the sake of good example. The heavenly Father, who created everything and preserves it in order, is order itself. Every disorder must displease him' (1960/II/4; cf II/3). And all this remains true even though the work does not seem particularly important: 'Work: hundreds of little "unimportant" matters, but they are part of my position and so part of God's will; so I must do them with preciseness, joy and love, everything with apostolic intentions' (1967/IV/2).

One special aspect of work is stressed repeatedly, the need for progress: 'Nor must I fall into the rut of a life of ease, mediocrity and self-sufficiency' (1966/IV/3). It is interesting to note that this thought is mentioned repeatedly in the meditation on the hidden life of Jesus in Nazareth in connection with the words: 'and Jesus increased . . .' (Lk 2:52): 'The hidden life also has much to tell me . . . The second thing is progress: always ready to be taught, whatever the source of the wisdom, so long as it is wisdom' (1963/IV/4; 1964/III/4). 'Progress: even in my old age I must try to make progress—in wisdom and grace. So always be willing to learn!' (1967/IV/2). In the retreat made just before he became a cardinal the principle of progress is explained in this way: in my work 'I must make constant efforts to advance in wisdom and grace. Wisdom: human and worldly wisdom—I must not fall behind in my knowledge and my subject. But must try at least to keep up with developments, and for apostolic reasons: I must not endanger the standing of authority by knowing too little' (1959/IV/1). A year later, as a result of the situation created by his elevation to the College of Cardinals, speaking of his interest in his professional work, he says characteristically: 'I must forgo my private interests (academic work and study), in so far as my professional work demands. I will devote myself entirely to what my present task demands' (1960/IV/2). Just three months before he died the author returns to the idea of progress: 'In quietness and seclusion I must perform my daily and weekly tasks, but I must always try to advance in wisdom by the study of topical questions, informative reading, discussion with others. "Always ready to learn"' (1968/IV/3).

2) One very important concern, and one that is sometimes quite a problem for men with a heavy burden of work, is care for their health and relaxation. The problem is how to be reasonable in one's approach to work, bearing in mind one's strength, and so taking care of one's health, without becoming a hypochondriac. Amongst the 'disorders' for which the author believes he must reproach himself he mentions: making 'too many demands on myself without regard to my strength...' (1963/I/3). Hence the principle: 'A reasonable practical care for my health and strength, but no indulgence or laziness' (1960/III/2); 'try, as long as possible, to conserve my strength for my work and not be unreasonable!' (1967/II/1–2.) The following reason is given for this principle: 'Nor must I be extravagant with my powers; they belong to him and I must keep them for him as far as I can without on the one hand being fearful and scrupulous, but also without making too many demands on them without sufficient reason. They belong wholly to God and only to him' (1964/I/1). A further explanation: 'our Lord's example shows me how I too should take care of my strength: "he was in the stern, asleep on the cushion". I owe the Church a reasonable concern for my strength and capacity for work. Certainly no one is indispensable, but it is often difficult enough for the authorities to find a replacement and so perhaps create a vacancy somewhere else. So I must rest in order to be able to work, but after my rest I must work all the harder' (1961/V/3). The practical consequences of this: 'Relaxation: this is also a duty. Recreation, sleep, walks, exercise' (1964/III/4). In the meditation on the multiplication of the loaves: 'Here our Lord shows his heart: in the first place in the way he treats his disciples. After their work he wants to give them a rest and time to recover. Holiday time and daily recreation are also in accordance with our Lord's will. "Come away... and rest a while"!' (1966/VI/2.)

3) One other aspect of human life, a thing of great value and something greatly desired, is what is variously termed recognition, success, honour, fame etc. The author knows that 'all external glory is super-

ficial and means nothing' (1960/V/1). In the meditation on our Lord's triumphant entry into Jerusalem he writes: our LORD 'sees better than I ever can what is really genuine in this procession and how many join in just because it is a feast. He sees too that this procession will only irritate his opponents more and make them more implacable' (1962/VI/4). He knows too how dangerous the pursuit of honour can be and 'how many [priests and religious] come to grief because of . . . ambition' (1966/VII/4). But all this does not mean absolute renunciation. He knows that even honour, success and recognition are part of the social life of men and that it is often God's will that they should be accepted. He is not afraid to admit to himself: 'I must not be blind to the fact that in a short time I have achieved a world-wide reputation' (1962/V/4). Indeed he is aware of his responsibility to care for this side of his life and work as well. Meditating on the word of the gospel, that Christ 'increased . . . in favour with God and man', he writes: 'I must not lose the good will and sympathy of my fellow-men, nor of those who work with me, through harshness, hardness or prejudice, especially now during the Council. There are higher interests at stake and I must take care of them with love' (1963/IV/4).

But at the same time he realizes that Christ chose the way of humiliation and shame and is determined to imitate our Lord in this—where his position and the circumstances allow it. Now as a result of these considerations we have the following principles. In the first place there is the goal and the mission: the will of God: 'This is my motto too in my position, not honour, or recognition or possessions, but to do the will of the Father in every situation in which he places me' (1960/III/4). 'I exist only for him and his interests, and the consequences of this for me, whether recognition and praise or blame and scorn, are of no account. For God and God alone!' (1960/I/1).

But since he knows how much man's lower nature thirsts for honour, he often comes back to the resolution not to seek honour in any of its forms. Not in his vocation from God: in this 'it is not so much a question here of dignity and honour—a greater external dignity is scarcely possible now; but of solid work in the service of the Church and of souls' (1963/V/2). In the meditation on the annunciation and thinking of the attitude of the angel he writes: 'He has no thought for himself, for his dignity or position. He has no desire to be anything but God's servant. A glorious example for every member of the hierarchy, and also for me! No seeking for honour, respect or possessions; to be nothing but God's delegates and servants of the Church and of souls' (1968/III/2). Nor in his work: 'Nor expect that I shall always have lasting success. They were amazed at our Lord but then they let him go. After the multiplication of the loaves they wanted to make him king and the next day even many of his disciples left. Do not look for applause' (1960/IV/3). 'As far as it depends on me, I must avoid everything that is sensational, striking, extraordinary, and simply work for the Church and its interests, working in a way that does not allow any influence from egoism, self-seeking, ambition or any other earthly motives' (1966/IV/3; cf 1968/IV/3).

Another side of the quest for honour is the fear of the refusal of recognition, the fear of negative judgment, of criticism. On this point the author writes: 'I am in the public eye: a city set on a hill, more than ever. So I must give no cause for criticism, for objections, whether in something I do or in the way I do it, on the other hand I must not be afraid of criticism' (1961/V/2). I must not allow myself to be put off or disturbed in my loyalty and devotion to our Lord ... by fear of criticism or disapproval and so on' (1964/VII/2). 'The important thing for me is to make my judgment on the basis of clear and objective criteria and always and everywhere to have the courage to stand by this judgment. It is only in this way that our Lord in his Church will be preserved from pain' (1963/VII/3).

But one must also be capable of accepting signs of honour in the right way and without coming to any harm. According to the author this art consists in remembering one's goal in all its forms and at all times, in relating signs of honour to this goal and at the same time cherishing the desire to follow where possible in our Lord's footsteps. 'Whatever I do, whatever success I have, whatever people do in my honour, it is not to be attributed to me but to him who "has done great things for me"' (1962/III/4). Referring to our Lord's triumphant entry into Jerusalem on Palm Sunday the author writes: 'this is a triumphant proccession for our Lord and he, "gentle and lowly in heart", accepts it because this is his Father's will as he had expressed it long ago through the prophet.— Often enough I am in a similar position, having to put up with festive processions and celebrations. I do it because I see God's will in it and can hope that some good will come out of it' (1962/VI/4). 'I cannot avoid men's esteem; but it must never in any circumstances be the driving force behind my action: I may admit it, but not desire it or seek it. May our Lord crowned with thorns give me the grace for this' (1966/VII/4). 'And if honour and recognition come my way, then they are not to be directed to my person but to the achievement. So altogether unselfish and serving only the great work. And so with our Lord putting up with any abuse, every cross and self-denial. Behold I am here: dispose of me!" (1960/III/2).

This desire and intention to follow in Christ's footsteps is shown especially in the constantly repeated resolution to lead—as far as depends on him and as far as the circumstances permit—a quiet, retired, hidden life. This preference for the hidden life can already be seen in the fact that without fail each year's retreat includes a meditation on the hidden life of Christ in Nazareth. This may at first sight seem to be in striking contrast with the extremely public life that circumstances forced the author to lead, especially the circumstances of his work for unity. But it does show that all the pomp and circumstance was not sought but simply accepted as part of his office and work. For his part he would have preferred to be 'a cardinal of quiet prayer' (1960/IV/2), but was brought out of the quiet life by his work and remained more or less constantly in the limelight. With this in mind let us look at those passages that are mainly concerned with this point. Three months before he became a cardinal the author writes without any inkling of what lay before him: 'Our Lord lived and worked quietly in Nazareth. No one who was unaware of his secret could even guess who he was, and he was only known at all within his own narrow circle of acquaintance. This is the model for the years God may still grant me. I live as far as I can a retired life in my room; I only appear in public when I have to and I do not talk about myself' (1959/IV/1). In the first retreat after his elevation he says the same thing: 'Here (in Nazareth) is a wonderful programme for my daily work. I must not go out of my way to appear much in public; I will be a quiet working cardinal as far as the circumstances permit' (1960/IV/2). And it is the same the following year with the addition: 'Invitations: reserved, moderate, modest, friendly' (1961/IV/2; cf 1963/IV/4). And the year after that, with reference to our Lord's example, he says: 'I must love this quiet life' (1963/IV/3). Two years before his death: 'after the busy years a time of seclusion has now come for me ... As far as it depends on me I must avoid everything that is sensational, striking, extraordinary' (1966/IV/3; cf 1968/IV/3).

The other particularly difficult way of following the crucified master's attitude to honour and reputation was the resolution, according to the circumstances, not to defend himself against negative judgments and criticism, and to say nothing. The meditation on our Lord's conduct before his judge leads the author to the conclusion: 'So our Lord's silence is well calculated. And this in circumstances where his honour and his life are at stake!' There follows the application to his own case: 'And in my case the occasions when I feel I have to justify and defend myself are often matters of such little importance. How often it does not matter at all whether I am right or wrong! This will be particularly important in the Council where I must be completely objective, and unbiassed, and kind and friendly to everyone, as our Lord would be, even to those who have different opinions. So there must be no suggestion of taking offence or being sensitive, "but he was silent". Apart from this I must not forget that I have promised our Lord so often to practise the third way of subjection' (1964/VII/3; cf 1966/VII/4).

The special applications we have discussed in this chapter will have shown sufficiently that the principles of the last chapter on the attitude to creation and all that is good in it, and to the 'world' in the pejorative sense of the word, affect the details of everyday life and can be applied there too. It will also be clear how easy it is to err on one or the other side in applying them. So what is needed is a great deal of calm thought and above all light from above in order to find the right path, as the author himself clearly states: 'In general it will be possible to say that whatever is naturally more difficult, that is, mortification and self-conquest, will be more likely to achieve the purpose. But even this must be considered according to supernatural principles. The positive values contained in "created reality" can often suggest the opposite. Taking all in all, then, I must proceed with deliberation and let myself be guided on every occasion by supernatural principles. "Speak, Lord, for thy servant hears" ' (1966/I/3).

CHAPTER 22

'Watch and pray, that you enter not into temptation'

The dangers that threaten us from the side of the 'world' and the fight that we have to wage against it are serious and by no means easy. And yet they are not the most serious or dangerous thing. Behind the 'world' stands the one through whom sin and concupiscence entered into man's life—and through whom the result of sin, that is the 'world' in the pejorative sense of the word, was created—namely 'the prince of this world' (cf Jn 14:30) and of 'darkness' (cf Eph 6:12). The author is well aware of this fact, which is anyway a teaching of the faith. In the struggle against the world and temptations 'it is not just a matter of psychology; behind everything there are the two great powers: God and Satan' (1960/V/3). In the meditation on the 'Two Standards' we read: 'It is also important for me never to lose sight of the workings of the evil spirit, even in me' (1963/VI/2). In the meditation on the mission of the apostles and the task given them by our Lord we read, after the mention of preaching the kingdom of God: 'we must "cast out devils"—but the devil dresses differently today: in scientific clothes, in the guise of false humanism, or all sorts of philosophical systems. We must unmask him' (1961/V/4).

The author is also aware that the life of the Christian, and all the more of the apostle, is exposed to the temptations of this 'wicked spirit'. 'It was the "Spirit", the Holy Spirit, who led our Lord into the desert, "in order that he might be tempted". This temptation was to show that we are not safe against the attacks of the evil spirit even in the holiest places (if our Lord is not, should an ecclesiastical dignitary be!) . . .' (1960/V/2). On other occasions the author speaks of the same thing using the words: 'difficulties' and 'storms' to which the Church, and therefore the life of every individual, is exposed: 'The Church is always exposed to storms, even when, like the apostles, it is where (and how) our Lord wants it. The disciples are not to be better off than their master. The history of the Church confirms this: 'there has not been a century without difficulties and struggles' (1964/V/2). 'Today all over the world there is a storm and a violent storm against God and the Church. This must not mislead me' (1961/V/3). The evil spirit tries his best to make use of the last and decisive hour of human life. So the author adopts the Church's prayer for the dying: 'May the Lord himself protect me from the evil enemy and lead me to eternal life!' (1966/II/4).

But it is not all a question of open battle and visible storms. The life and work of the Christian and of the apostle are often exposed to the secret influence of the evil spirit, who is always changing his guise, so that we have continually to unmask him (cf 1961/V/4). After saying that it is important for him never to lose sight of the activity of the evil spirit, even in himself, he at once explains that it is not simply a case of unusual things but of everyday affairs: 'In so very many cases it is up to me to make the right decision, right not only for me but for the Church and for souls. Although I make my decisions under the inspiration of the Holy Spirit, it is also possible for the evil spirit to influence me. And so I must be cautious in everything and always keep the principles of the faith in mind when I judge my "first movements" and have to decide for or against, in this way or that. So I must consider things carefully in the examination of conscience as well, discuss them with others and make every effort myself to see things clearly, so that I may not fall "into the snare of the devil" ' (1963/VI/2). Elsewhere, after enumerating various sorts of 'disorders' he continues: 'I must take careful note of these "more refined" movements and tendencies of the mind and make an effort to overcome them positively. This will not be possible without a great gift "for distinguishing between different spiritual influences" ' (1963/I/3).

In the last but one passage quoted the author also named the main ways of fighting against the deceit and attacks of Satan. Let us look at them more closely. The first thing is not to be afraid but to proceed with courage and trust: the storms and struggles of the Church 'must not mislead me. The thing is to fight the storm and fight it with courage and confidence. Our Lord does not sleep but he wants us to work and fight for him' (1961/V/3). 'In the midst of difficulties my trust is our Lord. He has sent and sends me the Holy Spirit also: "what you are to say will be given to you in that hour" ' (1966/V/4). Therefore certainty of victory as well: 'The gates of hell shall not prevail' (1959/VI/2). The Church always emerges victorious from these difficulties. 'Why is this? Our Lord is always praying for it, always living to make intercession for us. He guides it invisibly and visibly and comes to its aid at the right moment. But the disciples must row hard, do their duty, and, even if sometimes they make a mistake, our Lord overlooks it, if only they mean well. Our Lord, praying and watching, is our strength and salvation' (1964/V/2).

There is also need for watchfulness and prayer. In the meditation on the denial of Peter and the flight of the disciples, he writes: 'Are my retreat resolutions to be as ineffectual as the protestations of the disciples? I must remember our Lord's warning: "watch and pray that you may not enter into temptation"—that you may be preserved from danger' (1967/VII/1-2; cf 1960/V/3). But it must be a prayer that is inspired by faith, trust and therefore courage. Our Lord overcomes the storms 'through the work of his apostles by strengthening their arms. And so we can and must pray to him not like sinking men in a shipwreck but like good oarsmen. The history of the Church teaches me that he has overcome a thousand storms through his disciples, and often he has intervened suddenly himself: and there came a great calm. So faith, courage and confidence' (1961/V/3).

But more than supplication is needed, a life inspired ever more profoundly by the word of God is necessary: 'the strength to do all this (to overcome temptations) is given me by the "Word of God", that is, the supernatural way of looking at things. Above all I must aim at an interior life, based on the "Word of God", and further a life of prayer. I shall always receive strength and grace from this source' (1960/V/2). So it is a case of deepening the 'principles of faith', which enable one to recognize and unmask the deceits of the devil (cf 1963/VI/2). The cardinal writes in a similar vein in the meditation on Christ's attitude in the temptations in the wilderness: my work 'particularly at the Council . . . will have to be a matter of opposing the materialism of the age, of reminding the faithful of the need for a spiritual and supernatural life and warning them against the manifold temptations to attachment to the goods and honours of this world. "It is written": make sure that the teaching of the gospel is preached clearly and understandably and that all pastoral work has a practical but supernatural direction. The Spirit of Christ against the spirit of the prince of this world. If ever the struggle was necessary, then it is today—under the leadership of Christ' (1962/V/2).

Finally, the fight against those allies of the devil that live in us, concupiscence and the 'world'. The temptations of Christ in the wilderness show not only that we are open to temptations but also 'where the temptations lie. There are three temptations: to a comfortable life, to glory and honour, and to power' (1960/V/2). The author applies this thought at once to himself: 'In my high position too I must be lonely, must not mix with the "world", must not seek the things of this world, but must give an example of simplicity and modesty. This means too that I must avoid all pomp . . .' (1962/V/2). 'I must not be a "prince of the Church", having a good time, leading a comfortable life and not exerting himself; on the contrary I must lead a simple, moderate and modest life, as far as that is consistent with my position. I must not be the sort of cardinal who looks for popularity and publicity, always wanting to be in the limelight and anxious to have people dance attendance . . . I must not be domineering, authoritarian, insisting on controlling everything, but must carry out the tasks of my position with love' (1960/V/2). And of great importance is the patience so strongly recommended by Christ himself in the gospel: 'I shall bear difficulties that come from without in imitation of our Lord: "if they persecuted me, they will persecute you", "by your endurance you will gain your lives" '

(1966/V/4). But the decisive thing is love for our Lord: Satan's interest 'lies in preventing me from carrying out this plan fully. So all the more watchfulness, perseverance and prayer. The basic driving force must be love for our Lord, who goes before me with his noble example' (1960/V/3).

So we see that the cardinal offers us in brief compass all the essentials on the subject of temptations and the fight against him who was 'a murderer from the beginning' (cf Jn 8:44). We find here the belief in the fearful reality of an evil power opposed to God, which is active in the history of mankind from its beginning and to the attacks of which every individual is inevitably exposed. We find the principles by which this struggle is to be carried on and the weapons to be used. The teaching put forward by the author is seen to be clearly based on the Word of God, especially on a study of the life and teaching of our Lord. Thus the struggle against temptation is part of the imitation of Christ and an essential contribution to the fight that Christ himself waged against the 'prince of this world' (cf Jn 12:31) and the 'power of darkness' (cf Lk 22:53) and which now through the Church he will carry on to the end of time.

CHAPTER 23

'The first and most perfect of Christ's assistants'

The reader will already have noticed the importance the cardinal attaches to the role of Christ's mother, when he is meditating on the life, death and glory of Christ. In the eight-day retreat, the choice of mysteries to be meditated on is mostly left to the interest and taste of the retreatant. So it is significant that Bea often chooses those mysteries where Mary is in the foreground—the annunciation, the visitation, the marriage feast of Cana—or where she is one of the main protagonists: the nativity, the presentation in the temple, the finding of Jesus in the temple, and devotes special attention to the role of our Lady. But even in the meditations where Mary is not exactly at the centre of things, for example in the incarnation, on Calvary, and in the appearances after the resurrection, he likes to stress her part in the event.

This has nothing to do with sentimentality, which was quite foreign to his character: it is based on a deep faith, and primarily on the conviction, derived from the gospel account of the annunciation, of Mary's place in God's plan of salvation and her extremely close relationship with Christ. He expresses this conviction in the meditation on the annunciation: 'The first and also the most perfect of [Christ's] assistants is his mother Mary. She is the ideal for collaboration with the divine King: the handmaid of the Lord at the side of the Servant of the Lord; the poor woman of Nazareth at the side of the one who had nowhere to lay his head; the purest, the holy, the immaculate at the side of the one who was the pure God-Man. This is her real greatness and at the same time the key to the mystery of Nazareth' (1959/III/2). From which he concludes: 'The others who cooperate with him, the apostles and the priests, are copying her and only in this way are they real apostles' (id). So we read again and again that Mary is the model for his life and apostolate: for example in the annunciation, Mary's attitude is called 'the great model for my work in God's vineyard' (1962/III/3; cf also 1968/III/2). Mary is 'the unparalleled model for us all' (1962/VIII/1).

But since Mary and her life and suffering in union with our Lord are so constantly in the mind of the retreatant and accompany him so to speak every step of the retreat, it is obvious that what he has to say about the mother of Christ and his own relationship with her represents to some extent a summary of all that he has said about his relationship with God and with Christ, with the Church, his fellow-men and the world: in all this Mary is his model, the one on whom he can depend for motherly help.

Relationship with God

In this context Bea repeatedly stresses that in all the events related in the gospel Mary appears as the humble and obedient handmaid, devoted to God to the point of heroism. 'Mary too wants to be nothing but "the handmaid of the Lord". All the great promises concerning her Son make no impression on her; she only wants to know how God's will can be fulfilled in her' (1968/III/2). 'On hearing the angel's message, she has no answer but this: "the handmaid of the Lord" and the "fiat", which is so rich in consequences, but at the moment she does not think of all the difficulties that it involves. It is the will of God and that is why she agrees, not because of the dignity and greatness that is connected with it and on the other hand in spite of the worries and sufferings that this fiat involves. It is enough for her that God wills it this way. If her Son is to be the "Servant of the Lord", then she will be the handmaid (of the Servant) of the Lord' (1961/III/3). 'But Mary only thinks of one thing: "let it be to me according to your word", obedience to the will of God. This is the centre of her heart. Nothing else concerns her, neither honour nor position. But with all this she is still prudent. What does God want of me in these concrete circumstances? "How can this be?" This is an example of the application of the will of God in the concrete situation' (1966/IV/1). 'She hears things that are really tremendous. But she does not pay attention to them, only to the question whether it is the will of God and does not contradict another will of God—that she should remain a virgin. When she is sure of that she has only one word to say: "fiat"; for she is nothing but a "handmaid of the Lord".—This is the great model for my cooperation in God's work' (1962/III/3).

This attitude of humble obedience to God's will accompanies her throughout her whole life. At the birth of our Lord: 'Bethlehem teaches me total, unreserved and unswerving devotion to the will of God. The child in the crib knows all the details of the fulfilment of this will of God . . . Mary and Joseph probably have a general idea of what it is all about but no detailed knowledge of what it will bring them and mean for them. But Mary says: "Behold, I am the handmaid of the Lord; let it be to me according to your word," and with that she accepts everything that is to come, including the separation from her Son and his cross . . . At the crib in Bethlehem there are no outbursts of sentiment, no signs of softness, just the stern and strict will of God, which demands devotion without qualification and without recantation. This must now be my plan of action more and more consciously . . .' (1964/III/2). In the presentation in the temple, as well, Mary does not yet see clearly into the future, 'but she too offers her first-born Son absolutely and without conditions. And old Simeon tells her explicitly that she has to join in her Son's sacrifice and so closely that a sword will pierce her own soul. And she too, worthy of her Son, says without hesitation her "fiat". I must share the sacrifice of the Son and his mother—through my self-sacrificing work for him and his Church, even if this entails effort, strain and all sorts of suffering for me' (1960/IV/1). Speaking of Jesus taking leave of Mary at the beginning of his public life the author notes: 'Of course Mary felt all the sorrow of this parting but here too she says her "fiat" ' (1968/IV/4). To sum up, 'she remained the handmaid of the Lord throughout her life right up to the time when she stood beneath the cross. Therefore he who is mighty has done great things for her! I must also be a servant of the Lord in all things and at all times, as our Lord himself was the Servant of the Lord' (1967/III/2). We shall come later to speak of Mary's share in Christ's cross.

A number of other traits are closely connected with the basic approach we have just described. In the first place a deep faith. The presentation in the temple 'is also a mystery of faith, of a loving but quiet, almost hidden, faith, both in the case of our Lord and also of Mary and Joseph, and finally of Simeon and Anna. They all know the nature and mission of our Lord, but they are all silent and behave as if they know nothing of it. For Mary this is true of her whole life: in all things she is the quiet, humble, modestly retiring woman, who does not stand on her dignity, "my secret to myself" . . . My life too must be a life of quiet, humble faith, not making anything of itself, but in all things standing by what is revealed to it without being concerned with what people think' (1968/IV/2). Similarly in the meditation on Christ's birth: 'Everything is difficult for the Holy Family, but I cannot imagine that they had any thoughts or uttered any sound of complaint or criticism . . . Mary and Joseph accepted all the unpleasantness, disappointment and disagreement in a spirit of faith. They have God's word through the angel and they know that their child is the Son of God. This is the basis of their faith, which nothing can shake, but which on the other hand instils into them the greatest reverence in all that they see and suffer . . .' (1968/III/4).

In the passages quoted it is the quiet modesty and humility of our Lady before men that is stressed; but the cardinal also insists on her humility before God, in connection with the Magnificat. In the presence of Elizabeth, Mary receives '. . . . under the inspiration of the Holy Spirit the first confirmation of her dignity as the mother of God: "the mother of my Lord"—and what is her answer? She admits it: he "has done great things for me . . . all generations shall call me blessed" (as you, Elizabeth, have done). But she realizes and admits too that all this is not her doing but the result of the omnipotence, the holiness and the mercy of God . . . I too can say "he has done great things for me". Whatever I do, whatever success I have, whatever people do in my honour, it is not to be attributed to me but to him who "has done great things for me"' (1962/III/4).

Purity of soul is the essential preparation for cooperation with Christ; the author touches on this point only in passing but still repeatedly and expressly. Mary is 'the purest, the holy, the immaculate at the side of the one who was the pure God-Man' (1959/III/2). Again at the annunciation we read that Mary 'is not aware of the dignity and greatness that is already hers (Immaculate Conception); she is pious, humble and pure' (1961/III/3). In connection with the 'threefold colloquy', in the meditation on sin, he says: 'There was no sin in Mary's life, not even venial sin. That was her privilege . . . There were no disorders in the life of Mary or of Jesus. As described by scripture everything in her life is ordered and well-weighed up, to the last detail' (1960/II/4).

Next to purity of soul and closely connected with it comes unselfishness, which desires the gifts received from God only for the purpose intended by God: 'Magnificat: Mary is quite aware of what God has done for her and rejoices over it, but "in the Lord": she knows and admits that *he* is the great and holy one. Humility is truth. She also knows that these gifts of hers are for Israel's benefit, for God's People. What the Lord gives me is also not for me but for the Church and for souls' (1968/III/3).

Then comes virginity. In one of the texts we have quoted the author insists that Mary regards virginity quite definitely as God's will for her: she asks herself if what she has been told 'is the will of God and does not contradict another will of God—that she should remain a virgin' (1962/III/3). Elsewhere this idea is developed: Mary 'does not say: "I have not known my husband", but: How shall what is to happen in the future come about? She knows that by God's will she is dedicated to virginity. Here we see the expression of all Mary's profound greatness. This consideration is a new incentive for me to honour Mary as my great model and to imitate her virtues faithfully' (1968/III/2).

'The noblest of Christ's assistants'

The notes do not tell us much about Mary's relationship with Christ; as we shall see, they deal at length with the union of the mother with her Son in his suffering and beneath the cross, but apart from that there is little about her relationship with our Lord. What little the cardinal does say, however, betrays a certain suppressed ardour suggesting a depth of feeling that confined itself to few words. Speaking of the difficulties that accompanied the birth of Christ he says: 'Patiently Mary leaves everything to God, however difficult and incomprehensible she finds it all. It is her good fortune and happiness to be allowed to serve him whom she now carries in her chaste arms. She does not ask for more' (1960/III/4). On the subject of the birth itself he says: 'With what love and happiness and care did Mary take the child in her arms! In the Mass I hold the same Saviour in my hands—with faith, as Mary bore him in faith, but also with love, as she loved him with a mother's love' (1961/III/4). And finally: 'Mary was able to lift the child from the crib and pray: "through him, with him and in him . . . all glory and honour . . ."' (1966/IV/2).

The notes deal at length with the position and role of Mary in the work of the redemption—obviously with a view to the practical consequences of this doctrine for the retreatant's attitude to Mary. We have already seen the main text about Mary: 'As the first and also the most perfect assistant of Christ' (1959/III/2). In the meditation on the annunciation the author remarks: 'The greatest event in the history of the world, the incarnation, begins in as unlikely a way as could be imagined: in Nazareth a young girl, an angelic apparition . . .' (1963/IV/2). But then he sums up very concisely the greatness of this event: 'But in reality it is all immeasurably great: the virgin is full of grace and by her fiat she brings the divinity and humanity together: hypostatically in her blessed body and mystically in the Church . . . And little Nazareth becomes this day the centre of the world. Indeed "he who is mighty has done great things"! The most important thing for me is to let myself be used, however God wants to use me, in practice the unreserved fiat of my heart and my will' (id). With reference to the Magnificat he writes: Mary 'realizes and admits too that all this is not her doing but the result of the omnipotence, the holiness and the mercy of God (1962/III/4). Then he gives a magnificently concise review of the consequences of this event for Mary's position in the historical Church: 'This power, holiness and mercy God has now placed in her hands, and the whole history of the Church, of the saints, of those in need of help and of sinners is a proof of this' (id).

In this light he interprets the role of our Lady in various Gospel events. In meditating on the visitation, he stresses her maternal and obliging kindness: 'Mary has not received any instructions to do this: it is her mother's heart that has brought her to Elizabeth's house. With her she brings a blessing for mother and child' (1962/III/4). Elsewhere he points out that she went 'in haste' to her cousin, and then continues: ' "into the hill country": must help my neighbour even if it involves sacrifices. She "greeted Elizabeth": although she knows what God has done to her, she greets her relative before she is greeted herself: significant for me; in all things I must be obliging . . . and bring blessings wherever I go, even without being asked' (1968/III/3). From Mary's behaviour at the miracle at Cana the author learns amongst other things: 'What great power our Lady has over the heart of our Lord! And this is an unimportant matter; I have often far greater and more important requests. Why do I not approach Mary with unlimited trust and through her Jesus?' (1964/IV/3).

Mary's attitude to the 'world', to the things after which it yearns, the things it loves and seeks, can be seen over and over again in the passages that have been quoted about her fundamental approach to God and his will. At the annunciation Mary does not look for honours and dignities, she is not afraid of suffering and trouble, she only wants to be the humble handmaid of God and to carry out his will faithfully (cf 1968/III/2; 1961/III/3; 1966/IV/1; 1962/III/3; 1964/III/2; 1960/IV/1). It is not just that she accepts her poverty and her unknown and hidden life submissively from God's hands; when she is chosen by God for the highest dignity, she makes nothing of herself and continues to be a quiet, retiring, modest woman, loving her hidden life (cf 1968/IV/2).

But Mary's attitude to the world finds its most positive expression in her wholehearted participation in the cross of Christ. As we mentioned above, it is precisely this side of the life and destiny of the mother of Christ that the author deals with repeatedly and at length. Already at the birth she feels with Joseph 'all the effects of poverty—"in utter destitution"—but they make the journey in the spirit of faith, remembering the great events of sacred history' (1959/III/3). This theme is specially developed in the meditation on the presentation in the temple: 'Mary was also shown her way of the cross on this day: a sword shall pierce thy soul. Up to this moment she had no doubt a general idea of what was involved: now she knew it through the words of a man speaking to her as a prophet. And soon she was to experience it: the flight into Egypt, Jesus lost in the temple, the separation . . . sorrowful mother, pray for me' (1961/IV/1). ' "A sword will pierce through your own soul also"; she is to share in the contradiction that her child will meet. She is not merely a passive onlooker' (1964/III/3; cf 1967/IV/1). And now the deeper reason for this share: 'And Mary, who is nearest to Christ, is immediately drawn into the struggle: a sword of sorrow will pierce her soul—she is altogether innocent; but she must suffer with him because she stands by him. This is the destiny and the programme of those who want to show greater enthusiasm for him. It is also my great programme. Fiat! Fiat!' (1965/III/1). Again: 'For Mary this day is the beginning of her share in her Son's suffering, her "compassion". Joyfully she goes up to the Temple, not because she has to, but because her heart leads her there. But she cannot yet read the heart of her child . . . The words of old Simeon reveal to the mother the thoughts of her Son. He knows that he is the salvation, the light and the glory. But he knows too that this means struggles, suffering and death. This is what Simeon now says to his mother: "set for the fall and rising of many in Israel, and for a sign that is spoken against", and his mother is to have her share in this: "and a sword will pierce through your soul also". So begins the mother's way of the cross at the side of her suffering Son, and it will end on Calvary: "By the cross stood his mother Mary." She is the first and noblest of those who join in the Lord's work; and so she must make the same sacrifices as he does . . . this is my lot too. Holy mother, pierce me through, in my heart each wound renew of my Saviour crucified' (1959/III/4; cf 1960/IV/1).

There is a foretaste of this sombre future in the tension between her and her child when he remains in the temple: 'he stays in the temple without saying anything to his mother: this is a moment of tension, for which neither of them is responsible: it is a duty that the Father has imposed on him to show his mother that her maternal rights are limited and that the day will come when the Father will claim him altogether. "About my Father's business"!' (1963/V/1). But naturally it is only at the foot of the cross that she tastes this bitter reality in all its depth: 'Of all who accompanied our Lord on the way and stood by the cross Mary is the greatest: the queen of martyrs. Here the prophecy is fulfilled: "a sword will pierce through your own soul also"; but the sorrowful mother stood by the cross of her Son, and so she has become for us all the unrivalled model in carrying the cross. But in every cross and suffering she has also become our powerful mother and mediatrix' (1962/VIII/1). He meditates on the words Jesus addressed to his mother from the cross and says: 'It is difficult even to imagine all that entered into and weighed on his mother's heart at that hour. Only she and our Lord know that. And our Lord does not say anything about this: he lets her bear this pain in silence. He gives her only one sign of his love; he takes care of the mother he is now leaving behind and gives her his favourite disciple as a son. This is a scene of such divine dimensions that it is difficult to think of it in human terms' (1959/VII/4).

But it is precisely this deep and indescribably painful participation in her Son's passion that sets the seal on her place in the redemptive work of the Church. In the meditation on the Crucifixion, Bea writes: 'It is particularly noticeable how in the midst of all the pain and agony of the cross our Lord thinks of others . . . and finally his blessed mother, who has followed him to the foot of the cross: "Behold, your son". In her he gives his beloved disciple and us all a mother, his mother, who has now become our mother too' (1961/VII/4). 'From that moment his holy mother at the foot of the cross, the "pietà", became the mother of mercy, our life, our sweetness and our hope' (1960/VIII/1). 'At the foot of the cross Mary became my mother: I must belong to her like her crucified Son. The devotion to the mother of sorrows is familiar to me from my childhood: I must remain faithful to it now in the last years of my life as well . . .' (1960/VII/4).

The author has already shown how by his love and kindness the risen Christ comforts his own, and founds and builds up the Church; we see now how Mary is drawn into this activity of his: 'But after that he next consoles those standing nearest the cross, especially his holy mother. She is raised to a real heavenly ecstasy, united to her Son with a love that is beyond all human understanding. Now she is not only the mother of Jesus; she is also the spouse of Christ, of his mystical body' (1962/VIII/2). 'When he appeared to Mary he must have given her to the Church as mother and patroness. "Queen of heaven, rejoice"' (1961/VIII/2). And again: there is 'comfort too for Mary. It is true she does not need it in the ordinary sense of the word; she has suffered with him, but also hoped and realized that he would rise again. And now he is with her and shows her, his mother, what is to happen in the future: she who suffered with him is now to be the mother of the Church as well. The Lord's brethren are her children too and she will accept them as she accepted our Lord. So I must put my work under her special patronage. All the baptized are her children, whether they are aware of it or not. Under your patronage!' (1960/VIII/2.)

Looking back over what this chapter has shown, the first point to notice is how firmly the author's meditations are based on scripture, how they spring from it. He stresses just those traits that we see in scripture, in describing Mary's relationship with God: the humble obedience of the handmaid of the Lord, her humility, purity and virginity. So too with his description of Mary's relationship with Christ: her close union with him, her cooperation in his work, her share in his suffering, during his life and at the foot of the cross. He also sees her position as the mother of Christ's brethren, of all the faithful and of the Church, revealed in the words that Christ spoke on the cross to his mother and John. This is the foundation of his personal relationship with Mary and of his veneration and devotion for her; he writes that he is taking this devotion 'as a source of strength and grace' out of the retreat (1960/VIII/1). 'Through Mary I put my resolutions in the hands and heart of our Lord for him to bless them as he blessed the disciples and their work before his ascension' (1964/VIII/3).

CHAPTER 24

The Holy spirit: 'my life, my light, my strength'

Perhaps all this may make Cardinal Bea's religious life seem complex to many readers: how could he possibly keep so many factors in mind, and put them into practice as well? Where does anyone get the strength to lead such a serious and self-sacrificing life? Must not this have made his life unusually complicated? And yet very many people, who knew him personally, knew and admired his extraordinary simplicity and straightforwardness. How is all this possible? The retreat notes give the clear answer: the ultimate secret of this extraordinarily rich character lies in the Spirit of Christ which dwelt and worked in him in a hidden way. The notes reveal a lively faith in the Holy Spirit and a constant union with him: Bea appeals to him again and again and keeps himself ready for any call of the Spirit, following his inspirations faithfully.

As an introduction we quote a general text which gives a picture and, as it were, a symbol of the cardinal's view of the position and work of the Holy Spirit in the Church, and in each of its members. In the meditation on Christ's ascension he writes: 'The mood of our Lord and the apostles as they go to Mount Olivet is now quite different from what it was on Maundy Thursday. Not as though everything had already been achieved. On the contrary: their work is only just beginning. Our Lord sees in front of him the world still lying in darkness. It must be enlightened by faith and warmed by love. This is now the task of the disciples' (1964/VIII/3). How can a work of this nature be left to these men? 'But he can hand it over to them with one great consolation. The Holy Spirit will come upon them, the "power from on high", and he himself will be with them to the end of the world'. The Holy Spirit is after all the Spirit of Christ and his role is central: 'Our Lord has complete power over the Church; he remains with it for ever. But he exercises this power through the Holy Spirit, whom he sends' (1965/V/3). So the activity of the Holy Spirit remains the deciding factor in the continuation of Christ's work in the Church and through the Church, and so too in its individual members and through them.

Bea then applies this to his own life and work: 'And I must help in carrying out this task: this is my vocation, already as a Jesuit and a priest and now in my very special position. The Holy Spirit has enlightened me in this retreat on this precise point and my "decision" lays special emphasis on this' (1964/VIII/3). This conviction gives rise again and again to the resolution, expressed now in one way, now in another: 'I will cultivate devotion to the Holy Spirit in a very special way. He is the life of my soul, my light, my strength, and every day I have urgent need of his help' (1963/VIII/2).

This faith in the Holy Spirit, his work in the Church and its individual members, has its firm foundation in passages from the New Testament, on which the cardinal meditated repeatedly and on which he based his life ever more profoundly. First he stresses the role of the Holy Spirit in the life of Christ himself. Christ at his baptism 'already possessed the fullness of the Holy Spirit, and this is indicated by the appearance of the dove' (1964/IV/1). On the subject of the temptations in the desert: 'It was the "Spirit", the Holy Spirit, who led our Lord into the desert, in order that he might be tempted' (1960/V/2; cf also 1964/IV/1). In a reference to Christ's sacrifice on the cross: 'And it is said of him: "the blood of Christ, who through the eternal Spirit, offered himself ... to God" (Heb 9:14)' (1964/IV/1). Apart from this of course it is made clear that Christ promised the Holy Spirit (cf 1959/VI/4; 1968/VI/4). But above all he insists that 'the Holy Spirit is a fruit of the redemption'—a subject to which the author devotes two special meditations (cf 1963/VIII/2; 1966/VIII/3; cf also 1959/VIII/2). In one of these he says: 'The source of the Holy Spirit is the pierced heart of our Lord on the cross. Before this the Spirit was not yet active as he is now. But today, as his different names show, he pervades all "spiritual" life' (1966/VIII/3). He 'is the Spirit of the risen Christ' (1966/VIII/2).

Now we can look more closely at the action of the Holy Spirit in men. In the meditation on Christ's baptism, after mentioning that Christ already at that time possessed the fulness of the Holy Spirit, he continues: '... at the baptism the Holy Spirit comes to take up his abode in us, and he remains with us, as long as we do not drive him away by sin. So I must have a particularly high regard for the sacrament of baptism, both for myself and in my preaching' (1964/IV/1). 'When I speak of "grace", I must not think only of the accident of which the theologians speak: grace is the Holy Spirit living and working in my soul' (1966/VIII/3). This idea is then explained more fully: 'Baptism is not only a purification ("baptism of water") but above all the coming of the "fire", the Holy Spirit. With baptism he begins his great work of redemption: incorporation into Christ, and so a temple of God, like Christ a child of God with all the graces resulting for us from that' (1968/IV/4).

Like Christ in the gospels and St Paul in his epistles the author also emphasizes the essential condition for this indwelling, the fulfilment of the will of God: 'But there is a condition for all this: that I should do the "will of the Father", not only in great things but in such a way that all my daily activity is the fulfilment of the divine will, so that in a way

I can say with our Lord: I have "accomplished the work which thou gavest me to do". This must be the quintessence of this year's "decision" ' (1968/VI/4).

The action of the Holy Spirit is not restricted to baptism. He does not dwell passively in men but continues to work, guiding the whole of spiritual life and the apostolate and making it fruitful. Our Lord gives 'me the Holy Spirit, who dwells in my soul as in a temple and gives me the strength and grace that our Lord allows me. The Spirit of fortitude but also the Spirit of truth: may I keep the faith always before my eyes and so live from faith. You in me and I in you! Come, Holy Ghost' (1959/VI/4). From this he concludes: 'I must allow myself to be guided and directed by the Holy Spirit: "for all who are led by the Spirit of God are sons of God". I must, then, listen to the voice of the Holy Spirit when he speaks to me, even if he asks me to make sacrifices and bear crosses. He also led our Lord into the wilderness . . . So I must also let myself be guided and led by the Holy Spirit and listen to his voice faithfully. Hence I must pay particular attention to devotion to the Holy Spirit' (1964/IV/1; cf 1963/VI/2).

In particular it is the Holy Spirit who equips the apostles for their task, confirms them in it and guides them. On the strength of our Lord's promise and the Pentecost miracle the author states: 'The capability is given them [the apostles] by the Holy Spirit' (1968/V/1). 'And finally he promises them "the power from on high", "promised by the Father", the Holy Spirit, so that they may be his witnesses to the ends of the earth' (1961/VIII/3). Speaking of the apostles' main failings, 'pride, ambition and impatience', he says 'but it was the Holy Spirit coming on them at Pentecost who completed the work' (1959/V/1). The Spirit is also the strength of the apostles in time of persecution: 'Our Lord does not make any idyllic promises to the apostles: they are not to be any better off than he. But they can have confidence in the Holy Spirit. He will give them light and strength' (1963/V/4). So, Bea tells himself, 'in the midst of difficulties my trust is our Lord. He has sent me and sends the Holy Spirit also: 'what you are to say will be given to you in that hour" ' (1966/V/4).

The author then applies these thoughts to himself: the Holy Spirit is my light and my strength. He lets me take part in his search into the depths of the Godhead; it is through him that I know what I do know about God, in theology and contemplative prayer' (1966/VIII/3). In the meditation on the farewell address he writes: 'More than that, he gives me the Holy Spirit, who is in me and remains in me and recalls to my mind what our Lord has said to me in this retreat: this means not only theological truths but the practical lessons of the spiritual life' (1968/VI/4). 'So like the apostles I can conclude the retreat "with great joy" in the expectation that the Holy Spirit will give me light and strength, that *he* will be the "power from on high", making it possible for me to be a true and faithful apostle of the Lord: "you will be witnesses to me": and that I can always and everywhere bear genuine and fitting witness to our Lord' (1959/VIII/3).

Of course the cardinal is also aware that the two principles he has so far explained could be misunderstood in two ways. So he himself supplies the necessary clarification: 'but I must be open to [the Spirit's] influence. And it is not only the "flesh" that can put obstacles in his way, but lack of mortification, self-denial, in short the denial or neglect of the cross. Therefore this "cross" is so important for me. The works of the "flesh" (Gal 5:19–21) are where the cross is not; while the "fruit of the Spirit" exists where I "crucify the flesh". "If I live by the Spirit, let me also walk by the Spirit" ' (1966/VIII/3). In practice this means following Christ faithfully: 'If I tread the path of humility, of self-conquest, of patience in suffering and unpleasantness, in short the way of the imitation of Christ, and work on myself so that I keep ever closer to this path, then I may be certain that the Holy Spirit is living and working in me, even if I have no subjective experience of this. But I must pray too that this influence of the Spirit within me may become stronger and more effective' (1963/VIII/2). If in this way irregular tendencies are combatted, and indeed where possible excluded, and I follow Christ, then the Holy Spirit can make sure 'that I keep the faith always before my eyes and so live from faith' (1959/VI/4); then he is in a position to recognize God's will in 'the commands of my superiors, through the circumstances and conditions in which I have been placed, and through clear interior promptings' (1959/I/4). Nor does the guidance of the Holy Spirit dispense me from 'proceeding with prudence and caution', in place of whims there must be 'considerations of faith and reason, which I can follow, unhampered by personal considerations'. Similarly 'I must take careful note of these "more refined" movements and tendencies of the soul and make an effort to overcome them positively. This will not be possible without a great gift "for distinguishing between different spiritual influences" ' (1963/I/3). 'So my task is to find the right path and keep to it. And this is no easy task. To do it I need first of all light and strength from God: so I must pray, especially to the Holy Spirit, to the Virgin most prudent and the Seat of Wisdom . . .' (1964/I/3).

Lastly he must not forget the following: 'Although I make my decision under the inspiration of the Holy Spirit, it is also possible for the evil spirit to influence me.' From this it follows 'and so I must be cautious in everything and always keep the principles of the faith in mind when I judge my "first movement" and have to decide for or against, in this way or that. So I must consider things carefully in the examination of conscience as well, discuss them with others and make every effort myself to see things clearly, so that I may not fall "into the snare of the devil" ' (1963/VI/2). But the Holy Spirit stands by me in this struggle against the evil spirit too: 'The Spirit of Christ against the spirit of the prince of this world: if ever the struggle was necessary, then it is today—under the leadership of Christ' (1962/V/2).

Bea also warns against one further possible misunderstanding: 'I must not forget that others have the Holy Spirit as well and that he works in a different way in different members of the Mystical Body, in each according to his function. This can also be seen in the history of the Church: in the last centuries he guided the Church in very different ways and led to interior renewal, and he will also continue to do so (1963/VIII/2). From this he draws the practical conclusion: 'So I must see where and how he is working and then cooperate generously, even if I do not feel naturally inclined that way. The Spirit breathes where he will!' (id.)

What the notes tell us about the place and the role of the Holy Spirit in the life of Cardinal Bea is far removed from any fanaticism, illuminism, and from any exaggerations and misunderstandings. His statements are based on the deep and solid foundations of faith, above all on what the New Testament records about the life of Christ and on the Pauline theology of the Holy Spirit. They are also far from any arbitrariness: belief in the Holy Spirit and his action, and union with him go hand in hand with the struggle against the principles of the 'flesh', which is opposed to the Spirit; to his devotion to the Holy Spirit the author joins serious and cautious consideration and a careful 'discernment of spirits'. and finally he warns against the naïve thought that he is the only one to possess the Spirit: he expresses his faith in the whole range of the Spirit's activity in the Church and in all its members, and wants to treat this with respect, to recognize, cooperate with and further it. Thus the statements in the notes about the Holy Spirit bear the seal of God himself. For 'God is light and in him is no darkness at all' (1 Jn 1:5); 'God is not a God of confusion but of peace' (1 Cor 14:33) and the God of love itself (cf 1 Jn 4:8).

CHAPTER 25

'My death will not be lonely'

Scarcely anything can test a man's convictions and attitudes and try their genuineness and cohesion like the moment when he is confronted by death. It was the cardinal's habit, in nearly every retreat, to put himself mentally face to face with death. Apart from brief references, the notes contain six meditations on death and two on the 'particular judgment', that is the judgment of each individual as opposed to the general judgment at the end of time.

We look first at his general view of death. 'I am not afraid of it; in fact I welcome it because it will take me to the Lord' (1959/II/4). 'In my eighty-first year death must not be a stranger to me, but rather a welcome guest whom I expect every day' (1961/II/4; cf 1962/II/4). Not that he is under any illusions about the outcome of the judgment on this occasion. He devotes whole meditations to the theme of the judgment, and they show how conscious he was of its seriousness. One begins with the well-known words of the Book of Wisdom: 'Severe judgment falls on those in high places' (Wis 6:6), and continues: 'I must apply these words to myself as well. For almost the whole of my life as a religious and a priest I have been in a position of responsibility and today more than ever. Hence "severe judgment"—certainly much more severe than for an ordinary man, who simply carries out his domestic duties. When I am dead a great deal will be said and written about me. This is of no importance, but what is of importance is the judgment the divine judge passes on me. How shall then my life appear? Who the saint my prayer to hear, when the just himself shall fear?' (1962/III/1.) 'When the Lord calls me I shall stand before his judgment seat as I am at that moment. His mercy has accompanied me until death and even in death. But now I am not standing in front of the merciful Saviour but in front of the stern Judge who sees right through me and judges me according to what I am at the moment. So everything depends on my ability to pass the test at that moment' (1961/III/1). From a meditation like this the author immediately draws the practical conclusions about the way in which he must prepare himself for death—a point to which we shall return later.

In spite of this view of the judgment and also of death, which is dictated by faith itself, the author looks towards death 'with confidence': 'I am now at the end of my life. So I look forward with confidence to this end and to what comes after. As long as I can work, I shall do so with all my strength, and suffer and endure too. But then I hope to hear the words "enter into the joy of your master" ' (1960/VIII/2). The principal reason for this confidence is his trust in God: 'I look upon the approach of death with tranquillity and confidence: God has given me so many graces and he will not abandon me then' (1967/II/1–2). This trust in God is explained more fully, in the first place with reference to his own sins: 'I can only commend my past confidently to God's mercy. He knows how things stand and I have been through this often enough in my general confessions' (1959/II/1). 'The sins that have already been forgiven in confession do not count any more, nor do the venial sins of which I have earnestly repented' (1961/III/1). 'I appeal to God's mercy for my sins and failings' (1961/II/4). Then with reference to the 'good works': 'As for what I take with me: their works follow them. I shall place them confidently in our Lord's hands, for whom I have done them' (id). It is in this sense that he can write: 'I must be prepared for it by having a clear conscience and concentrating on the fulfilment of the task that God has given me: the dying prayer of our Lord: "Father . . . glorify thy Son . . . I have manifested thy name to the men whom thou gavest me . . . having accomplished the work which thou gavest me to do." I must then look towards death with great confidence, indifferent as to when, how and where it comes' (1962/II/4).

A further reason for his confidence is belief in what God has revealed to us about eternal happiness. 'It is death that frees me from the worries and labours of this life' (1961/II/4); it brings the good news: 'Let us go to the house of the Lord' (1962/II/4): for 'my true home is in heaven' (1966/II/4). Death is the way to 'the transfiguration that awaits me too' (1961/VI/2), a transfiguration 'of the body too . . . when I rise from the dead' (1959/VI/2). Death is 'what leads me to our Lord' (1959/II/4; of 1961/II/4), and to 'the Blessed Trinity' (1961/II/4; cf 1963/III/4), where I shall hear the words 'enter into the joy of your master' (1960/VIII/2), where I shall 'see him face to face' (1966/VIII/4). It is at death that I shall be granted 'a share in the life of the Blessed Trinity and so infinite happiness and eternal blessedness' (1962/I/3), in other words 'a share in the divine blessedness' (1959/I/1).

From this outlook, which is so deeply rooted in the faith, arises a longing, expressed again and again in biblical exclamations: ' "Who will deliver me from this body of death?"; "My desire is to depart and to be with Christ." This is the frame of mind with which I want to meet my death, whenever and however it may come' (1963/III/4). ' "My desire is to depart and to be with Christ". "Let us go to the house of the Lord" ' (1962/II/4). 'Come, Lord Jesus' (1961/III/4).

But according to this view of death, based on faith, it is essential that death should find a man ready, and so he should prepare himself for it. Since retreats are aimed principally at the practical side of religious life, this point is discussed repeatedly and at length. First: preparation is necessary and involves every aspect of life: 'I cannot prepare death like a lecture or a talk, but I must always be ready for it. And I can and must make an indirect preparation by my life: my work, my prayer, my sufferings' (1967/II/1–2; cf 1961/II/4). 'At the moment I must still work out my salvation in fear and trembling' (1963/III/4; cf Phil 2:12).

The meditation on judgment suggests that 'it is fortunate that I have been able to serve our Lord for so many years!' (1961/III/1), and turns his mind to preparing for the judgment: 'These, then, are the conclusions I can draw from this: 1) do my best to avoid all venial sins, even the slightest; 2) always do God's will faithfully, in whatever form it comes to me; 3) always make my examination of conscience and confession well; 4) cultivate the love of our Lord in myself more and more. Enter not into judgment with thy servant, Lord!' (1961/III/1). In the same context, we read: "But I must keep these words before my eyes: "but if we judged ourselves truly, we should not be judged". So no illusions about myself, gratefully accepting every well-meaning criticism from others and seeing what is true in the criticism of ill-wishers. But judging myself in my examination of conscience and in confession!' (1963/III/4.) 'But I must daily 1) ask myself in the examination of conscience whether I am prepared; 2) pray in the examination of conscience and after Mass that I may be prepared' (1962/II/4). 'Nor must I forget my sins: examination of conscience, monthly recollection, confession and, as a penance, great patience in the face of the difficulties and obstacles that old age brings with it. I can draw strength from the Church, whose child I am, and from the sacraments, especially the Eucharist, and I can draw light from the Church's teaching' (1959/II/4).

In this connection, too, he again insists on the necessity of the interior life. Thinking of the 'more severe judgment' that awaits him because of his position, he writes: 'This retreat must definitely help me, in spite of all exterior activity and success, to do everything in a truly supernatural spirit, in a spirit of recollection and union with God, in a spirit of deep faith. Then my judgment, on which all depends, will be such that I can face my heavenly Judge. But only then! Mere outward activity and eternal success, even in religious matters, is not the decisive thing for "those in high places" ' (1962/III/1).

Then the need for spiritual freedom and so for detachment from all earthly things is stressed: 'I have nothing to leave behind: I know that all fame etc is vain, and I have long since left flesh and blood, money and property. In my will I shall soon dispose of what I have as cardinal' (1961/II/4). 'Death does not mean a separation for me. I have already given up everything that could involve separation' (1963/III/4; cf 1959/II/4). Another term for detachment and a means of realizing it is the daily 'dying to oneself'. 'I must make death real even during my life: every day must see my old self die a little, a "dying to myself" by self-denial, mortification and self-conquest. And the other way of bringing this about is increasing familiarity with the idea of heaven, so that this may become my real home even now' (Phil 3:20) (1966/II/4). What is needed more than anything is 'a love of God that is always growing and nourished by an ever-increasing faithfulness in carrying out God's will. Even in my last years this will not be possible without a struggle and self-denial' (1959/II/4).

Will not this vivid awareness of death limit the ability to work and the joy in work? On the contrary. In fact it is while meditating on the thought of death that the cardinal writes: 'I wait for it, not in idleness but working all the time until the Lord calls me' (1961/II/4). 'In the meantime, however, I do my work and do it as if I had to do it for a long time yet, and so perfectly and exactly that there is no difficulty in someone else continuing it. God does not need me especially; but as long as he uses me I shall do my part until I can no longer do it. Work while there is light. The thought of death should also make me kind, not to win men's affection for myself but to distribute all the gifts that God has placed in my hands' (1962/II/4). This profound faith leads him repeatedly to express the wish that the last summons should reach him in the course of his work: 'May it come to me in the midst of my work' (1959/II/4). 'So I hope to be ready every day to be called: and preferably in the midst of my work' (1961/II/4).

This devotion to work until the last moment is in the first place due to this consideration: 'My time on earth must also be a time of laying up treasure for myself in heaven. My real heavenly treasure is not the honour that I receive from men nor my reputation, nor all the titles and decorations, but the deeds, which follow me. So now I must labour with Christ and for Christ, as long as he gives me strength for it. This is the best way I can prepare for death' (1966/II/4). The zeal for work also comes from the desire to be ready for death, 'concentrating on the fulfilment of the task that God has given me', in order to be able to say with our Lord his 'dying prayer': 'Father . . . glorify thy Son . . . I have manifested thy name to the men whom thou gavest me . . . having accomplished the work which thou gavest me to do' (1962/II/4; cf also 1960/VII/4; 1961/II/4). After saying 'the seventy-nine years that he has given me tell me that he will soon be calling me to eternity', he concludes: 'So no hesitation in carrying out the programme, always keeping in sight the greater thing that he wants to give me, namely himself' (1959/I/3).

On one occasion he explains in rather surprising terms what he means by a 'happy death'. In the meditation on Christ on the cross he exclaims: 'Happy the dying man who can be even a little like him! . . . He is really a king in the way he bears it all. He shows no sign of his cruel sufferings, but he does show his noble patience and his truly divine love. We can see this mainly in his words: they are the words of someone in complete control, as if he had nothing at all to suffer himself. It can hardly ever have happened that a dying man resembled him in this way. And his love goes out above all to his enemies, who have brought him to the cross; to the men crucified with him and only then to his mother and the beloved disciple' (1967/VII/3).

Such a death is also full of hope and confidence. For even in death 'the mercy of our Lord follows me' (1961/III/1). Again: 'And then I hope the prayer may be answered: "May Christ Jesus smile upon you and welcome your coming; and may he appoint a place for you among those who stand ever near him"' (1961/II/4; cf 1959/II/4). 'And at this moment Mary will "turn her eyes of mercy towards me"' (1959/II/4). 'Nor will my death be lonely: "go forth, O Christian soul; may the angels and saints, and our Lord himself, welcome you". Every holy Communion should be a viaticum so that I shall not die without the viaticum even if I die suddenly: "may the Lord himself protect me from the evil enemy and lead me to eternal life!" If I live like this I shall be able to die "with joy and satisfaction"' (1966/II/4).

Let us sum up briefly: Cardinal Bea's attitude to death and his approach to this aspect of human life is based on his faith, his trust and his love. Faith makes him look on death as a welcome guest, a friend who will lead him to our Lord. For death opens up to him the way to God's great promises, to a share in the blessedness of God himself. Reliance on God's mercy and love gives him confidence with regard to his sins and the future course of his life, and above all with regard to the outcome of the last decisive struggle at the hour of death. This trust and love arouse a fervent longing for that happy hour of the eternal meeting with God and Christ. And this longing spurs him on not only to prepare himself for death, to be ready at all times, but at the same time to work with greater devotion and carry out the work given him by God ever better and more perfectly. This appreciation and mastery of death through belief, trust and loving devotion to God allow him to live even now in his true home in heaven, always ready to undertake the last journey there. Ready, also, to live and work for Christ with all his strength as long as need be, until he has wholly and completely carried out the task that God has given him in Christ.

Epilogue

Two days before Pope John died, I accompanied Cardinal Bea, as his secretary, on his last visit to the pope. From what the cardinal said later, the dying man scarcely recognized him; at any rate he did not manage to say anything that the cardinal could understand. But among the other people we met in the ante-room there was an Italian lawyer, Vittorio Vermese, a former Director-General of UNESCO. He told the cardinal that on 20 April 1963 (two months before the pope's death) he had been received in a long private audience. And amongst other things, the pope had said to him: 'Just think what a great favour God bestowed on me in letting me discover Cardinal Bea.'

In fact Pope John had met Cardinal Bea for the first time in March 1959 at an audience when the latter had been presented to him as a consultor of the Holy Office (as it was then), together with the rest of the staff. But Pope John did not make him a cardinal because of his acquaintance. As the cardinal stated in an interview in Spring 1960, the pope took this step mainly as a mark of respect for his predecessor, Pius XII, whose confessor Bea had been for the last thirteen years of his pontificate. Yet it soon became clear how like-minded the two men were: from the first audience the pope granted the new cardinal on 9 January 1960 they understood each other perfectly. The close spiritual sympathy that existed between the two was altogether confirmed by later events in connection with the Council. It is a generally recognized fact that few people understood Pope John's idea of the Council and worked so hard to put it into practice as did Cardinal Bea.

But we also have some special proof of this relationship. In his book *Ecumenism in the Council*, Bea recounts that on 15 October 1962 Pope John received Bishop Fred Pierce Corson, at that time President of the Methodist World Federation, in audience. Bishop Corson described the course of this audience in the following words: 'At the audience that Pope John, now eighty-one years of age, granted me, I told him how surprised I was to find him so robust and strong, so capable of conveying to others on every occasion a feeling of trust and a profound spiritual peace. He replied that he had found a source of constant renewal in the Book of the *Imitation of Christ* by Thomas à Kempis and above all in the third book, chapter 23, and he quoted the main points of this chapter. "Now, my son ... always try to do the will of others rather than your own. Always choose to have less rather than more; always make for the lowest place and take rank below all others. Let your constant prayer and desire be that the will of God may be perfectly accomplished in you. The man who does all this crosses the frontier of the land of peace and inward rest." At this I told him that I hoped he would send this message to all Christian pastors. He answered that he would be delighted if I would pass this on to my pastors as his special message.' This Bishop Corson did in a leaflet bearing a fine photograph of John XXIII on the front and containing on the two inside pages an account of his audience and the text of the relevant chapter of the *Imitation of Christ*.

It is fascinating to find exactly these thoughts taken from the same chapter of the *Imitation*, in the cardinal's notes. After an honest investigation of the 'irregular tendencies' that still remained in him and a resolution to examine himself in this respect in the daily examination of conscience in order to try to overcome them, he continues: 'Basically it is the search for the "four things that bring great peace" (*Imitation* III, 23): 1) to do the will of others rather than your own; 2) choose to have less rather than more; 3) always make for the lowest place and take rank below all others; 4) let your constant prayer and desire be that the will of God may be perfectly accomplished in you. This is true even in my present position, sometimes perhaps more in my frame of mind than in external actions. It tells me that I must fight every urge to do my own will, every inclination to look for approval and recognition, every irregular desire to have and possess something, at its very beginning, at its root, so that I can face all these things with interior freedom' (1961/I/4).

Is it just chance or is it something more than this that the cardinal, like Pope John in his *Journal of a Soul*, has left us such a rich collection of spiritual notes? It is all the more surprising with Bea, since he was extremely reserved in matters pertaining to his soul and his interior life. It was never the author's intention to share with others the intimate mysteries of his relationship with God and Christ, and I believe we can regard their possession as a gift from God. In his providence and kindness God the Father wanted to give us a self-portrait of the cardinal of unity, and one that came mainly from the inspiration of the Holy Spirit. In these notes we have over and over again the great joy of discovering new and unexpected traits in this unusual character, of discovering aspects, until then completely unknown, of the personality of Augustine Bea, religious, priest and apostle. This self-portrait should be for all of us—his brethren, colleagues, all who knew him and loved him, indeed all his brothers in Christ—an affectionate memorial and one that should accompany us through life as a model, a light and an incentive.

After the Requiem for Cardinal Bea, held in St Peter's, Pope Paul VI received the numerous well-known people who had attended the service as representatives of the non-Catholic Churches and ecclesial communities. Amongst other things the pope told them: 'We must think of

Cardinal Bea as still present among us.' In these notes the cardinal is present, in his words, in his life with Christ in God. They were not written for others. We have the privilege of sharing in what is most profound and sacred in man, his conversation with God.